Paris City Councillors in the
Sixteenth Century

Paris City Councillors in the Sixteenth Century

The Politics of Patrimony

Barbara B. Diefendorf

PRINCETON UNIVERSITY PRESS

PRINCETON, NEW JERSEY

Published by Princeton University Press, 41 William St.,
Princeton, New Jersey
In the United Kingdom: Princeton University Press,
Guildford, Surrey

Library of Congress Cataloging in Publication Data will
be found on the last printed page of this book

Publication of this book has been aided by a grant
from the Publications Program of the National Endowment
for the Humanities

This book has been composed in Linotron Garamond

Clothbound editions of Princeton University Press books
are printed on acid-free paper, and binding materials
are chosen for strength and durability

Printed in the United States of America by Princeton
University Press, Princeton, New Jersey

To Elizabeth and Jeffry

Contents

List of Tables

Acknowledgments

IN STUDYING the Parisian elite, I have benefited from the advice and encouragement and, I would hope, the wisdom of friends and family, teachers, colleagues, and students. Certain of these persons deserve special mention. First and foremost, I am grateful to Natalie Davis, who not only directed the dissertation on which the book is based but is also responsible for my first real introduction to sixteenth-century France. She has shared generously of her time and learning. I am grateful as well to Gene Brucker, who read each chapter of the dissertation with gratifying care and made many insightful suggestions. Nancy Roelker has also spent many hours with my city councillors, and my work has profited from her great knowledge of sixteenth-century Paris and its magistracy. Robert Descimon, Jonathan Dewald, Ralph Giesey, Orest Ranum, and Denis Richet have also offered useful suggestions at one stage or another of this project.

Many librarians and archivists have assisted me in this work. I would like to single out Mme Catherine Grodecki of the Minutier central at the Archives nationales for particular thanks. Institutional support for the project has been supplied by the Alliance française de New York, the American Council of Learned Societies, and the Graduate Schools of the University of California at Berkeley and Boston University. I appreciate their assistance. Catherine Bergstrom and Jean Gahan performed typing chores with admirable patience.

Lastly, the two persons to whom this book is dedicated. My aunt Elizabeth Rosenfield has contributed to this book in many ways. As an experienced editor, she has helped to purge the book of unnecessary gallicisms, jargon, and obtuseness. As a trained lawyer, she has helped me to see the integral relation between the law and the society in which it functions. But above and beyond these contributions, the book is dedicated to her because of the person she is and the affection I bear her. My husband, Jeffry Diefendorf, has contributed to this project in more ways than I can name. From the first tentative formulations of the thesis to the final editing tasks, he has thoughtfully heard and patiently read innumerable variations on the theme. While I am very grateful for the confidence with which he supported this project, I am no less grateful for his always constructive critical suggestions. For these and other reasons this book is for him.

The responsibility for any errors of fact or interpretation is my own.

A Note on Manuscript Sources and Abbreviations

WHEN CITING manuscript sources in the footnotes, I have used the abbreviation of the archive, followed by the designation of the general series or collection and then by the number of its subdivision, followed by folio or page numbers and/or dates of contracts. The names of the principal parties are also given if they do not already appear in the text. The dates of contracts are expressed in the French style, that is to say, with the day first and then the month and the last two digits of the year. Unless otherwise specified, all years refer to the sixteenth century. The dates of documents have been left in the old style, as they appear in the sources. In the text, however, references to dates have been brought into alignment with our contemporary calendar and the abbreviation "(n.s.)" (new style) has been added to advise the reader of the change.

Subtitles and titles of series have been omitted from the footnotes for the sake of brevity. They can be found in the bibliography.

The following abbreviations and short forms are used in the notes:

A.C.	Paris Custom of 1510
AN	Archives nationales
Annales	*Annales. Economies, sociétés, civilisations*
BN	Bibliothèque nationale
BSHP	*Bulletin de la Société de l'histoire de Paris et de l'Ile-de-France*
Carrés	Carrés d'Hozier
D.b.	Dossiers bleus

£	*Livres tournois*
Min. cen.	Minutier central
MS fr.	Manuscrits français
MSHP	*Mémoires de la Société de l'histoire de Paris et de l'Ile-de-France*
N.a.	Nouvelles acquisitions
N.C.	Paris Custom of 1580
P.o.	Pièces originales
Reg. BV	*Registres des délibérations du Bureau de la Ville de Paris*

Map of Paris known as the "Tapisserie" (approximately 1540). Source: Bibliothèque nationale.

Introduction

HISTORIANS have long recognized that the bourgeoisie of sixteenth-century Paris produced some of the most illustrious dynasties of the *noblesse de robe* of Old Regime France. They have recognized as well that the ties of kinship played an important part in the success of these families. And yet, despite the burgeoning literature on elites and the family in French history, little work has as yet been published on the families that constituted the dominant elite of the largest city and political capital of the sixteenth-century French monarchy.[1] Ironically, the very importance of the role played by Paris and its inhabitants in many of the major events of French history may have contributed to this gap in the literature. In seeking out new areas of history to explore, it is easy to overlook those that are seemingly most familiar. Moreover, the study of Parisian social history poses problems that are not encountered in the study of provincial towns. It is difficult if not impossible to extricate the social and political structures of the French capital from those of the monarchy itself. It is, however, precisely because of the unique role of Paris in the French state that a study of the governing elite of this city assumes an importance that transcends the local context.

The present study seeks to enlarge our understanding of

[1] Denis Richet and some of his students have undertaken a large-scale, computer-assisted analysis of the Parisian notability, but the results of their research have not yet been published. For a discussion of this research, see Denis Richet, "Aspects socio-culturels des conflits religieux à Paris dans la seconde moitié du xvie siècle," *Annales* 32 (1977):764-89. Much of the recent literature on French elites is discussed in a review article by J[ohn] H. M. Salmon ("Storm over the Noblesse," *Journal of Modern History* 53 [1981]:242-58), while an excellent bibliography on the family in early modern France is provided in Gerald Soliday, ed., *History of the Family and Kinship* (Millwood, N.Y., 1980), pp. 76-94.

French history through an examination of the character and behavior of the dominant elite of Paris during a crucial period in the development of the French monarchy. In order to understand the means by which the families that composed this elite achieved their preeminence and maintained it through successive generations, I have explored the ways in which participation in civic affairs, career choices, matrimonial arrangements, and inheritance practices served the ambitions of this group. The study is principally archival in character. The initial conceptualization of both problem and approach and certain points of interpretation of course owe much to my reading of recent secondary works on social structures, the family, and the law. If there are relatively few references to these works in the body of the text, it is because as my work on the Parisian elite progressed I found that it took on a shape and contour of its own, a shape dictated by the nature of the archival sources and the information they yielded. Attempts to bring in frequent comparisons with the results of studies of other cities and other social groups, studies that are inevitably based on different sorts of data and bounded by different parameters, would have diffused the focus of the book, and I found the subject at hand to be large, complex, and important enough to stand alone.

Indeed, the first problem in dealing with the Parisian elite was to reduce the scope of the undertaking to manageable proportions by focusing research on a limited segment of the local elite and a limited period of time. This was important for several reasons. In the first place, it is extremely difficult to define the boundaries of the Parisian upper classes. Unlike the patriciate of many German and Italian cities during the Renaissance, the Parisian elite had neither a clearly defined juridical status nor carefully controlled membership requirements to set it apart from the two hundred thousand or more other inhabitants of the metropolis on the Seine.[2] The prob-

---

[2] There are no reliable figures on the size of the Parisian population in the sixteenth century. At the start of the century, the city was still recovering from the prolonged crisis of the Hundred Years War, which, according

lem of defining a Parisian notability according to social or professional status is further complicated by the city's role as the capital and administrative hub of the French monarchy. To avoid these problems, I have focused this study on the ninety men who held office in municipal government as *conseillers de l'Hôtel de Ville* between the years 1535 and 1575. Nomination to the office of councillor in the Hôtel de Ville was almost by definition a mark of elite standing in the city. Without formal legislative authority, the body of twenty-four councillors served as advisors to the principal officers of the Parisian municipality—the *prévôt des marchands* and four *échevins*. The office was in theory elective, but in practice it was co-optive, with a strong tendency toward hereditary function by the second half of the sixteenth century. In spite of the narrow recruitment—or because of it—the men named to the council were by birth or alliance members of prominent and well-respected Parisian families. Several of the city councillors were famous men in their own right, among them the humanist Guillaume Budé, the jurist Christophe de Thou, and the chancellor Michel de L'Hôpital. At least in terms of prestige, the city councillors well merited their nickname of the city's "little Senate," and these ninety men were indisputably a part of the Parisian elite.[3]

The time period for this study was chosen because it lies at the heart of an important period of social and political transition in the French monarchy. The specific years for city

---

to the most reliable estimates, saw a medieval city of some 200,000 reduced by half by the first quarter of the fifteenth century. Rebuilding, at first slow, gradually accelerated in the later decades of the century, so that the city had in all probability nearly returned to its earlier peak by 1500 (Jean Favier, *Paris au xve siècle* [Paris, 1974], pp. 61-62). This growth continued in the sixteenth century, despite renewed outbreaks of the plague. Even the most conservative estimates give Paris a population of 200,000 at the end of the sixteenth century, while others go as high as 400,000 or more (Pierre Chaunu, *La Mort à Paris* [Paris, 1978], p. 198; Pierre Lavedan, *Histoire de Paris* [Paris, 1967], p. 32). In my own opinion, the conservative estimate is probably the more accurate.

[3] Albert Miron de l'Espinay, *François Miron et l'administration municipale sous Henri IV* (Paris, 1885), p. 161.

council membership (1535-1575) were determined by methodological considerations as well. City records are incomplete before the 1530s; a reliable list of city councillors cannot be established for the earlier period. The register at the Châtelet of notarial contracts involving transfers of property (*insinuations*), a prime source for this research, was only begun in 1539 after the ordinance of Villers-Cotterets. The terminal date, that on which the last of the city councillors studied was nominated to office, was chosen to avoid the confusion of social and political issues that occurred as the quarrels between Politiques and Ultra-Catholics polarized Parisian society in the later decades of the century.[4] The religious turmoil of the middle decades of the sixteenth century must of course figure into any study of French society in this period. However, because the Parisian elite remained so firmly Catholic, religious issues are touched on here only as they affected relationships within some of the councillors' families.

Because this is a study of families, the careers and marriages of the city councillors' offspring are as important as those of the councillors themselves. Therefore, the temporal limits of the study are necessarily carried beyond the forty-year period from which the city council membership was drawn. Indeed, in its broadest terms, the period under consideration spans the entire sixteenth century and the first decade or more of the seventeenth. Guillaume Budé, probably the oldest of the city councillors in the group, began his career with the office of *secrétaire du roi* in 1497, while the sons of some of the younger city councillors did not come of age until the

---

[4] The problems of the League demand special attention, and since this period has already attracted more scholarly attention than other portions of sixteenth-century Parisian history, it seemed reasonable to stop short of it. See Elie Barnavi, *Le Parti de Dieu* (Louvain, 1980); J[ohn] H. M. Salmon, "The Paris Sixteen, 1584-94," *Journal of Modern History* 44 (1972):540-76; and Peter M. Ascoli, "The Sixteen and the Paris League, 1585-91" (Ph.D. dissertation, University of California at Berkeley, 1972). Denis Richet has attributed his research on the Parisian nobility to a desire to understand the social background of the participants in the League ("Conflits religieux," pp. 764-65), and Roland Mousnier has also had students at work on various aspects of the period of the League in Paris.

early years of the seventeenth century.[5] The middle and later decades of the sixteenth century are the decades central to this study, however.

This was a crucial period for the French monarchy. Despite the divisive effects of religious schism and civil war, there were developments in the middle and later part of the sixteenth century of critical importance to the later strength of the absolute monarchy. Among these developments, the rapid expansion of the bureaucratic apparatus upon which centralized government depended and the growing power and prestige of the body of professional civil servants must be singled out. Although the growth in the number and status of the professional bureaucracy has its roots back in the medieval period, this process accelerated dramatically in the sixteenth century as the overt practice of venality encouraged the multiplication of governmental offices. Other important developments were the institutional reforms begun by Francis I and Henry II and continued, albeit somewhat erratically, during the reigns of the last Valois kings. The imposition of monarchical authority in realms previously left to local administration and custom is of particular significance. Finally, theoretical foundations necessary to the extension of absolute powers by the Bourbon monarchs were laid during this period.

These developments were felt particularly in Paris, the administrative heart of the kingdom. The increasing prominence of the officerial hierarchy, for example, was especially obvious in Paris because of the location there of the sovereign courts and the central fiscal bureaucracy. There was a decline in the role of merchants in the highest strata of civic government and a corresponding increase in the role of officers to the king. The institutional reforms of the French monarchy affected the Parisian elite on two accounts: as officers of the king and as his subjects. Directly, as members of the royal bureaucracy, or indirectly, as members of an administrative

---

[5] *Nouvelle biographie générale*, s.v. "Budé."

body frequently consulted by the king, they participated in the formulation of a number of these reforms. In this respect, the individual contributions of Michel de L'Hôpital while chancellor and Christophe de Thou, charged with the codification of customary law, stand out, but many other city councillors, their closest relatives, and friends helped to shape the policies and powers of the central government.

Paris was at this time, as Paris has always been, an intellectual as well as a political capital, and in the sixteenth century, the center of intellectual ferment was in the ranks of the professional bureaucrats. Among the king's officers were a number of worldly and educated men who encouraged the revival of classical learning in France and who had much to do with the flowering of French arts and letters and, most importantly, with the emergence of a new vision of history and a new appraisal of the nature of political power and sovereignty.[6]

All of these developments—intellectual, political, and social—are particularly important because they affected both private values and public ambitions. They determined what was considered desirable, worthwhile, worth striving for. Since ambition is in large measure dependent upon the opportunities a society offers and the value placed upon them, an examination of the mechanisms for social advancement and maintenance among the Parisian elite inevitably involves an examination of social values. And, because a value system cannot operate in isolation from the social and political structures around it, there will be inevitable parallels between the principles from which notions of personal achievement and the principles from which notions of collective success are derived. There will also be parallels between the means judged

---

[6] Among the more important works on the contribution of the royal officers to political and historical theory are William F. Church, *Constitutional Thought in Sixteenth-Century France* (Cambridge, Mass., 1941); Julian H. Franklin, *Jean Bodin and the Sixteenth-Century Revolution in the Methodology of Law and History* (New York, 1963); Donald R. Kelley, *Foundations of Modern Historical Scholarship* (New York, 1970); and George Huppert, *The Idea of Perfect History* (Urbana, Ill., [1970]).

most desirable for effecting private ends and those judged
most desirable for effecting public ends. Thus we shall see in
the study that follows repeated parallels between the role of
the family and that of the state, between the role of the father
and that of the king. These parallels exist because the institutions of family and state, and the roles of father and king,
were based on common principles, those of order, authority,
hierarchy, responsibility, and respect for tradition.

The ninety men whose careers and families are the subject
of this study did not profit equally from the process of change
in sixteenth-century politics, economics, and society. Some
of these men had brilliant careers and promoted their children
to still more prestigious positions; others knew less success
for themselves and their heirs. But despite the varying levels
of individual achievement, all can be seen to have operated
within fundamentally the same system of priorities and values. These priorities and values were not, however, charac-
teristic of this group of ninety men only. Many of the conclusions drawn from the behavior of this group are also valid
for other local notables—for other important city officers, for
other officers of the sovereign courts and at the higher levels
in the royal administrative and fiscal bureaucracies (especially
among those who were Parisian by birth or considered themselves so by adoption), and for the wealthier merchants and
bourgeois rentiers of the city.

A few definitions are important to the work that follows.
I have used the term "family" in its most common usage
today, that is, to refer to "the group of persons consisting of
parents and their children, whether actually living together
or not; in [a] wider sense, the unity formed by those who are
nearly connected by blood or affinity."[7] This definition is more
appropriate for the aims of this study than is the sixteenth-
century usage, which referred primarily to the household and
included servants as well as kin. For purposes of clarity, the
term "lineage" is used instead of "family" when reference is

---

[7] *Oxford English Dictionary*, 1971 ed., s.v. "family."

made to a group of persons claiming descent from a common ancestor, and "kin" is used for persons more distantly related by blood or marriage.[8]

As I have already said, the precise boundaries of the Parisian elite cannot be defined. For a working definition, however, I would say that a man should meet all or nearly all of the following criteria to be considered a part of the local elite. He should be Parisian by birth or at the very least have married into a family long known and respected in the city. Even if possessing country estates, he should consider Paris his principal residence. He should himself hold civic office as prévôt des marchands, échevin, or city councillor, or he should be a direct descendant or brother of one of these city officers. By profession, he should be an officer of the sovereign courts, an important member of the administrative and fiscal bureaucracy, or one of the highest officers of the Châtelet, although he might also be a very wealthy merchant (probably a wholesaler, although a few jewelers might qualify) or a rich rentier living off landed income or bonds. The size of this group is necessarily small. Only 305 persons held office as prévôt des marchands, échevin, and city councillor in sixteenth-century Paris. Even if this number is doubled several times over to include the closest relatives and most influential associates of these men, we are speaking of only several thousand persons in a city whose population was somewhere between 200,000 and 300,000 persons. I have used the term "notability" in a rather broader sense to include persons of somewhat lower civic or monarchical office and somewhat less wealthy merchants and rentiers. This would include persons who were

---

[8] For an excellent discussion of the concepts of "family," "lineage," and other terms of kinship in Old Regime France, see Jean-Louis Flandrin, *Familles: Parenté, maison, sexualité dans l'ancienne société* (Paris, 1976), pp. 17-21. See also Edward Britton, "The Peasant Family in Fourteenth-Century England," *Peasant Studies* 5 (1976):5-6; Peter Laslett and Richard Wall, eds., *Household and Family in Past Time* (Cambridge, England, 1972); and Robert Wheaton and Tamara K. Hareven, eds., *Family and Sexuality in French History* (Philadelphia, 1980), pp. 6-9.

named as "bourgeois" representatives to city elections but did not otherwise participate in civic affairs.

The term "bourgeois" presents special problems, for even in the sixteenth century the term had several, overlapping definitions. Two definitions are particularly important here. The first definition of "bourgeois" is a juridical one. In the Old Regime, the right to call oneself a "bourgeois de Paris" (or "bourgeois" of some other city) was a privilege formally accorded by the city government to persons who had resided in the city at least a year and who owned property, paid taxes, and served in the militia there.[9]

By this definition, artisans, merchants, and officers of the king, even those who were noblemen, were proud to style themselves "bourgeois de Paris" in the sixteenth century. Lists of the *notables bourgeois* summoned to assist in municipal elections, tax levies, and other important civic affairs demonstrate that the quality of bourgeois covered a wide range in the sixteenth century. Merchants and officers of the king—from simple *clercs* to presidents of Parlement—predominate, but an occasional carpenter, baker, or other artisan also appears in the earlier part of the century.[10] The term "bourgeois de Paris" was thus more precisely an indication of legal status than one of social standing.

The second definition of "bourgeois" is a functional definition by which the term referred only to those residents of the city who lived off the income from lands and investments without exercising any profession or trade. This is the sense in which Henry II meant the term when, in 1554, he speci-

[9] *Reg. BV*, 12:79, describes the process of obtaining certificates of bourgeoisie under Henry IV. See also François André Isambert, *Recueil général des anciennes lois françaises depuis l'an 420 jusqu'à la Révolution de 1789* (Paris, 1822-1833), 2:675, for the earliest known ordinance (1287) regarding bourgeois status. Antoine Jean Victor Le Roux de Lincy, *Histoire de l'Hôtel de Ville de Paris* (Paris, 1846), pp. 295-353, enumerates the royal ordinances concerning the privileges of the bourgeoisie. More concisely, the *Ordonnances des rois de France de la troisième race* (Paris, 1723-1849), 19:176 (*Edit de 1528*), gives a summary of the privileges.

[10] *Reg. BV*, 2:357.

fied that the city council was to include ten officers of the
king, seven merchants, and seven notable bourgeois.[11] As the
confusion produced by this edict indicates, sixteenth-century
usage was not always as clear-cut as the ruling implies. The
city officers were clearly not accustomed to thinking of royal
officers, merchants, and bourgeois as mutually separate and
exclusive categories. The status of simple bourgeois was often
a temporary one—the status of a retired merchant or officer,
or that of a man in transition from mercantile to officerial
functions. Moreover, a man who held an office that provided
little remuneration or who derived income from commercial
ventures and bonds equally might define himself alternately
as a merchant or officer or as a bourgeois. Still, it is necessary
to have a term to refer to those persons who were, temporarily
or not, living primarily off their investments. For purposes
of clarity, I have substituted or appended the term "rentier"
when this definition of "bourgeois" is required.

By limiting my use of the term "bourgeois" to these juridical and functional definitions, I do not mean to ignore the
social connotations that the term had even in the sixteenth
century. When the maréchal de Saint-André wanted deliberately to insult the son of the city councillor Pierre Perdrier,
he called him a *bourgeois de petite condition*.[12] Nor do I mean to
dodge the question of social tensions that lies behind this
example. The Parisian elite occupied a position in the social
hierarchies of sixteenth-century France that many historians
would consider to have been fraught with tension. Since the
publication of Roland Mousnier's important *Vénalité des offices*
in 1945, relations between the newly ennobled officers of the
king and the old aristocracy and between the king's officers
and the lesser bourgeoisie from which they sought to dissociate themselves have gradually been given a well-merited

[11] *Reg. BV*, 4:341-42, citing edict of May 1554.
[12] Lucien Romier, *Jacques d'Albon de Saint-André, maréchal de France 1512-
1562* (Paris, 1909), pp. 195-97; also cited in Roland Mousnier, *Etat et
société sous François I et pendant le gouvernement personnel de Louis XIV* (Paris,
1966).

attention.[13] Though Mousnier's argument that there was an essential antagonism between the old nobility and the recently ennobled officers is based primarily on evidence from the seventeenth century, such works as Davis Bitton's *French Nobility in Crisis* have shown that many of these tensions may have already been present in the sixteenth century.[14] Recently, other scholars have staked out conflicting positions on the issue; they have renewed the controversy but have not resolved it.[15] My research on the Parisian elite cannot resolve the issue either, although it inclines me more toward the view that antagonistic relations with the traditional nobility and the lesser bourgeoisie did not play a major role in the thinking or activities of the Parisian elite.[16] Members of this group did not view the social system as a single hierarchy or ladder, and they did not see the path of their ambitions as being

[13] Roland Mousnier, *La Vénalité des offices sous Henri IV et Louis XIII* (Rouen, 1945). In his more recent works, Mousnier has returned frequently to the idea that an essential antagonism opposed the traditional nobility and the newly ennobled members of the royal bureaucracy, "a conflict not only between two levels in the hierarchy but also between two types of profession and two different ways of life" (*The Institutions of France under the Absolute Monarchy*, trans. Brian Pearce [Chicago, 1979], pp. 202 and 207).

[14] (Stanford, 1969).

[15] Stressing the antagonism that the mercantile bourgeoisie felt for the social-climbing members of the royal bureaucracy, as well as the tensions between this group and the old nobility, George Huppert has attempted to cast the argument in new terms by defining the robe officers as a "new class" and labeling this class the "gentry" (*Les Bourgeois Gentilshommes* [Chicago, 1977]). Robert Harding (*Anatomy of a Power Elite* [New Haven, 1978]), Jonathan Dewald (*The Formation of a Provincial Nobility* [Princeton, 1980]), and James Wood (*The Nobility of the Election of Bayeux* [Princeton, 1981]), are among those who have recently posed important challenges to the view that there was an essential antagonism between robe and sword, but because the first deals principally with political rather than social relations, while the second two are local studies, it is difficult to extrapolate a general conclusion from them.

[16] I hope in a future study of religious violence in Paris during the early years of the Wars of Religion to explore more fully the underlying social and political tensions in the city. It is possible that this work will cast a somewhat different light on the role of the governing elite of the city and their relations with other elites and with the less privileged inhabitants of the city.

barred by the position of the traditional nobility. The sources on which I have relied most heavily—notarial records and personal papers—show few signs of tension between the Parisian elite and the groups above and below them on the social scale. As the chapters that follow will show, the image that emerged from all of my sources was that of an elite which, fortified by an impressive degree of family solidarity, was secure in its role in both city and monarchy and confident in its dealings with other groups.

PART I

Portrait of a Municipal Elite

1. City Government: Institutions and Politics

Nostre ville est la nef royalle, nostre prévost des marchans en est le pilotte, les eschevins en sont les voiles, les fleurs de lys et la croix blanche en sont les enseignes. Mais certainement nul vent ne la peut remuer que celuy seul qui sort de la bouche du roy ou de ses lieutenans et gouverneurs. —*Le Livre des marchands*

PARIS in the sixteenth century was the center of the French monarchy. Though the king's household was not yet stationary, ambling like the medieval court from one royal residence to another and lingering more frequently in the gracious châteaux of the Loire valley than amidst the noisome activity of the metropolis on the Seine, Paris remained the heart of the realm. More than a symbol, "the glory of France, and one of the noblest ornaments of the world," as Montaigne expressed it,[1] Paris was a functioning capital, a city that bustled with the business of the king.

If the Valois monarchs were frequently absent, the administrative and judiciary organs of the monarchy were nonetheless securely rooted in the capital. At the heart of the city, on the Ile-de-la-Cité, the Palais de Justice buzzed with the activity of the sovereign courts. Coffers in the Tour d'Argent of the Palais and in the Louvre held the king's treasure, and the responsibility for the royal accounts was likewise centered in the capital. Men of ambition were drawn to Paris from all corners of the realm and beyond: bankers from Tuscany, merchants from across the Rhine, students, and provincial law-

[1] Michel Eyquem de Montaigne, *Essais* (1588), bk. 3, chap. 9. All English quotations from Montaigne are taken from Donald M. Frame, trans., *The Complete Essays of Montaigne* (Stanford, 1958) and are cited as "(Frame, p. 743)."

yers converged upon the capital in search of knowledge and wealth. The great nobles of the kingdom, princes of the church, and representatives of foreign courts kept lavish townhouses in the city to be near the official, if not permanent, residence of the king. From the greatest courtiers and magistrates to the lowest clerks and the peddlers of lace and ribbons in the courtyard of the Palais, the character of Parisian life was indelibly stamped by the city's role as the capital of France.

There was, however, another side to Parisian life. For all its cosmopolitan airs, there still existed within the metropolis a nucleus of native Parisians who looked upon the city not just as the hub of France but as their own town and home. It is this locally oriented Parisian society that concerns us here; in particular we are concerned with its upper crust— the local elite whose family names appear and reappear throughout several centuries of parish, confraternal, and municipal records—and with the ways in which family ties functioned in the sixteenth century to promote personal standing, political success, and financial advancement. Before examining the structures of this elite society, we need a clear picture of the political and institutional framework in which it existed.

The French kings recognized that the security of Paris and the well-being of her citizens were too important to be left to agencies whose responsiveness to the royal will could not be guaranteed. In consequence, they fostered the creation of a complex administrative structure that allowed the city only limited autonomy. Appointive officers directly responsible to the crown assumed control of the vital functions of police and justice, while the elected officers of the Parisian bourgeoisie took on subsidiary tasks such as supervising commerce and collecting taxes. The division, however, was neither clear-cut nor simple. The agencies of king and city overlapped in function and in personnel. It is the purpose of this chapter to examine the institutional structures of the municipality and their relationships to crown and citizenry. These relationships will be examined in three different contexts: first, in the context of the evolution of the municipal administration from the medieval period to the sixteenth century; second, in the context of election procedures and the selection of municipal personnel; and third, in the context of the behavior of city officers when confronted with the monarchy's escalating demands for funds. In this way we can begin to understand the nature of the role played by the Parisian elite in the affairs of the city and the kingdom.

The Structure of Municipal Government

The focal point of municipal politics in the sixteenth century was the Hôtel de Ville, or city hall. An awkward pastiche of medieval and Renaissance styles, the building itself serves as an appropriate symbol of the times. In the 1530s Francis I imposed upon the city his plan for a new city hall. Designed in the lavish style of the Renaissance, it reflected the youthful exuberance and determined authority of the king rather than the more conservative tastes of the city fathers.[2] Because of financial pressures, however, construction of the new building faltered and ground to a halt, and for most of the century the Hôtel de Ville retained a somber medieval mien behind its Renaissance façade.

Like the building in which it functioned, the city administration remained essentially medieval in structure. At the head of the city's government was the prévôt des marchands, or merchants' provost. He derived his functions from the gradual evolution of the medieval Hansa, the Marchandise de l'Eau, which he represented. Originally a purely mercantile association controlling shipping on the Seine, the Hansa had gradually evolved into a municipal administration with broad-based responsibilities for public services, welfare, and security.[3] The term "prévôt des marchands" was rather outdated

[2] Reg. BV, 2:164-65.
[3] Frédéric Lecaron, "Les Origines de la municipalité parisienne," MSHP 7 (1880):105-106. Fifteenth-century city records give lists of the "marchands hansés," and the term still occasionally occurs in the sixteenth-century city registers.

by the sixteenth century, as the prévôt represented a bourgeoisie that was by no means strictly mercantile in its orientation. Like his medieval predecessors, however, the prévôt des marchands was responsible for the regulation of commerce, the direction of public works, the organization of the militia, and the collection of taxes. He was assisted in these tasks by four échevins, or aldermen. In principle, at least at the end of the sixteenth century, the first échevin was responsible for municipal finances, the second for provisioning the city, the third for public works such as pavements, lighting, and fountains, and the fourth for the personnel and correspondence of the municipality.[4] It is not, however, certain that these administrative distinctions were adhered to in practice.

The prévôt des marchands and échevins were elected for two-year terms, with two of the four échevins elected each year so that there would always be some experienced men among them. Greater continuity was provided by the permanent employees of the Hôtel de Ville, the *greffier* (secretary), the *receveur* (treasurer), and the *procureur de la ville* (the officer charged with representing the city's interests in Parlement and other governmental agencies). The daily routines of administration were largely carried out by the *sergents* (police officers) of the Hôtel de Ville and by the district agents, the *quarteniers*, one from each of the city's sixteen *quartiers*. The quarteniers, in turn, relied upon *cinquanteniers* and *dizainiers* to help run the militia, supervise tax collection, and otherwise handle problems at the district level. Together, the prévôt des marchands, four échevins, the greffier, and sixteen quarteniers were known as the *corps municipal* or Bureau de la Ville.

For important affairs, particularly those dealing with finances, personnel, and defense, the Bureau de la Ville was assisted by a council of twenty-four local notables. These were the conseillers de la ville, the city councillors who, for the years 1535 to 1575, are the subject of this study. The office

---

[4] Miron de l'Espinay, *François Miron*, p. 158.

itself dates back to the year 1296, when a standing council of twenty-four *proudoumes de Paris* was first elected to assist the prévôt des marchands and échevins with the city's business.[5] The councillors were in many respects only second-level city officers. They possessed no formal legislative power. Rather, they served as advisors to the members of the *corps municipal*. They did not even attend municipal assemblies on a regular basis but had to be summoned specially. Thus the importance of the city councillors lay in the prestige of the men named to this office rather than in the functional significance of the office itself.

The city councillors were not the only advisors consulted by the Bureau de la Ville on important civic issues. Remonstrances to the king, the levy of new taxes, and other questions of great importance were often handled by even larger municipal assemblies. On occasion, members of the sovereign courts, university officials, and representatives of the major ecclesiastical corporations of the city were also invited to be present at civic meetings to voice their opinions on issues that concerned them.[6] There is a certain cynical truth in Henri de Carsalade du Pont's appraisal of this practice as an attempt on the part of the city to distribute the blame if matters went ill.[7]

City officers received no salary for the performance of their functions, but they did enjoy certain privileges and honoraria. For example, the city councillors, along with the prévôt des marchands and other major officers, were traditionally given on the occasion of their entry into office a velvet purse of silver coins stamped with the emblem of the city. They also received cloth for new robes when a royal marriage or formal entry into the city was celebrated, and candles and spices were ritually distributed to them at Christmas and other holidays.[8]

---

[5] Lecaron, "Origines," 7:112-13, citing MS "Coutumes de la ville," AN, KK10.

[6] See, for example, *Reg. BV,* 7:61.

[7] Henri de Carsalade du Pont, *La Municipalité parisienne à l'époque d'Henri IV* (Paris [1971]), p. 43.

[8] *Reg. BV,* 2:307, 344, and 344n; 3:160.

In 1574 the allotment of candles and spices was replaced by a cash payment.[9] In addition, the city councillors enjoyed certain legal and fiscal prerogatives. In 1538, for example, the king granted them the right of *committimus* (the right to have lawsuits tried in the upper courts) and an exemption from the tax on salt for personal and household use.[10] Many of the functions of the Hôtel de Ville overlapped those of the officers of the Prévôté of Paris appointed by the king. Often referred to simply as "the Châtelet" because they had their offices in this medieval fortress, the officers of the Prévôté protected royal interests in the city and exercised police and judicial functions in the name of the king. The term "police" must be understood here in its broadest sense. The officers of the Châtelet were responsible not only for the maintenance of public order and the prosecution of criminals, they were the supervisory agency for all matters relating to the general health, security, and prosperity of the city's inhabitants. As such, their responsibilities frequently coincided with those of the Hôtel de Ville in the marketplaces, ports, and other areas of the city where questions of public health and welfare were at issue. In addition to these duties, the Châtelet functioned as a tribunal for both civil and criminal affairs, and its decisions could be appealed only in the Parlement of Paris, the highest judicial body in the realm.

The highest officer of the Châtelet, appointed by the king, was the prévôt, but since the prévôt was an important nobleman, the position was primarily honorific. It was the prévôt's

---

[9] Ibid., 7:221, 215. The prévôt des marchands received £280, and the échevins, procureur, greffier, and receveur received £140. The city councillors were also paid in coin after this date, but the size of the payment is not known.

[10] Ibid., 2:308. The value of these privileges was limited. The great majority of city officers already enjoyed the privilege of *committimus* because of their status as royal officers, and, according to Martin Wolfe, the salt tax was not burdensome in the sixteenth century (*The Fiscal System of Renaissance France* [New Haven, 1972], p. 335). The city councillors were allowed the measure of one *sétier* (equal to several hundred pounds) of salt free of tax, but Wolfe's calculations show that the tax on even such an enormous purchase would have amounted to less than £3.

first assistant, the *lieutenant civil* who oversaw the day-to-day administrative routine of the city. A *lieutenant criminel* was responsible for matters of police and criminal justice, and beginning in 1544 a *lieutenant particulier* was appointed to relieve the *lieutenants civil* and *criminel* of some of their increasing burdens.

Under the direction of the *lieutenant civil*, the *commissaires enquêteurs* of the Châtelet (literally, examining officers; functionally more like policemen) tended to the daily routines of civil order and welfare.[11]

Just as they overlapped in functions, the Prévôté of Paris and the Prévôté de la Marchandise overlapped in personnel. Between 1535 and 1575, at least four of the men who served as *lieutenants civils* and *criminels* were also city councillors, échevins, and even prévôts des marchands.[12] Concern was occasionally expressed about a conflict of interest between the functions of municipal officers and those of the king's officers in Paris, but this issue was not taken very seriously.[13] Throughout this period a very large proportion of the city officers were by profession officers of the administrative and judicial agencies of the crown, and any attempt to avoid duplication of personnel in civic and royal office would have drastically changed the character of city government.[14] Neither the king nor the entrenched city hierarchy stood to benefit from such a change.

The Parlement of Paris was primarily a judicial body, the

[11] Gaston Zeller, *Les Institutions de la France au xvi* siècle* (Paris, 1948), p. 175.

[12] Thomas de Bragelongne, Martin de Bragelongne, Jean Morin, and Nicolas Luillier. All but the first were prévôts des marchands as well as échevins and city councillors.

[13] *Reg. BV*, 5:3 and 3n. Since the *Traité de la police* of Nicolas de Lamare (4 vols. [Paris, 1705-38]), historians have tended to view the Châtelet and the Hôtel de Ville as competitive and in continual conflict. Carsalade du Pont used the example of the early seventeenth-century prévôt des marchands François Miron, who was simultaneously *lieutenant civil*, to disprove this notion, but he appears unaware of these earlier precedents of multiple officeholding in the Châtelet and the Hôtel de Ville (*Municipalité*, p. 41).

[14] See Chapter 2, on professional activities of city officers. The Edict of Fontainebleau of October 1547 forbade royal officers to hold civic office, but little attempt was made to enforce the edict (see *Reg. BV*, 3:100).

highest of the sovereign courts, but it also had a legislative role from which it derived a role in the administration of the capital. Unlike the Châtelet, however, the Parlement played a role in city affairs that did not normally involve day-to-day administrative activities. Though its mandate was a broad one, the Parlement of Paris was too busy functioning as the highest sovereign court of the kingdom to concern itself on a regular basis with municipal business. Moreover, its structure was ill-suited to the performance of administrative tasks. The role of Parlement was rather that of overseer and intermediary, intervening at will when a problem in the city or a potential crisis came to the attention of the *parlementaires*. Concerned with everything from the price of firewood or the danger of plague to the choice of officers for the local militia, directives issued by Parlement during the sixteenth century aimed at the maintenance of order in the city and the well-being of its citizens. The execution of these directives was left to the municipality, but the parlementaires kept a watchful eye on the city, and records of the city council contain a number of letters from Parlement reprimanding the municipal officers for laxness in their duties.[15]

The other sovereign courts and other agencies of the central administration—the military governor of Paris, for example—occasionally intervened in municipal affairs in a manner similar to that of the Parlement. The king and his councils also kept a close watch on the business of the Hôtel de Ville

[15] J. H. Shennan (*The Parlement of Paris* [Ithaca, 1968], pp. 86-97) gives a generally good overview of the intervention of Parlement in municipal affairs, but the importance of the role of Parlement in city affairs appears disproportionately large because it is viewed in isolation from the other jurisdictions in the city. The origin of parlementary intervention in municipal affairs is unclear, but Gaston Zeller (*Institutions*, pp. 179-80) assures us that this authority was commonly exercised in towns having Parlements in the sixteenth century. Zeller's assumption is that the Parlements were able to dominate the city agencies by their greater dynamism and prestige, rather than because of any explicit authorization. Paul Robiquet, on the other hand, attributes the calm acceptance of the "rather haughty influence of Parlement" by the city officers to the overlapping membership of these two bodies (*Histoire municipale de Paris* [Paris, 1880], 1:297).

and frequently sent letters to the prévôt des marchands and échevins to direct their activities. As one might expect, the monarchy was particularly active in municipal affairs during times of civil strife or when war threatened. The king's intervention on such occasions was not limited to matters of supreme importance; he dictated even such details as curfew hours in the city and the size and patrol patterns of the night watch.[16] The king's interest in municipal affairs, moreover, extended to purely domestic concerns: commercial policies, provisioning, even necessary repairs to the sewer system might occasion missives from the sovereign to the Bureau de la Ville. Indeed, city records for the first three-quarters of the century indicate that the impetus for major public works projects and reforms of public administrative agencies, as well as measures for the maintenance of public order and tranquility, was nearly always provided by either the king or Parlement rather than by the Hôtel de Ville.[17]

The important role played by the monarchy in municipal affairs was not new in the sixteenth century. As the favored residence of the Capetian kings and the nucleus around which they built their kingdom, Paris had never known the independence from superior authority enjoyed by other municipalities with similar roots in the merchants' guilds of medieval towns.[18] That the city was denied administrative independence did not mean that the Capetian monarchs did not further the creation of a municipal government in Paris. Quite the contrary: the kings and the merchants of the Paris Hansa recognized very early the mutual benefits of close cooperation, and the gradual extension of the powers of the Hansa was the product of a long series of accords between the monarchy and the merchants.[19] By the late thirteenth cen-

[16] See, for example, *Reg. BV*, 7:368-70.
[17] A notable exception is the formation of a consular court in 1563 (*Reg. BV*, 5:321, 352-56).
[18] Henri Pirenne, *Medieval Cities* (Princeton, 1952), pp. 179-80.
[19] Raymond Cazelles, *Nouvelle Histoire de Paris de la fin du règne de Philippe Auguste à la mort de Charles V* (Paris, 1972), pp. 107 and 117; Lecaron, "Origines," 7:105-106.

tury, the officers of the Hansa were concerning themselves with the general interests of the Parisian bourgeoisie and not just with the river trade. Their headquarters, the Parloir aux Bourgeois, functioned as a kind of bureau for commercial affairs, a meeting place for the city's corporations, and a lobbying agency for mercantile privileges.[20] The Parloir aux Bourgeois also began to perform many of the functions of municipal administration, expanding its traditional responsibility for ports and quays to the construction and maintenance of roadways, fountains, fortifications, and other public works. The monarchs used the Parloir aux Bourgeois to collect taxes levied on the city's inhabitants, and kings and Parisians alike tacitly accepted the right of the Parloir to act as the representative agency of the city's bourgeoisie.[21]

Even during the period between the late thirteenth century and the Hundred Years War, however, which many historians have considered the apogee of the Parisian bourgeoisie and the period in which the prévôt des marchands and échevins appeared as "the most real power, if not the highest," the role of the monarchy in Parisian affairs should not be underestimated.[22] Although extensive mercantile privileges and administrative and judicial powers were granted the Parloir in order to ensure its continued support of the financially embarrassed and politically vulnerable monarchy, each concession was carefully weighted so that the dominant power remained with the crown. Public works projects gave the Parloir added responsibilities without any real increase in authority, and the control retained by the monarchy was emphasized by the fact that all of the tax concessions granted to support municipal affairs were of limited duration, renewable only at

[20] Robiquet, *Histoire*, 1:21-22; Lecaron, "Origines," 7:110-13; Georges Huisman, *La Juridiction de la municipalité parisienne de Saint Louis à Charles VII* (Paris, 1912), p. 22.

[21] Le Roux de Lincy, *Hôtel de Ville*, pp. 99-176: "Sentences du Parloir des Bourgeois."

[22] Cazelles, *Histoire de Paris*, pp. 117, 216-17. See also Lecaron, "Origines," 7:163-67; François Olivier-Martin, *Histoire de la coutume de la prévôté et vicomté de Paris* (Paris, 1922), 1:52.

the king's pleasure.[23] Moreover, in an era when nobles, religious corporations, and independent communes commonly exercised extensive rights of seigneurial justice, the juridical authority of the Parloir was not impressive. The records of the Parloir aux Bourgeois show that its basic jurisdiction was limited to commercial matters.[24] There is little evidence to support the traditional claim, voiced as early as the sixteenth century, that the prévôt des marchands had once shared the authority of the prévôt of Paris over ordinary civil and criminal justice in the city.[25] The most important check on the powers of the prévôt des marchands and échevins, however, was that the city had no charter guaranteeing municipal liberties. Time and again the city had to petition the king to reconfirm the traditional privileges of the bourgeoisie. No matter how old and customary these privileges, they were at the mercy of the royal will.[26]

It is within this historical framework that we can best un-

[23] Le Roux de Lincy, *Hôtel de Ville*, pp. 259-73: a list of official acts.

[24] Ibid., pp. 99-176. See, for example, documents cited pp. 152, 156, and 162. See also Huisman, *Municipalité*, pp. 110-47.

[25] *Reg. BV*, 3:209-10; accepted by Lecaron, "Origines," 7:167; questioned by Huisman, *Municipalité*, p. 203. The role played by the Parloir in the late thirteenth and early fourteenth centuries as a tribunal judging successions and other matters of private law, usually cited to support this argument concerning earlier judicial powers, is commonly misinterpreted. It was the usual practice before the codification of customary law in the sixteenth century to refer cases where the custom was uncertain to groups of respected local residents. The records of the Parloir suggest that it was in this capacity and not as judges by right that the Parloir decided private law cases. Called in on cases as "arbitre arbitrateur, ou amiable compositeur," the Parloir assembled "en conseil de bones gens et de sages" to express its understanding of customary practice in Paris. These cases provide further evidence that the Parloir was the accepted representative of the bourgeoisie but do not prove that it had extensive juridical authority. (See, for example, Le Roux de Lincy, *Hôtel de Ville*, pp. 106-109 and 119: documents.)

[26] Charles VI proved that this was no idle threat when in 1383 he abruptly abolished the Parloir on the ground that its officers had provoked the tax revolt known as the revolt of the "Maillotins." The prévôt des marchands and échevins were not officially reestablished until 1412. (*Ordonnances*, 5:685-87: Ordinance of January 27, 1383; 9:668: Ordinance of January 20, 1412; Favier, *Paris*, pp. 129-45; Lecaron, "Origines," 8:183-97.)

derstand the functioning of the Bureau de la Ville over the centuries. Rather than a powerful, independent force defending its integrity against the assaults of the monarchy, the city government was in fact an agency of limited mandate, dependent for its very existence on the toleration that the kings accorded it for the sole reason that it served their own purposes well.

The Selection of City Officers

In any assessment of the relationship between municipal government and monarchical authority, it is necessary to know who the city officers were and how they were selected. In the case of sixteenth-century Paris, it is important to look not only at the formal electoral process but at the informal practices that might have subverted this process from within and the external forces that might have impinged upon it from without. Only after determining who had a stake in the selection process can we begin to judge whose interests the municipal government did in fact serve.

As a survey of electoral procedures will show, the number of those who could aspire to the red and tan robes of the prévôt des marchands was very small indeed, and the number who could help to select these officers was not much larger. Although the authority of the *corps municipal* in matters relating to police, finance, and welfare extended to all persons in the city, there was no basis for popular participation in municipal government. Even those who had acquired the privilege of bourgeois status in the city had no right to participate in municipal elections or politics. The privilege of voting in city elections, like the privilege of attending council meetings, was only enjoyed at the invitation of the officers of the Bureau de la Ville.

The election of the prévôt des marchands and échevins was complicated and indirect. Besides the *corps municipal* and the city councillors (together known as the *corps de ville*), the electorate included only two bourgeois from each of the sixteen quartiers. By no means the elected representatives of the local populace, these thirty-two bourgeois were chosen from a list of names supplied for each quartier by a district assembly. This assembly consisted of the dizainiers and cinquanteniers and eight additional delegates hand-picked by the quartenier.[27] The selection of these bourgeois electors was thus determined by the district officers, and in any event, the thirty-two bourgeois made up only a minority of the electorate, outnumbered by the prévôt des marchands, échevins, councillors, and quarteniers. City elections were consequently by their very structure subject to the domination of those already in power.

The more permanent city offices—those of the greffier, receveur, procureur, quarteniers, and councillors—were in principle also elective. The term of office was indefinite and normally extended until death or resignation for old age or senility. Election procedures for the first three offices followed the form of the échevinal elections, and the election of the quarteniers imitated this ritual on a district level except that the mandate of the local officers assembled with the chosen bourgeois representatives extended only to the nomination of three candidates for the office of quartenier; the final choice was left to the corps de ville.[28] This provision was important because it ensured the higher officers a greater measure of control over the lower ones. It demonstrates once more that the locus of power in city politics was always high. In any event, by the middle of the sixteenth century, these semipermanent offices changed hands more frequently through resignation than through election, as the holders of these offices had gradually acquired the implicit right to name their successors. The consent of the corps de ville was required,

---

[27] *Reg. BV,* 4:201-207. Similar descriptions can be found for nearly any year around the dates of August 16-19 in the *Registres.* Mid-fifteenth-century rules specified that the corps de ville elect the bourgeois delegates from the list supplied by the quarteniers (Lecaron, "Origines," 8:207, citing ordinance of July 25, 1450). By the sixteenth century, however, it was customary to draw lots for these positions.

[28] See, for example, *Reg. BV,* 2:82-83 or 3:152-53.

but consent was almost always easily obtained if the designated successor was judged capable of executing the duties of the office and if certain formalities were observed.

The election of city councillors differed in several important respects from that of other city officers. In the first place, only the prévôt des marchands, échevins, and incumbent councillors could vote for new city councillors. Neither quarteniers nor the bourgeoisie of the city had any say in the matter. Secondly, the city councillor could in theory resign only in favor of his son, son-in-law, brother, or nephew, although a number of exceptions to this rule could be cited.[29] In such cases, however, the council was usually careful to protect itself by the technical device of refusing to accept the resignation proffered in favor of someone who was not a close relative but at the same time voting to elect the designated candidate as a tribute to the outstanding career of civic service of the resigning member.[30] Informal practice thus permitted the resignation *in favorum* even where a strict interpretation of the regulations forbade it.

Although venality was strictly forbidden where city office was concerned, the evidence suggests that money did sometimes change hands. The permanent offices, particularly those connected with the city's fiscal operations, were most likely to be abused. In 1576, for example, the city receveur, François de Vigny, was accused of selling his office for 50,000 francs.[31] On several occasions the accusation of venality extended to the office of city councillor. For example, in 1536 one of the échevins protested the reception of Jean Courtin as city councillor and asked that he be made to swear that he

---

[29] Of the ninety men who were members of the city council between 1535 and 1575, approximately one in six appears to have been the designated successor of a councillor to whom he was not closely related.

[30] *Reg. BV,* 5:522.

[31] According to the chronicler Pierre de L'Estoile, the purchaser was in a precarious financial situation, and it was only reasonable to assume that he would attempt to recuperate his costs at the public expense (*Journal pour le règne de Henri III {1574-1589}*, ed. Louis Raymond Lefèvre [Paris, 1943], p. 127). See also *Reg. BV,* 8:23-29.

had not paid for the office. Only after long debate and the intervention of Parlement was the oath administered and Courtin accepted.[32]

When the Catholic League took over Paris in May of 1588, one of the first actions of Henry of Guise and the revolutionary commune was to declare an end to venality in city office. Asserting that most of the city officers were then acquiring office by purchase, the league proposed to fill all future offices by election and to limit the term of city officers, including the city councillors and quarteniers, to two years or some other fixed duration.[33] It is impossible to judge how much truth lies behind this accusation of widespread venality, for the political motives of the league in setting up a revolutionary commune obscure the facts of the issue. Certainly there was not the open sale of office that occurred in the monarchical bureaucracy. Whether or not it was common to accept cash for one's resignation, however, the very facility with which city councillors named their own successors in the second half of the century indicates that they had a proprietary attitude toward their civic functions.

It is clear, moreover, that whatever corruption of the electoral process there was took place within the period we are studying. Among the city councillors named to office prior to 1550, at least twenty-three were elected, while only nine are known to have benefited from the resignation of a previous city councillor. During the 1550s there were five elections and seven resignations. Between 1560 and 1575 there were only seven elections—two of which occurred because of the

[32] Ibid., 2:223, 226, 251. There is also evidence that, at least by the 1570s, the office of city councillor was considered to have a monetary value even within the family. Just a month before his death in November 1576, Louis Huault resigned his office as city councillor in favor of Claude de Faulcon, the husband of his eldest daughter. When Huault's estate was divided between his widow and five children in 1578, the office of city councillor was treated like a dowry or other advance on the paternal succession and was deducted from the inheritance rights of the eldest daughter. The value assigned the office was £1,000. (AN, Min. cen. VI:59 [19/8/78]: partage.)

[33] Reg. BV, 9:134-35.

sudden need to replace men expelled for Protestantism—while twenty-seven city councillors acquired their positions by virtue of resignation.

The patrimonial nature of succession to office was further enhanced after 1581 by the practice of resignation *en survivance*. Following a procedure by that time common in the royal bureaucracy, the officeholder resigned his position to a son or other close relative with the understanding that he was to continue to exercise the functions of the office himself until he died or was incapacitated, at which time the survivor would automatically receive the office. The practice was first introduced into municipal affairs in April 1580, when conferred upon the quartenier Jacques Kerver in special recognition of forty-nine years of civic service.[34] When the city councillor Bernard Prevost asked to resign *en survivance* sixteen months later, there was no question of its being a special favor. Four other city councillors immediately stepped forward to make identical requests, and at the same meeting it was agreed in principle that such resignations would in the future be accepted.[35]

The right to name one's own heir to office was not, however, one that could be fully relied upon. City records show that technicalities could be found that would serve to disallow a candidate that the other members of the corps de ville did not favor, even though the resignation was in principle acceptable. In 1564, for example, the councillor Nicolas de Livres resigned directly in favor of his son instead of tendering his resignation to the prévôt des marchands with the stipulation that his son be named, as he was required to do. The resignation was disqualified for this oversight, and since Livres had died in the meantime, another candidate was chosen. On other occasions, the same technical error was conveniently overlooked.[36]

When a councillor either did not choose to name his suc-

---

[34] Ibid., 8:236.
[35] Ibid., 8:263.
[36] Ibid., 5:433. Cf. ibid., 3:21-23; 7:445.

cessor or died before he could do so, it was customary to name the prévôt des marchands to the available slot on the council, provided, of course, that he was not already a city councillor. The same honor was occasionally extended to the échevins. At least seven of the ninety councillors being studied here were elected to the council during their terms as prévôt des marchands and another ten during terms as échevins. Only one man who was prévôt des marchands during these middle decades of the sixteenth century was not also chosen as city councillor, and approximately half of the échevins eventually became councillors.

The rules that covered the resignation and election of the city councillors and such customs as the election of the prévôt des marchands to the council ensured the domination of municipal politics by a small group of men. The right to name one's successor, combined with the necessity of having the designated candidate accepted by the prévôt des marchands, the échevins, and one's fellow councillors, fostered a sense of corporate identity on the part of these most prestigious city officers. It kept the individual councillors from viewing their offices as but a form of personal property, while at the same time it encouraged family traditions of civic service.

The only threat to the entrenched hierarchy of city officers in municipal elections came not from below, from the bourgeoisie and the district-level officers, but from above, from the king. The newly elected prévôt des marchands and échevins had to be approved by the king before they could be invested with their offices. At times, the kings went beyond their right to approve elected candidates and interfered directly in the election process. Such interventions can be traced back at least to the reign of Charles VII. Both Charles and his son, Louis XI, occasionally sent the Bureau de la Ville letters that "recommended" in the strongest possible terms a candidate for city office.[37] It is significant, however, that Charles and Louis were respectful enough of Parisian traditions—or

[37] Favier, *Paris*, p. 422n.

merely cautious enough—to choose their candidates from among the city's notables. Most of their candidates were, in addition, men who had been previously elected to municipal office. Furthermore, when the monarch's nominee was not elected, as sometimes happened, the matter was allowed to drop quietly. Neither Charles VII nor Louis XI tried forcibly to impose unacceptable candidates on a reluctant city council.[38]

Whether through principle, political wisdom, or simply because they were more concerned with their wars with the Hapsburgs and their pleasures in the Loire valley than with the politics of their capital city, the three kings who followed Louis XI showed little inclination to meddle in the internal affairs of the Hôtel de Ville. Francis I intervened only once, in 1536, when battles lost in Picardy had put the very security of the capital in jeopardy. He asked that the prévôt des marchands be retained for another term so that an experienced man would have charge during the troubled times. The king specifically provided, though, that this was a one-time affair and that he did not wish to abrogate the city's privileges or to set unfortunate precedents for the future. Even then, the king's request was put to Parlement before being accepted by the city.[39] Not until the second half of the century, when the monarchy's fiscal and political problems became acute, did the French kings once more intervene persistently in the domestic politics of their capital.

The issue was reopened in 1556, when Henry II questioned the election of the new prévôt des marchands. Admonished by the city's representative that not since the reign of King Louis XI had any candidate been chosen who lacked a plurality, Henry accepted the election results, replying that he had no wish to interfere with the privileges of the bourgeoisie.[40] The next year, however, and in each of the other two elections held during his lifetime, Henry II used his "absolute power"

[38] Ibid., pp. 426-27n. Le Roux de Lincy, *Hôtel de Ville*, p. 158, and Robiquet, *Histoire*, 1:271-72, note only the occasions on which Louis XI successfully imposed his candidates.
[39] *Reg. BV*, 2:272-73.
[40] Ibid., 4:445.

to substitute a candidate receiving fewer votes for at least one of those elected by the city officers.[41] Henry was consistent in neither the reasons he gave for his interference nor in the candidates he selected. In 1559 his first choice for échevin was the very man whose election by the Bureau de la Ville he had overturned in 1557.[42] He did, however, consistently name as échevin men who had received some votes in the city election and who had some experience in the affairs of the Bureau de la Ville—just as Charles VII and Louis XI had chosen men of experience and standing likely to be acceptable to the other city officers.

Henry's widow, Catherine de Medici, likewise meddled in municipal elections. Her first attempt to intervene, in 1563, was ignored by the city, a defeat she accepted without comment.[43] A more serious confrontation occurred the next year, when Catherine ordered election procedures changed in all French towns. Henceforth, two men were to be elected for each municipal position in order that the king might make his own choice between them. The officers of the Paris Bureau de la Ville at first resisted this move, carrying out the city elections in the traditional manner and sending remonstrances to the king. Ignoring the city's complaints, Charles IX sent letters naming the next prévôt des marchands and échevins. The letters were delivered by the governor and lieutenant for the king in Paris, the maréchal de Montmorency, who appeared personally before the assembled Bureau de la Ville in order to ensure compliance with the king's will. After a final plea to Montmorency, the city officers yielded. The terms of their compliance indicate clearly their understanding of the nature of monarchical authority. Having been instructed by the king that, their remonstrances notwithstanding, he wanted those named in his letters to be prévôt des marchands and échevins, they were prepared to obey.[44]

[41] Ibid., 4:494.
[42] Ibid., 5:39-40.
[43] Ibid., 5:274-75.
[44] Ibid., 5:444-58. Catherine de Médicis, *Lettres*, ed. Hector de la Ferrière and Baguenault de Puchesse (Paris, 1880-1909), 2:214.

In the elections that followed, the royal prerogative of naming the prévôt des marchands and échevins was again claimed, but with a bit less insistence each year. Within a few years, the candidates with the most votes were regularly confirmed by the crown.[45] Indirect means, like letters "recommending" candidates, were again used effectively to influence elections, but direct confrontation was avoided. The issue surfaced again at the Estates General of Blois in 1577. The deputies for the Third Estate, under the presidency of the Paris prévôt des marchands and city councillor Nicolas Luillier, sought the free election of all prévôts des marchands, échevins, and city governors and the removal from office of those who had not been freely elected.[46] The grievances of the Third Estate had little effect, however, and the monarchs continued on occasion to interfere in city elections.

It is significant, however, that throughout this period royal intervention in municipal elections operated consistently within the framework of the political hierarchies already established within the city. The monarchs were not attempting to undermine these hierarchies but rather to ensure that the persons named would be those most trustworthy in their loyalty to the crown.

The Hôtel de Ville and Royal Finances

A keener appreciation of the relationship between the municipal officers and the monarchy can be reached by looking more closely at one of the main functions of the municipal officers, that of collecting taxes for the king. The city's tax burden, which was one of the most volatile political issues of this period, offers a particularly good opportunity to evaluate the conflicting loyalties of the municipal officers and the tensions that underlay their attitude toward the crown.

Tax collecting was one of the most important services that the city government provided the monarchy. Not only was

[45] *Reg. BV*, 5:514, 574-76, 600-603; 6:47-48, 134.
[46] BN, MS fr. 10871, fol. 116: article 440.

the city responsible for the collection of a number of indirect taxes such as the *aides* on fresh and salt-water fish, wine, and various other products sold in the city, it was also responsible for the apportionment and collection of any direct taxes laid upon the inhabitants of the capital. During the sixteenth century these functions, routinely performed by the Bureau de la Ville for several centuries, absorbed a larger and larger share of the bureau's attention as the embattled and extravagant Valois monarchs drained the revenues from traditional sources and invented new levies besides.

A number of these levies were disguised as "loans" or "free gifts." At one point, Henry II ordered the Parisians to bring their silver plate to the Hôtel de Ville to serve as collateral for bonds being sold to raise money for his wars.[47] Charles IX seized upon the city's custom of offering a gift to a newly crowned monarch to demand that the Bureau de la Ville offer his brother d'Anjou, recently chosen King of Poland, a present worth at least £150,000 (*livres tournois*). Gifts previously offered kings assuming the French throne had never exceeded about £10,000.[48] Free gifts and loans had a certain advantage for the populace over direct taxes; they did not set a precedent. Nevertheless, whatever they were called, the financial demands the king placed on the city had to be met by taxes— direct, indirect, or a combination of the two—imposed upon the city's residents.

Indirect taxes had long provided the income for public works projects, the local militia, and other municipal expenses. The king granted the Bureau de la Ville the farm of various *aides* for stipulated periods of time, and the city in return shared the receipts with the crown.[49] If funds proved insufficient, the city had to seek further tax allocations from the king, for only the crown had the right to impose taxes. During the

[47] *Reg. BV*, 4:264, 265, 282-84.
[48] Ibid., 7:89. The sum, eventually reduced to £50,000, was still owing in 1574, when Charles IX died and d'Anjou became Henry III, King of France. For earlier gifts: Ibid., 1:221-22, 3:153n.
[49] Ibid., 1:7-8.

course of the sixteenth century, however, the city was obliged
to ask for new *aides* more and more frequently, and the largest
share of this tax money went to pay the extraordinary sub-
ventions demanded by the monarchy rather than to meet ordinary, local expenses.

For the first three decades of the century, the demands of
the crown were moderate. Except for the levy of £150,000
urgently required in 1528 to help ransom the sons of Francis
I held captive in Spain, the special loans and gifts accorded
the monarchy by the Hôtel de Ville were generally in the
neighborhood of £20,000 to £30,000.[50] These sums began to
escalate dramatically in the 1530s, and by mid-century they
had undergone an approximate tenfold increase. Intended primarily to finance the state's war effort, the levies demanded
of the city during the second half of the century figured in
the hundreds of thousands rather than the tens of thousands
of livres. During the reigns of Henry II and his sons, the
Bureau de la Ville was almost continually occupied with the
raising of one or another extraordinary contribution to the
crown. Seldom was one effort finished before another had begun. In 1575 alone the city contributed more than a million
livres in forced loans and taxes.[51]

The potential revenue from indirect taxes having long since
proved insufficient, the monarchy increasingly demanded direct taxes of the city, despite the exemption from the *taille* (a
tax on the Third Estate) and from other head taxes traditionally enjoyed by the inhabitants of Paris. Resembling the *taille*
in everything but name, the *capitations*, *soldes*, and other direct taxes raised in the city were distributive taxes; that is to
say, the king and his councils decided the sum of money
required and apportioned this total among the various local
administrative bodies for collection. In Paris this responsibility fell to the Bureau de la Ville, which then divided the
city's quota among the quartiers. The district officers were

    [50] Ransom money from 1528: see ibid., 2:13. Other "loans" and "gifts":
see ibid., 1:32, 80-83, 193-95, 201-202, 230, 276-77; 2:146.
    [51] Wolfe, *Fiscal System*, p. 116.

directed to select assistants from among the bourgeoisie to help compile neighborhood tax rolls according to the amount each person (or each household) could presumably afford. Because the principle of a continuing obligation to make direct contributions to the crown was not accepted by the city officers, no standing tax rolls were kept. City law required that the rolls be burned after the collection was completed. Therefore, the cumbersome process of apportionment had to be repeated each time direct taxes were demanded by the king.[52]

The officers of the Hôtel de Ville habitually resisted attempts at direct taxation, protesting as a matter of principle that such taxes violated the city's traditional privileges and as a practical matter that the poverty of the city's inhabitants caused tremendous resistance to the collection of head taxes. In 1557, for example, the Bureau de la Ville warned the king that there was danger of popular sedition if he persisted in demanding a *capitation* of the city's already beggared residents.[53] There was nothing unusual about the city protesting the funds demanded by the king; indeed, remonstrances were a virtually automatic response to extraordinary taxes levied on the city, and the frequency with which these complaints resulted in an immediate moderation of the sum demanded suggests that the kings expected to bargain a bit with the city and planned their financial demands accordingly. Direct taxes, however, were protested with particular vehemence.

The reasons given the king by the Bureau de la Ville in protesting direct taxation were no doubt justifiable: popular resistance to direct taxation and the cumbersome apportionment system had made for enormous difficulties in collecting these levies. On the other hand, the possibility that these officers were acting more from selfish motives than from civic concern should not be discounted. As wealthy citizens, the

[52] *Reg. BV,* 2:22, for example, indicates that the city was quite concerned that no standing rolls be kept. Elaborate precautions were devised to protect the rolls drawn up for the collection for the ransom of the king's sons in 1528. The lists were to be kept in a locked chest and burned as soon as the collection of funds was completed.

[53] Ibid., 3:125; 4:481-82, 507-508.

city officials could expect to pay a large share of any proportional head taxes, while revenues raised off articles of general consumption—*aides* on fish or firewood, for example—hit hardest at the poor. Certainly there appear to have been selfish motives behind the decision of the municipal assembly in 1573 to set the highest individual assessment of the *capitation* at twenty livres, thirty if it later proved necessary, despite the insistence of the quarteniers that the required total of £50,000 could never be met if the richest inhabitants did not contribute at least forty livres apiece.[54]

Besides the repeated use of the *capitation* and frequent escalations of indirect taxes, the Bureau de la Ville became increasingly involved during this period with another sort of financial device in aid of the central government, the *rente sur l'Hôtel de Ville*. Even more than the welter of stopgap measures, the free gifts and forced loans, the *rentes* on the Hôtel de Ville contributed to the ultimate destruction of the fiscal stability and the political credibility of the Valois regime.[55]

Rentes sur l'Hôtel de Ville were bonds sold to private citizens bearing an annual interest normally set at 8.3% (the *denier douze* or twelfth penny) paid from the income from selected taxes—on salt, for example, or wine. The Hôtel de Ville was in theory only the middleman: the king turned the designated revenues over to the city to disburse to the purchasers of *rentes* (*rentiers*), and the city had merely to "lend its name" to the affair. Historians generally agree that the king chose the Hôtel de Ville as the vehicle for this money-raising scheme because the city's reputation for fiscal responsibility was expected to attract more purchasers than would have been attracted by bonds issued in the name of the financially shaky monarchy.[56]

Originating in 1522, *rentes* on the Hôtel de Ville were not extensively used until the reign of Henry II. By the time of

[54] Ibid., 7:138-40.
[55] Bernard Schnapper, *Les Rentes au xvie siècle* (Paris, 1957), is the best source on this subject.
[56] Ibid., pp. 152-53; Wolfe, *Fiscal System*, p. 93.

the last Valois king, Henry III, however, this financial expedient had been so overused and so much abused that it was difficult to find purchasers for the *rentes*. The city officers found themselves caught in a double bind: the king demanded that they find new purchasers for the bonds, but they could no longer hope to assure investors of regular interest payments. The desperate kings had assigned as collateral for the *rentes* such distant and uncertain sources of income as the city treasuries of Toulouse and Montpellier and revenues extorted from a reluctant and uncooperative clergy.[57] When interest payments fell seriously in arrears in 1576, the officers of the Hôtel de Ville addressed strongly worded remonstrances to the king, lamenting the plight of "Frenchmen of all estates":

ecclesiastics, princes, gentlemen, bourgeois, artisans, nursing orders, widows, minors, orphans, colleges, communities and people of all sorts, [who] freely and with good will placed their goods and funds at your service and aid in your urgent necessity and that of your predecessors

And a good many, to do this, sold their houses, lands, and possessions; sometimes at low and base price. Others were by your command forced and constrained by us, the prévôt des marchands and échevins, and by violent compulsion and soldiers garrisoned at their own expense in their own homes [forced] to bring their funds to contribute, [funds] which they often had to borrow from their friends or sold their possessions and properties to provide.[58]

The anger of the city officers in 1576 and their embarrassment at the ignoble role they had been forced to play in procuring funds for the king contrasts sharply with the earlier acquiescence of the *corps municipal* in *rentes* on the Hôtel de Ville. Until royal abuses made it impossible to find purchasers, it had seemed easier to lend the city's name to bond issues than to raise further tax monies. These *rentes*, moreover, appeared a good investment opportunity to wealthy Parisians, and many city officers had invested heavily in them. When

[57] Wolfe, *Fiscal System*, pp. 115 and 154; Schnapper, *Rentes*, pp. 172-73.
[58] *Reg. BV*, 7:387.

the worsening financial straits of the crown made interest payments increasingly erratic, the municipal officials were thus
concerned for their own purses as well as for the city's reputation for fiscal responsibility. Complaining that parents were
being obliged to take their children out of school, marriages
were being broken up, and heirs were having blood-feuds
because funds they had been solemnly promised were not being
paid, the city officers were speaking for themselves and their
peers.[59]

It does not necessarily follow, however, that the officers
were any less sincere in speaking also for the old man who
went hungry because he had invested all he had in *rentes*, for
the country gentleman in despair because he had traveled miles
to Paris for his money and had to return empty-handed, or
for the nursing orders that had to turn away the poor souls
they could no longer afford to shelter.[60] Concerned for their
own fortunes and families, the city officers were nevertheless
anxious for the peace and prosperity of the realm. Protests
against abuses of the *rentes* increased in rhythm with the general tenor of complaints about the extravagance of the crown
and the corrupt practices of the agencies of government. From
the early years of the century, when city officials regularly
but respectfully asked that tax burdens be lightened because
times were hard, to the years of religious war, when the complaints were bitterly angry, the tone of the remonstrances
hardened dramatically. In 1575, for example, complaints about
a new troop tax presented to the king by the municipal assembly included an impassioned outcry against the "universal
corruption in all estates and orders of the realm"—against
simony in the church, venality in the judiciary, and brutality
in the police and armed forces, as well as against fiscal mismanagement in royal agencies.[61]

Uncomfortably poised between city and crown, the municipal officers recognized the importance of cooperation with

[59] Ibid.
[60] Ibid.
[61] Ibid., 7:313-15.

the monarchy for their own personal success and for the city's welfare, but they were not willing blindly and silently to serve a grasping power that despoiled all it touched.

Municipal Government and the Parisian Bourgeoisie

So far the officers of the Hôtel de Ville have been discussed for the most part in relation to the higher authority of the monarchy. But what about the relationship between the Bureau de la Ville and the Parisians in whose name they governed? Whose interests did the Bureau de la Ville in fact represent?

Clearly the more prosperous artisans and merchants of the city had good reason to feel positively about the Hôtel de Ville, for the *corps municipal* had continued in the sixteenth century to serve as their lobbying agent with the monarchy, defending the city's commercial interests and the traditional privileges of the Parisian bourgeoisie. When ships belonging to Parisian merchants were confiscated in Flanders in 1528, for example, it was through the Prévôté de la Marchandise that these merchants secured the king's aid in obtaining their release. In 1563 the city government brought to the king's attention the request of the local businessmen for a special court to try commercial cases, a privilege already enjoyed by Lyons, Toulouse, and Rouen. The monarchy respected the right of the Hôtel de Ville to present the views of the city's merchants and on occasion even actively sought the opinion of the local businessmen through the agency of the Hôtel de Ville, as in 1548, when Henry II asked the city officers to deliberate with local merchants and bourgeois about a proposal to create a bank in the city.[62]

The Prévôté de la Marchandise did not, however, look after the interests of the mercantile elite alone; it represented all of the Parisians who enjoyed high social and economic standing—the bourgeois who lived off investment revenues, mem-

[62] 1528: Ibid., 2:9; 1563: Ibid., 5:321; 1548: Ibid., 3:107-108.

bers of the liberal professions, officers of the sovereign courts, even nobles residing in the city (except, of course, the higher nobility, which had a more direct path to the ear of the king). The city officers, for example, repeatedly defended the exemption from the *ban* and *arrière ban* long enjoyed by residents of the capital.[63] Since the *ban*, the obligation for military service that holders of fiefs owed to the king, applied only to those who possessed noble properties, the issue was one of concern to only the very highest levels of local society.

At just what level of society did a Parisian begin to look upon the officers of the Hôtel de Ville as his agents and allies? This is a difficult question to answer, for the sources that reflect public opinion during this period are scanty. The journals and diaries that we have from Parisians living in the sixteenth century are all products of the same social milieu as the city officers; they view the city hierarchy from the top and not from below.[64] A couple of popular songs and pamphlets satirize the Hôtel de Ville, but they are evidently motivated by polemical (usually Protestant) religious sentiments and cannot be assumed representative of the population at large.[65]

[63] Ibid., 1:138-40, 173-79; 2:175-78; 4:525-27.

[64] Pierre de L'Estoile, for example, the most famous Parisian chronicler of the late sixteenth century, was related to a family that held city office through both his stepfather, François Tronçon, and his brother-in-law Jean Tronçon. Jean and François were both sons of the city councillor and prévôt des marchands Jean Tronçon. BN, MS fr. 32589 Saint-André: *fiançailles* of 16/6/65 (Tronçon/L'Estoile) and *fiançailles* of 12/5/60 (Tronçon/Monthelon); AN, Y107, fol. 213v°: marriage contract of 6/4/60 (Monthelon/Tronçon).

[65] "Chanson de Marcel, prévôt des marchands," in *Recueil de chants historiques français*, ed. Antoine Jean Victor Le Roux de Lincy (Paris, 1842), 2:294-98. "Le Livre des Marchands," usually attributed to Louis Régnier de la Planche, and published in La Planche's *Histoire de l'estat de France, tant de la république que de la religion sous le règne de François II*, ed. Edouard Mennechet (Paris, 1836), vol. 2. Individuals connected with city government are satirized in some of the poems and *placards* collected by L'Estoile, but the attacks are on their professional or personal behavior and not on their roles in civic life. A single, inconclusive bit of evidence suggesting a tradition of popular respect in the city for its highest officer is to be found in a saying repeated by the Swiss student Thomas Platter, who visited Paris in 1599. Describing in his journal the structure of city government in

The lists of participants in civic ceremonies, however, suggest that a sense of positive identification with the government of the Hôtel de Ville extended at least through the organized corporations in Paris. The municipal government, having itself originated in the medieval corporate structures of the city, traditionally accorded a conspicuous role in civic ceremonies to the artisanal and mercantile corporations. The ceremonies organized for the entry of Henry II in 1549 are typical: two hundred and fifty printers, two hundred stone masons and carpenters, and as many dressmakers were chosen by their guilds to take part in the festivities. In lesser numbers, representatives of more than sixty corporations—from pastry chefs to grain carriers—dressed in their finest to parade the colors of their guilds through the streets of the city.[66]

These ceremonies may seem frivolous to a generation that does not take pageantry seriously, but they were in fact a brilliant public relations device for the monarchy and the municipality alike. Enlisting the participation of the common people while at the same time dazzling them with the glory of their sovereign and his regal entourage, these festivities heightened a sense of popular involvement with the municipal organization while simultaneously raising the king in his majesty even farther above his subjects.

In surveying the institutions of city government and some of the political issues that concerned municipal officers in the middle of the sixteenth century, I have stressed the continuity with medieval traditions and underlined the ways in which a functional balance was maintained between monarchical and municipal authority. In the sixteenth century, as in earlier periods, city government functioned in close cooperation with the king. The king remained, as he had always been, the dominant partner in the alliance. The city's role as tax col-

Paris, Platter wrote that the person of the prévôt des marchands is "sacred." "When someone happens accidentally to break something, they say to him, 'you will never become prévôt des marchands.' " (L. Sieber, "Description de Paris, par Thomas Platter le jeune, de Bâle [1599]," *MSHP* 23 [1896]:181.)

[66] 1549: *Reg. BV*, 3:164-65.

lector gave it a certain de facto leverage to use in bargaining
with the crown, and the city officers' right to remonstrate
with the king allowed them to vocalize their grievances, but
ultimately the city's powers were limited by the prevailing
theory of the "absolute powers" of the monarchy. It is important to appreciate that these theoretical limits on municipal authority were accepted by the city officers because of
their understanding of the nature of monarchical authority.
They were also accepted by the city officers because it was to
their advantage to do so. Whatever pride they had in traditions of municipal liberties, the city officers could easily recognize that service to the crown offered a far greater potential
for reward than service to the municipality. It was only natural that they should have wanted, as far as possible, to be of
service to the king through their service to the city.[67]

[67] A very different view of relationships between civic and monarchical
agencies is given in Orest Ranum, *Paris in the Age of Absolutism* (New York,
1968), p. 28.

2. The City Councillors: A Collective Portrait

Mannequins, Hennequins, ridicule canaille,
Fils de l'aune et du poids, des comptoirs, des étaux. . . .
—1576 verse cited by L'Estoile

As WE HAVE SEEN in the previous chapter, election procedures in the Parisian municipality allowed a small number of families to dominate civic politics. It is the purpose of this chapter to examine the social and professional character of the families that made up that unofficial, self-selecting elite, first by studying the family background of the participants in city government and then by investigating their occupational pursuits. A number of questions present themselves: Was the Prévôté de la Marchandise in the sixteenth century still the organ of the merchants of Paris? What role did the growing legions of royal officers play in civic affairs? And to fill in the portrait that emerges from this study of family ties and careers, what were the styles of living and the values of these men, their social aspirations, their charitable activities and religious beliefs, their urban dwellings and country estates? To understand the care with which they planned for the success of their offspring, we must know something about the city councillors not only in the Hôtel de Ville but in their work, their parishes, and their homes.

Family Ties in City Government

Before turning to the ninety men who were city councillors between 1535 and 1575, let us take a broader look at participation in municipal politics in sixteenth-century Paris. As near as can be calculated from surviving records, a total of 305 persons held office in the Hôtel de Ville of Paris during the sixteenth century as prévôts des marchands, échevins, and city councillors.[1] (Many held more than one of these offices; they are counted only once.) It is thus obvious that only a very small percentage of the city's residents ever had the honor of being named to the highest offices of the Hôtel de Ville. On the other hand, since the number of city offices was limited, it was not possible for a very large proportion of the population to hold these offices. A relevant question, then, might be to ask how much turnover there was in city office.

The prévôt des marchands and four échevins served two-year terms, so a maximum of 250 persons could have held these offices during the course of the sixteenth century. In fact, 215 persons held these offices during this period; thus the turnover rate was 86%. The city councillors served unlimited and often lengthy terms (the mean for the eighty city councillors whose dates of nomination and resignation are known is 15.4 years), but it is significant that only 30% of the city officers served as both prévôt des marchands or échevin and as city councillor.[2] Given the mechanisms that favored the acquisition and retention of office by a narrow

[1] Calculations are based on a list of officers drawn from BN, MSS fr. 32359 and 32840 and reconciled with data drawn from the *Reg. BV* and other sources. None of these lists is entirely accurate, particularly for the period before 1530. The lack of a standard orthography and the frequency with which sons bore the same first name as their father also create certain problems of identification. Despite possible errors, the ratios produced by these figures should be sufficiently accurate for comparative purposes.

[2] The following table shows the frequency with which very short or very long terms were served by the ninety city councillors studied.

Number of Years Served on City Council

Years	Number of Councillors	Years	Number of Councillors
0-4	16	30-39	7
5-9	16	40 or more	2
10-19	25	cannot compute	8
20-29	16	Total	90

TABLE I
Family Ties among the City Officers of Sixteenth-Century Paris

No. of persons in family holding office	No. of families	% of families	No. of persons
1	140	46%	140
2	29	19	58
3	11	11	33
4	8	10	32
5	6	10	30
6	2	4	12
Total	196	100%	305

elite, the number of individuals who held high city office in the sixteenth century is somewhat greater than might have been expected.

What then of the number of families involved in high city office? For the time being, let us limit our inquiry to the paternal line. For the purpose of these calculations, patronyms will be used as a convenient, though not a perfectly accurate, measure of family ties.[3] Table I shows the distribution of civic office among the 196 patronyms borne by the 305 men who served as prévôts des marchands, échevins, and councillors in the sixteenth century. As can be seen here,

[3] In only five cases does it appear possible that surnames were shared by men related only distantly, if at all: Boucher, Le Breton, Le Clerc, Le Comte, Prevost. Genealogical information on the ninety city councillors and their families has been compiled from a wide variety of sources: from genealogical records and remaining parish records at the Bibliothèque nationale, from notarial records in the Archives nationales, from the Y series of Châtelet records, and from such published documentary sources as the *Reg. BV*, the *Epitaphier du Vieux Paris* (Emile Raunié and Max Prinet, 4 vols. [Paris, 1890-1914]), and the *Collection de documents pour servir à l'histoire des hôpitaux de Paris* (Léon Brièle, 4 vols. [Paris, 1881-1887]). Some use has been made of secondary sources such as the genealogies in Edouard Maugis, *Histoire du Parlement de Paris de l'avènement des rois Valois à la mort d'Henri IV*, vol. 3 (Paris, 1916), and Chaix d'Est-Ange, *Dictionnaire des familles françaises anciennes ou notables à la fin du xix* siècle*, 20 vols. (Evreux, 1909-1929), but I have been cautious about accepting these statements without documentary evidence to back them up.

nearly half of the city officers were the sole members of their families to serve in high municipal office during the course of the century, and nearly two-thirds had at most one other direct relation in the paternal line in city office. The mean number of city officers per family is only 1.6.[4] This figure seems low, in view of the ease with which city councillors could, through most of the sixteenth century, resign their positions in favor of close relatives.[5]

On the other hand, though these averages are low, Table 1 also shows that there were some families in the city that were repeatedly active in sixteenth-century politics. Six members of the Le Lievre family and six Prevosts held high city office.[6] Five members each of the families of Bragelongne, Hennequin, Luillier, Sanguin, de Thou, and Viole, and four members each of another eight families served as prévôts des marchands, échevins, and councillors in the 1500s.[7] Most of these families participated in municipal office continuously for half a century or more, and their role in city politics is even more impressive if we go beyond the limits of the sixteenth century.

The Luillier family, for example, first attained the échevinage in 1444;[8] over the next two centuries at least a dozen members of the family held high city office. We do not have records of the fifteenth-century city councillors, but we do know that three members of the Luillier family served as échevins during that period, and from the time Eustache Luillier, sieur de Saint-Mesmin, became prévôt des marchands and a city councillor in 1504 until his great-great-great-grandson

---

[4] The mean is somewhat lower (1.3) if we consider only prévôts des marchands and échevins and somewhat higher (1.7) if we consider just councillors.

[5] Adding in the next level of city officers, the quarteniers, does not noticeably change the patterns of participation.

[6] It is, however, possible that Pierre Prevost was not related to the five Prevosts de Saint-Cyr. The appendix provides a complete list of the sixteenth-century city councillors.

[7] Aubery, Du Drac, Marle, Montmirail, Neufville, Paillart, Palluau, Perrot.

[8] Jean Luillier, échevin in 1444 and 1446 (BN, MS fr. 32359, fol. 5).

Geoffroy Luillier, sieur d'Orville, resigned as city councillor in 1646, there was virtually always at least one member of the family in city office.[9] Only four members of the Du Drac family served as city officers in the sixteenth century, but their combined terms as city councillors spanned all but eleven years of the century. Similarly, the Le Lievres were present on the city council during all but about twenty years of the century, and the families of Prevost, Bragelongne, Paillart, de Thou, and Viole were represented on the city council continuously from at least the 1530s to the turn of the century. As the resignation of city councillors in favor of family members became increasingly common in the second half of the sixteenth century, the number of families that held onto office as city councillor through multiple generations increased. The families of Hennequin, Palluau, Aubery, and Perrot all tended toward hereditary officeholding from the time they first achieved the rank of councillor in the middle decades of the sixteenth century until after the start of the seventeenth century. The Aubery family was still active in civic affairs in the eighteenth century. Félix Aubery, the marquis de Vatan, prévôt des marchands in 1740, was a direct descendant of Jean Aubery, a mercer, échevin in 1559 and a city councillor five years later.[10]

It was not just the possibility of keeping an office in the family through resignation, however, that accounts for the unusual prominence of a small group of families in city pol-

[9] After Eustache, his eldest son, Jean, sieur de Saint-Mesmin and Boulancourt, became a city councillor, serving more than three decades before he resigned in 1563 to his son, Nicolas. Nicolas resigned *en survivance* to his son, also named Nicolas, in 1583, and the latter served until 1615, when the branch of Saint-Mesmin and Boulancourt died out with him. That same year, however, Geoffroy Luillier, sieur d'Orville, a great-grandson of Eustache through a younger branch, was made a city councillor, and his son and grandson followed him. Several of these men, as well as several other members of the family, also served as prévôts des marchands and échevins during that period.

[10] A. Trudon des Ormes, "Notes sur les prévôts des marchands et échevins de la ville de Paris au xviiie siècle (1701-1789)," *MSHP* 38 (1911):107-223.

itics. While certain families held office for a number of decades continuously, others appear sporadically through several hundred years of city records. The Marles, Neufvilles, and Sanguins first held civic office in the first half of the fifteenth century, and members of these families were repeatedly named to municipal posts during the next century or more. The Marles and Neufvilles, however, never did develop strong traditions of hereditary officeholding, and the Sanguins only began to do so during the latter third of the sixteenth century.

The disproportionate role of a small number of families is particularly evident on the city council. All sixteen of the families that had four or more members in city office during the sixteenth century were represented on the city council between 1535 and 1575, and members of these sixteen families composed more than two-fifths of the total number of city councillors for this period. The city council, then, was not a microcosm of Parisian officialdom but had at its core a markedly narrower and more ingrown elite. This inbred quality was due in part, but only in part, to the resignation rule. Fifteen of the thirty-eight men who were members of these sixteen families were city councillors because of the resignation of a father or brother, but twenty-three were apparently freely elected.[11]

The city councillors also came most often from old city families with a long history in city politics. At least thirty-one of the ninety city councillors under discussion are descended in the paternal line from men who were either prévôts des marchands or échevins in the fifteenth century or city councillors in the year 1500, the first year for which membership in the category of city councillor is recorded. Another seventeen are descended in the maternal line from men whose families served in city government before 1500. More complete records of municipal personnel and more extensive ge-

[11] In theory, a city officer absented himself from any vote involving a close relation, but it is impossible to determine whether or not this rule was consistently observed.

nealogical data on the city councillors would doubtless show
a still higher rate of kinship.

Despite the generally patrimonial and patriarchical nature
of sixteenth-century society, relationship through the maternal lineage was important to the cohesion of the Parisian elite.
More than a third of the councillors in this study are known
to have had maternal ascendants in families active in city
politics.[12] Relationship acquired through marriage was even
more significant. Fifty-two percent of the marriages made by
the ninety city councillors allied them with families that appear on the lists of sixteenth-century prévôts des marchands,
échevins, and city councillors. If we count men instead of
marriages, the figure is still higher: fifty-three city councillors
(59%) made at least one marriage within the civic elite.[13]

The sum of these relationships is impressive: at most only
one councillor in eight was neither the son, son-in-law, nor
grandson of a member of a family active in city politics.[14]
Even this statistic understates the complex family ties of the
city councillors. Louis Huault, for example, though neither
the son, son-in-law, nor grandson of a city officer, was the
stepson of a Sanguin, the brother-in-law of a Hacqueville,
and the great-grandson of a Luillier. All of these families were
active in city affairs by the mid-fifteenth century. Huault's
ties to the civic elite were further cemented by the alliances
of two of his children with the offspring of prominent city
officers.[15]

[12] Thirty-one of the ninety city councillors amounts to 34%. Only sev-
enty-three mothers are known, so the figure in fact represents 42% of the
known cases.

[13] Fifty-three (59%) city councillors married women bearing names on
the lists of fifteenth- and sixteenth-century city officers; thirty-six did not;
one did not marry. If we count total marriages instead of men, the proportion is somewhat smaller (52%).

[14] I have been able to trace no such relationship for J. Aubery, Boucher,
Cressé, Du Gué, Guyot, O. Hennequin, Huault, Le Prestre, J. Prevost I,
Tanneguy, and Tronçon. It is likely, however, that such relationships do
exist in at least some of the cases.

[15] His only son married the daughter of Adrien Du Drac, and a daughter
married the son of Thomas de Bragelongne. The documents on the Huault
family contained in the BN, P.o. 1542 appear accurate, but those in the

The multiple ties linking Huault with the municipal elite are typical. Many of the councillors' families had lineal or marital ties to three or more other prominent city families. At least a dozen of the councillors' families could claim ties to one branch or another of the Luillier family. Jean Luillier de Boulancourt alone had kinship with at least ten of the men who served with him on the city council, not including his father, who served before him, and his son, who served after him. Similarly, Pierre Croquet had a father, a brother, two brothers-in-law, and a son-in-law on the city council, and two of his daughters married the sons of city councillors.

In theory, a man had to be a native of Paris to be elected to municipal office.[16] In practice, however, there appear to have been several exceptions to this traditional rule among the city councillors. Michel de L'Hôpital was a native of Auvergne and had come to Paris to make his career there only a dozen years before he was elected to the city council; Oudart Hennequin had been a merchant in Troyes before his move to the capital.[17] In each case, however, it seems likely that there were family ties that caused the Bureau de la Ville conveniently to overlook the required native status. When L'Hôpital was elected to the council, his father-in-law, Jean Morin, long a city councillor, was prévôt des marchands. Oudart Hennequin was a brother-in-law of Jean Luillier de Boulancourt by Luillier's first wife, but more importantly, Hennequin's non-Parisian origins may have been obscured by the long association his family had had with notable Parisian

---

BN, Carrés 345 are often falsified. See also AN, Min. cen. VI:36: marriage contract of 2/11/66 (Huault/Faulcon); VI:44: marriage contract of 21/6/71 (Huault/de Beauvais); VI:48: marriage contract of 18/1/73 (Huault/Bragelongne); VI:58: marriage contract of 22/1/78 (Huault/Du Drac); and VI:79: *Inventaire après décès* of 17/12/77 (Louis Huault de Montmagny).

[16] Le Roux de Lincy, *Hôtel de Ville*, p. 157.

[17] Michel de L'Hospital, *Oeuvres complètes*, ed. Pierre Joseph Spiridion Duféy, 5 vols. (Paris, 1824-1826; reprint ed., Geneva, 1968), 2:518. For Hennequin: Académie des sciences morales et politiques, Paris, *Collection des ordonnances des rois de France: Catalogue des Actes de François Ier* [hereafter cited as *Actes de François I*], 10 vols. (Paris, 1887-1908), 5:537 (no. 17437); and 6:731 (no. 22716).

families. Members of the Hennequin family, both merchants and officers, had begun to move to Paris by at least the second half of the fifteenth century and, by the end of the century, had made alliances with such families as the Baillets, the Luilliers, and the Hacquevilles. Oudart's uncle, Pierre Hennequin, a lawyer in Parlement, married into the Marle family, and either Pierre or it may have been his son, also named Pierre, was elected to the échevinage in 1529. When Oudart was elected to the city council in 1549, it is likely that his fellow members had long forgotten that he was not a native of the city.

We can see, then, that although there was no formally constituted patriciate in Paris, the highest city offices were dominated by a small nucleus of interrelated families. The elite circle was not entirely closed. It was occasionally possible even for a man not born in the city to gain admittance to this prestigious group—if he or members of his family married into the circle. It was also sometimes possible to work one's way into the highest city offices through years of service in lesser municipal offices, but the incidence of working up through the ranks was more rare than has sometimes been supposed.

Of ninety councillors studied, only five, all of them merchants, served as quarteniers before acceding to higher municipal office.[18] It is possible that some city councillors in the early decades of the sixteenth century had themselves been quarteniers or were descendants of quarteniers in the fifteenth century. Since there are no existing records of these officers for the fifteenth century, this cannot be determined. It is clear, however, that the prospects of a quartenier in the sixteenth century working his way up to the office of city councillor or prévôt des marchands were not good. Thirty-six percent of the 126 men who were quarteniers between 1500 and 1600 were eventually elected échevins, but only 7 men (6%) became city councillors, and none became prévôt des mar-

[18] Denis Barthelemy, Jean Barthelemy, Jean Croquet, Jean Le Lieur, Claude Le Lievre.

chands.[19] And indeed, not all of the quarteniers who eventually became city councillors can be considered to have worked their way up through the ranks. Of the seven quarteniers who became city councillors, only two were the first members of their families to achieve this office. The other five were the sons, brothers, or sons-in-law of men who already held the office of city councillor.

Did it, then, take more than one generation to work up through the ranks? Apparently not. Nomination to the office of city councillor was far more often a matter of family ties than a reward for services rendered. A man with the right connections might be elected prévôt des marchands even if neither he nor his father had ever held office in the city; a quartenier without the proper family connections could scarcely hope to rise higher.

Occupation and Social Status

An edict issued by Henry II in May 1554 ordered that membership in the city council include ten officers of the king, seven bourgeois, and seven merchants. The first election of a city councillor after this edict shows what consternation the king's demand caused in the corps de ville: the councillors could not decide who belonged in what categories. They debated whether or not lawyers in Parlement were to be counted as officers of the king and quarreled over who was a bourgeois and who a merchant. Jean Croquet, an ex-merchant, claimed bourgeois status but protested that, although he had not done business for ten years, he was not about to deprive himself of the possibility of engaging in commercial enterprise in the future if he so desired. The question of the

[10] It should not be surprising that a far greater number became échevins than councillors. Though the office of échevin might in some respects be considered a higher office than that of a city councillor, it should be remembered that the councillors enjoyed a lifetime of prestige and did little work for the city. The échevins, on the other hand, had only two years of glory and a lot of hard work. The office was thus a lesser reward for a quartenier than a councillorship would have been.

status of lawyers recalled an earlier debate over whether or not a young man who had completed legal studies but not yet defended a case in Parlement was or was not an officer of the king. These questions were never resolved. It became apparent that no matter how the counting was done, the quota for officers was filled and those for bourgeois and merchants were not, and so, deciding that either a merchant or a bourgeois could be elected, the corps de ville simply dodged the issue.[20]

Since the agents of the monarch were no more consistent in enforcing this law than they had been in other sporadic attempts to intervene in city elections, the edict never seriously affected the composition of the city council. Indeed, after this one election, it was ignored. The interest of the edict, then, lies not in its effect on council membership but in the confusion provoked in the corps de ville by the necessity of defining its membership according to occupation.

If the officers of the Hôtel de Ville could not agree on how they fit into three apparently straightforward occupational categories, how much more difficult is it to categorize them professionally from a distance of four hundred years. There are inevitable gaps in the documentation that make it impossible to trace the progress of an individual's career with the precision desired. In addition, and most important, it is difficult to determine how best to divide the various occupational pursuits of the councillors into categories suitable for comparative analysis. The tripartite division ordered by the king presents the problem of distinguishing retired merchants living off their investments from nobles living off landed properties, both of whom would serve in the city council as "bourgeois de Paris"; also it lumps together all of the king's officers from the simple counselor in the Châtelet to the chancellor of the kingdom, the most prestigious robe officer in the realm.

To solve these problems without going to other extremes and employing so many diverse categories that no meaningful

[20] *Reg. BV*, 4:154, 341-42.

comparisons could be made, I have devised a seven-part schema. I should emphasize, however, that the basic distinctions are occupational and not social; they relate to the nature of the functions performed and not to the social standing of the man performing them. It should not be assumed, for example, that a man from category five (in Table 2), a nobleman who held no office, was accorded less respect than a man in categories one through four. Social status in the sixteenth century was far too complex to be reduced to two variables; and Table 2 is not intended to be a vertical scale of social standing. In order for the cumulative totals of officeholding to be meaningful, officers of the king have been grouped together at the top of the list. Noblemen without office have been listed after the officers of the king, whatever their rank. The question of nobility is not, however, to be slighted. It is merely deferred to the end of this section. I should also point out that the councillors are categorized in Table 2 according to the highest occupational level they attained during the time they were members of the city council. The broader question of the

TABLE 2
Occupational Activities of the City Councillors

Occupation	No. of officers	% of officers	Cumulative %
High officers: presidents of sovereign courts; maîtres des requêtes, etc.	18	20%	20%
Middle-level officers: sovereign court counselors	24	27	47
Middle-level officers: chancellory, royal administration	13	14	61
Lower-level officers & liberal professions	12	13	74
Nobles without office, or with office in the royal households	5	6	80
Bourgeois de Paris: rentiers	5	6	86
Merchants	13	14	100%
Total	90	100%	

professional advancement achieved by the councillors over the entire course of their careers will be discussed in the next chapter.

For the purposes of Table 2, I have considered anything above (but not including) the level of counselor in Parlement as "high office." As chancellor of the kingdom, Michel de L'Hôpital is of course included in this group, as are Nicolas de Neufville, who served in a number of prestigious positions during his long career as a counselor of the Conseil Privé, and Claude Marcel, who attained the rank of *intendant* and *contrôleur général des finances*.[21] A majority of the officers in this category were presidents of the sovereign courts, but the office of *maître des requêtes*, held by four city councillors, is also included. Though somewhat lower in status than the presidents of Parlement, the maîtres des requêtes enjoyed the privilege of hereditary nobility and consequently rank closer to the presidents of Parlement than to the counselors, who only acquired hereditary nobility in the third generation of counselors.[22]

Eleven of the middle-level officers of the sovereign courts were counselors of Parlement, and three were *maîtres des comptes*. The others included in this group also held positions in the sovereign courts—the Cour des Aides, the Eaux et Forêts,

[21] See Zeller, *Institutions*, p. 117; and Wolfe, *Fiscal System*, pp. 267-68, on the functions and standing of the *intendants des finances*.

[22] Jean Richard Bloch, *L'Anoblissement en France au temps de François Ier* (Paris, 1934), pp. 75-77. François Bluche and Pierre Durye (*L'Anoblissement par charges avant 1789* [La Roche sur Yon, 1962], 2:19-20) correctly point out that the nobility of officeholders was only implicit or customary in the sixteenth century. The first edicts explicitly regulating the noble prerogatives of royal officers date from the seventeenth century. There is thus a certain ambiguity about the status of royal officeholders in the period under discussion, an ambiguity reflected in the frequently contradictory interpretations of contemporary historians. Because I am concerned primarily with relations between officeholders and merchants, I have chosen to treat this presumed or customary nobility as real. From the perspective of officeholders who enjoyed the privileges of nobility or the bourgeois merchants who envied them, it was real—regardless of the counterarguments of the old landed nobles or the differences in status that continued to separate the newly ennobled officeholders from the old landed nobility.

and the Cour des Monnaies, as well as Parlement and the Chambre des Comptes. The status of these offices was sufficient to confer the privileges of personal, gradual nobility.[23] All of the thirteen middle-level officers of the chancellory and royal administration were secrétaires du roi. Despite this apparent homogeneity, there are important differences among the officers grouped in this category. The office of secrétaire du roi automatically brought its purchaser noble status. Consequently it was often acquired by men who had no desire to serve actively as administrators but simply wanted to enjoy the privileges of noble status.[24] Some secrétaires du roi did, however, have official responsibilities in the chancellory, and others simultaneously held other offices in the royal administration.

The largest single group among the "lower officers" is that of the lawyers in Parlement. Seven of the twelve men grouped in this category were lawyers in the Parlement of Paris, and four served as officers of the Châtelet. Also included in this category is Louis Braillon, a *médecin ordinaire du roi*. It should be pointed out that all of the men categorized here as "lower officers" nevertheless enjoyed positions of some standing compared with the lowest rank of Parisians qualified to call themselves officers of the king: the notaries, police officers, and bailliffs of the Châtelet. Indeed, as *lieutenants civil, criminel*, and *particulier* for the Châtelet, Jean Morin, Thomas de Bragelongne, and Martin de Bragelongne held the highest ad-

---

[23] The Cour des Monnaies did not have the prestige of the other sovereign courts, but it was officially raised to the level of a sovereign court in 1552, so I have considered it the equal of those jurisdictions. The auditors and correctors of Comptes were also of somewhat lesser status than other officers of that court, but they did share the privilege of personal nobility (Zeller, *Institutions*, p. 242; Bluche, *Anoblissement par charges*, 2:28).

[24] The best source on the secrétaires du roi is Hélène Michaud, *La Grande Chancellerie et les écritures royales au 16ᵉ siècle* (Paris, 1967). As Bloch points out (*Anoblissement*, pp. 84-87), the situation of the *notaires et secrétaires du roi* was somewhat ambiguous in the sixteenth century, because the letters patent of 1484, which accorded them noble status, were not registered for nearly a century. Still, their prerogatives appear to have been generally recognized.

ministrative positions in the Prévôté of Paris beneath the prévôt himself. The main criterion used here to distinguish
between "middle" and "low" office is the privilege of at least
personal nobility. Those who by virtue of their office possessed personal or hereditary nobility have been classed no
lower than "middle" officers; those who did not have this
status, as "low" officers.

Five of the city councillors were noblemen who did not
hold judicial or administrative office during the time they
were on the city council, although three of the five held robe
office at other times in their lives. One of the five, Guillaume
de Marle, also had the honor of being an officer of the royal
household, a *maître ordinaire de l'hôtel du roi*, during the time
he served on the city council, although it is difficult to determine how much importance to attach to this honor. During the sixteenth century, the title "maître d'hôtel" did not
necessarily imply service at court or even the receipt of a
stipend. The title was sometimes even given to men of nonnoble standing as a reward for financial or other services.[25]

Those who are listed in Table 2 as merchants are men who,
as far as can be determined, still described themselves as
"marchands, bourgeois de Paris" at the end of their careers.
The line between the categories of merchants and simple
bourgeois is not, however, a perfectly clear one. According
to seventeenth-century city records, for example, Louis Abelly
was still a merchant when he was elected to the échevinage
in 1577, but all of Abelly's personal records and *rente* receipts
as well as the contemporary city records list him as just
"bourgeois de Paris."[26]

The records do not usually specify to which of the city's
mercantile corporations the merchants on the city council belonged. As was common with important merchants in the
city, they are usually identified only as "marchands, bourgeois de Paris" in both municipal and personal records. Most
of those whose corporate affiliations can be identified, how-

[25] Zeller, *Institutions*, p. 101; Bloch, *Anoblissement*, p. 82.
[26] *Reg. BV*, 16:230; and 18:147.

ever, belonged to one or another of the prestigious *Six Corps* that stood at the summit of the city's mercantile hierarchy. The Larchers and Jean Le Sueur were drapers, Denis Barthelemy a grocer, the Auberys wholesale mercers, Pierre Poulain a mercer-jeweler, and Claude Marcel a goldsmith. Only Claude Le Prestre, who sold wine and saltwater fish, was not a member of the *Six Corps*.[27] Though we have few specifics on the extent and nature of their trade, all evidence suggests that the merchants on the city council were among the most prosperous and important merchants in the city. The Le Lieurs, for example, were an important family of Rouennaise origin, one branch of which had already by the sixteenth century acceded to robe office. The scale of affairs conducted by Robert Le Lieur can be gauged from the fact that in 1524 he excused himself from some city business on the ground that he had to attend to the twenty shiploads of salt he was expecting momentarily in Rouen. The Le Lievres, the Barthelemys, and the Marcels were also long known among the Parisian bourgeoisie.[28] An indication that Pierre Croquet was among the wealthier merchants of the city is provided by a tax roll from 1572. Assessed at the maximum rate allowed, he was taxed at £300. Only a few persons were so highly taxed, and most were noblemen and officers of the king.[29] As a final indication of the position of the city councillors among

[27] In the second half of the sixteenth century, the *Six Corps* consisted of the *drapiers, épiciers, merciers, pelletiers, bonnetiers*, and *orfèvres* (*Reg. BV*, 7:414). Concerning Ge. Larcher: Brièle, *Documents*, 3:224-25; Gu. Larcher: AN, Y91, fol. 129v° (4/7/45); Le Sueur: *Reg. BV*, 5:284; Barthelemy: Ronda Larmour, "The Grocers of Paris in the Sixteenth Century: Corporations and Capitalism" (Ph.D. dissertation, Columbia, 1963), p. 160n; Aubery, Marcel, and Le Prestre: Georges Denière, *La Juridiction consulaire de Paris; 1563-1792* (Paris, 1892), p. 87; Poulain: *Reg. BV*, 5:355.

[28] Le Lieur: Ibid., 1:287; Le Lievre: Emile Coornaert, *Les Français et le commerce international à Anvers* (Paris, 1961), p. 234; Barthelemy and Marcel: Antoine Jean Victor Le Roux de Lincy and Lazare Maurice Tisserand, *Paris et ses historiens aux xive et xve siècles* (Paris, 1867), pp. 353-63.

[29] BN, MS fr. 11692, fol. 57v°. Apparently Croquet refused to pay this high tax, for he was later assessed £1,200, quadruple the original amount, for delinquency. See Maurice Vimont, *Histoire de la rue Saint-Denis de ses origines à nos jours* (Paris, 1936), 1:210; also *Reg. BV*, 6:374-75n.

the mercantile elite of the city, four of the nine merchants on the city council who were still alive in 1563, when the consular court for commercial affairs was formed, had the honor of being named as judges and consuls of the court.[30] Despite the prestige of some merchants, this group formed a small minority on the city council. As one can see from Table 2, almost three-quarters of the members of the city council between 1535 and 1575 were officers of the crown. Not only was city government dominated by royal officers, it was dominated by royal officers of important and prestigious rank. Three-fifths of the city councillors held at least the ennobling office of secrétaire du roi or a counselorship in one of the sovereign courts. Though the latter position did not confer immediate hereditary nobility, the traditional importance attached to the judiciary functions of the sovereign courts gave their officers a prestige generally considered to outweigh that of the secrétaires du roi. Only one out of seven of the city councillors was a merchant at the end of his service on the council (although, as we shall see, a somewhat larger number began their careers as merchants), while members of the liberal professions, officers of the Châtelet, and lesser officers in the sovereign courts and royal households together accounted for but another seventh.

The tax list from 1572 gives at least a partial insight into the question of how closely the financial standing of those taxed was related to their occupational status.[31] The tax roll does not represent the actual wealth of the city residents but rather their apparent wealth as perceived by the city officers and bourgeois responsible for the assessments. Despite the likelihood of occasional inaccuracies, the record of perceived wealth is instructive; we see in it the city councillors as they were seen by their contemporaries, who had to judge from

---

[30] J. Aubery, C. Le Prestre, C. Marcel, C. Aubery. Denière, *Juridiction consulaire*, p. 509.

[31] BN, MS fr. 11692: "Compte du don de Trois cens mil livres tournois octroie par la Ville de Paris au feu Roy Charles dernier decede en l'annee 1571 [1572]."

external displays of prosperity and could not peek inside the family coffers.

Only half of the ninety men chosen for this study were still alive in 1572, but it has been possible to identify thirty-six members of the group and seven of their widows on the 1572 list. Of these forty-three individuals, nine paid the maximum tax of £300. Except for the merchant Pierre Croquet and the widow of the nobleman Thierry de Montmirail, those who paid the maximum tax were all high officers of the king. Below that level, however, it is impossible to find any association between occupation and taxation. The lowest tax paid by a city councillor was £30, the rate assessed the lawyer in Parlement Jean Le Breton. A *général des monnaies*, an *avocat du roi* in the Cour des Aides, and a young merchant paid only £40 each. Seven city councillors paid between £50 and £90. Their occupations ran the gamut from merchandise to the office of president in the Cour des Aides. The same spread can be found among the eight individuals who paid between £100 and £140, the six who paid from £150 to £190, and the eight who paid from £200 up to, but not including, the maximum. The tax roll shows, then, that we cannot make any automatic assumptions about a relationship between apparent wealth and professional standing. It also shows that, while men of great wealth did make up a significant proportion of the city council, a large fortune was not necessary for nomination to this office.

This is not to suggest that the city councillors were not individually as well as collectively wealthier than the average Parisian. Quite the contrary. Their individual wealth, as indicated by taxes paid, was considerably greater than average. The mean tax paid by residents of the quartier of Macé Bourlon, a prosperous but typical quartier in the old mercantile heart of the city, was £22, £8 below the lowest tax paid by a city councillor and far beneath the mean for this group, which was £158 (the median was £160). Even in the quartier of the Marais under the direction of Charles Maheut, perhaps the wealthiest neighborhood of the city and one in which a number of city councillors resided, the mean tax was only £39. Still, it is important to know that, whatever their wealth compared with that of the average Parisian, the city councillors were not uniformly men of exceptional wealth. If nine city councillors paid the maximum tax, eleven paid less than £100, and the tax registers abound with the names of persons of comparable or greater riches.[32]

In evaluating the professional standing of the city councillors, it is only reasonable to ask how the composition of the council changed over the years we are studying. Table 3 is an attempt to answer this question by charting the occupational make-up of the council at ten-year intervals. To give a somewhat broader perspective, I have carried the analysis down to 1595 and as far back as 1515, although the year 1525 had to be omitted because of incomplete records.

It would be unwise to read too much into Table 3. Aside from the edict of 1554, there was no attempt in the sixteenth century to maintain any particular occupational balance on the council. Members were not likely to resign from the city council because of professional promotions either, except for a small number of very high royal officers who found that their responsibilities to the king left no time for civic service. Consequently, it is only natural that there should be some fluctuation in the various categories because of changes in personnel and the progress of individual careers.

For the most part the council seems to have been relatively consistent in its composition. There is, however, a long-term trend that appears significant: the council became noticeably

---

[32] Historians have sometimes accused the city officers of using their position to lower their own taxes. (See, for example, Larmour, "Grocers," p. 170.) Although it is impossible to remove all suspicion of such behavior, my study of the 1572 tax roll suggests that the accusation is unwarranted. The city councillors who paid the lowest taxes are those whom other sources indicate to have been the least wealthy and powerful. While it is possible that the collective pressure exerted by the city's elite served to keep the maximum tax rate fairly low in proportion to their true ability to pay, it does not appear likely that individual city officers tried to profit personally from their positions by using pressure or influence to keep their tax rates low.

TABLE 3
Occupational Make-up of the City Council at Ten-Year Intervals

Occupation	1515[a]	1535	1545	1555	1565	1575	1585	1595
High officers	4	4	2	3	2	6	7	5
Middle-level officers: courts	7	11	8	7	8	6	6	8
Middle-level officers: administration	2	—	2	4	2	6	7	4
Lower-level officers & liberal professions	6	4	5	3	4	4	2	3
Nobles without office	—	—	2	2	2	1	1	2
Bourgeois de Paris: rentiers	—[b]	—	—	2	2	—	1	1
Merchants	5[b]	5	5	3	4	3	1	—
Total	24	24	24	24	24	26[c]	25[c]	23[d]

[a] The list for 1515 is based on a compilation of names in the *Registres*, which are incomplete in this period, and BN, MSS fr. 32359 and 32840. From 1535-1585, lists of membership are taken from city records as of August 16 of the year cited, the date of the annual election of the échevinage.

[b] Incomplete records make it impossible to distinguish between merchants and the bourgeois in 1515.

[c] There are more than twenty-four councillors in these years because two councillors who were dropped in 1569 as suspected Huguenots were reintegrated after the pacification of 1570 but the two who had been elected to replace them were not dropped.

[d] There were only 23 councillors in 1595 because Nicolas de la Place, a counselor in Parlement, was exiled for his participation in the League and not allowed to rejoin the Council until 1599. (*Reg.BV*, 12:111-12).

more top-heavy over the course of the century. There is a gradual but significant decline in the number of lower officers and merchants on the city council. At each checkpoint in the first half of the century we find five merchants among the city councillors. By 1585 there was only one; by 1595 none. Indeed, after the death of Claude Le Prestre in 1594, twelve years were to pass before a merchant was again named to the city council.[33] Certainly, the decline in merchants was not in any way made up for by an increase in the number of bourgeois rentiers. By the end of the century, the city councillors were an illustrious lot indeed.

An important mark of social status was the claim to noble

[33] BN, MSS fr. 32840, fols. 52-55; and 32359, fols. 51-54.

rank, and it is important to identify what proportion of the city councillors were noblemen. The task of identifying the nobles on the city council is complicated, however, by the presumption of noble status in the sixteenth century, the ease of its usurpation, and the tendency of upwardly mobile families in the seventeenth and eighteenth centuries to conceal the true status of their sixteenth-century ascendants. The process of gradual ennoblement, which applied to many officers in the sovereign courts, also makes it difficult to distinguish true nobles from commoners.

In the seventeenth century, a man called upon to defend his noble status had to prove that his ancestors were gentlemen. In the sixteenth century, on the other hand, a man living nobly was presumed a noble unless it could be demonstrated that his father or grandfather had engaged in trade, paid the *franc-fief*, the *taille*, or other taxes from which the nobility was exempt, or otherwise displayed signs of *roturier* (nonnoble) origin.[34] Since all Parisians were exempt from the *franc-fief* and the *taille*, it was possible for a man whose father and grandfather had lived off their investments as bourgeois to insinuate himself into the ranks of the nobility merely by living like a nobleman.[35] The confusion, tension, and loss of potential revenue for the crown that resulted from this system gradually became clear, and by 1600 it was forbidden for a person to style himself *écuyer* (the lowest title of nobility) or to pass himself off as a gentleman unless his father and grandfather had exercised the profession of arms.[36] In the meantime, however, the laxity of the system encouraged the usurpation of the titles of nobility by those who had no right to them.

Any man rich enough to buy noble property might in the hope of being taken for a nobleman call himself "sieur de . . . ," even if his father and grandfather—or he himself—

[34] Bloch, *Anoblissement*, pp. 25-33.
[35] Mousnier, *Etat et société*, p. 207. This right was upheld in 1572 (*Reg. BV*, 6:440 and 440n).
[36] Bloch, *Anoblissement*, p. 33.

had engaged in trade. The term "sieur de" could be legally used by anyone who owned a seigneury, and it did not in itself constitute usurpation. Thus, for example, Jean Barthelemy could legitimately call himself "sieur du Plessis-Belleville" even though he was but a retired merchant. Even the form "seigneur de" did not necessarily indicate nobility.[37] The elder Nicolas Perrot apparently capitalized on the prestige gained by his election as prévôt des marchands in 1556 to style himself "Nicolas Perrot, seigneur des Carneaulx et du Courtil" or even "noble homme Nicolas Perrot, seigneur des . . ." instead of plain old sire Perrot, though there is no indication that he gave up commerce, nor was the office of prévôt des marchands an ennobling office at that time.[38]

Some individuals found it difficult to resist going one step further and adding the noble title "écuyer." Two city councillors, Jean and Claude Aubery, appear to have been guilty of such usurpation in 1570, when they claimed in Claude's wedding contract the status of écuyer.[39] Although Jean Aubery had acquired the seigneuries of Troussay in 1556 and Trilleport-les-Meaux in 1569, he was still a grocer and not entitled to the noble appellation "écuyer."[40] Jean's son Claude was also a grocer at the time of his marriage and for several years thereafter. He is identified in *rente* receipts as late as 1574 as "marchand, bourgeois de Paris," and in 1576 he was elected judge of the merchant's consular court.[41] Claude was finally ennobled in 1578 by the purchase of the charge of

[37] Marcel Marion, *Dictionnaire des institutions de la France aux xviie et xviiie siècles* (Paris, 1923), p. 506.

[38] In 1577 Henry III did grant nobility to the corps de ville, but François Bluche has determined that this act remained a dead letter because it was not registered by Parlement (Bluche, *Anoblissement*, p. 33). It is not clear whether the honorific "noble man" adopted by Perrot constituted usurpation. Originally the term did indicate nobility, but it was gradually debased until, by the seventeenth century, it was applied primarily to commoners. On Perrot: *Reg. BV*, 4:445-49; BN, P.o. 2242 Perrot à Paris, nos. 13 and 19.

[39] BN, D.b. 36 Aubery, fol. 122.

[40] BN, Nouveau d'Hozier 15 Aubery, fol. 16.

[41] BN, P.o. 122 Aubery, no. 38 (19/7/74); Denière, *Juridiction consulaire*, p. 299.

secrétaire du roi.[42] These false claims in the marriage contract were accepted as part of the proofs of nobility submitted by Claude's great-grandson in 1697 and 1705. Tracing the family back to "Jean Aubery, écuyer, seigneur du Troussay," the official genealogy implied that the family had its origins in the landed nobility and not in the ennoblement of an ex-merchant in 1578.[43]

In other cases, there is evidence that documents presented to the royal genealogists by descendants of city councillors were tampered with or altered. For example, there is the case of Philippe Le Lievre, a lawyer in Parlement and the first of his family to abandon commerce for the liberal professions. The qualification "honorable femme," indicating bourgeois status, which had preceded the name of his mother, Charlotte Menisson, in his marriage contract was later erased from that document.[44] Similarly, the qualities of Oudart Hennequin and his father Michel at the time of Michel's death in 1520 were effaced in the documents concerning Michel's estate in the *Dossiers bleus* (genealogical records used to prove nobility) of the Hennequin family to conceal the fact that Oudart had been a merchant before he became an officer of the crown in 1521.[45] The secret is well concealed in the Hennequin family papers and is betrayed only by letters patent of Francis I issued in 1521 allowing Oudart Hennequin, newly appointed *contrôleur général des finances d'Outre-Seine,* one year to dispose of any merchandise he still had in his possession "in view of the commerce that he then exercised."[46]

More common, but fortunately more transparent, than falsified legal records are fictitious genealogies or boastful hints about a family's proud past. For example, the Longueils, parlementaires since 1380, traced their origin to the old Norman nobility and not to the Dieppoise seller of salt fish from whom

[42] Abraham Tessereau, *Histoire de la Chancellerie* (Paris, 1710), p. 206.
[43] BN, Nouveau d'Hozier 15 Aubery, fol. 16; D.b. 36 Aubery, fol. 122: *Preuves de noblesse.*
[44] BN, P.o. 1718 Lièvre, no. 283: extract of contract of 1/1/50.
[45] BN, D.b. 354 Hennequin, fol. 187v°.
[46] *Actes de François I,* 5:537: *Lettres* of Paris, 28/12/28.

TABLE 4
Effective Nobility among the City Councillors

Status	No. of councillors	% of total
Effectively noble	50	56%
Privileged	13	14
Unknown	4	4
Commoners	23	26
Total	90	100%

they were in fact descended. Even so respected and honorable a man as Jacques-Auguste de Thou was not above boasting that his family was descended from the old knightly nobility, when in fact they stemmed from the échevinage of fifteenth-century Tours. One genealogy of the Bragelongne family went so far as to trace their origin to a cadet son of the counts of Nevers in the eleventh century.[47]

Despite occasional pretense of knightly ascendants, most of the councillors' families can be traced back to the bourgeoisie of Paris, Troyes, or the towns of Normandy and the Loire valley; and those who were noble were so because of office and not because of lands. A number of these wealthy bourgeois families possessed seigneuries in the fifteenth century without being noble. Consequently, in constructing Table 4, which summarizes the social status of the city councillors, I have discounted the uncorroborated evidence of family trees and genealogical dictionaries and relied instead upon primary sources that were less likely to be falsified, such as contracts, rente receipts, city records, and the procès-verbaux of the Paris Coutume. A category of "unknown" has been included for those cases in which primary materials provided insufficient evidence.

There is also a category in Table 4 labeled "privileged per-

---

[47] Longueil: François Bluche, Les Magistrats du Parlement de Paris au xviiie siècle (1715-1771) (Paris, 1960), p. 93; de Thou: Jacques-Auguste de Thou, Mémoires, ed. Joseph François Michaud and Jean Joseph François Poujoulat (Paris, 1838), p. 283; and Salmon, Society in Crisis, p. 104; Bragelongne: Chaix d'Est-Ange, Dictionnaire, 3:961.

sons" to take account of the tacit process of personal or gradual ennoblement that operated in the sixteenth century. In 1485 the king gave the secrétaires du roi the right to enjoy the privileges of immediate hereditary nobility by virtue of their office. Although this right had not been explicitly extended to the highest officers of the crown—the chancellor and *secrétaires d'Etat*, the presidents of the sovereign courts, and the maîtres des requêtes—these officers were also assumed to be noble in the "first degree" in the sixteenth century, while counselors in Parlement and the Cour des Aides, maîtres des comptes, and the *trésoriers généraux de France* were granted only the personal privileges of nobility with their acquisition of office. These privileges did not become hereditary until the third generation, after two successive generations in the family had each exercised the charge for more than twenty years.[48] Councillors counted as "privileged," then, are those who enjoyed the personal privileges of the nobility without being able to pass these privileges automatically to their children.

At least twenty-six city councillors, 29% of the group, came from families presumably or effectively noble. The length of time that these families had enjoyed the privileges of nobility varied considerably. A few families, the Du Dracs and the Longueils among them, had been noble since the late fourteenth century.[49] In many more cases, it was the father or grandfather of the councillor who was ennobled. In nearly all of these families, however, the original ennoblement came through office, either through gradual ennoblement in the sovereign courts or the immediate ennoblement of the secretaries to the king and higher officers of the crown. Fifteen councillors were the first members of their families to acquire hereditary nobility. Most of these men purchased their nobility with the office of secrétaire du roi, the quickest and easiest path to noble status for the wealthy bourgeois of the sixteenth

[48] Bloch, *Anoblissement*, p. 76; Bluche, *Anoblissement par charges*, p. 9.

[49] Du Drac: AN, MS fr. 32359, fol. 8; Longueil: J. François Bluche, *L'Origine des magistrats du Parlement de Paris au xviiie siècle* (Paris, 1956), p. 93.

century. In another nine cases, it is unclear whether a councillor inherited or acquired his noble status, and thirteen councillors enjoyed personal but not hereditary nobility. Discounting the four whose claims to nobility are doubtful but cannot be conclusively proved or disproved, seventy percent of the city councillors enjoyed the privileges and prestige of either personal or hereditary noble standing. Only twenty-three councillors, little more than a quarter, were definitely commoners. Even if all of the unknowns were roturiers, the number of unknown cases is too small to affect these totals significantly.

Three of the city councillors—Nicolas de Neufville, Guillaume de Marle, and Jacques de Longueil—had the additional honor of being named *chevaliers des Ordres du Roi*.[50] The two Du Dracs bore the title "vicomte d'Ay," the lowest of the titles of dignity. Their forefathers had borne this title for at least two generations.[51] Moreover, two city councillors, Augustin Le Prevost and Nicolas de Neufville bore the title of "baron." The prestige of this appellation cannot, however, be accurately known, for the rank was not yet a part of the official hierarchy of noble titles.[52]

The emphasis placed here upon the privileged status of the majority of city councillors should not be allowed to obscure the distance that still separated the old nobility of the sword, descendants of medieval knights, from the new nobility of the robe, men ennobled for the administrative or juridical functions they performed. Whatever their legal privileges, royal officers were not the social equals of the old landed nobility. Still, what concerns us here is less the social differences between robe and sword than the distance that set apart

[50] Neufville was treasurer of the Ordre de Saint-Michel for years (*Reg. BV*, 6:36); Marle does not appear to have been named to the Ordre de Saint-Michel until after he resigned from the city council in 1564 (*Reg. BV*, 6:188); Longueil was named *chevalier* of the Ordre de Saint-Michel in 1578 (Abbé Lebeuf, *Histoire de la ville et de tout le Diocèse de Paris*, ed. M. Augier [Paris, 1883-1893], 3:17).

[51] AN, MS fr. 32359, fol. 8.

[52] Zeller, *Institutions*, p. 18.

the Parisian elite from the great majority of their fellow Parisians. The social distance between nobles and nonnobles on the city council is also important.

Just how significant was the distinction between noble and roturier? This question will come up again in the chapters on the careers, marriages, and estates of the councillors' families. But first, a collective picture of the councillors' style of living and social values, a brief look at their urban dwellings and rural properties, their charitable activities, and religious beliefs.

Urban Residences and Rural Properties

Unlike the quarteniers, who, as representative officers of the administrative districts of the city, had to reside in the quartier they represented, the city councillors could live anywhere in the city. From the information that is available on the street or at least the parish of more than two-thirds of the councillors,[53] it is apparent that most of the councillors chose to live in the heart of the medieval city, within about a kilometer of the city hall. Though the city had long since expanded beyond the twelfth-century wall of Philip Augustus, the only neighborhood outside the old boundaries that was popular with the city councillors was the Marais, a fashionable and spacious quarter that had grown up in the later Middle Ages around the royal palaces of the Tournelles and Saint-Pol.

As in many medieval and early modern cities, the neighborhoods of Paris were for the most part heterogeneous. Some neighborhoods, however, were most popular with members of a particular professional group. At least nine of the merchants on the council lived in the city's traditional commer-

[53] Artisans and lesser merchants commonly listed their street and parish in notarial contracts; officers of the king did so more rarely in the sixteenth century. Often they gave their residence simply as "Paris," so for this social group notarial contracts are not as fruitful a source of residential patterns as one might expect.

cial district around the Halles and the rue Saint-Denis. The house of Antoine Le Lievre, for example, faced directly onto the noise and bustle of the marketplace from behind the pillory of the Halles. Claude and Jean Palluau, Gervais Larcher, and Claude Le Prestre resided on streets leading from the Halles to the rue Saint-Denis, while Louis Abelly, Pierre Croquet and Claude Le Lievre lived directly on the rue Saint-Denis, and Jean Le Sueur lived south of the Halles on the place aux Chats. The two jewelers, Claude Marcel and Pierre Poulain, lived on the pont aux Changes, where the moneychangers and jewelers of the city had displayed their glittering wares for four centuries.[54]

Only four councillors are known to have resided among the scholars and clerics of the left bank: the elder Augustin de Thou, his son Christophe, Michel de L'Hôpital, and the younger Nicolas Perrot. All four were officers of the crown schooled in the law, and it is not surprising that they chose to live in the left-bank parish of Saint-André-des-Arts, a neighborhood long popular with parlementaires for its convenience to the Palais de Justice.[55]

The most popular neighborhoods, however, were those nearest the Hôtel de Ville, in the parishes of Saint-Merry, Saint-Jean-en-Grève, Saint-Gervais, and Saint-Paul. More than half of the councillors whose residences are known lived in these four parishes. Merchants and nobles alike resided in the old parish of Saint-Merry. In 1564, for instance, the grocers Jean and Claude Aubery and the president of Parlement, René Baillet, lived on the rue neuf Saint-Merry.[56] Moving eastward from Saint-Merry, the districts of the city became more aris-

[54] A. Le Lievre: *Reg. BV*, 4:153-54; Palluau, Le Prestre, Abelly, Croquet: BN, MS fr. 11692; Larcher: Brièle, *Documents*, 3:224-25; C. Le Lievre: AN, P.o. 1718 Lièvre, nos. 286-87; Le Sueur: *Reg. BV*, 5:284; Marcel: Denière, *Juridiction consulaire*, p. 294; Poulain: AN, MS fr. 32591 Saint-Paul.

[55] Morin and Tanneguy: BN, MS fr., 32585 St. Landry; de Thou, Perrot, L'Hôpital: BN, MS fr. 32589 Saint-André.

[56] Aubery: Denière, *Juridiction consulaire*, pp. 288 and 299; BN, D.b., 36 Aubery, fol. 96vᵒ; Baillet: AN, M622: *Preuves de noblesse*, Potier (14/9/64).

tocratic in character. Even the parish of Saint-Paul was not, however, homogeneously aristocratic. The wife of Guillaume Larcher and the widow of Denis Barthelemy, two of the merchants on the city council, gave Saint-Paul as their parish in 1577 and 1581 respectively.[57]

The quartier around the old Hôtel de Guise (where the National Archives now stand) was an especially prestigious one and a favorite with wealthy officers of the king. On the rue de la Bretonnerie, for example, the average tax paid in 1572 was £76.6, more than three times the average for the mercantile quartier Macé Bourlon. One-third of the sixty-six taxpayers on the street paid more than one hundred livres in taxes.[58] In 1572, eleven city councillors or their widows lived in this quartier, the quartier Charles Maheut, which stretched from the rue du Temple to but not including the rue vieille du Temple and from the rue de la Verrerie out almost to the old enclosures of the Temple. Their taxes averaged £211.

Though there is only scanty evidence to suggest that some Parisian families had a local political base in a city neighborhood comparable to the clannish identification of major Florentine families with various districts of that city, several Parisian families can be identified with a specific neighborhood over a period of many generations.[59] For example, the allied families of Luillier, Baillet, Hennequin, and Nicolay were prominent residents of the quartier Charles Maheut. Not only the major branches of these families but secondary branches, cousins, and in-laws abounded in the neighborhood.[60] It may be more than coincidental that these families were among the most noted supporters of the Guises, who also had their headquarters in this neighborhood. On a somewhat lesser scale, the Bragelongne family and their allies were concentrated in the rue Saint-Antoine and neighboring streets of the parish

[57] Larcher: AN, MS fr. 32591 Saint-Paul; Barthelemy: AN, Y123, fol. 51v° (24/6/81).
[58] BN, MS fr. 11692, fol. 191.
[59] On Italian patterns, see for example Gene Brucker, *Renaissance Florence* (New York, 1969), pp. 23-24.
[60] BN, MS fr. 11692, fols. 183-204.

of Saint-Paul, while the closely related Longueil and Mont-mirail families resided in the streets just east of the church of Saint-Gervais.

We should not, however, exaggerate the level of residential stability in the city. While it is true that many councillors did live in one house or neighborhood and associate them-selves with one parish church over long periods of time, others can be traced through several different quartiers or parishes. Furthermore, while married sons and daughters sometimes lived in the same neighborhood, even under the same roof as their parents, it was not uncommon for married offspring to live in another part of the city.

Wherever the councillor lived in the city and whatever his profession, his townhouse was likely to resemble those of the other wealthy bourgeois of the city, at least in its general layout and external appearance. The basic floorplan indicated by the *inventaires après décès* of the councillors is simple.[61] On the ground floor were the principal living room (*salle*), the kitchen, one or more small storage rooms, and perhaps an-other, smaller living room. The living room might overlook either the street or the courtyard that provided the back of the house with light and air and sometimes a garden. A mer-chant also had his shop (*boutique*) on the ground floor. On the second floor were three or more bedrooms (*chambres*), often adjoined by smaller rooms or wardrobes, and studies. Wealthy families often had a special room where arms were kept and sometimes a *comptoir*, a room for the money coffers. Some-times there were additional floors, and often there was one or more additional building behind the court, used variously for further housing, storage, or stables, and joined to the main building by a covered gallery. Cellars beneath the main house provided for the storage of wine and wood.[62]

    [61] See also Pierre Couperie and Madeleine Jurgens, "Le Logement à Paris au xviᵉ et xviiᵉ siècles," *Annales* 17 (1962):488-500.
    [62] For a typical merchant's dwelling: AN, Min. cen. XX:78 (13/2/69): *Inventaire après décès* of Jean Le Sueur. The house of a middle-level officer: AN, Min. cen. CXXII:187 (18/1/52): *inventaire après décès* of Anne Tron-çon, wife of Robert Saint-Germain. The house of a very wealthy royal

Usually the *chambres* are described only as "overlooking the court" or "overlooking the street," but occasionally one can tell how they were used by the family. For example, the four daughters of Louis Huault, sieur de Montmagny, shared one room, while their brother had his own room with an adjoining study, and Huault and his wife had the largest room.[63] Madeleine Potier and Bernard Prevost had no children of their own, but one of their nephews had his own room in their house at the time Prevost died.[64] About a dozen servants are mentioned in the Prevost inventory, but unfortunately there is no indication of what rooms they used or where they slept.

As housing became increasingly expensive in the sixteenth century, there was a tendency to divide the large old houses of the city, renting out the building behind the court, if there was one, or rooms in the main building.[65] It is impossible to know whether or not all of the city councillors owned their own homes and retained the whole house for their own use and that of their servants. Although the names of parents and children, brothers and sisters, and other relatives often follow one another on the 1572 tax list, it is not usually possible to determine whether these relatives shared a single house or merely resided on adjoining parcels of land. And while property donations often mention the gift of half a house or less, joint ownership does not necessarily indicate joint tenancy. It would appear, however, from a donation made to Adrien Du Drac by his father-in-law in 1549, that even the properties of the wealthy were sometimes being divided. Thomas Rapponel, a secretary to the king, donated his large house and garden on the rue de la Chapelle de Bracque to his daughter

---

officer: AN, Min. cen. LXXXVII:139 (23/7/63): *Inventaire après décès* of Jean Luillier.

[63] AN, Min. cen. VI:79 (17/12/77): *Inventaire après décès* of Louis Huault de Montmagny.

[64] AN, Min. cen. LXXXVI:159 (10/10/85): *Inventaire après décès* of Bernard Prevost.

[65] Couperie, "Logement," p. 493. On rising housing costs: Emmanuel Le Roy Ladurie and Pierre Couperie, "Le Mouvement des loyers parisiens de la fin du Moyen Age au xviiie siècle," *Annales* 25 (1970): 1,002-1,023, especially Table 1, p. 1,021.

Charlotte and her husband, Adrien Du Drac, with the express provision that the property not be divided "like a number of buildings in the city." According to Rapponel, these subdivisions resulted in overcrowding, the spread of infectious disease and lack of fresh air, and the eventual division of the property itself, which ruined "all the beautiful and old houses of the city."[66]

Though it was not until the seventeenth century that it became the fashion among the wealthy nobles of the robe to have elegant townhouses, built of stone like miniature castles around a *cour d'honneur*, at least some of the sixteenth-century Parisian elite must already have had large and luxurious homes.[67] Nicolas de Neufville, for example, hosted the king for dinner in 1562, and both he and his father lent their home near the Louvre on numerous occasions for the lodging of visiting aristocrats. According to the chronicler known as the Bourgeois de Paris, Mencia Mendoza, the wife of Count Henry of Nassau, arrived in Paris in the suite of Marguerite of Austria in 1530 "with her entourage which is about eighty horse, both men and women, and went to the house of Monsieur de Villeroy, trésorier de France, by the command of the king." They remained there about a week at the expense of the crown.[68] In 1559 the Duke of Alba and members of his entourage were lodged at Villeroy's during the festivities that accompanied

[66] AN, Y94, fol. 206v° (5/4/49).

[67] Indeed, the *cour d'honneur* and the *porte-cochère* of the seventeenth-century townhouse, designed to accommodate in style the visitor arriving by carriage, were unnecessary in the sixteenth century, when most visiting was still done on foot or on mule or horseback. The carriage was an invention of the mid-sixteenth century, but its use within the city did not become popular for some time. Jacques-Auguste de Thou related in his memoirs that his mother was the first person in Paris, after the queen and Henry II's natural daughter Diane, to own a carriage, but she only used it to go to her country house and never within the city (de Thou, *Mémoires*, p. 331).

[68] "Journal de ce qui s'est passé en France durant l'année 1562, principalement dans Paris et à la cour," *Revue Rétrospective*, Ser. 1, 5 (1834):198. Françoise Lehoux, "Le Livre de Simon Teste, correcteur à la Chambre des Comptes au xvie siècle," *Bulletin philologique et historique du comité des travaux historiques et scientifiques* (1940-1941), p. 168n.

the wedding between Elizabeth of Valois and the King of Spain.[69] In 1568 this "large house containing several buildings, courts, wells, galleries, a chapel, stables, garden and other buildings" was acquired by the duc d'Anjou from Nicolas de Neufville and his brother Jean for £50,000.[70] Even a small sampling of inventories after death reveals that there were great contrasts in the luxury with which the houses of the city councillors were appointed. For example, when Bernard Prevost, a president of Parlement and member by birth and alliance of very wealthy families, died in 1585, his townhouse contained furnishings valued at 1,984 *écus* (£5,952), not counting tapestries, books, silver plate, or jewels. The tapestries alone were worth 1,587 écus, and the silver plate 1,405 écus. The book collection (primarily law and theology) was large, though the individual volumes were apparently neither luxuriously bound nor rare. The value of the books was fixed at 172 écus, and together with jewelry worth 754 écus, these possessions amount to 5,902 écus (equalling £17,706).[71] Renée Nicolay, the widow of the president of the Chambre des Comptes Jean Luillier, enjoyed a similarly luxurious style of living. The household possessions and jewelry in her estate were valued at 5,166 écus (£15,498) on her death in 1585, and this does not include the half of the household effects that had been claimed by Luillier's heirs after his death in 1563.[72] On the other hand, the furnishings belonging to Jean Le Sueur, a merchant-draper, amounted to only £2,746, including tapestries, silver plate and jewels.[73]

While it is true that Le Sueur died sixteen years before Prevost, inflation could account for only a small fraction of this difference in standards of living. Or perhaps it might

[69] *Reg. BV*, 5:29 and 30n.

[70] *Reg. BV*, 6:36 and 7:9n.

[71] AN, Min. cen. LXXXVI:159 (10/10/85): *Inventaire après décès* of Bernard Prevost.

[72] AN, Min. cen. III:175 (30/8/85): *Partage des meubles* of Renée Nicolay, widow of Dreux Hennequin, then of Jean Luillier. Also AN, Min. cen. LXXXVII:139 (23/7/63): *Inventaire après décès* and *partages* of Jean Luillier.

[73] AN, Min. cen. XX:78 (13/2/69): *Inventaire après décès* of Jean Le Sueur.

better be called a "standard of luxury," for to all appearances Jean Le Sueur lived well in his amply furnished house on the place aux Chats. The value of his furniture alone (£432) may be small compared to that of Prevost (£5,952) but it is of a scale not incomparable to that left in 1606 by Louis Abelly, a wine merchant who acquired office as secretary to the queen mother (£800).[74]

In general, then, we can say that the homes of the city councillors were at the least comfortable and at the best luxurious. They were large enough to permit the individual family members, or at least the adults, some measure of privacy (though it is difficult to know just what value was placed on personal privacy in this society), and even to allow married children to live with their parents without too much strain. And despite their wealth, the city councillors were by no means shut off from the life of the city. Residing in the heart of medieval Paris, in houses that opened onto the busy streets, marketplaces, and bridges of the town, and traversing the city on foot or muleback, the city councillors were in daily contact with the lively activity and heterogeneous population of the city in a way that the seventeenth and eighteenth-century elites, locked behind the portes-cochères of their elegant mansions and riding in their carriages, were not.

Though the orientation of the city councillors' lives and activities was to a large degree urban, more than two-thirds of the councillors owned noble properties in the environs of Paris or elsewhere in France. More than a third of the merchants and bourgeois on the city council managed to acquire seigneuries, and four out of five of the royal officers possessed at least one noble property.[75] Many city councillors owned more than one seigneury; André Guillart, for example, owned at least fourteen.[76]

[74] AN, Min. cen. X:3 (26/9/1600): *Inventaire après décès* of Louis Abelly.

[75] Eight out of twenty-four merchants and bourgeois; fifty-three of sixty-six officers of the crown.

[76] Arlette Jouanna, "André Guillart, Sieur du Mortier, de l'Isle et de l'Epichelière," in Roland Mousnier et al., *Le Conseil du Roi de Louis XII à la Révolution* (Paris, 1970), pp. 245-46; AN, Y107, fol. 245 (21/9/66).

The principal seigneuries of several councillors lay at some distance from the capital, in the regions from which their families had originally come. Raoul Aymeret, for one, inherited the seigneury of Gazeau near Niort, and the most important of André Guillart's possessions lay near Le Mans. Others had properties in Champagne and the Loire Valley. The large majority of rural properties owned by the councillors, however, lay within about seventy kilometers (forty-four miles) of the city. They served as summer, holiday, and retirement retreats while also providing foodstuffs, income, and status. A circle inscribed around Paris with its center at Notre Dame and a radius equal to the distance to Compiègne would have enclosed most of these estates.

Moreover, at least twenty of the councillors had properties within about twenty kilometers of the heart of the city—an area now within the urban agglomeration of Paris. Pierre Perdrier's seigneury of Bobigny, cultivated in vines and grain during the Old Regime, is now an industrial suburb of the city, as are Louis Huault's property of Montmagny and Christophe de Thou's estate of Stains near Saint-Denis. Bonneuil, another property of Christophe de Thou, has been enveloped by the airport of Le Bourget, while south of Paris overlooking the Seine, the Viole family's land at Athis is now bordered by the runways of Orly. Sceaux and Sèvres, once belonging to city councillors, are residential suburbs, while, somewhat further from the city, the properties of Roquencourt, L'Etang-la-Ville, Fourqueux, and Chambourcy have retained a more rural air because of their proximity to the parks of the royal palaces of Versailles, Marly, and Saint-Germain.[77]

Table 5 categorizes the councillors according to the number of generations that their principal seigneury had passed in direct descent in their family. If the councillor was com-

[77] Bobigny: Lebeuf, *Paris*, 2:634-38; Montmagny: Lebeuf, *Paris*, 1:586-87; Stains: Lebeuf, *Paris*, 1:580-82; Bonneuil: AN, Y94, fol. 382 (4/3/49); Athis: Lebeuf, *Paris*, 4:412-20; Sceaux: Lebeuf, *Paris*, 3:456; Sèvres: Lebeuf, *Paris*, 3:14-17; Roquencourt: Lebeuf, *Paris*, 3:156-59; L'Etang-la-Ville: AN, Y131, fol. 193vº (22/3/89). The principal estates of the city councillors are listed in the Appendix.

TABLE 5
Noble Properties of the City Councillors

Properties	No. of cases	% of total
Inherited:		
Acquired at least by grandparents	22	24%
Acquired at least by parents	16	18
Acquired by councillor	11	12
Uncertain when acquired	13	14
None owned	28	31
Total	90	99%

monly associated with more than one title, I have used either the property whose name the councillor most frequently adopted or the oldest of his known properties. Thus, for example, Jean Bochart is counted for Noroy, which his grandfather acquired in 1482, even though he most often styled himself after the more important seigneury of Champigny. Champigny had only passed through one generation in direct descent.[78] Similarly, Jean Luillier, seigneur de Saint-Mesmin et de Boulancourt, is counted for Saint-Mesmin, because Saint-Mesmin was inherited from his grandfather, while the date of acquisition of Boulancourt, the title he most often bore, is unknown. The comparative importance of the two properties is irrelevant. It is clear that each generation of Luilliers from Jean's father to his grandson alternated the titles of Boulancourt and Saint-Mesmin with the simple purpose of distinguishing father from son.

I should point out, however, that Table 5 does not necessarily show the oldest seigneury owned by a councillor's family. In the first place, it only goes back two generations, and, secondly, a number of city councillors were younger sons and as a consequence did not inherit the oldest properties of their line. Jacques de Longueil, for example, inherited Sèvres, which

[78] Bochart's mother, Jeanne Simon, inherited the greater part of the family's holdings there from her uncle, Jean Simon, the bishop of Paris (Georges Louet, *Recueil de plusieurs arrests notables du Parlement de Paris* [Paris, 1712], 1:412-14).

his father, the president of Parlement Jean de Longueil, had only acquired in 1535, rather than the magnificent family estates of Maisons and Rancher, which had been in the family more than a century.[79] As Table 5 demonstrates, more than two-fifths of the city councillors inherited at least one of their noble lands, and nearly a quarter inherited properties that had already been in their families for several generations. Many of these acquisitions date from the second half of the fifteenth century, the period for which Guy Fourquin found the greatest increase in the holdings of jurists and administrators in the countryside around the capital.[80]

According to Fourquin, there was never a sudden dispossession of the nobility by enriched bourgeois, at least not in the Paris area. There was, rather, a gradual osmosis between the high bourgeoisie and the old nobility, an osmosis apparent as early as the thirteenth century. The holdings of Parisians in the surrounding countryside generally remained small, however, until the later part of the fifteenth century, when, for the first time, the nobles of the robe were able to buy entire domains. His research shows, moreover, and my findings would seem to confirm, that a rich bourgeois first placed his fortune in royal office and only later began to acquire important rural properties. "The administrative fortune precedes the territorial fortune [in this area]."[81]

It should not, however, be assumed as a consequence that the highest officers had the greatest properties. Michel de L'Hôpital, for example, never did acquire a comfortable fortune but was instead continually pressed for funds. He paid

---

[79] Maugis, Parlement, 3:170.

[80] Guy Fourquin, Les Campagnes de la région parisienne à la fin du Moyen Age (Paris, 1964), pp. 465-73.

[81] Ibid., pp. 152-53, 470, 409. For the role of the Parisian bourgeoisie in the surrounding countryside, see also Yvonne Bézard, La Vie rurale dans le sud de la région parisienne de 1450 à 1560 (Paris, 1929); Bernard Guenée, Tribunaux et gens de justice dans le bailliage de Senlis à la fin du Moyen Age (Paris, 1963); Jean Jacquart, La Crise rurale en Ile-de-France, 1550-1670 (Paris, 1974); and Marc Venard, Bourgeois et paysans au xviie siècle (Paris, 1957).

only £2,000 for his seigneury of Champmoteux in 1560, apparently selling what remained of his inherited properties in Auvergne in order to make the purchase.[82] The house that he built there was handsome but far from opulent, and the lands on which it stood were meager for a man of L'Hôpital's standing. By contrast, Jean Palluau, a merchant before he became a secretary to the king in 1549, left several seigneuries, one of which was valued at more than £24,000 in 1589.[83]

For the most part, the acquisition of rural properties proceeded gradually, through piecemeal purchases and additions to inherited properties. The system of land tenure around Paris, in which properties were divided and subdivided into tiny parcels, made necessary this piecemeal system and was in turn reinforced by it. An entire seigneury rarely consisted of a solid block of land, but was usually composed of a multitude of small plots, interspersed with properties owned by others. The property that Jean-Baptiste de Courlay inherited at Vitry was composed of 185 separate parcels of land in fifty-five different fields, yet it totaled only 125 *arpents* (approximately 125 acres).[84] Many of the city councillors—perhaps most—were still adding bits and pieces whenever they could to properties inherited from fathers and grandfathers. At the same time, they also purchased new seigneuries whenever and wherever they could. A wealthy family sometimes had its properties concentrated in one particular region, but it was nevertheless more common for them to be scattered in several directions around the city. It is beyond the scope of this study to evaluate the role of the city councillors as landlords, but it is worth noting that it would have been impossible for any of the councillors who owned a number of properties to take a very active part in the supervision of his scattered holdings. Even the smaller landlords, and Courlay was certainly among them, had either to employ professional overseers or to lease

[82] L'Hospital, *Oeuvres*, 1:274-75 and 294n: contract of 2/8/60.
[83] AN, Y131, fols. 193v°-96 (22/3/89). Also BN, *Carrés* 479 Palluau, fol. 188-89v°: extract of donation of 22/3/89.
[84] BN, P.o. 886 de Courlay, nos. 55-109 (4/12/93): *partage*.

out entire estates to local farmers or businessmen, who were better placed to negotiate with tenants and collect the rents and produce due them.[85]

Charitable Activities and Religious Beliefs

Records of charitable and lay religious institutions in the city suggest that the families most active in municipal politics also assumed the broadest responsibility for local charities. In 1505 the administration of the Hôtel Dieu was confided to a board of lay governors elected by the Bureau de la Ville and invested by the Parlement of Paris. The *gouverneurs* were supposed to be "bons personnages et gens de bien," and it is not surprising that many of those chosen were city officers. At least ten of the city councillors being studied served on this board.[86] Following the model of the Hôtel Dieu, the orphanage of the Enfants de Dieu (usually known as the Enfants Rouges), founded in 1536 by Marguerite of Angoulême, confided the election of its governing board to the Bureau de la Ville. Among the governors of the Enfants Rouges were the city councillors Adrien Du Drac, Jean Prevost, and Christophe de Harlay.[87] City officers and other members of their

[85] For a typical lease: AN, Min. cen. VI:48 (15/3/78): *Bail à ferme* by Renée Nicolay, the widow of Jean Luillier, of all of the revenues of her property at Champçenais to Pierre Barre, a merchant living at Colummiers in Brie, for the sum of 633-2/3 écus plus one *muid* (a large barrel) of wheat and one of oats each year.

[86] *Reg. BV*, 1:103-105, 108-109. Board members included J. Croquet, Guyot, R. Le Lieur, Le Prestre, C. Le Sueur, D. Barthelemy, Marcel, Ge. de Marle, J. Palluau, N. Perrot I (*Reg. BV*, 3:131 and 4:183; Brièle, *Documents*, 3:173, 181, 302, 336, 357). It is probably no coincidence that the proportion of merchants among this group is high. In 1614, the drapers' corporation complained that "merchants are employed ordinarily only in those civic duties which are onerous and have no access to the honorable ones. For they are made to administer the receipt and payments of the poor, they are established as judges and consuls, they are chosen as masters and wardens of their guilds and for several other functions where there is not a penny to be earned, but on the contrary they spend their own money and leave their business for the public profit." (Larmour, "Grocers," p. 163, citing AN K675, no. 20.)

[87] *Reg. BV*, 6:346-47, 3:231-32.

families were also involved in the commission created by Parlement in 1543 to study the problem of poor relief in the city, in the consequent establishment of the Bureau des Pauvres in 1544, and in the extension of the hospital system that grew out of this concern over poor relief.[88] In 1566 three of the five governors of the orphanage of Saint-Esprit were city councillors.[89] City councillors were also active in professional and civic confraternities and in the charitable activities of their local parishes, where they served as officers of the lay confraternities that had charge of the upkeep of the church and the collection of alms.[90]

The city councillors and their families donated money as well as time to the poor and sick of the city. In 1549, for example, Oudart Hennequin and his wife donated an inheritance amounting to more than 2,000 écus to serve as alms to the poor of Paris, "leurs freres et seurs chrestiens, presens et advenir."[91] Though this was the largest donation found in the records so far, gifts and legacies of several hundred livres or more to the Hôtel Dieu and other local charities were not uncommon.[92]

Councillors also contributed to their parish churches, not

[88] Ibid., 3:26 and 26n; Michel Félibien and Guy Alexis Lobineau, *Histoire de la ville de Paris* (Paris, 1725): *Preuves* 2:622, 711.

[89] AN, Min. cen. VI:35: *Délibération* of 18/8/66.

[90] J. Paillart I: *marguilleur* of Saint-Merry in 1539 (BN, P.o. 806 Le Cointe, no. 40); J. Aubery: *marguilleur* of Saint-Merry in 1551 (BN, D.b. 36 Aubery, fol. 96v°). In 1551, Thomas Bragelongne was doyen of the select *grande confrérie Notre-Dame*, and in 1567, Christophe de Thou had this honor. Other members are also listed in Antoine Jean Victor Le Roux de Lincy, *Recherches sur la grande confrérie Notre-Dame aux prêtres et bourgeois de la ville de Paris* (Paris, 1844), pp. 112-13.

[91] AN, Y94, fols. 217v°-18 (19/2/49).

[92] From the records of the Hôtel Dieu: J. Luillier: £145 and £500 legacies in 1563 (Brièle, *Documents*, 3:318); Marcel: 83 écus in 1578 (Brièle, *Documents*, 3:357); Poulain: £250 legacy (Brièle, *Documents*, 3:343); Ja. Sanguin: £300 legacy on death of wife (Brièle, *Documents*, 4:29); J. Aubery: legacy of £400 (Brièle, *Documents*, 3:343). Charlotte Rapponel, wife of A. Du Drac: donation to the hospital of the Trinity of portions of two adjoining houses, rue du Temple (AN, Y111, fol. 129 [13/12/70]). J. Luillier: £300 *rente* for the *communauté des pauvres* (AN, Min. cen. LXXXVI:53 [11/1/60]: *Constitution de rente*).

only endowing masses for the salvation of their souls but supporting the construction and upkeep of church buildings. Members of the Hennequin and Baillet clans donated the funds for the south façade of the transept of the new church of Saint-Merry, constructed in the 1520s to meet the needs of the rapidly growing parish, and placed there the fine window of Saint Peter at the door of the Temple.[93] Also impressive was the contribution of the Tronçon family to the church of Saint-Germain-l'Auxerrois. The central chapel of the apse, begun at the expense of the draper Jean Tronçon in 1504 was completed after 1531 by his son, the city councillor of the same name. Known variously as the chapel of the Passion, the chapel of Our Lady of the Consolation, or the chapel of the Tomb because of the sculpture by Jean Soulas of Christ being placed in the tomb (commissioned by the elder Tronçon), this chapel was one of the most important sixteenth-century additions to the church of the royal parish.[94]

The staunch Catholicism of the Parisian populace in the sixteenth century is well known, and the role that city officers may have played in such fiercely partisan violence as the massacre of Saint Bartholomew's Day is notorious, but it would be a mistake to assume that the city councillors were uniformly Catholic in their personal faith or unmoved by the prevailing currents of dissent. Although a large majority of the city councillors were indeed faithful Catholics, several are known to have been at least temporarily attracted to Calvinism, and a greater number had close relatives who openly adopted the new beliefs. It is clear in studying the families of the city councillors that even in this solidly Catholic city the religious schism of the century cut deeply and turned brother against brother, father against son, and even husband against wife.

In the Du Drac family, for example, Catholic devotion caused two of the daughters of city councillor Adrien Du Drac to retire to convents upon the deaths of their husbands. One

---

[93] Amédée Boinet, *Les Eglises parisiennes* (Paris, 1958) 1:401 and 420.
[94] Ibid., 1:267.

of these daughters, the widow of the parlementaire Jacques Aurillot, became known as a "ligueuse enragée" and died "en odeur de sainteté" in 1590.[95] By contrast, Adrien's oldest son Olivier is the only city councillor known by his own admission to have been a Protestant (though he had retired to his estates in Brie and was no longer a city councillor at the time he made the admission). In February 1585, in the contract for his second marriage, Olivier Du Drac, chevalier et vicomte d'Ay, and his bride Madeleine Le Charron promised each other and God to "persevere in the true faith" even if it meant abandoning all of their possessions and fleeing France.[96]

Two city councillors, Guillaume de Courlay, a secrétaire du roi, and Nicolas Du Gué, an avocat du roi in the Cour des Aides, were removed from both civic and royal office in March 1569, in compliance with the king's edict excluding from office anyone who had made profession of the Reformed faith.[97] It is not known whether Du Gué or Courlay were among the royal officers who protested their exclusion and attended mass in hopes of regaining their offices, but like all of those similarly excluded, they were returned to their positions in 1570 as a consequence of the Peace of Saint-Germain. Du Gué resigned as a city councillor within a year of his return but retained his position as avocat du roi throughout the renewed religious strife of the 1570s. Courlay retained both civic and royal office during this period. Unfortunately, these superficial facts offer little insight into the true religious beliefs of these two men. Were they wrongly accused of Calvinism in 1569? Or, if they were indeed Protestants in 1569, did they subsequently abandon their faith under pressure? On the basis of the present evidence, there is simply no way to answer these questions.

There is also some uncertainty about the beliefs of two of

---

[95] *Dictionnaire de biographie française*, s.v. "Du Drac." The other daughter was Marguerite Du Drac, the widow of the city councillor Augustin Le Prevost.

[96] AN, Y126, fols. 338v°-40 (27/2/85).

[97] *Reg. BV*, 6:116-21.

the most famous members of the city council, Michel de L'Hôpital and Guillaume Budé. Suspicion that L'Hôpital was overly sympathetic to the Protestants, who counted his wife and daughter among their converts, was in large part responsible for his removal as chancellor. Suspicion about Budé was aroused after his death, when his testamentary request for a quiet burial at midnight without the usual pomp of a Catholic funeral was revealed and later when his widow and several children took refuge in Geneva.[98] However, scholars who have closely studied the activities and writings of these two men have generally concluded that they were sympathetic to but not adherents of the Reformed Church. Perhaps the best comment on L'Hôpital's beliefs is Theodore Beza's statement that L'Hôpital had "glimpsed the light but not received it."[99]

André Guillart, sieur du Mortier, was also rumored to be a Protestant. A letter written in 1564 by Sarron, the secretary to the Spanish ambassador to France, mentions the "miraculous conversion" of Guillart and accuses him of having previously been "among the most favored of the Admiral and those of his sect."[100] The author of a recent study of Guillart is, however, probably more correct in concluding that Guillart was not a Protestant but rather a man of "that family of minds that later acquired the name of Politiques."[101] It is likely that as a youth Guillart was influenced by the theologian and humanist Josse Clichtove, who was the tutor of his elder brother, Louis (later the bishop of Chartres), at the College of Navarre. Louis and his father, Charles Guillart, a president of the Parlement of Paris, were among Clichtove's prin-

[98] It does not seem, however, that the testament itself can be considered a Protestant document, affirming as it did his confidence in the intercession of the Virgin Mary and the saints Paul and Mary Magdalene (Madeleine Foisil, "Guillaume Budé [1467-1540]," in Roland Mousnier et al., *Le Conseil du Roi*, p. 285). See also J. Ravenel, "Testament de Guillaume Budé (1536)," *Bulletin de la Société de l'histoire de France*, 2e partie, 2 (1835):225-27.

[99] L'Hospital, *Oeuvres*, 1:281.

[100] Jouanna, "Guillart," p. 242, citing *Mémoires de Condé*, 2:198: letter of Sarron, secretary to Perrenot de Chantonnay (16/4/64).

[101] Ibid.

cipal patrons, and a number of his works, including the *Antilutherus*, were dedicated to members of the Guillart family.[102] While there is no proof that André shared the vision of a reformed and responsive Catholic Church that Clichtove impressed upon his brother Louis, it is tempting to speculate that the teachings of the French reformers helped produce the moderate and open spirit that allowed André Guillart to serve Catherine de Medici as an emissary to Catholics and Protestants alike.[103]

It would seem that Guillart, like Budé and L'Hôpital, was accused of Calvinism as much because of dissent within his close family as because of his own actions or beliefs. At least as early at 1561, Guillart's daughter-in-law, Marie Robertet, openly attended Reformed services in Le Mans, where the Guillart family properties were situated. His son Charles, who took over as bishop of Chartres from his uncle Louis, was also suspected of Calvinism.[104] Condemned for heresy by Pius V in 1566, Charles Guillart took advantage of the strong Gallican sentiment of the period and managed to have his excommunication revoked.[105] He was able to hang onto his bishopric until shortly after Saint Bartholomew's Day, when public outcry against a preacher he had invited to speak led to his hasty retreat under a hail of stones. He resigned shortly thereafter.[106] André Guillart's eldest son, André II, remained a Catholic, but Marie Robertet apparently managed to indoctrinate their eldest son, Louis, with her Reformed views. In

[102] Michael J. Kraus, "Patronage and Reform in the France of the Préréforme: The Case of Clichtove," *Canadian Journal of History* 6 (1971):49-54. See also the abbot E. Haye's "Notes historiques sur Chartres et le diocèse pendant l'épiscopat de Louis et de Charles Guillart (1525-1553, 1553-1573)," *Mémoires de la Société archéologique d'Eure-et-Loir* 10 (1896):241-71, on Louis Guillart's reforms.

[103] Guillart served as ambassador both to Rome and to London; he was also sent on missions to the French Protestants. Along with L'Hôpital, he was among those responsible for securing the release of Condé after the Tumult of Amboise (Ibid., p. 430; Jouanna, "Guillart," pp. 236 and 242).

[104] Haye, "Chartres," p. 430.

[105] Nancy Lyman Roelker, *Queen of Navarre: Jeanne d'Albret* (Cambridge, Mass., 1968), p. 240n.

[106] Haye, "Chartres," pp. 458-59; Jouanna, "Guillart," pp. 241-42.

1578 André Guillart II disinherited Louis and gave him some property from Marie Robertet's dowry on which to live, in the hope that he would "retire from the company of Marie Robertet, who is the principal cause of his debauchery and [the] corruption of his morals."[107] These hopes went unanswered. In 1579 Louis married into a Protestant family, wedding Marie Raguier, the daughter of Marie de Béthune.[108] By contrast, there are no visible signs of tension over religious belief in the marriages of either L'Hôpital or Budé. The testament of L'Hôpital makes clear his devotion to his wife and confidence in her.[109] He was likewise devoted to his daughter, his only child, who was also a Protestant. Guillaume Budé's large family was divided. Several sons, including the oldest, and at least one daughter, a nun, remained Catholic, while three other sons and several daughters accompanied his widow, Roberte Le Lieur, to Geneva. Another Protestant daughter remained in France and offered shelter on her estates to Huguenots during the civil wars.[110]

These were not the only councillors whose families were divided by religion, however. There was also schism within some of the merchant families of the council. François Perrot (the son of the elder Nicolas Perrot) and his wife Nicole Croquet (the daughter of Pierre Croquet) were condemned by Parlement in their absence and sentenced to death in September 1562, along with Nicolas Croquet, his wife, and Jacques Gobelin (the brother, sister-in-law, and brother-in-law re-

[107] AN, Y120, fols. 273v°-74v° (20/11/78).
[108] AN, Y121, fol. 53v° (31/8/79). André Guillart signed the contract, as he was required to authorize his wife's donations, but the generous portion Louis was given came entirely from his mother, and there was no sign of *rapprochement* between father and son.
[109] L'Hospital, *Oeuvres*, 2:517-31.
[110] Nancy Lyman Roelker, "The Appeal of Calvinism to French Noblewomen in the Sixteenth Century," *Journal of Interdisciplinary History* 2 (1972):416. Other sources on the Budé family genealogy include *Reg. BV*, 3:15; BN, P.o. 547 Budé; David O. McNeil, *Guillaume Budé and Humanism in the Reign of Francis I* (Geneva, 1975); and Foisil, "Budé," pp. 277-91. Errors and inconsistencies in these and other sources, however, make it difficult to be more precise about Budé's offspring.

spectively of four city councillors).[111] The reason given for the sentence was that after having been banished from the capital as suspected Huguenots, they were seen at Meaux at a time when some religious images were broken and churches pillaged there.[112] A month later the king stayed the order for their arrest and execution on the ground that their families would have been unduly penalized by the order:

Inasmuch as the said arrest being executed, it would be a perpetual mark against them, their family and relations, for which they would be constrained to abandon our kingdom, and because we hope to obtain some good service in the future, as our predecessors have in the past from some of them, and also because their relatives have certified us of the will that they have to purge themselves of the affair imposed upon them. . . .[113]

The affair had already resulted in the arrest of the city councillor Pierre Croquet by the local militia. Forced to surrender his horse and arms, Pierre was only released after supplying proof that he had not deviated in his fidelity to the Catholic church.[114] The fact that he had close relatives who were notorious Huguenots did not terminate Pierre's political career in the city. He remained on the city council even though his brother Nicolas returned to Paris and played an important role in Protestant agitation in the city. Convicted with his in-laws Philippe and Richard Gastines for having lent their house to the celebration of the Protestant rites of Holy Communion, Nicolas Croquet was executed on the place de Grève

[111] Paul Guérin, "Délibérations politiques du Parlement et arrêts criminels du milieu de la première guerre de religion (1562)," *MSHP* 40 (1913):70-71 and 71n. See also BN, P.o. 2242 Perrot à Paris, no. 20 (13/6/59): marriage contract; BN, P.o. 944 Croquet, no. 49; *Reg. BV*, 2:149; AN, Y114, fol. 169v° (13/12/70).

[112] Guérin, "Délibérations," pp. 70-72: Letter of 15/10/62, signed Charles and Robertet. The order for Huguenots to leave Paris is reproduced in the *Reg. BV*, 5:126-27, and the incident at Meaux is probably the incident referred to *Reg. BV*, 5:128-29 (8/7/62).

[113] Guérin, "Délibérations," pp. 70-72.

[114] Ibid., p. 74n.

in June 1569.[115] François Perrot also returned to Paris for a time. A *rente* receipt of 1567 lists him as "bourgeois de Paris" and the guardian of a child by his deceased wife, Nicole Croquet.[116] Perrot had not, however, abandoned his beliefs. Leaving Paris again, he lived for many years in Venice, where he wrote propaganda for the Huguenot cause and translated the *Traité de la vérité* of Du Plessis-Mornay. Other members of the Perrot family were also Protestants, including at least one son of the younger Nicolas Perrot and possibly his wife.[117]

Another city councillor who was closely related to a victim of Catholic wrath was Cosme Luillier, though he did not live long enough to know that his brother-in-law, Pierre de la Place, a president of the Cour des Aides, was martyred in the massacres of Saint Bartholomew's Day.[118] Likewise, Pierre Perdrier, another councillor, did not live to know that his

[115] A. de Ruble, "Journal de François Grin, religieux de Saint Victor (1554-1570)," *MSHP* 21 (1894):50 (30/6/69): Croquet and the two Gastines were hung and strangled "pour hérésies saccagemens et argent par eulx baillés aux rebelles et ennemys de Dieu et du roy." See also Brulart, "Journal," p. 205. Athanase Josué Coquerel, *Précis de l'histoire de l'Eglise Réformée de Paris* (Paris and Strasbourg, 1862), p. 67, citing de Thou, asserts that Parlement would willingly have kept the penalty light, but the public demanded the death of the Huguenots. The house of the Gastines was ordered destroyed and a pyramid erected to mark the event. The displacement of this marker two years later, ordered by the king to conciliate the Protestants after the Peace of Saint-Germain, touched off a series of riots in the capital. *Reg. BV*, 6:398-435, gives a self-serving and not entirely accurate recital of these events. It is generally suspected that the city officers did not put their best effort into either the quiet removal of the pyramid or the suppression of the ensuing riots.

[116] BN, P.o. 2242 Perrot à Paris, no. 29. This would appear to have been the daughter, Esperance, who married Robert Hurault, the grandson of Chancellor de L'Hôpital in 1582.

[117] Eugène Haag and Emile Haag, *La France protestante* (Paris, 1846-59), 6:312. Richet, in "Conflits religieux," p. 767, says both Nicolas Perrot father and Nicolas Perrot son were Huguenots. I have not been able to confirm this from other sources. If the younger Nicolas Perrot was a Protestant, he must have renounced the faith before 1569, for he was not removed from the city council along with Du Gué and Courlay. Haag and Haag, 8:195-98, says that Nicolas may have been Protestant and that his wife, Claude Goyet, definitely was.

[118] Haag and Haag, 6:312; AN, Y93, fol. 104v°.

son was responsible for the death of the maréchal de Saint-André in the battle of Dreux.[119]

Since few records have come to light upon which to base a systematic inquiry into the question of Protestantism among the Parisian elite, we must settle, at least for the present, for these known incidences. Obviously, this is less than satisfactory. There are few Protestants we can identify who were not either members of very famous families (like the Budés and L'Hôpitals) or celebrated in their own right as martyrs, warriors, or propagandists for their cause (the case of Croquet, Perdrier, and Perrot, respectively). Just totaling the cases discussed above (and assuming that Courlay and Du Gué were indeed Protestants in 1569), however, we find that nineteen city councillors were themselves Calvinists or had immediate relatives or in-laws who adhered at some point to the Reformed faith.[120] Although this is only a small minority of the total number of city councillors, it is probable that there were other Protestants among these ninety families who did not leave such a clear trace on the records. I am not suggesting that the Hôtel de Ville was riddled with heresy. Far from it. But it is important that we should be aware that even within the staunchly Catholic Parisian elite there were dissenters, and that many persons who were themselves faithful Catholics may yet have been influenced in their behavior toward their families and in their attitudes toward the religious strife of the era by the knowledge that their own houses were divided.

[119] Jean Perdrier, sieur de Mezières et de Bobigny. Jacques-Auguste de Thou, *Histoire universelle depuis 1543 jusqu'en 1607* (London, 1734), 4:481. The incident is also related in Romier, *Jacques d'Albon*, pp. 195-97 and 380; and Mousnier, *Etat et société*, 1:184 and 211.

[120] Besides the city councillors mentioned in the text, Le Clerc was the brother-in-law of Nicole Croquet, Le Cointe was the father-in-law of Courlay, Le Prevost the brother-in-law of Du Drac, Morin the father of L'Hôpital's wife, and N. Perrot II the brother of François Perrot.

PART II

Professional Advancement

3. The Careers of the City Councillors

O que Marcel est un grand maistre!
Aussi bien tost nous verrons naistre
Force apprentif de son escole.
—1585 verse cited by L'Estoile

FOR PURPOSES of analysis, career choices, matrimonial arrangements, and successional patterns will be dealt with separately in the next three parts of the book. It is important, however, to realize that these three aspects of family planning are closely interrelated, not only in their psychological, motivational aspect but in their financial aspect as well. A man's marriage and his first important professional position quite often occurred simultaneously, or nearly so, and the financial settlement of the marriage was frequently instrumental in advancing a man's career. The influence and contacts of the newly acquired in-laws could serve this same purpose.

The subject of this chapter is the nature of the advancement a man might achieve in his own career and the means by which this promotion was accomplished. The collective portrait of the councillors' careers presented in the last chapter will be expanded to show how the councillors advanced over the course of their careers and to compare their success with that of their fathers. The disparate nature of the councillors' careers might at first seem a handicap to such an undertaking. There are, however, compensatory advantages in that this diversity allows us to examine the attitudes of both businessmen and royal officials toward their place in society and to see the similarities in the ambitions of all of these men.

Then, as a complement to the collective portrait and an

aid to further analysis, the career of one man, an ambitious merchant who became one of the highest financial officers of the realm, will be studied in more detail.

Occupational Mobility

In order to measure occupational mobility, Table 6 presents a cross-tabulation of the early career of each city councillor against his highest known occupational achievement. "Early careers" are defined according to the principal employment or professional quality of a man at about the time of his first marriage. This point was chosen because a man's occupation is more frequently known at the time of his marriage

TABLE 6
Professional Advancement of the City Councillors

	Early career								
Peak occupational achievement	High office	Middle office: courts	Middle office: administration	Low office & liberal professions	Nobles without office	Bourgeois de Paris: rentiers	Merchants	Total: peak achievement	Percentage
High office	—	13	4	4	—	—	1	22	24%
Middle office: courts	—	11	4	3	—	1	1	20	22
Middle office: administration	—	—	7	3	—	—	3	13	14
Low office & liberal professions	—	—	—	12	—	—	—	12	13
Nobles without office	—	1	—	—	4	—	—	5	6
Bourgeois de Paris: rentiers	—	—	—	—	—	—	5	5	6
Merchants	—	—	—	—	—	—	13	13	14
Total: early career	0	25	15	22	4	1	23	90	99%
Percentage:	0	28	17	24	4	1	26	100%	

than at other points in his early life. Moreover, the occasion of marriage appears to have had a symbolic association with youthful maturity and independence among the upper reaches of the Parisian bourgeoisie in the mid-sixteenth century. This fact makes it an appropriate point at which to assume that a man was seriously engaged upon but still at the start of his life's work, an assumption that will be further discussed in the chapter on marriage. It is important to add here that most city councillors appear to have married for the first time between their mid-twenties and mid-thirties, often around their thirtieth year. [1]

Beginning the study of a man's career at the point of his marriage and not necessarily with his first known occupation also helps to avoid a problem that arises in evaluating the careers of the lawyers in Parlement. Since admittance to the bar in Parlement was a prerequisite to the office of counselor in Parlement, it can be assumed that all counselors in fact began as lawyers. Only a few, however, pleaded cases at the bar long enough for us to consider that they had careers as lawyers before joining the ranks of the judges. Counselors in Parlement who did first make a name for themselves as lawyers, such as Christophe de Thou, are counted in Table 6 among those who began in the liberal professions, while a larger number of parlementaires are counted among those who began in the middle-level judiciary posts.

In those few cases for which I have no certain knowledge of a man's career before he was middle-aged, I have used his first known position instead of his position at the time of his marriage. It is possible, for example, that Simon Cressé worked as a jeweler alongside his father before he gave up commerce to live "nobly" as a bourgeois de Paris. Since there are no primary materials that prove he was a jeweler, however, he has been categorized according to the documentary evidence that he was a bourgeois rentier. It is likely, then, that Table 6 somewhat overstates the levels at which councillors' careers

---

[1] See Chapter 5.

began and, as a result, understates the advancement they achieved.

As one would expect, none of the city councillors began their careers in high office. More than a quarter of them (twenty-five men, or 28%), however, appear to have taken office in the sovereign courts at a fairly early age. This is a significant proportion. It indicates that one must look closely at the family background of the city councillors, for surely it is only among the higher levels of the robe that we can expect to find young men acquiring the dignity of counselors in the sovereign courts by the time they were of age to marry. It is also significant that more than half of these twenty-five counselors in the sovereign courts eventually attained the highest judiciary and administrative positions in the kingdom. Moreover, it is worth observing that the proportion of city councillors who began their careers in the sovereign courts and eventually attained high office is far larger than the proportion of those who began with offices in the chancellory or other areas of the royal administration and eventually attained high office.

Although a majority of those who began with careers in the liberal professions or lower offices remained in this category, these positions could also serve as springboards to greater personal success or as temporary positions for sons of important officers destined eventually to succeed to the paternal dignities. For example, the three members of the de Thou family who were on the city council between 1535 and 1575 all made a reputation at the bar before acceding to royal office. Though family ties and royal favor played a certain role in this success, personal merit was also a significant factor, particularly in the case of Christophe de Thou.

To judge from Table 6 there was only a moderate amount of mobility from the lower offices into the middle-level court offices, the chancellory, or the royal financial administration, but it is perhaps at this point that the sources are most deficient. It is likely that some of the men whose careers were not recorded before they achieved the distinction of membership in Parlement or in the college of the secrétaires du roi did in fact begin with lower offices. I should also caution that, because of the way occupational categories are defined in Table 6, significant professional mobility is not always apparent. A man could make considerable advancement in his career without his categories in the table changing. This is particularly true in the case of the lower offices. Martin and Thomas de Bragelongne and Jean Morin, for example, all rose from minor offices in the Châtelet to lieutenancies in the Prévôté de Paris, the highest offices in the Châtelet beneath the prévôt himself, but since these positions were still in the lower jurisdiction of the Prévôté and not in the sovereign courts, the three men are still counted in Table 6 as "lower officers." Both the deficiencies of the sources and the inadequacies of categorization, then, tend to bias Table 6 toward occupational stability.

Despite this bias, there is significant mobility shown on both the top and bottom levels of the chart. Five of the twenty-three councillors who began their careers as merchants achieved at least middle-level positions in the courts and chancellory. Three merchants purchased the ennobling office of secrétaire du roi, one became a maître des comptes, and yet another rose to become a member of the king's privy council and an *intendant des finances*.

Another aspect of the professional mobility of the city councillors is shown in Table 7. Because it is important to consider mobility in terms of the occupational mobility of the family as well as that of the individual, the highest career achievement of each councillor is compared here with the highest known occupation of his father.

Table 7 illustrates some of the complexities of the social and professional make-up of the city council in the mid-sixteenth century. It shows a high level of mobility, particularly among the sons of merchants and lower officers, but it also shows that an important proportion of the city council was made up of high and middle officers of the robe who were themselves sons of high and middle robe officers. Seven of the

TABLE 7
Careers of the City Councillors Compared with the Careers of their Fathers

Councillor's peak occupational achievement	Father's peak occupational achievement							Total	Number unknown
	High office	Middle office: courts	Middle office: administration	Low office & liberal professions	Nobles without office	Bourgeois de Paris: rentiers	Merchants		
High office	7	7	4	2	—	—	2	22	—
Middle office: courts	—	9	2	3	—	—	4	18	2
Middle office: administration	—	1	3	1	1	—	4	10	3
Low office & liberal professions	—	2	—	2	1	1	3	9	3
Nobles without office	1	—	1	—	3	—	—	5	—
Bourgeois de Paris: rentiers	—	—	—	—	—	—	5	5	—
Merchants	—	—	—	—	—	—	13	13	—
Total	8	19	10	8	5	1	31	82	8

city councillors who attained high office were themselves the sons of high officers, and eleven were the sons of middle-level officers. Only four were the sons of lesser officers and merchants. And yet, the fact that four men were able to make this enormous professional leap is in itself important. It is also significant that, though only thirteen city councillors were themselves merchants at the end of their careers, at least thirty-one councillors were the sons of merchants. As Table 7 indicates, an ambitious merchant family could rise far in just one generation.

The stability shown in Table 7 is as important as the mobility. It is not surprising that a large proportion of high officers were themselves the sons of high officers. Such continuity is to be expected in a society in which honors and social status were for the most part inherited. It is perhaps surprising, however, that the sons of the highest officers of the crown, themselves destined for important functions in the monarchy, did not abandon the municipal arena for the monarchical arena. That they did not do so indicates that municipal affairs should not be considered to have been a proving ground or a lesser sphere of activity for those unsuited or ineligible for more important tasks. Membership in the city council was an honor and civic service a responsibility accepted even by those who had higher honors and other responsibilities.

The family careers have not been traced here beyond the careers of the councillors' fathers. To do so would only reinforce this image of mixed stability and mobility. Though some of the families of the city councillors had achieved their professional distinction only recently, a number of the most active families in municipal affairs—the Du Dracs, the Luilliers, and the Marles among them—could trace their membership in the sovereign courts to at least the first decades of the fifteenth century. Proud of their Parisian roots as well as their robe traditions, members of old robe families did not disdain to hold municipal office alongside ambitious and upwardly mobile merchants and petty officers. Ambition and tradition were not incompatible in civic office.

In many respects, the career patterns of the city councillors and their families would seem to typify the patterns of mobility described by Roland Mousnier in his studies of early modern French society:

It was necessary, for the most part, to raise oneself by degrees, from commerce to finance, from finance to a low office in the judicature or an office of secretary to the King. Then one could hope to accede to the magistrature, to office as lieutenant general of the *bailliages* or offices of the sovereign courts, then to those of *maître des requêtes* and to the Council of State. This usually required three, four generations, generally four generations.[2]

[2] Roland Mousnier, *Les Hiérarchies sociales de 1450 à nos jours* (Paris, 1969), pp. 73-74.

Only an exceptional man could make it from commerce to the Conseil d'Etat. More likely, but still rare, was the possibility that the son of a merchant might accede to high royal office, as did Jean Prevost, a president of the Chambre des Requêtes of Parlement and the son of a merchant of Blois, or Pierre Hennequin, a president of Parlement and the son of a merchant of Troyes.[3] Most often there were three or more generations between an ancestor in commerce and a descendant in high office.

It is also true that financial office was an important step in the transition from commerce to judiciary office in a number of these families. The history of even the most established parlementaire families often leads back to financiers at some point. André Guillart, a maître des requêtes, for example, was the grandson of a receveur général of the Count of Maine.[4] The Luilliers and the Sanguins were famous as money changers in the late fourteenth and early fifteenth centuries, and even the Longueils, though parlementaires since 1380, were descended from a Dieppoise merchant and officer of the salt monopoly.

The ease with which these patterns can be recognized should not, however, lead us to unwarranted generalization. Linear models for social mobility such as Mousnier's can be useful tools for analysis, but we should not forget that they can also distort reality by reducing a complex situation to a few set categories hierarchically arranged. The elegance of this linear model should not lull us into accepting the progression as an inevitable lock step leading from merchandise to finance, then to low, middle, and high office. Few families in fact fit the model exactly; and even the families that most closely resemble the model often skipped a generation or two in the progression. As we have seen, a wealthy merchant did not have to become a financier in order for his son to obtain judicial office, nor was low judicial office or the office of secretary to the king a necessary prerequisite for magisterial office, at least

---

[3] Prevost: Bluche, *Magistrats du Parlement*, p. 360; Hennequin: *Actes de François I*, 6:731 (December 1543).
[4] Jouanna, "Guillart," p. 231.

as far as this sixteenth-century elite was concerned.[5] The careers of the city councillors also show the importance of distinguishing among the various types of financial office a man might hold. The financial bureaucracy had its own hierarchy, and enormous differences separated petty functionaries such as the farmers of minor *aides* from important officers of the king's finances such as the trésoriers généraux, who were ennobled for their functions, or the *intendants des finances*, who were members of the Conseil d'Etat. Only the lowest officers of finances—the receveurs, élus, commissaires, and contrôleurs of various regions or departments of the fiscal services— were likely to view low judiciary office as a step up in society, and even these officers often moved directly into the sovereign courts.

We must also remember that linear models can distort reality by narrowing the perspective from which a situation is viewed. By accepting the idea that early modern French society was ordered around "the social esteem, dignity, and honor accorded by consensus to a particular social function,"[6] we emphasize prestige at the expense of the economic and political factors upon which the social hierarchy was based. An auditor of the Chambre des Comptes could aspire to become a maître des comptes or even a president of that court because he would draw a higher salary, demonstrate greater professional competence, and have a higher level of responsibility in the procedures and decisions of the court. Not only desire for social esteem but also professional, financial, and political motives encouraged a move from commerce to royal office.

The first step from commerce into royal office was often tax farming.[7] While still a merchant, a man might purchase the right to collect taxes on one of the taxable commodities

---

[5] As late as 1588, the avocat général du roi in the Chambre des Comptes recognized the right of an ex-merchant to hold office as a maître des comptes, providing he had not engaged in trade within the previous four years (Arthur Michel de Boislisle, *Chambre des Comptes* [Nogent-le-Rotrou, 1873], p. 188).

[6] Mousnier, *Hiérarchies*, p. 74.

[7] Pierre Jeannin, *Merchants of the Sixteenth Century*, trans. Paul Fittingoff (New York, 1972), pp. 61-63.

brought into the capital or another city. Thus, for example, the father of Louis Abelly, a wine merchant, purchased in 1539 the right to farm the *aide* on the wine sold at retail in the quartier of the Grève in Paris.[8] Because the collector of *aides* had to go down to the docks and into the houses and cellars of the merchants of the city to inspect for illegally imported merchandise, it was useful to have a man familiar with the trade serving in this office.[9] Success in the farming of taxes often led to other positions in the fiscal administration. The profits of tax farming could be invested in venal office, and the experience adapted to other administrative functions. Because the royal financial bureaucracy grew so rapidly under the stresses of monarchical extravagance and prolonged warfare in the mid-sixteenth century, there was ready opportunity for a man enriched by trade and tax farming to invest in venal office.

This career opportunity would not, however, have attracted many prosperous merchants had social and financial incentives not encouraged the abandonment of commerce for office. Rich Parisian merchants might not have turned so often from business to royal office had the profits of commerce been more certain and the risks less great. Certainly there were some large fortunes to be made in business, but French commercial and banking techniques in the mid-sixteenth century were such that large-scale business endeavors required the prolonged risk of enormous sums of capital.[10] When Jean Charpentier, one of the most important Parisian drapers, died in 1585, for example, his heirs inherited £134,000 in outstanding notes that had to be collected from 184 merchants scat-

[8] *Actes de François I*, 4:30 (10/8/39).

[9] Only occasionally does there seem to have been an awareness of a potential conflict of interest in having tax collectors who were otherwise associated with the product for which they collected taxes. In 1568, for example, the butchers were forbidden to bid on the right to collect the tax on hooved animals sold in the city (*Reg. BV*, 6:3).

[10] Coornaert, *Commerce*, pp. 246-47. See also Larmour, "Grocers," especially pp. 125-28 on the profits of commerce.

tered from Toulouse to Rennes.[11]Repeated outbreaks of war made commerce particularly risky in the sixteenth century. In 1528, for example, the city councillors Denis Barthelemy and Claude Le Lievre were among a group of merchants who complained to the Bureau de la Ville that goods they had shipped to Flanders had been seized illegally, although there had been no declaration of war. There had even been confiscations of merchandise in France by French soldiers and seamen. The angry merchants protested these seizures as "contrary to all justice and reason."[12] It is not surprising that a man as he grew older might wish to place his money in investments that appeared more secure or that a man who feared his son had not the same flair for business that he had might choose to train this son for a less risky career.

The worries and insecurities of the business community were well expressed in the petition a group of Parisian merchants addressed to the king through the Bureau de la Ville in 1548. The petition was in opposition to the proposal to create a bank in the city from which the monarch might borrow funds. One of the main objections of the merchants to a bank was that it would destroy commerce, because, they argued, men would prefer to let their money earn 8% in the bank instead of risking it in business ventures:

As for commerce, which cannot be conducted without great care and diligence, under the hazards and doubtful events of fortune, and even most often to little profit—such as four or five percent—it would be entirely abandoned; and few persons would be found who would not prefer to put their money in the bank, to live in their houses off the profit that they would draw, in joy, repose, and security, rather than to undertake traffic in merchandise in distant

---

[11] Roger Gourmelon, "Etude sur le rayonnement commercial des marchands drapiers parisiens au xvi⁰ siècle," *Bulletin philologique et historique (jusqu'à 1610) du Comité des travaux historiques et scientifiques*, 1961 (1963), p. 266. The city councillor Jean Le Sueur, also a draper, left £33,000 in outstanding notes on his death in 1569. This was more than four times the value of the inventory he had on hand at the time (AN, Min. cen. XX:78 [12/2/69]).

[12] *Reg. BV*, 2:9.

regions, laboring with body and mind, and in continual danger and peril of shipwreck, highway robbery, and other unforeseen events.[13]

Even if the merchants understated the profitability of commerce in order to make their case sound stronger, the fear of risk that underscores their argument has a ring of truth about it.

A further reason that a man might choose to leave business for office in the royal bureaucracy was that he saw in the service of the king a better chance to protect his fortune and that of his family. Position in the royal bureaucracy gave a man not just social status but political influence as well. An officer of the crown was more likely than a merchant to have his requests heard by the king, his opinions solicited by other officials, and his aid sought by those of lower standing. The facts of political life were clear. In a centralized monarchy, power radiated from the throne. The only way to share in this power was to approach as near as one could to the center.

In centuries past, the merchants had had a collective tool for political leverage in the Prévôté de la Marchandise. Long before the sixteenth century, however, the membership in the city government had come to be dominated by royal officials and the Prévôté itself had shown its weakness to the king. The Bureau de la Ville still served the merchants of the city to the extent that it consulted them on important questions, presented their petitions to the king, and even occasionally guaranteed them a certain right to representation in its councils, but it could do little more. It could not make the merchants a powerful and respected force in the state; it could not give them the pride and status that might have kept them from abandoning trade for royal service.

The desire for political leverage, then, as well as the desire for financial security worked with the desire for social elevation to turn merchants away from commerce and toward service in the royal bureaucracy. In quitting commerce merchants were following a logical path of career advancement and mak-

[13] Ibid., 3:108.

ing useful skills available to the state. For the most part the same drives for professional success and social elevation operated within the bureaucracy itself.

Claude Marcel: A Case Study of Ambition and Favor

The career of Claude Marcel, a goldsmith and jeweler on the pont aux Changes when elected to the city council in 1564, illustrates the dramatic advancement that was possible for a wealthy and ambitious man in mid-sixteenth-century Paris. A talent for finding money for the desperate monarchy enabled Marcel to rise from jeweler to *intendant* of the king's finances and trusted advisor to Catherine de Medici in less than a decade. Still a merchant in 1566, Marcel first served the king in an official capacity in November 1567, as receiver of the subsidies the clergy had promised the crown.[14] While continuing to serve as receiver of taxes collected from the Gallican Church, Marcel gradually assumed a number of other financial responsibilities in the royal households. By 1570 he was appointed *receveur général des finances de la Reine mère* and commissioned with the collection of the forced loans the king had levied on certain of his subjects.[15] In the fall of 1571, he was raised to the status of treasurer in the queen mother's household, and by the end of 1572, he was a member of the king's privy council and *intendant de ses finances*.[16] Within just six short years, then, Marcel had been admitted to the small circle of men who determined and executed the financial policies of the last Valois. The success of his career, moreover, was rewarded by social success—at least in some circles. When Marcel's daughter was married in 1577, the lewd behavior of the courtiers at her wedding reception scandalized bourgeois Paris, but the presence of the king and three queens at the

[14] Léo Mouton, *La Vie municipale au xvie siècle. Claude Marcel, prévôt des marchands* (Paris, 1930), p. 66, citing BN, MS fr. 14757, fols. 1, 9, 90.

[15] BN, P.o. 1836 Marcel, nos. 23-26: *rente* receipts for 1570.

[16] Mouton, *Marcel*, p. 94; BN, P.o. 1836 Marcel, nos. 32, 36-40, 42, 45; BN, MS fr. 32581 Saint-André: baptism of Claude de Mesmes (24/11/72).

festivities signified how far the ex-jeweler had come up in the world.[17]

The career of Claude Marcel might be viewed as an exception to the usual process of advancement. To be sure, his rise was extremely rapid, lofty, and dependent upon royal favor rather than the traditional networks of family ties and patronage. Yet a closer look shows his career to be less of an exception than it might seem. In fact, it was not mere personal magnetism or political favoritism that took him so quickly to the top, as some historians, intrigued by the possible role Marcel played in the events of Saint Bartholomew's Day, have assumed. Marcel possessed a whole array of skills and experiences that made him a valuable servant to the king. An examination of his career can give us insights into the relationship between commerce and royal office, civic service and royal favor.

If it was Marcel's skill at collecting gold and silver ducats that later endeared him to the Valois kings, it was his talent at fashioning objects of these precious materials that first brought him to the attention of the royal family. Born about 1520 into a family long known in the Parisian bourgeoisie, Claude Marcel became a master of the goldsmiths' guild in 1544. It was a natural career choice for Marcel: his father was also a goldsmith. He chose as his first wife the daughter of another member of the corporation.[18] One of the most prestigious guilds in the city, the *orfèvres* differed from the great merchant guilds in that the members were craftsmen and artists as well as dealers in goods made by other hands. Apparently Marcel was skilled at his craft. Though none of his works are known to have been preserved, he is said to have been one of the best goldsmiths of the period and a favorite

---

[17] L'Estoile, *Journal pour le règne de Henri III*, p. 157.

[18] Jacqueline Hotman, the daughter of Pierre Hotman (Mouton, *Marcel*, p. 12; BN, P.o. 1836 Marcel, no. 166). Though I have frequently used the term "jeweler" as a convenient translation of "orfèvre," the sixteenth-century orfèvre was primarily a maker and seller of gold and silver objects, while articles of personal adornment and precious gems were the province of the *joailliers*.

of Catherine de Medici, who served as godmother to one of his six daughters. According to Léo Mouton, whose little study of Claude Marcel is the only work that gives Marcel more than a passing mention, Catherine was still *dauphine* when she first became the patron of the young goldsmith.[19] However uncertain this may be, it is clear that Marcel was known and liked at court at least by 1557, when he was named échevin at the express request of the king.[20]

Beyond facilitating his acquaintance with the royal family, Marcel's early career may have helped his later advance in several ways. In the first place, his career as a jeweler gave him his earliest administrative experience. Because of the high intrinsic value of the materials with which they worked, the orfèvres were subject to close scrutiny both from their corporation and from regulatory agencies of the crown. In 1553 Marcel was elected *garde* of the jewelers' corporation. In this capacity, he had regularly to inspect the works produced by the city's orfèvres, evaluating the alloys used and taxes paid as well as the craftsmanship involved.[21] This work was done twice weekly at the Hôtel de Ville, where the hallmarks were stamped on the approved pieces. Frequent visits to the jewelers' shops were also required. The administrative responsibilities involved in performing these functions were good experience for Marcel and brought him into contact with officials of both municipal and monarchical government. When Henry II ordered the Parisians to bring their silver plate to the Hôtel de Ville in 1554 to serve as security for loans he was raising to finance his wars with Charles V, Claude Marcel was one of the two jewelers selected to appraise the pieces brought in.[22]

[19] Mouton, *Marcel*, pp. 25, 27-28. Mouton assumes, though without offering evidence, that it was the first daughter who was the queen's godchild, because it was she who bore the same Christian name as the queen.

[20] *Reg. BV*, 4:494.

[21] Mouton, *Marcel*, pp. 21-23.

[22] *Reg. BV*, 4:299; Félibien, *Histoire*, 5:288-89. The Département des Etampes at the Bibliothèque nationale possesses a manuscript copy of the *registre* of silver furnished the king: "Charles IX . . . Vaiselle d'argent fournie par les bourgeois de Paris au Roy. Registre depuis le 6ᵉ aoust jusqu'au 30 octobre 1562." It is perhaps worth noting that Marcel's own

Marcel's first official service to the king's treasury was thus as a jeweler and not as a tax collector.

It was quite natural that Marcel, as a worker in precious metals, should become involved in the minting of coinage. Like his father and uncles before him, Marcel was a member of the confraternity of the *monnoyeurs* of Paris.[23] His main position in the confraternity was that of *essayeur général des monnaies* (an inspector of weights and values), and it was in this capacity that he served on the commission appointed by the king for the reformation of the currency in 1559.[24] A thorough knowledge of currency regulations no doubt later proved useful to Marcel as a tax collector and financier, and service on this royal commission again provided valuable experience and contacts.

The culmination of Marcel's career as a merchant/craftsman can be seen in his election in 1566 as judge of the consular court run by and for the city's merchant community.[25] Only the third man to serve as judge of the recently created commercial court, Marcel was the sole orfèvre elected to this function in the sixteenth century. The vast majority were wholesale drapers, mercers, and grocers, the cream of the Parisian merchant community. Marcel's position among this group confirms his high standing among the city's commercial elite and indicates that he was at the top of his craft when he abandoned it in November 1567 to collect subsidies promised the king by the Gallican church.

Well before this time, however, Marcel's sphere of activity and influence had broadened from trade organizations to community service. In 1555 he was named treasurer of the Bureau

contribution to the forced loan was valued at over £6,000—ten times the size of the contributions of other city officers (fol. 76).

[23] BN, MS fr., N.a. 11904. Mathieu Marcel and his brothers Geoffroy and Pierre were received into the confraternity in 1521 and 1524.

[24] BN, MS fr. 18501: "Formulaire manuel à l'usage d'un officier des Monnaies," 1529-1577. Copy inscribed "Claude Marcel, essaieur général." Mouton, *Marcel*, p. 36, citing BN, MS fr. 19505.

[25] Denière, *Juridiction consulaire*, p. 509. The consular court was formed to settle commercial disputes of £500 or less in value without the time and expense of regular court proceedings.

des Pauvres, and in 1556 the officers of the Bureau de la Ville made Marcel gouverneur of the Hôtel Dieu.[26] In 1557 Marcel was named échevin. Marcel's debut as a city officer occurred under a cloud. As a candidate for the échevinage in 1557, Marcel received fewer votes than the city councillor Pierre Croquet but was chosen instead of him at the request of the king. The city officers apparently accepted the king's orders without remonstrance, perhaps because of the emotional climate engendered by the king's military disaster at Saint-Quentin only a week earlier.[27] Fearful for the safety of the city and the realm, the officers of the Bureau de la Ville probably had little inclination to quarrel with the king over the city's traditional electoral freedom. Although Marcel first entered city office by royal command rather than popular vote, it should not be assumed that he was disliked by his fellow officers. Quite the contrary; it seems likely from the study of royal intervention in city elections that Marcel placed high on the list of candidates.[28] Furthermore, Marcel's election just the previous year to the board of governors of the Hôtel Dieu would suggest that the city officers had confidence in his abilities.

During the decade following his first nomination as échevin, Marcel devoted many hours—too many hours, by his own account—to civic affairs. In 1560 he was reelected to the échevinage by popular vote. Wishing more time for his own affairs, he accepted his reelection only on the understanding that he was merely to serve out the remaining year of the term of an échevin deposed for his Protestant faith.[29] A year later, however, the king and queen mother ordered Marcel, along with several other city officers, continued in

[26] *Reg. BV*, 5:248n; Brièle, *Documents*, 3:357.

[27] *Reg. BV*, 4:493-99.

[28] The top two candidates were the younger Augustin de Thou and Pierre Croquet, both of whom belonged to families active in city government since the first part of the sixteenth century. Croquet had been a city councillor since 1553.

[29] *Reg. BV*, 5:142.

office.[30] Marcel's reaction to this order is significant, for it shows that, whatever his ambitions, he was not afraid to oppose the wishes of the king. While the Bureau de la Ville complied willingly enough with the king's command and re-elected Marcel, Marcel himself protested loudly that he had already served the city as best he could as treasurer of the poor and through three years as échevin. He begged to be excused from a further term. Marcel's protests were sent to the Chambre du Conseil of the Chambre des Comptes, where they were received without sympathy, and Marcel was threatened with imprisonment in the Conciergerie if he refused to take office as required.[31] Still under protest, Marcel consented to serve one more year. When that additional year had passed, Marcel was again asked to remain as échevin by his fellow officers of the Hôtel de Ville, the maréchal de Montmorency (on the part of the king), and the Parlement of Paris. Adamant in his refusal, Marcel succeeded at last in his wish to resign.[32] He had, however, been elected city councillor two months earlier, so he was not entirely freed from municipal duties.

Marcel's election as city councillor further confirms his popularity with his fellow officers of the Hôtel de Ville. Seizing upon a technicality to invalidate the resignation of a dying city councillor in favor of his son, the corps de ville chose Marcel instead to fill the vacancy.[33] Since this office was more of an honor and less of a burden than the échevinage, Marcel accepted the nomination without protest. And he did not voice any complaint when elected prévôt des marchands in 1570.[34]

It is not entirely clear whether Marcel was freely elected to the Prévôté de la Marchandise or whether he was appointed by the king. To all appearances, he was legitimately chosen,

[30] Ibid., 5:275.
[31] Ibid., 5:282-84.
[32] Ibid., 5:456-59, 459n, and 473-74.
[33] Ibid., 5:433.
[34] Ibid., 6:176-77.

but the actual vote is not recorded, and the city records state rather ambiguously that the election results were presented to the king, who opened them and announced, "qu'elle [sa majesté] auroit voullu et ordonné pour Prevost des Marchans led. Sʳ Marcel."[35] It is not clear if "the aforesaid Marcel" was the majority candidate or merely the king's choice. The former possibility, however, seems most plausible in view of the fact that the election occurred just one week after the Peace of Saint-Germain pledged the king to a cessation of hostilities against the Protestants. Since Marcel's violent opposition to the Protestant party was well known, it seems unlikely that the king would have overridden the city's vote to name him prévôt des marchands at the very moment he was trying to calm the religious passions of his subjects. On the other hand, the strongly Catholic city officers might well have seized upon the occasion of the city elections to signal their disapproval of the royal declaration of truce by choosing a known Catholic hothead. In any event, it seems evident that Marcel's position was based on more than his being a docile favorite of royal policy makers.

The role of city office in Marcel's rise in the royal bureaucracy is a complex one. On final appraisal, however, it would seem that his influential position in city politics bore less relation to his later success as a servant of the crown than might be suggested by his first appearance on the municipal scene as the royal candidate in 1557. In an indirect way, however, participation in city government probably was related to Marcel's success. More than ten years intervened between Marcel's commission to appraise the silver plate brought into the City Hall and his appointment as receveur of church taxes. During this time, he held a series of municipal offices that not only gave him valuable administrative experience but raised his standing among his community at large, among the local elite, and with the crown. Though the Marcels were an ancient and respected family among the Parisian bourgeoi-

[35] Ibid.

sie, they were not, prior to Claude's success, in the ranks of those who held the highest offices in the city in the sixteenth century. Marcel's new standing in the ranks of the civic notability must inevitably have changed his relationship with the royal family. Garbed in the traditional robes of the city officials, Marcel was no longer a mere tradesman employed to make beautiful objects for the queen's pleasure; he was at the head of a government that, although subject to the crown, was ancient enough, powerful enough, and rich enough for its officers to be treated with respect by even the monarch himself.

The ceremonial role of Marcel as prévôt des marchands must also have had the psychological effect of putting some distance between his early life as a craftsman and his later posts at court. Consider, for example, his role as prévôt des marchands in 1571 when Charles IX and his bride, Elizabeth of Austria, made their ceremonial entrance into the capital. Dressed magnificently in his fur-trimmed robes of red and tan velvet and attended by four footmen dressed in his own colors of black and white, Marcel rode through the streets of the city on a mule draped in gold-fringed velours. At the high point of the elaborate procession, Marcel knelt before the king and presented him with the keys to the city.[36] This traditional gesture is one of respect, honor, and even obedience on the part of the city's highest officer and of the city itself, but it is the gesture of a host and a man of standing, not that of a lackey. Office in the Hôtel de Ville thus reinforced Marcel's personal stature as well as furthering his professional ambitions and allowed him, once royal office was obtained, to be the king's servant, and not just the queen mother's jeweler.

As a city officer, Marcel used his abilities to serve simultaneously his own ambitions, the city's interests, and the de-

<hr />

[36] Ibid., 6:281-82. Victor E. Graham and W. McAllister Johnson, *The Paris Entries of Charles IX and Elisabeth of Austria* (Toronto, 1974), contains documentary material not included in the account of the entries published in the *Reg. BV.*

sires of the royal family. During his several terms as échevin and while a city councillor, Marcel frequently served as an intermediary between the municipal and monarchical governments. On a number of occasions, the king used Marcel to inform the city of the political affairs of the state and the needs of the crown. In turn, the officers of the Hôtel de Ville often selected Marcel to deliver their messages and remonstrances to the king.[37] Marcel's influence with royalty, moreover, apparently went beyond his official role as the city's favorite emissary to the court. For example, a Huguenot epigram related in the memoirs of L'Estoile gives Claude Marcel the credit (or blame) for convincing the king in 1568 to create a sixth presidency in the Parlement of Paris for Pierre Hennequin in exchange for Hennequin's generous contribution of £60,000 to the royal coffers.[38] An anecdote from 1572 illustrates the relationship of jocular familiarity that existed between Claude Marcel and the royal family by this time: "One day when he [Marcel] had gone in the name of the city to ask Catherine de Medici to attend the fireworks of the Saint's Day of Saint John on the place de Grève, he approached Marguerite of France, then twenty years old, and, taking hold of her under the chin, he brusquely told her 'you're invited too, little girl.' "[39]

Despite the assertion of Georges Denière that Marcel was a tool of the Guises, I have not been able to find any sign of close ties between the Guise family and Marcel prior to 1577, when the wedding reception of Marcel's daughter was held in the Hôtel de Guise.[40] I suspect that Marcel, although an ardent Catholic, was too devoted to the Valois dynasty to have been a true Guisard. Clearly his advancement in the royal administration was achieved through Catherine's sponsorship and his place in city government through both popular vote and royal prerogative. Moreover, if the dates of Marcel's

---

[37] For example, *Reg. BV*, 4:529-30 and 5:296, 317, 402, 404.
[38] L'Estoile, *Journal pour le règne de Henri III*, p. 149.
[39] Denière, *Juridiction consulaire*, p. 72.
[40] Ibid. L'Estoile, *Journal pour le règne de Henri III*, p. 157.

professional advances are compared with the periods of greatest Guise influence at court, it is clear that the Guises could not have been his main patrons, at least not in the period prior to Saint Bartholomew's Day. While it thus appears inaccurate to call Marcel the "tool" of the Guise family, there is no doubt that because of his staunchly Catholic political beliefs Marcel sometimes indirectly served the cause of the Guises.

The active role that Claude Marcel played in Catholic politics in the city can be documented as far back as 1561. He was then the head of a group of Parisian notables who sought out the king at Saint-Germain to ask the release of a monk arrested for incendiary and seditious sermons against the Huguenots.[41] In 1562 Marcel was captain of a dizaine in the Parisian militia and as such took part in the sometimes brutal repression of Huguenot dissent in the city.[42] In 1570 a popular song satirized Marcel as the leader of a group of rich and rabidly Catholic Parisian merchants eager to stamp out the Protestant heresy once and for all. The song clearly indicates that the economic leverage of these merchants could threaten as well as benefit the monarchy and suggests that Charles IX may have found himself in an awkward position when Marcel was elected prévôt des marchands just a week after the pacification of Saint-Germain:

> Marcel, speaking with the king,
> Said to him, "Sire, by my faith,
>   Well I see
>   And also believe
> That our good city
> Will go to the dogs
> If you do not take care of
> This [Protestant] gospel."
>
> (Chorus) You will go to mass,
>   Huguenots, or Marcel will sell

[41] *Reg. BV*, 5:108-109.
[42] Ibid., 5:129-30, 130n.

His belongings and hastily
Leave France.
"What, Sire! don't you know
That I save you ducats
For your affairs,
Not being too unhappy
To do still more for you?
If you wish to employ us
You will never have to raise
A single denier."
(Chorus)
"For I am more than 500 strong
Who have our coins ready
Handsome and heavy
And of the largest [denominations]
For the war we wish you to make
Against these Huguenots,
In order to chase them out quickly
And we'll help."
(Chorus)[43]

One occasion on which Marcel may have used his political power as prévôt des marchands to counter the king's plans for pacification is the affair of the Croix de Gastines. One of the concessions made the Protestants in the Peace of Saint-Germain was the promised removal of the monument to religious hatred known as the Croix de Gastines, which marked the destruction of a house on the rue Saint-Denis where Reformed services were said to have been held.[44] As early as August 1571, the officers of the Hôtel de Ville and the Châtelet had been ordered by the king to tear down the monument.[45] Despite the king's increasing anger, the city officers procrastinated throughout the fall, insisting that the Parisian populace

[43] Le Roux de Lincy, *Chants*, pp. 294-98.
[44] See Chapter 2, n. 114. Nicolas Croquet, the brother of Jean and Pierre Croquet, was martyred for his participation in these services.
[45] *Reg. BV*, 6:363n.

would not allow the Croix de Gastines removed.[46] They offered instead to move the pyramid and cross to the cemetery of the Innocents, but even this action was repeatedly postponed. By the time the removal was begun in mid-December, public agitation had grown to such a pitch that violent rioting broke out in the city. The account of this affair given in the *registres* of the Bureau de la Ville is decidedly self-serving, first making excuses for the delays and then glorifying the role of the prévôt des marchands and échevins in putting down the riots.[47] In spite of the "official" account, it is hard to avoid the conclusion that if the city officers had been determined to preserve the Peace of Saint-Germain and the peace of the city they could have avoided these troubles by acting quietly and decisively months earlier.[48] And though there is no direct evidence, it is hard not to suspect that Marcel, as prévôt des marchands, was guilty of tolerating or even encouraging the delays.

Whatever Marcel's role in the affair of the Croix de Gastines, it is clear that as prévôt des marchands he could act decisively—even imperiously—when he chose. Just four months later, in the spring of 1572, an arrest made by Marcel—a seemingly inconsequential incident—sparked off an angry quarrel over jurisdictional rights between the Châtelet and the Hôtel de Ville. Protesting that Marcel had wrongly arrested one of his agents, the *lieutenant civil* of the Châtelet, Gabriel Miron, complained that "Marcel was everything in Paris and did everything, and that the children ran through the streets saying that he was the vice-king [*vice roy*]."[49]

We can see, then, that Marcel, strong-minded and staunchly

---

[46] Ibid., 6:380.

[47] Ibid., 6:398-434.

[48] Letters addressed to the city on December 15 by the king, the queen mother, and the duc d'Anjou suggest that the royal family was of the same opinion: those responsible for moving the cross were guilty of procrastinating and dissembling. Had the cross been moved promptly and quietly, there would have been no occasion for public unrest. Ibid., 6:421-22.

[49] Jean de La Fosse, *Journal d'un curé ligueur* (Paris, [1865]), p. 141.

Catholic, owed much to the dynasty but cannot be considered the blind instrument of its policies. As the song from 1570 suggests, Marcel's influence among the Parisian bourgeoisie and his ability to provide funds for the ever penurious Valois gave him a certain leverage where the crown was concerned. The monarch stood to gain as much from Marcel as Marcel did from the monarch. Thus it hardly seems plausible to attribute Marcel's remarkable career, as some historians have, to his purported role as the prime link between the court and the Hôtel de Ville in the planning and execution of the Saint Bartholomew's Day massacres. The evidence on which to judge Marcel's role in the tragic events of Saint Bartholomew's Day is, unfortunately, both incomplete and inconclusive. City records do not mention Marcel's presence in the Louvre late on the night of August 23, when Charles IX and Catherine de Medici gave orders to the newly elected prévôt des marchands, Jean Le Charron, to call out the militia, close the city gates, and prepare to take action against the seditious rebellion planned by the Huguenots. Other accounts of the episode agree, however, that Marcel was not only present but more active in the receipt of orders and commission of duties than was Le Charron.[50] The Venetian ambassador recounts a conversation between Marcel and the king concerning the number of troops that he could raise for the king's defense and the speed with which he could raise them.[51]

[50] Reg. 7:10-11. De Thou, *Histoire*, 6:395-96, acknowledges that Le Charron was prévôt des marchands, but he adds that Marcel was the one charged with transmitting the orders to the captains of the quartiers because he was known to be a friend of the queen and the court, and it was judged that the public would have confidence in and obey his orders without question.

[51] James C. Davis, ed. and trans., *Pursuit of Power* (New York, 1970), p. 242. Ilja Mieck builds upon this account an argument that Claude Marcel was responsible for raising an unofficial band of auxiliary troops to aid the duc de Guise in the slaughter of the Huguenot nobility in the quartier Saint-Germain. It is his theory that Marcel's auxiliaries and not the city's militia were responsible for touching off the popular massacres, which began as they crossed the bridges of the city. Although careful to point out that the evidence on Marcel's personal role in the affair is not

In his short biography of Marcel, Mouton concludes that Claude Marcel probably remained at the Hôtel de Ville throughout the events that followed, as was the custom for city officers in times of public turmoil—a reasonable if unproven conclusion. At least this conclusion is more credible than the equally unproven assertion of the popular historian Philippe Erlanger that Marcel was a fanatic, eager to lead personally the massacre of the heretic Protestants.[52] Because the sources are incomplete and inconsistent, we are left to wonder what share of the blame Marcel must bear for that awful night and what role this one incident played in his later career. We shall never be certain whether or not the confidence Catherine de Medici had in Marcel's influence over the Parisian bourgeoisie and his devotion to the crown was a decisive element in the rash plan to slaughter the Protestants gathered in the city. Be that as it may, Marcel's active and varied public career should caution us against placing too much emphasis on the massacres as an element in his success.

From this summary of his career, then, it can be seen that the rise of Claude Marcel, which at first glance appeared to be based on mere personal or political favor, can be accounted for quite reasonably in terms of professional skills and experience. Before entering the king's service, Marcel was highly experienced in administrative routines. His duties as an officer of the jewelers' guild, the mint, the Hôtel Dieu, the Hôtel de Ville, and the consular court of the merchants provided him with progressive and valuable training in those matters which are the perennial concern of bureaucratic officialdom. Through these lesser positions, he learned to cope with jurisdictional disputes, fiscal inadequacies, hierarchical authority, and other sorts of red tape. In fact, he followed a familiar, logical path from commerce to royal office. Like

conclusive, Mieck clearly makes him the villain of the piece. ("Die Bartholomäusnacht als Forschungsproblem: Kritische Bestandsaufnahme und Neue Aspekte," *Historische Zeitschrift* 216 [1973]: 73-110.)

[52] Mouton, *Marcel*, p. 134. Philippe Erlanger, *St. Bartholomew's Night*, trans. Patrick O'Brian (New York, 1962), p. 152.

other merchants who sought financial office, Marcel put his business acumen into the service of the king. From his first royal commission appraising the silver plate brought into the Hôtel de Ville, it was but a short step into office as a tax collector. Success in tax collecting led to positions of increasing responsibility in the royal financial bureaucracy. Indeed, the career of Claude Marcel is unique only in its rapidity; he recapitulates in a decade what took others several generations. The advances made in Marcel's career were consolidated by the careers and marriages of his children. His son Claude took up office as a maître des comptes and married into the well-connected Le Picart family. His son Mathieu went into the service of the duc d'Anjou, brother to Henry III, serving first as his secrétaire ordinaire and then as a général des finances. He later became a counselor in the Grand Conseil and, under Henry IV, served as intendant des finances and conseiller d'Etat. Surprisingly, Mathieu died unmarried. The eldest of Marcel's six daughters also appears to have died unwed. The other five, however, all made suitably impressive matches, marrying officers of the royal households and courts. By these alliances, the Marcel family was connected with such important Parisian families as the Hacquevilles and the Longueils. In this aspect, too, Marcel's career is typical rather than unique.[53]

Whether we look at the individual case or at the collective record of the city councillors, it is clear that the dominant elite of sixteenth-century Paris was well placed to take advan-

[53] Catherine Marcel died unwed. Denise married René Dollu, a secrétaire du roi and maître de la Chambre aux Deniers. Marguerite married Louis de Hacqueville, sieur de Vicourt, in 1577. He became a *gentilhomme servant la reine* in 1579. In 1578 Marie Marcel married Jean Le Veau, sieur de la Brochère, a counselor in Parlement. She later remarried with Nicolas de Longueil du Rancher, whose first wife had been the daughter of Pierre Croquet. Germaine Marcel married Raoul Le Féron, sieur d'Orville, in 1582. At the peak of his career, Le Féron was a secrétaire des finances du roi. Marcel's youngest daughter, named Denise like her older sister, was married in 1597 to René Le Meneust. He became a maître des requêtes and a president of the Parlement of Bretagne. (BN, D.b. 424 Marcel; P.o. 1836 Marcel, nos. 43, 56, 166; D.b. 442 Le Meneust, fol. 4; Carrés 253 Le Féron, fols. 135-41. Mouton, *Marcel*, pp. 160-68, 185-88, 210.)

tage of the opportunities for financial and professional advancement offered by the expanding bureaucracy of the kingdom of the later Valois. Moreover, civic service and career promotion tended to be mutually reinforcing. For a merchant or member of the liberal professions, participation in municipal affairs could provide a variety of experience—financial, administrative, and political—that could facilitate not just a step onto the ladder of royal office but perhaps several steps. For the son of a royal officer already destined to follow his father in service to the king, civic service offered experience, visibility, and evidence of maturity. Furthermore, though participation in municipal government went hand in hand with the professional success of the city councillors, it was not simply a stepping stone to be used and left behind. The members of the sixteenth-century Parisian elite continued to play an active role in their city whether they obtained high royal office or remained merchants or members of the liberal professions.

Although the evidence here is sufficient to show that there was upward mobility and that municipal service often played a role in that rise, we cannot at the same time point to any significant change in the pattern of occupational mobility over the period we are studying. The tendency for wealthy Parisian merchants to abandon trade for royal office is evident as early as the fourteenth century, and it is not until the early seventeenth century that the ability of merchants to acquire royal office and of royal officers to acquire still higher offices appears to have been seriously impaired.[54] Similarly, the tendency for royal officers to supplant merchants in city government dates back at least to the first half of the fifteenth century and was checked only in the second and third decades of the seventeenth century, when new men of mercantile and petty officerial status began gradually to replace the descendants of the sixteenth-

[54] Cazelles, *Histoire de Paris*, p. 107; Mousnier, *Vénalité*, pp. 342-43, 360-62.

century city councillors in municipal office.[55] Within the sixteenth century, the ease with which royal office could be acquired doubtless fluctuated with the price and availability of
office and with the general economic condition of the kingdom.
It is clear, however, that through most of the century there
was ample room for mobility for an individual who was well-
placed, respected, and in possession of sufficient means.

[55] Favier, *Paris*, pp. 130 and 242; Carsalade du Pont, *Municipalité*, p.
52; AN, MS 32359, fols. 53-58.

4. Fathers and Sons

Un père deux fois père employa sa substance
Pour enrichir son fils des trésors de science;
Et couronnant ses jours de ce dernier dessein
Joyeux il épuisa ses coffres et son sein,
Son avoir et son sang. . . .
—Agrippa d'Aubigné

THE CHOICE of a career for one's sons, like the choice of a son's marriage partner, was quite naturally accepted as a parental responsibility by the middle and upper classes of sixteenth-century France. In legal documents, personal letters, and diaries, we read of men being "destined" by their fathers for the church, the army, or the courts. Though many fathers did not live to see their sons' destinies fulfilled, they planned with care for the future careers of their young sons. Depending upon a man's background and character, the decisions he made about his sons' careers might be based upon family tradition, personal ambition, or a careful study of the sons' natural aptitudes. What was best for each child had to be weighed against what was best for the family as a whole. The family's finances had also to be considered, particularly if there were a number of children for whom provision had to be made. A study of the decisions parents made about the careers of their children therefore helps us to understand not only relationships between fathers and sons but also the role of the individual within the family and of the family within the society.

One of the most challenging aspects of this enquiry is the difficulty of relating theory to practice. An important body of theoretical literature dealing with all aspects of family life, including the education of children and the selection of their vocations, has been left by the leading intellectuals of the period, the humanists. More than just abstract theorists, the humanists were perceptive observers of Renaissance society. Their writings therefore give us valuable insights into the concerns and actions of their contemporaries. Humanist opinion is particularly pertinent in this study, because the Parisian elite included some of the most important French humanists. At the same time, it is very difficult to determine to what extent the theories of the humanists actually influenced child rearing among the Parisian notability.

There is no doubt that the humanists influenced the curriculum taught in the colleges of Paris. Beginning in the early sixteenth century, a new emphasis was placed on classical literature and rhetoric in the medieval *collèges*, and in 1530, at the instigation of Guillaume Budé and other French humanists, Francis I founded the special school for classical studies that is now the Collège de France. We know, moreover, that the new style of pedagogy advocated by Budé in his letters to his sons found a receptive audience among at least some members of the Parisian elite. The city councillor Jean Courtin, for example, appears to have received a humanistic education much like that prescribed by Budé for his own sons. Indeed, Courtin may even have shared the preceptor of Budé's son Dreux, his friend and contemporary.[1] The publication in 1520 of Budé's *Epistolae*, which included letters to the sons of friends and relatives encouraging them in their studies as well as letters to his own sons, brought Budé's theories on education to a broader public. The issue of new, enlarged editions in the decades that followed indicates that Budé's theories were well received.[2] We cannot conclude from this that the theories of the humanists had an important prac-

[1] Louis Delaruelle, *Répertoire analytique et chronologique de la correspondance de Guillaume Budé* (Paris, 1907), no. 76: letter to Jean Courtin (Amboise, 20/11/20).

[2] *Epistolae Gulielmi Budei regii secretarii* [Paris, 1520]; *Epistolae . . . posteriores* [Paris, 1522]; *Epistolarum Latinarum, Lib. V.* [Paris, 1531]; *Epistolae graecae* [Paris, 1574]. See letters to François and Christophe Le Picart, to Claude and François Robertet, to Pierre Séguier, and others.

tical influence. We can try, however, to determine the extent
of this influence from literary sources, memoirs, and diaries
that reveal how decisions affecting career choices were made
in individual cases. Unfortunately, such sources are rare and
throw light on only a few select cases. The collective experience that can be analyzed from notarial records necessarily
leaves motives unknown. Ultimately, then, it is impossible
to say with confidence whether there was a meshing of theory
and practice or why each followed the path he did. However
incomplete the final picture, it is nevertheless important to
consider the evidence provided by all three types of information available: the theories of the humanists, the personal
testimony of letters and memoirs, and the collective experience of the city councillor families as a group.

Humanist Ideas on Vocation and Family

French humanists, like their Italian predecessors, approached the question of career planning from two distinct
and potentially contradictory angles. They were concerned in
the first place with personal vocation—with the suitability of
the individual for the career he was to undertake—but they
were equally concerned with parental authority—with the right
of the father to determine his son's career. The concern for
personal vocation emerges most clearly in humanist treatises
on education, which commonly stress the need to develop the
child's natural talents and provide him with a well-rounded
education, an education for citizenship as well as scholarship.
The humanists also tied the emotional bond between father
and son to the questions of education and career.

Many of the basic educational theories built on by French
humanists such as Rabelais, Montaigne, and Pasquier were
first set out in the fifteenth century by Pietro Paolo Vergerio,
Leon Battista Alberti, and other Italian humanists. Vergerio,
for example, taught that a child's talents and temperament,
revealed at an early age, should be carefully cultivated and
that a man's career should be in harmony with his "natural

disposition." Vergerio deplored the coercion of sons into un-
suitable careers and praised his own father for allowing him
to become a scholar despite the objections of his kin.[3] The
freedom to choose one's own career was not, however, widely
acceptable in a society with a strong tradition of parental
authority. The potential conflict between individual character
and paternal will implicit in the argument against forced vocations had somehow to be resolved if humanist views on
education were to be favorably received. The Italian humanists effected the necessary reconciliation between the principles of self-determination and the principles of parental authority by attributing to the father the responsibility for
discovering the natural inclinations of his sons and so guiding
their education that these gifts might be developed. For example, in his treatise *Della Famiglia*, Alberti argued that the
well-being of the entire family was dependent upon the development of the special abilities of each of its members. It
was the duty of the head of the household to study and interpret the signs of his sons' talents and to lead them into the
most fitting professions. In Alberti's opinion, a father who
placed his children haphazardly into careers for which they
were not suited endangered his family's reputation and standing.[4]

It was not in a spirit of slavish imitation that French humanists drew upon the pedagogical theories of the Italians.
Rather they borrowed because they felt they faced some of
the same problems, and the solutions devised by the Italians
appeared equally apt for the French situation. Like the Ital-

[3] Richard M. Douglas, "Talent and Vocation in Humanist and Protestant Thought," *Action and Conviction in Early Modern Europe*, ed. Theodore
K. Rabb and Jerrold E. Seigel (Princeton, 1969), pp. 271-72. William
Harrison Woodward, *Vittorino da Feltre and other Humanist Educators* (Cambridge, Mass., 1964), pp. 36, 36n, 182-92, 202, and 202n.

[4] Douglas, "Talent and Vocation," p. 274. Leone Battista Alberti, *The
Family in Renaissance Florence, a Translation of "I Libri della Famiglia,"* ed.
and trans. Renée Neu Watkins (Columbia, S.C., 1969), pp. 56-62 and
86.

ians, the French had to resolve conflicting demands between personal independence and family solidarity.

The best known educational treatise by a French humanist is Michel de Montaigne's essay for Diane de Foix, "Of the Education of Children," first published in 1580. Acknowledging the difficult burden of bringing up children, Montaigne warned that it is easy to mistake the early signs of a child's natural inclinations. His advice was to "guide them always to the best and most profitable things, and to pay little heed to those trivial conjectures and prognostications which we make from the actions of their childhood." Montaigne's essay nevertheless reflects the humanist concern for the development of individual character. It was important, in Montaigne's opinion, that those responsible for the child's education be continually attentive to the capacities and character of their charge; the tutor must listen as well as talk to his pupil. "It is good that he should have his pupil trot before him, to judge the child's pace and how much he must stoop to match his strength." Montaigne suggested cynically that the tutor whose pupil preferred idle stories to wise conversations or the tricks of jugglers to armed combat should "strangle him early, if there are no witnesses, or apprentice him to a pastry cook in some good town, even though he were the son of a duke." He was serious nonetheless in advancing "Plato's precept that children should be placed not according to the faculties of their father, but according to the faculties of their soul."[5]

Like earlier Italian and French humanists, Montaigne believed that training in physical skills and social graces was necessary to the development of the whole being. Thus the program he prescribed for the son of Diane de Foix closely resembled that set out by Rabelais more than half a century earlier, lacking only the Gargantuan measure. Under his humanist tutors, Rabelais's fantastic giant rose at four in the morning for a day filled with intellectual and physical exer-

---

[5] Montaigne, *Essais*, bk. 1, chap. 26 (Frame, pp. 109, 110, and 120).

cises. In addition to a full program of studies, he learned to
sing and to play musical instruments, to swim and to ride
horseback, to use all the weapons of the soldier and all the
tools of the artisan.[6] Similarly, in the curriculum he set out
for the son of Diane de Foix, Montaigne determined that

Even games and exercises will be a good part of his study: running,
wrestling, music, dancing, hunting, handling horses and weapons.
I want his outward behavior and social grace and his physical adapt-
ability to be fashioned at the same time with his soul. It is not a
soul that is being trained, not a body, but a man; these parts must
not be separated.[7]

The same humanist idea, the development of the whole
man, is evident in the educational program Guillaume Budé
outlined for his sons. Budé directed the preceptor of his oldest
sons to allow his charges frequent game sessions and to take
them for walks in the city in order to relax them and to teach
them the ways of men. In his letters to his son Dreux, Budé
repeatedly cautioned that the study of letters alone did not
form a man of the world. He insisted that his son learn good
manners and the ways of polite society along with his Latin
and Greek. Alluding to his own difficulties in accommodat-
ing himself at a late age to the demands of court life, Budé
urged Dreux to acquire from childhood those qualities that
would help him to get ahead in life. Recommending that
Dreux seek the company of cultivated men and the practice
of worldly games, Budé asked, in a word, that he "bow to
the customs of the century." These counsels were given in
spite of Budé's own dislike for court life. They represent a
realistic appraisal of the skills necessary for success in the
service of the Valois kings and an acceptance of the desirability of entering into this service. Budé justified the pressure
he placed on Dreux on the grounds of the superior qualities
of mind and character he recognized in him. While it appears

[6] François Rabelais, *Gargantua*, chaps. 23 and 24; in *Oeuvres complètes*,
ed. Jacques Boulenger and Lucien Scheler ([Paris], 1955).
[7] Montaigne, *Essais*, bk. 1, chap. 26 (Frame, p. 122).

that the youth was driven more by his father's ambitions for him than by his own desires, at least there was some attempt to ensure that the child was suited to the career for which he was destined.[8]

A greater consideration for individual abilities was shown by the Parisian humanist Etienne Pasquier for his five sons. In the famous letter "Sur la profession d'avocat," addressed to his eldest son, Théodore, Pasquier acknowledged that he had "destined" Théodore for the law from the time he started college, "not just because I had received some benediction for this from God, but inasmuch as from your infancy, in making you disclaim, I found you extremely well disposed for it." Pasquier was pleased to have his eldest son follow in his own footsteps, and he liked the thought of a profession passing from father to son; "not, however, that I would wish to make that a perpetually stable rule, except insofar as I should find the children so inclined; for above all one must not do violence to their natural character, otherwise it would be like the ill-bred giants who wished to make war against the heavens."[9]

The careers of his other sons were planned with the same care. When his third son, Pierre, rebelled against the career at court that was intended for him and ran away to Italy, Pasquier calmly recalled the parable of the prodigal son and paved the way for Pierre to become instead a soldier, a profession for which the youth was better suited.[10] Likewise, when his youngest son thought he wanted to be a cleric, Pasquier allowed him to try monastic life until he was convinced, as his father had always been, that he had no religious vocation.[11]

[8] Delaruelle, *Répertoire*, no. 28: letter to Guillaume Du Maine (Lyons, 16/4/19); and no. 81 (Blois, 24/12/20); no. 31 (Montpellier, 9/5/19); no. 98 (3/6/21); no. 75 (Amboise, 20/11/20); and no. 92 (7/2/21): letters to his son Dreux.

[9] Etienne Pasquier, *Lettres*, in *Les Oeuvres*, 2 vols. (Amsterdam, 1723): bk. 9, letter 6. (Also in Dorothy Thickett, ed., *Lettres familières d'Etienne Pasquier* [Paris, 1974], pp. 156-57.)

[10] Ibid., bk. 7, letters 1-3; bk. 10, letter 2; bk. 11, letter 3 (Thickett, *Lettres familières*, pp. 90-95, 178-79, 189-92).

[11] Ibid., bk. 11, letter 5.

Pasquier, moreover, encouraged his friends to allow their children's careers to be determined by their individual abilities. Reassuring a friend who had sent her son off to Paris, Pasquier wrote that he would watch over her son like his own, "while waiting until by the growth of his age and discretion we can know to what employment his natural character will dispose itself."[12]

Pasquier's letters, which display time and again his belief that a child's natural talents should govern his destiny, throw a new light on his often cited opinions on parental authority. Pasquier was, indeed, a firm believer in the authority of parents over their children. He strongly supported Pierre Airault, the *lieutenant criminel* of Angers, when Airault wrote a treatise against the Jesuits, who had allowed his son into their order despite his explicit disapproval. Agreeing with Airault that "the child cannot take religious vows without the express consent of his father and mother," Pasquier argued that the obedience of a son to his father is a godly thing due a father from his children as obedience to God is due from us all.[13] This demand for obedience, however, appears less rigidly authoritarian if we consider the responsibilities Pasquier associated with fatherhood and the unselfish and loving concern that to him was an integral part of being a parent. In his view, a father must always have his child's best interest at heart. When Pasquier thought that his son Nicolas behaved arbitrarily in countering his daughter's romantic inclinations, he reprimanded Nicolas for exercising "not parental authority but absolute seigniory" and advised him that "we must love each of our children principally for his sake and not for our own."[14]

The emotional bond between father and child, evident throughout Pasquier's correspondence, is perhaps best expressed in the letter to Paul de Foix, the French ambassador

[12] Ibid., bk. 14, letter 6 (Thickett, *Lettres familières*, pp. 215-16).
[13] Ibid., bk. 11, letter 9 (Thickett, *Lettres familières*, pp. 195-97).
97).
[14] Ibid., bk. 22, letter 10 (Thickett, *Lettres familières*, pp. 408-409).

to the Pope, in which he asked de Foix to take the runaway Pierre into his service. "I am a father," he wrote, "when I say father to you, you can immediately judge the tyranny which nature exercises over me in favor of my children."[15] The same emotional response to parenthood pervades the letter written to Airault. The letter contains a reasoned defense of parental authority, but it is first and last a letter of sympathy and shared anguish for a father grieving over the disappearance of his son.[16]

That sixteenth-century French fathers felt love and affection for their children deserves to be mentioned, if only to avoid the impression that paternity was an arid institution existing only to perpetuate the family name and glory. Social and literary conventions discouraged the expression of sentiment between father and son, but the emotional bond was not in itself denied.[17] The custom of sending children away to school, of entrusting their education to preceptors or putting them in other households in their youth, was based not upon indifference or dislike of children but upon the fear that parents would be too indulgent with their own offspring. Montaigne, for example, wrote that "it is an opinion accepted by all, that it is not right to bring up a child in the lap of his parents. This natural love makes them too tender and lax, even the wisest of them."[18]

At the same time, Montaigne detested the customs that forced children to maintain a distant and formal relationship with their parents. He complained of the "austere and disdainful gravity" that was maintained toward children who

[15] Ibid., bk. 7, letter 1 (Thickett, *Lettres familières*, p. 90). See also bk. 7, letter 3; bk. 9, letter 2; bk. 10, letter 8; bk. 11, letter 9.

[16] Ibid., bk. 11, letter 9.

[17] Montaigne, *Essais*, bk. 2, chap. 8 (Frame, pp. 284-85, 287).

[18] Montaigne, *Essais*, bk. 1, chap. 26 (Frame, p. 112). See also Vergerius, *De Ingenius Moribus*, cited in Woodward, *Vittorino da Feltre*, p. 101. There is little evidence in the sources concerning sixteenth-century Parisian families, at least among the elite, to uphold the conclusions drawn about the brutal emotional climate of the sixteenth-century family in England by Lawrence Stone (*The Family, Sex, and Marriage in England, 1500-1800* [New York, 1977]), esp. pp. 99-101.

had come of age in the hope of keeping them "in fear and obedience," and he argued against "artificial and unnecessary" attempts to ensure respect, such as forbidding children to use the name of father, "as if nature had not already provided sufficiently for our authority." In an ironic reversal of Machiavelli's phrase, he added that "even if I could make myself feared, I would much rather make myself loved."[19]

The time and energy that a father spent supervising his son's education and career depended in part, of course, upon his own temperament and character. Jacques-Auguste de Thou, for example, complained at one point that his father was too wrapped up in public affairs to take time for his own family.[20] On the other hand, Guillaume Budé, whose single-minded devotion to his studies has given rise to a number of anecdotes, was nevertheless a devoted and attentive father. We have already seen with what care he planned the education of his sons, but it seems that he had affection as well as concern for his family. In 1516, for example, he wrote to Erasmus that "domestic cares occupy me more than philosophy. What leisure, indeed, can a father have who is raising six sons, brothers of one unique sister, and who cherishes them particularly?" In 1519 Budé complained to Juan-Luis Vives that his new duties at court were keeping him from both philology and family life with his wife and children, and in 1522 when he was prévôt des marchands as well as a maître des requêtes of the king, he made a similar complaint to Erasmus.[21]

Regardless of personal temperament, however, a common sense of family pride and continuity encouraged sixteenth-century fathers to do everything possible to promote the careers of their sons. This attitude is typified in a remark made by L'Estoile about Pierre Séguier, second president of the

[19] Montaigne, *Essais*, bk. 2, chap. 8 (Frame, pp. 284-85, 287).
[20] De Thou, *Mémoires*, p. 294.
[21] Desiderius Erasmus, *La Correspondance d'Erasme et de Guillaume Budé*, trans. Marie Madeleine de La Garanderie (Paris, 1967), p. 57 (no. 403); similarly in 1519, p. 185 (no. 915); and in 1522, p. 236 (no. 1328) and p. 239 (no. 1370). Delaruelle, *Répertoire*, no. 43: letter to Juan-Luis Vives (19/8/19).

Parlement of Paris and a member of an old Parisian family. According to L'Estoile, Séguier created an office of *audiencier* in the chancellory for one of his five sons, "although it was notoriously not in the public interest. He excused himself on the grounds of the great affection he had for his children and the need to establish them well."[22]

Pasquier strongly criticized the attitude of men like Séguier. He thought Parisian fathers in particular were guilty of harboring too great ambitions for their sons and of pushing them too early into careers for which they were not sufficiently mature. In his letter "Sur la profession d'avocat," Pasquier deplored his fellow Parisians who, "seeing themselves advanced in some estate, thought of nothing except to promote their children to higher estates." He especially deplored the "custom of the richest families of Paris" of purchasing offices for sons just out of the university. He assured his own son Théodore that he would do everything possible for his promotion, "as a good father," but urged the young man to forget about family connections and conduct his fortune as if it depended upon himself alone, for "there is nothing which ruins the Parisian so often as the opinion he has of being the son of a father of some wealth and means."[23]

While one cannot deny the wisdom of Pasquier's counsel, it is easy to see how the structures of family and society encouraged just the sort of dependence upon parental wealth and connections that Pasquier warned against. The system of venal officeholding largely overlooked personal ability in favor of financial and political interest. Offices of the robe were not entirely closed to a man of more intellect than breeding, but parentage opened more doors than talent. It was not easy for one born and raised within the unique social climate of the capital to stand aloof from the values and opinions of his peers or to resist sharing greedily in the opportunities that wealth, connections, and a corrupt political system made available.

[22] L'Estoile, *Journal pour le règne de Henri III*, pp. 252-53.
[23] Pasquier, *Lettres*, bk. 9, letter 6 (Thickett, *Lettres familières*, pp. 156-62); bk. 7, letter 10.

The patriarchal and authoritarian family structure further encouraged sons to rely more upon the wealth and contacts of their fathers than upon their own talents, for even adult sons were often financially dependent upon their fathers. A man brought up to wealth and standing could not expect to earn enough in the early years of his career to meet his needs without help from his family.[24] Capital was required by those who wished to invest in business or royal office, and capital, property, or at least a generous allowance was required by those who chose to live nobly. A living allowance was also necessary for men who chose to make their way at the bar, in medicine, or in the liberal arts. Even those who entered the army or the clergy at any but the lowest levels required a stipend. Through his control of the purse strings, a father retained inordinate power over his son's career. It was to this power that Montaigne referred when he said that fathers did not need to rely upon "austere and disdainful" gravity to maintain control over their children. In Montaigne's opinion, "it [was] an injustice that an old, broken, half-dead father should enjoy alone, in a corner of his hearth, possessions that would suffice for the advancement and maintenance of many children, and let them meanwhile, for lack of means, lose their best years without making progress in public service and the knowledge of men."[25]

Montaigne's criticism of fathers who sought to maintain control over their children by hoarding their wealth suggests that paternal authority was at times used for selfish purposes and not just for the common good of the family. Indeed, Montaigne went so far as to accuse some fathers of being

---

[24] This is well illustrated by the inventory of possessions belonging to Jean de Montmirail, son of the city councillor Thierry de Montmirail. A counselor in the Châtelet, Jean was probably in his early or mid-twenties when he died in 1565 (n.s.). He still lived in his parents' house, and, according to his servant and lackey, his personal property consisted of only some articles of clothing (most of which were qualified as having been purchased by his mother), three swords, a handful of books, and a trunk. He had, moreover, recently pawned two robes and a ring for a total of twenty-six écus. (AN, Min. cen., III:124 [5/2/64]: *Inventaire des biens*.)

[25] Montaigne, *Essais*, bk. 2, chap. 8 (Frame, p. 280).

tight-fisted toward their sons out of jealousy "at seeing them appear in the world and enjoy it when we are about to leave it."[26] A son might seem a threat to his father, a warning of his own mortality. At the same time, however, he was the promise of the family's future and the sign of its immortality.

Vocation and Family: Three Accounts

We are fortunate to have the memoirs of three members of city councillors' families who left unusually revealing accounts of the personal and familial decisions that shaped their careers. These accounts are of particular interest because the three men are closely related. They are the son, son-in-law, and grandson, respectively, of city councillor Christophe de Thou: Jacques-Auguste de Thou, Philippe Hurault de Cheverny, and Cheverny's second son, also named Philippe Hurault. While we cannot assume that the case histories of these three men are typical of their social class, the nature of their ambitions and the way they are expressed in the memoirs give an insight into the nature of family relationships and the motives for professional achievement—at least within the upper reaches of the Parisian elite.

The professional attainments of Jacques-Auguste de Thou, who was a president of Parlement as well as a celebrated historian, his brother-in-law Philippe Hurault de Cheverny, who served as chancellor of the kingdom from 1583 until his death in 1599, and Cheverny's son Philippe, who became bishop of Chartres, place them at the very top of the social spectrum we are studying here. Though privileged by their high status and, especially in the case of the Huraults, by an unusually close relationship to the monarchy, the three came from a background typical of the city councillors as a group; that is to say, they came from bourgeois families ennobled several generations earlier for service to the king and linked to other

---

[26] Ibid.

noted robe families by multiple ties of kinship. Beneath the personal idiosyncrasies—the dreamy indolence of de Thou, the ravenous ambition of Cheverny, and the prideful self-sacrifice of the younger Hurault—we can detect a common chord of shared values in which the honor of the family and its solidarity sound the dominant notes. While they may have been manifested in many different ways, these values were doubtless shared widely by others of comparable background and achievement.

It is in the choice of a career by the first of this group, Jacques-Auguste de Thou, that we would expect to see the greatest influence of humanist thought, for both his father and he were thoughtful men whose scholarly pursuits were squarely in the humanistic tradition. And indeed, some influence of the humanists can be detected, although not perhaps in the ways or to the extent one would expect. In the career planning of the Huraults, such influence appears to have been almost totally lacking. The passion for family honor and advancement obscures all other motives and sentiments. Reading the memoirs of Cheverny and his son, one has the strong sense of being in the presence of those very ambitious Parisians that Pasquier so deplored.

In one very important respect, we must rule out a humanistic influence in the choice of career for all three of these men. The humanists taught that a man's career should be determined by his aptitude and personal inclinations, yet all three of these men were destined from the very cradle for ecclesiastical careers. They were placed in the church with the intention that they would succeed to important positions and clerical benefices held by collaterals and not because of their own inclinations. Careers were not, however, made simply by a decision at birth. Only the younger Philippe Hurault was to remain true to the destiny planned for him. Cheverny and de Thou were instead led by unforeseen events into secular careers.

Of the three, Cheverny was able to take the most active

role in shaping his own destiny. This is in large measure because his own father, Raoul Hurault, a royal officer and special emissary for Francis I, died only a few months after Cheverny's birth in 1528. He had ordered in his testament that two or three of his five sons and both of his daughters be given religious professions because he feared that his fortune would not provide "honestly" for all of them. It was assumed that Philippe, as the youngest child, would be one of the clerics, and he was put into minor orders as a child. His destiny changed when the untimely death of the two churchmen who were to have served as his benefactors left Cheverny with few benefices and an unpromising future in the church. With the agreement of his mother, he resolved to seek instead "through diligence and hard work, a more advantageous fortune for the estate into which he was born."[27] Apparently, Cheverny believed he could find patrons—or succeed without them—more easily in the world than in the church. If he was concerned about his own unsuitability for religious life, he made no mention of the fact, nor does he appear to have considered the question of a personal religious vocation in planning religious professions for his children.

It is significant that Cheverny's mother concurred in his resolution to leave the church and put what funds she could at his disposal. She had already placed two sons in the church, and her eldest son was childless and likely to remain so. Moreover, according to Cheverny, his mother had a special affection for him because she judged that he "could do better and achieve more than the others for the honor of the house."[28] The primary consideration of Cheverny's mother was thus the good of the family, just as this had once been the motive of his father in ordaining religious professions for his younger sons and was later to be Cheverny's own motive in planning the careers of his sons. Cheverny's concern for his own career—a standing worthy of his birth and an opportunity for

[27] Philippe Hurault, Count of Cheverny, *Mémoires*, ed. Joseph François Michaud and Jean Joseph François Poujoulat (Paris, 1838), p. 465.
[28] Ibid.

advancement—was a more personal ambition but was nevertheless consistent with the emphasis both he and his parents placed on family honor and status.

After completing his studies at the universities of Poitiers and Padua, Cheverny began his career in the suite of his cousin the archbishop of Tours, a counselor to the king. Here he intended to learn about the affairs of state and the conduct of wars and armies. Once again, however, an untimely death deprived Cheverny of his benefactor, and he had to seek a new path to success. He found this in the Parlement of Paris, where, at the age of twenty-four, he purchased the office of *conseiller clerc* from Michel de L'Hôpital.[29] Cheverny recognized that experience in the Parlement had been a stepping-stone to many important careers, and he set out quite deliberately to use it in this way himself. With scarcely concealed satisfaction, he points out in his memoirs that the persecution of suspected Huguenots then taking place upset the careers of many of his fellow parlementaires and permitted him to advance rapidly to the dignity of the *grand'chambre*. There he "tried always, in rendering justice, to gratify everyone and to oblige as many persons of quality as possible."[30]

After nine years in Parlement, Cheverny decided he was ready to go on to bigger and better things, and with the advice of his friends he purchased the office of maître des requêtes in the Hôtel du Roi. His tactics in this office, indeed throughout his career, remained what they had been in Parlement. He tried to please as many people as possible, but he sought in particular to be obliging to those who mattered most. Within a short time, the Cardinal of Lorraine showed favor to the young maître des requêtes, and Catherine de Medici soon became his principal patron, remaining so for most of her life.[31] Thus, though lacking a father to guide his career and losing his intended benefactors at an early age, Cheverny eventually attained the office of chancellor, the highest

[29] Ibid.
[30] Ibid., p. 466.
[31] Ibid.

robe office in the state, through his ability to use the patronage system to advantage.

The way in which Cheverny planned the careers of his children also illustrates the determination and ambition that drove
him. He wanted his eldest son, Henri, to have a career at
court. His second son, Philippe, was intended for the clergy
from the time of his birth. This intention was signified even
in the baptismal services. Choosing an important churchman,
the Cardinal de Birague, as young Philippe's godfather,
Cheverny had the impressive pastoral cross habitually worn
by the cardinal placed around the infant's neck as a sign of
his future vocation. Cheverny also destined an infant daughter
for the church, but he changed his mind when a marquis
asked for her hand in marriage. In planning these church
careers, Cheverny was not trying to dispose cheaply of children who might otherwise drain the family coffers. For each
child he had specific and prestigious ambitions. His daughter
Anne was intended to succeed his wife's sister, the abbess of
the rich abbey of Saint-Antoine-des-Champs outside of Paris.
For his son, Philippe, it was the bishopric of Chartres that
he coveted. The youth's schooling was directed toward this
goal, and to this end, Cheverny played ruthlessly on the claims
of friendship and family and, moreover, spent a good deal of
money.[32]

Before young Philippe was ten years old, Cheverny had
obtained promises from Henry III that on the death of the
incumbent, Nicolas de Thou (the uncle of Cheverny's wife),
the bishopric of Chartres would be reserved for Philippe. By
the time the boy was seventeen, Cheverny had procured four
prestigious abbeys for him. The abbey of Royaumont, for
example, was obtained from a distant cousin, an aged and
broken spendthrift, who succumbed to Cheverny's adroit flattery and resigned the abbey to Philippe in exchange for a
pension of £5,500 a year. Cheverny was quite frank in his
memoirs about both the financial settlements and the personal
leverage used to further his ambitions for his son. He wrote,

[32] Ibid., pp. 478-80.

for example, that he had "so well kept up the spirits and managed the affection" of the bishop of Chartres during an illness in 1596, two years before his death, that de Thou had resigned his bishopric in favor of young Philippe.[33]

Cheverny had not, however, reckoned with the opposition of the rest of the de Thou family to his scheming. They intended Chartres for one of their own line, and the bitter family quarrel that resulted from this rivalry was only settled when Cheverny offered to pay the de Thous a handsome pension for the bishopric. Acknowledging in his memoirs that the pension was excessive, Cheverny justified his actions on the ground of "the desire that I had to put that piece in my house, in order to consolidate the condition and fortune of all of my children and not to be embarrassed by anyone else in that region where all or most of my family's possessions lay."[34]

Family pride and the family fortune were thus the keys to Cheverny's actions. It should be noted, moreover, that the family's honor was not seen to reside in the eldest son and principal heir alone; Cheverny was concerned for the "condition and fortune" of all of his children. His concern for his children did not, however, extend to a concern for their personal wishes or inclinations. The bishopric of Chartres was coveted by the father and not by the son for whom it was intended. Left to his own devices, young Philippe would gladly have traded Chartres for the more adventuresome life of a knight of Malta. But the young bishop had been well schooled by his father. When Cheverny died in 1599, Philippe turned down the handsome offers that were made for his bishopric for "the same considerations that had brought my father to obtain and give me that dignity, for the fortune, the honor, and the good of our house all together obliged me to hold to it and to turn down all offers and dispositions to the contrary."[35]

[33] Ibid., pp. 566 and 549.
[34] Ibid., p. 566.
[35] Philippe Hurault, Abbé de Pontlevoy and Bishop of Chartres, *Mémoires*, ed. Joseph François Michaud and Jean Joseph François Poujoulat (Paris, 1838), p. 588.

Philippe expected to be consoled for the "onerous condition of bishop" by the role he would play in "the preservation and increase of our family." In this he was to be disappointed, for his brothers refused to apply themselves to the same goal. Cheverny had destined his eldest son for the court because he judged that it was vital to maintain the contacts and friendships he himself had cultivated there for so many years. Henri refused to recognize this duty, preferring to remain at Cheverny with his friends, so the young bishop took on this burden too. He would rather have continued his theological studies, but "I judged," he wrote, "that I should sacrifice myself to the general good of our family in embarking at court rather than letting the honor and friends that the deceased chancellor, our father, had left us be lost."[36] Once again it was the "general good of the family" that was invoked. Like his father, the bishop of Chartres believed that the family could only prosper if each member attained a position that offered not only personal dignity but political leverage and a chance to further the careers of other family members.

The career of Jacques-Auguste de Thou provides an interesting contrast to the careers of the ambitious Cheverny and his dutiful son. Though Jacques was obedient to his father and respectful of his family, he was neither as personally ambitious nor as concerned with family honor as his brother-in-law and nephew. His memoirs, more candid in some respects than those of Cheverny and less self-serving than those of the younger Philippe Hurault, show clearly the part that personal inclination played in his ultimate choice of career.

The third son of Christophe de Thou, Jacques was brought up in the household of his uncle Nicolas de Thou, archdeacon of Paris and later bishop of Chartres, with the expectation that he would succeed to the important clerical benefices held by his uncle. He did not begin to question this prospect until his mid-twenties, when his uncles first suggested that he

[36] Ibid.

abandon his clerical profession to marry. Jacques demurred, replying that he left his future "entirely to the will of his father." De Thou's docility may, however, have stemmed as much from indolence as obedience. In his memoirs, he admitted that he was "accustomed to the celibate life" and had no ambition beyond attaining some diplomatic post that would permit him to continue his travels. Though a man of twenty-six, he was more interested in his studies and his travels than in a career—within the church or without it. When his uncles brought up the subject again about a year later, however, Jacques did begin to question his vocation, writing of himself in the third person that "the estate for which one destined him and toward which he did not feel himself drawn seemed to him a heavy burden; the tranquil life toward which his penchant led him appeared sweet."[37]

De Thou was reluctant to assume the weighty responsibilities of high church office. He decided that it would be better to abandon "several apparent grandeurs, filled with an infinitude of troubles, to choose an easier sort of life, to marry, in short, when the occasion presented itself."[38] In making his decision to leave the church, Jacques also considered the question of a personal religious vocation. Several years earlier, a humanist friend of his father's had counseled him to think seriously about the estate he was embracing and to question his motives. He was advised to be certain that he had more care for "the glory of God and the incorruptible wealth of heaven than for that of the earth; for otherwise these great riches called benefices, which were abused by most persons and used only to satisfy their cupidity, would be a poison as mortal to his soul as to his honor."[39] De Thou was struck by the wisdom of this advice, and it figured in his ultimate decision to renounce his religious profession. As a motive for the change, however, the salvation of his immortal soul seems to have had less weight than the comfort of his mortal exist-

[37] De Thou, *Mémoires*, pp. 284-86, 296.
[38] Ibid., pp. 296.
[39] Ibid., p. 285.

ence. De Thou did not, in fact, dispose of the clerical benefices his father had provided for him until after he was irrev-
ocably committed to leaving the church, ten years after he
first began to question his motives for leading a religious
life.[40] In contrast, then, to Cheverny, who abandoned a clerical career because it promised too little distinction and sought
instead a higher fortune in the secular world, Jacques sought
release from a clerical profession that promised wealth and
power in favor of a more peaceable life in secular society.

The principles that most influenced Jacques's plans for his
career seem to have been a dutiful acceptance of paternal authority and a rather conventional belief in family solidarity.
As long as his father was alive, he refused to take any stand
on his own vocation. Once Christophe had died, Jacques was
open to the persuasions of his uncles, his mother, and his
brother-in-law Cheverny. (One cannot help suspecting that
Cheverny already had designs on the bishopric of Chartres
when he urged Jacques, the heir-apparent to the bishopric,
to leave the church.) It was his mother in particular that
Jacques sought to please when he agreed to seek the charge
of maître des requêtes as the first step toward a secular career.
Family sentiment was not, however, strong enough to lead
de Thou into a career he disliked. He agreed to his family's
proposals as long as they matched his own inclinations, but
when his uncle Augustin urged him to accept a *survivance*
(survivor's right) to his position as attorney general in Parlement so the office would stay in the family, Jacques flatly
refused. He was not suited, he told his uncle, to a position
requiring continual speeches and public appearances.[41]

Jacques's immediate family did not just advise him in his
change of professions; they had a formal, legal role in the
matter. In order for him to secure release from the vows he
had taken for minor orders, all of the members of de Thou's
family who might have an "interest" in the change had to

[40] Ibid., p. 318.
[41] Ibid., pp. 314 and 318-20. Augustin's only son had already refused
the position because of "inclinations opposées."

appear before an ecclesiastical court. It is clear from the list of those summoned, which included de Thou's mother, his brother, two brothers-in-law, and the widow of his eldest brother, that the interest involved was financial. As co-heirs to the estates of Christophe de Thou and his wife, Jacques's siblings and their spouses were bound to be affected by his release from the clerical vow of celibacy, and the court wanted to be certain of their consent to the change.

Canon law forbade the church knowingly to accept a religious profession that was not freely given, and coercion was ground for release from one's vows. Therefore, de Thou's mother and his uncle, the bishop of Chartres, had to swear that Jacques had only taken the vows for minor orders out of obedience to the will of his father and that, during the lifetime of his father, Jacques had often expressed repugnance for the clerical estate.[42] There was a certain irony in the case presented to the ecclesiastical court. Though the first part of the statement was true—Jacques had entered the church at the wish of his father—the second was not. Jacques had never protested his father's choice but had instead docilely submitted to his father's will. Because of his family's testimony, however, paternal authority, the principle that had dictated de Thou's obedient acceptance of a clerical career, became the principle upon which it was ended.

In both the Hurault and de Thou families, the right of the father to plan the careers of his sons was accepted without question, as was the principle that the family's prosperity depended upon the mutual cooperation of all of its members. In practice, however, only in the case of the younger Philippe Hurault did adherence to these principles require the sacrifice of personal preferences and happiness. Unforeseen changes in family situations allowed Jacques-Auguste de Thou and Philippe Hurault de Cheverny to pursue the careers they wished

---

[42] Ibid., p. 322. As a secular cleric, Jacques could inherit, but his estate would have been returned to his siblings on his death and any children would, of course, have been illegitimate and thus barred from the succession.

with the full support of their mothers and collateral relatives and without abandoning the principles of paternal authority and family solidarity.

It is nevertheless significant that in both of these cases the rigors of paternal authority were mitigated as a result of events that closed off some paths to success and opened others, rather than as a result of the application of humanistic teaching. The deviations from parental planning were opportunistic, due as they were to the premature death of intended benefactors and the death or childlessness of older brothers, and not to consideration of individual character. The humanist idea of personal vocation appears only fleetingly, as in Jacques-Auguste's rejection of an ecclesiastical career for which he had no calling. Even here it appears in a rather distorted fashion and in the context of the son's decisions, not the father's. While the humanists would have agreed with the principles of paternal and family authority that shaped these careers, they would not have approved the lack of concern for individual aptitude or the excessive ambition which these same principles served to justify.

The Careers of the City Councillors' Sons

With but a few exceptions, such as those discussed above, the question of motivation can be approached only indirectly in analyzing the achievements of the city councillors' sons. We must rely on what the sons did and not what they said or claimed to think. Inevitably, this leaves certain tantalizing puzzles. Consider, for example, the family of Guillaume Budé. If we evaluate the levels of achievement of Budé's seven sons according to the common standards of sixteenth-century French society, the family was downwardly mobile. Compared with Budé's own status as maître des requêtes, his sons had careers of little distinction. The eldest held the office of *avocat des requêtes de l'hôtel du roi*, a respectable but not very prestigious office, which Budé obtained for him before his death in 1540. Budé also obtained his second son's position as *valet de chambre du roi*, a relatively meaningless office that did not necessarily guarantee noble standing or entail actual service in the royal household.[43] A third son was a tax collector in Paris, two sons had religious vocations (one as a parish priest and the other as prior of Vitry-aux-Loges), and two became scholars. On the other hand, by Budé's standards as a humanist, his sons might well be termed successes, each in the field of endeavor to which he was suited. This is especially true of the two sons who were scholars: Louis, who became a professor of Oriental languages in Geneva, and Jean, a classicist and an active member of Geneva's governing circles. They contributed to the glory of letters and took an active part in civic affairs, as Budé himself had done. It would be wrong therefore to press our judgments too far.

Still, there are several important observations that can be made about this example. The most important is the realization that Guillaume Budé was in fact an anomaly among the maîtres des requêtes in that his position came as an unexpected, personal reward for intellectual achievement and not as the carefully planned culmination of an ambitious career helped along by a sizeable fortune and brilliant alliances. When Budé was called to court by Francis I in 1519, he accepted with mixed feelings. He did not want to abandon his studies but feared that in refusing the king's invitation he would wrong both his fellow humanists, who were often accused of being unsuited to the active life, and his family, whose condition might benefit from the honor paid him. He disliked life at court, however, and retired from it before his sons were of an age to profit from his connections there.[44] It would appear, moreover, that his sons did not have the protection and concerted aid of an extensive network of powerful relations. Budé's wife, Roberte Le Lieur, was the daughter of

---

[43] Zeller, *Institutions*, p. 101.

[44] Delaruelle, *Répertoire*, no. 87: letter to N. Leonicus (Romorantin, 11/3/21) and no. 90: letter to his son Dreux (Blois, 23/12/20); no. 165: letter to J. Colin (Paris, 6/12/29).

an ex-merchant living nobly.[45] Neither her family nor his closest kin were sufficiently highly placed to promote Budé's sons' careers after his death. Budé had many friends and distant relatives in high places, but apparently none was close enough to provide the sponsorship that a young man needed to make his way into the closed spheres of patronage and favor that englobed the French court. It is also pertinent that the religious schism of the Reformation had direct consequences for the careers of two sons and may have indirectly affected those of other sons by casting an element of suspicion on their activities. Finally, whatever part personal choice might have had in Budé's sons' careers, it is probable that financial necessity had an important effect on their aspirations and achievements. Indeed, even if Budé's frequent complaints of financial difficulties are exaggerated, he had to provide for ten children, only three of whom chose religious professions, and the portion that each received of his estate cannot have been munificent.[46]

Budé's brilliance as a scholar won him a position above that to which his family and fortune would normally have brought him. Intellectual achievement was not, however, the best asset out of which to fashion prestigious careers for seven sons in sixteenth-century France. As we shall see, the families that were upwardly mobile were those that were able to profit from the very advantages that the Budés lacked. They were the families whose successes were based less on personal achievement than on a network of patronage and family ties, the families that were able to profit or at least not to suffer from the political and religious turmoil, and the families that were either very wealthy or small enough that the patrimony did not have to be split into inadequate portions. What is perhaps surprising is the number of families that were so fortunately placed.

Table 8 displays in summary fashion the highest known

[45] Foisil, "Budé," p. 285.
[46] Delaruelle, *Répertoire*, no. 120: letter to Jean le Picart (21/9/21); Erasmus, *Correspondance*, pp. 68-69 (no. 435) (7/7/16).

professional achievements of the city councillors and their sons. The ninety city councillors are known to have had a total of 180 sons who lived at least to early adulthood. There is enough information on the careers of 156 of these sons to allow them to be classified by level of achievement. Twenty-four sons were not classified because of ambiguities in the available information or because they appear to have died too soon after their careers began for a meaningful classification to be made. The categories used in Table 8 differ in several respects from those used in previous tables analyzing the careers of the city councillors. A line has been added for clerical professions. Although it was permitted for a city councillor to be a cleric, none were clerics during the period we are studying, and therefore this category has not been needed. It has not been important to take into account military officers and courtiers, either, since none of the city councillors held a military com-

TABLE 8
Careers of the City Councillors Compared with the Careers of Their Sons
(Highest Professional Achievement)

Occupation	No. of councillors	% of councillors	No. of known sons	% of known sons	Known Sons with Secular Careers
High office	22	24%	34[a]	22	24
Middle office: courts	20	22	31	20	22
Middle office: administration	13	14	25	16	18
Low office & liberal professions	12	13	17	11	12
Nobles: no office, military and court	5	6	24	15	17
Bourgeois and merchants	18	20	9	6	6
Clerics	—	—	16[a](18)	10	—
Total	90	99%	156	100%	99%

[a] Two of the high officers of the crown were clerics. To avoid double-counting, they have been counted as high officers only but listed in parenthesis as clerics and not re-added to the total. Those clerics who held high church office (for example, bishops) have been classed as clerics.

mission and only one was an officer of the king's household.[47] Among the sons of the city councillors there were, however, some officers of the *bouche* and *chambre du Roi*, the royal guards, and other elite military establishments. Since all of these individuals were also noblemen, and since it would overburden Table 8 to create additional categories for courtiers and soldiers, I have grouped them with the nobles who did not hold robe office. I have also combined the category of "bourgeois" with that of the merchants to simplify the table somewhat.

Table 8 shows certain similarities but also important differences between the careers of the city councillors and those of their sons. If we consider only secular careers, we see that officeholding patterns for robe office among the sons as a group closely resemble those of the city councillors. The proportion of city councillors and sons in each of the categories of "high," "middle," and "low" office are within a few percentage points of one another, differences that have little or no statistical significance for a group this size. On the other hand, the percentage of sons associated with the traditional noble occupations—those serving as military officers or officers of the royal households or living nobly off their estates—is nearly three times that of the city councillors in this category, while the percentage of city councillors who are classified as simple "bourgeois" or merchants is more than three times as great as the percentage of sons in this category.

In order to interpret these statistics and to understand what they indicate about social mobility in the city councillors' families, it is necessary to look beyond aggregate figures in comparing fathers and sons. This is done in Table 9, which is a cross-tabulation of the highest known professional achievements of the city councillors and their sons.

Like Table 7, which compared the careers of the city coun-

----

[47] Zeller, *Institutions*, pp. 100-107, gives the best description of the domestic and military households of the king in the sixteenth century. The subject is too complex to permit discussion here, but it should be pointed out that there were important differences between the households of the sixteenth-century French kings and the more familiar establishments of Louis XIV.

TABLE 9

Careers of the City Councillors Cross-Tabulated with the Careers of Their Sons

	Sons' peak professional achievement									
~ncillor's Peak ~fessional ~ievement	High office	Middle office: courts	Middle office: administration	Low office & liberal professions	Nobles: military & courtly office	Bourgeois & merchants	Clerics	Not classified	Total	Total classified
~h office	23ᵃ	1	1	3	6	0	4ᵃ(6)	5	43	38
~ddle office: courts	5	13	5	2	5	0	6	6	42	36
~ddle office: ~dministration	4	5	12	1	8	0	4	4	38	34
~ office & ~iberal professions	1	8	4	3	1	0	1	5	23	18
~bles without ~ffice	1	0	0	1	3	0	0	1	6	5
~rgeois & ~nerchants	0	4	3	7	1	9	1	3	28	25
~al	34ᵃ	31	25	17	24	9	16ᵃ(18)	24	180	156
~f total	19%	17%	14%	9%	13%	5%	9%	13%	99%	
~f known	22%	20%	16%	11%	15%	6%	10%	–	100%	

Two of the high officers of the crown were clerics. To avoid double-counting, they have been ~nted as high officers only but listed in parenthesis as clerics and not re-added to the total. Those ~ics who held high church office (for example, bishops) have been classified as clerics.

cillors with those of their fathers, Table 9 shows both stability and mobility. On the whole, the sons of the high officers
managed very well to maintain positions as high as those their
fathers had held. Two-thirds of the sons of the high officers
of the crown themselves became high officers in the royal
bureaucracy. Moreover, two of the four clerics held the distinguished position of bishop of Chartres, and two of the six
classified among the "nobles" were *gentilshommes de la chambre
du roi*. Only five sons of high officers appear in categories that

suggest downward mobility, and four of these are sons of Guillaume Budé.

Stability is also the dominant note among the sons of the city councillors who held middle-level office in the sovereign courts and the chancellory. More than a third of the sons in each group followed in their fathers' footsteps. There were, however, opportunities for upward mobility. Five sons of counselors in the sovereign courts and four sons of secrétaires du roi attained high-level offices in the king's bureaucracy. Upward mobility is also apparent in the careers of the sons of low-level officers and members of the liberal professions. Thirteen of the eighteen known sons of low-level officers and members of the liberal professions reached secular positions that were clearly more distinguished than those held by their fathers. Many of the sons of the merchants and bourgeoisie were likewise upwardly mobile. Indeed, the careers of the sons of merchants on the city council illustrate well the "rush into office" so often remarked upon in studies of French society. Four out of the twenty-five members of this group became counselors in the sovereign courts, three became officers of the chancellory, and seven held office in a lower jurisdiction or were lawyers in Parlement.

In all groups, then, except perhaps the group of men whose fathers had already attained high robe office, there was a clear tendency toward upward mobility. There was also a small but significant trend among some families for some sons to leave robe occupations for occupations more frequently associated with the old nobility such as offices in the army or at court. Sons who were not upwardly mobile tended to remain on the same level as their fathers, and only a much smaller group were less successful professionally than their fathers.

The high level of stability among the top group of robe officers was in part due to the growing tendency toward hereditary offices in the sixteenth century. Even before the edict of the Paulette in 1604 made office automatically hereditary upon the payment of a fee, it was generally easy for a president of Parlement or other high official to acquire from the king a *survivance* that guaranteed his son's right to succeed to the office when he died. Thus, for example, André Guillart II, Antoine Guyot, Achilles Harlay, and Bernard Prevost became maîtres des requêtes and presidents of the sovereign courts by virtue of *survivances* their fathers made in their favor. Similarly, Jacques-Auguste de Thou acquired a *survivance* to the presidency held by his uncle Augustin de Thou II.[48]

At least as many of the city councillors' sons, however, attained high office through the informal favors and prestige they enjoyed as members of prominent magisterial families as through the formal tool of the resignation *en survivance*. A *survivance* only allowed a family to hold onto one office, it did not aid in the acquisition of further offices for additional sons, it was of no use if a man died while his sons were still very young, and it could not help a young man who aspired to a different office from that held by his father. In such cases, a man had to depend instead upon the prestige of his name and the pull of his family connections. Of course, a man had also to be willing to pay for his office, but a large purse was not enough to buy the highest offices in the realm. Only a man with the right family background and the right friends in the right places had the privilege of buying high office.

A man who had these important prerequisites, however, was well placed to benefit indirectly from his father's status, even after his father's death. Nicolas Luillier, for example, was not able to succeed to the presidency his father had held for thirty-five years in the Chambre des Comptes when the latter died in 1563 because the position had been suppressed in 1560 by the Edict of Orléans. Nevertheless, when a presidency in the court became available in 1567, it was offered to Nicolas.[49] As the grandson of a maître des comptes, the son of a president of the court, and the brother-in-law of the

[48] Shennan, *Parlement*, pp. 116-18. Guillart: AN, Y97, fol. 44v° (8/7/51); Guyot: AN, Y115, fol. 330 (11/5/74); Harlay: AN, Y114, fol. 252v° (1/7/73); Prevost: *Reg. BV*, 6:215n; de Thou: de Thou, *Mémoires*, p. 322.

[49] *Reg. BV*, 5:309n. The date of Jean Luillier's death is, however, incorrect. It should read 1563.

first president of the court, Nicolas Luillier was a logical candidate for the post. Family ties were likewise responsible for Oudart Hennequin's appointment as a maître des requêtes in 1603. A child when his father, Pierre Hennequin, died in 1577, Oudart was not able to follow him as a president of Parlement, but the family's important connections—including Oudart's marriage in 1597 with a daughter of Nicolas Potier de Blancmesnil—nevertheless assured him of a prestigious position in the robe.[50]

The careers of the middle- and lower-level officers also demonstrate the importance of strong collateral and affinal ties in maintaining or raising the family's social and professional level. As with the sons of high officers, only a minority of the sons of middle- and lower-level officers received their positions directly by their father's resignation *en survivance*. As far as the records show, only three of the counselors in the sovereign courts, five chancellory officers, and one or two lower officers resigned in favor of their sons.[51] The hereditary aspect is increased somewhat if we include the four high officers who resigned middle-level positions they held in the chancellory or Parlement in favor of their sons when they moved into higher office, but it is nevertheless clear that direct transmission of office accounts only partially for the tendency of the sons of city councillors to arrive at professional levels as high as or higher than those of their fathers.

More important than direct transmission, it would seem, were family traditions and conditions in the family environment that encouraged sons to follow the paths their fathers

[50] Oudart's paternal uncle, for example, was Henri de Mesmes, seigneur de Roissy et de Malassis, a counselor of state; and one of his brothers-in-law was Olivier Le Fèvre d'Eaubonne, a president of the Chambre des Comptes. Though a number of members of the Hennequin clan were compromised in the League (as, indeed, Oudart's father might have been, had he lived longer—he is described by L'Estoile as a "tool of the Guises"), other family connections went on to become trusted servants of Henry IV. (BN, D.b. 354 Hennequin, fol. 210; L'Estoile, *Journal pour le règne de Henri III*, pp. 153-54.)

[51] J. de Bragelongne, M. de Bragelongne, Courlay, Courtin, Du Drac, Perdrier, Saint-Germain, Viole, Vivien.

had taken. That the sons of officers in the central administration and judiciary were brought up to aspire to royal office seems clear. Their education and aspirations were directed from childhood toward this end, and in a state with a rapidly growing bureaucracy and a restricted, stagnant educational system, this was no small advantage; a sizeable portion of the family wealth was made available for purchase of office when the proper moment came, and in a state where few people had readily available funds, this was another distinct advantage. Their marriages, too, were arranged to consolidate the family's position in the royal bureaucracy. Arranging a marriage within one's professional circles had the advantage of reinforcing contacts for mutual favors and possible professional advancement. It also provided in-laws who had standing in the same professional circles, who shared many of the same values and priorities, and who could be counted on in the case of one's premature death to guide one's sons along paths leading into the royal bureaucracy.

This last point may seem a minor one, but it is in fact very important. Nearly a third of the seventy-two city councillors known to have had sons died while all of their sons were still under twenty-five, the age of majority according to the customary laws of Paris; and more than two-fifths died while at least some sons were still underage.[52] These early years were crucial in a young man's life, for the evidence suggests that it was in the mid-twenties that the sons of the city councillors most often obtained their first office. A man who had lost his father early did not need to worry about his future, however, if he still had uncles who could help him get ahead. He might even have benefited from his orphanhood by receiving his share of the paternal estate and using it to buy an office for himself.

A final aspect of the careers of the city councillors' sons that needs to be considered is the relationship between the

[52] Twelve had no sons; six are not known; twenty-three died while all of their sons were still minors; and eight while at least some of the sons were still minors.

professional achievements of firstborn and younger sons. There
is a tendency in studies of early modern French society to
view the career of the eldest son as distinctly more important
than the careers of the younger sons, the cadets. Certainly it
seems reasonable to assume that the eldest, favored in inheritance rights in noble families, would be destined for a more
prestigious career than his younger siblings. This assumption
pervades the literature and even the language of the Old Regime—is not "cadet" synonymous with both younger son or
brother and military officer in training?—and is found in recent works of social history as well.[53] A comparison of the
professional achievements of the firstborn sons of the city
councillors with their younger brothers has not, however, borne
out this assumption. In officerial families there was little if
any disparity between the professional achievements of eldest
sons and their younger brothers; in mercantile families the
younger sons may even have had the advantage.

The eldest son had certain initial advantages in robe families. He was usually considered the heir to his father's position or was first in line for any office acquired by his parents,
and as a result, his career advanced somewhat more rapidly
than those of his younger brothers. In the long run, however,
in the families I have studied, the cadets were frequently able
to equal or even outdistance the careers of their older brothers. Of twenty-four families in which two or more brothers
were officers of the robe, there were only four cases in which
the eldest brother had a distinctly higher office than those
held by his younger brothers.[54] In three further cases, the
eldest brother's office was only marginally superior to the offices held by his younger brothers. For example, Christophe
and Augustin de Thou were both presidents of the Parlement
of Paris, but Christophe, the elder, had the additional distinction of being first president. In twelve cases, at least one
younger brother held a rank equal to that of the eldest, and

[53] See, for example, Mousnier, *Hiérarchies*, p. 75, or Huppert, *Bourgeois
Gentilshommes*, p. 43.
[54] G. Budé, Courlay, Marcel, Ge. de Marle.

in five cases, it was the younger brother whose position was higher.[55] The oldest son of Claude Aubery, for example, became a maître des comptes, while one of the younger sons became a maître des requêtes and conseiller d'Etat and the other became a president of the Chambre des Comptes. Similarly, the eldest son of Martin de Bragelongne acceded to his father's position as *lieutenant civil* of the Châtelet, a nonnoble position, while three of the younger sons held ennobling office in the sovereign courts. One even became a president of the Chambre des Enquêtes in Parlement and a conseiller d'Etat. Clearly, then, in these families at least, any advantage in being the firstborn son was outweighed by other factors that made for professional advancement. Friends at court, prestigious alliances, maybe even hard work and good luck counted for more than primogeniture.

The evidence on mercantile families is admittedly slim. There are only six merchant and bourgeois families for which the careers of two or more sons are known. In five of these families, it was a younger son who had the most prominent career, and only in the sixth was it the eldest—and even this is not certain—who went on to become an officer of the king. The oldest son in four of these families followed his father into business, while one or more of the younger sons went on to become officers of the king. In the fifth family, three sons became officers, including the eldest, but he was merely a tax collector while two of his younger brothers were maîtres des comptes. Further examples can be found among the city councillors and their brothers showing the same trend. Nicolas Perrot I, Jean Barthelemy, and Gervais Larcher were all older brothers who remained merchants like their fathers while

[55] I have counted only those families in which two or more sons had functions that fit into the following four categories: 1) high robe office, 2) middle robe office in the courts or chancellory, 3) office in lower jurisdictions, lower office in sovereign courts, liberal professions, 4) merchants and bourgeois rentiers. The clergy and the military services each had its own hierarchy and cannot reasonably be compared with the status of royal officeholders, nor can the status of nobles who exercised no profession be reasonably compared.

their younger siblings went on to become counselors in the sovereign courts. Jean Tronçon, a counselor in Parlement, Nicolas Le Sueur, a greffier in the Cour des Aides, and Jean Palluau, a secrétaire du roi, were all the younger brothers of merchants. I have found no cases among the city councillors where not one of the younger brothers outshone the eldest.

The explanation for the upward mobility of younger rather than older sons in merchant families would appear to lie in the improvement of the family's financial status and the consequent increase in its social ambitions between the time when the first son's education and career had to be planned and the time when the last son was provided for—often a decade or more later—but it would be difficult to prove this theory conclusively. There may have been an element of family pride as well as financial advantage in taking the eldest son into the family business. However, the eldest son, even if he chose a business career, did not necessarily go into business with his father. The oldest son of Claude Le Lievre, for example, married a widow with £20,000 worth of merchandise as her marriage portion; it would seem likely that he took over her first husband's operations, rather than entering his family's business.[56]

The way in which these merchant families deployed their sons to the mutual benefit of all would seem well typified by the example of the Perrot family. The eldest son of a prosperous merchant, Nicolas Perrot I not only took over the family business with his stepmother, Marguerite de Thou, on the death of his father, but he later served as executor of his stepmother's estate, as guardian of his stepsister, and as general manager of the personal as well as the commercial affairs of the family. It was probably no coincidence that he married his stepmother's daughter by her first husband. While Nicolas managed the family fortunes, his younger brother, Miles, studied law and became first a lawyer and then a counselor in Parlement—a promotion no doubt helped by the family's close

[56] BN, P.o. 1718 Lièvre, no. 281.

connections with the de Thou family. In the next generation, Nicolas's own family was able to profit from these robe connections. His son, Nicolas II (who was probably the eldest son—the Perrots are the exception mentioned above), likewise became a counselor in Parlement, and several younger sons also held royal office. Though Nicolas I remained a merchant, his stature increased with the rise of his family and the important connections they acquired. Elected prévôt des marchands in 1556, he was the only prévôt des marchands in the sixteenth century who was not an officer of the king when elected to that office.[57]

There was one career that was most often—though not always—regarded as a role for younger sons.[58] That was the clergy. Among the city councillors' sons, however, there is little evidence to support the common assumption that the church served as a wholesale dumping ground for the superfluous offspring of large families. Only eighteen of the city councillors' sons, a mere 12% of the total, were clerics, and in only three families was there more than one son who went into religious orders. Though it is possible that the number of clerics among the city councillors' offspring is here somewhat understated—the child placed into a convent at an early age was the one most likely to disappear from his family's records—it is doubtful that a complete record would dramatically alter these statistics.[59] The church in general and monasteries in particular were not in high repute in this period of religious turmoil, and from the evidence we have seen of the professional success of the younger sons of the city councillors, it would appear that there were better opportunities for them elsewhere.

Of those sons who did become clerics, a very high proportion acceded to positions of high standing in the church.

[57] BN, P.o. 2242 Perrot à Paris, nos. 2, 4, 6; *Reg. BV*, 4:444-46.

[58] Eldest sons in the clergy included L. Guillart, brother of the city councillor; N. Prevost, son of Jean Prevost I; and N. de La Place, son of the city councillor.

[59] Since only a small percentage of these families included Protestants, it is doubtful that Protestant affiliation is an important factor here.

They were bishops and canons of cathedral chapters, abbots and priors of monasteries. Few of the councillors' sons were simple monks, and only one so far as I have been able to ascertain was in the lower clergy of secular orders. Those who were important churchmen commanded a large measure of respect and, in most cases, received a sizeable income from their clerical benefices. These benefices were considered almost as family properties, and children were put into clerical orders with the express purpose of providing an heir to the offices controlled by their collaterals or affines (as we have seen in the cases of Hurault and de Thou). These clerics, then, not only served the negative function of relieving their fathers of a claim on the patrimony, they effected a positive increase in the wealth and power that a family had at its disposition.

Are these career patterns typical of the Old Regime, or are they particular to the late sixteenth century? I believe that the latter is true, that the careers chosen by the city councillors' sons, the high levels of success they enjoyed in these careers, and the relation between the careers of eldest and younger sons are products of the economic and social nexus peculiar to the late sixteenth century. I would expect this to be especially true of the high officers of the crown, as is illustrated by Table 10. This table compares the careers of the sons of the high officers of the crown among the city councillors in the sixteenth century with the careers of the sons of the conseillers d'Etat in 1658 listed in a recent study of the Conseils du Roi.[60] It shows that both eldest and younger sons of the high officers among the city councillors in the sixteenth century were more often able to maintain the high level of office their fathers had obtained than were the sons of the conseillers d'Etat in 1658. Thirteen older sons and ten younger sons of city councillors held high office in the courts and the

[60] Virtually all of the high officers of the crown on the city council were members of the Conseil d'Etat, or the Conseil Privé, as it was most often called in the mid-sixteenth century, so, while my group does not have a perfect correlation with Mousnier's and is not a cross-section of the Conseil in one particular year, the comparison should nevertheless be a usable and useful one.

TABLE 10

Comparison of the Careers of the Sons of the High Officers among the
City Councillors (1535-1575) with the Sons of the
Conseillers d'Etat in 1658

	Eldest Sons		Younger Sons	
	City Councillors	Conseillers d'Etat	City Councillors	Conseillers d'Etat
High robe office	13[a]	2	10[a]	3
Middle office: courts	—	8	1	5
Middle office: administration	1	—	—	—
Low office & liberal professions	—	—	3	—
Nobles:				
Military	—	2	—	13[b]
Maison du Roi	3	1	1	—
No office	1	5	1	—
Clerics	—(1[a])	—	4(5[a])	10(19[b])
Total	18	18	20	31

SOURCE: For figures on sons of Conseillers d'Etat: Mousnier, *Conseil*, p. 27.

[a] One older son and one younger son were high officers of the crown and also clerics; to avoid double-counting, they have been counted as high officers only but listed in parenthesis as clerics and not re-added to the total.

[b] Nine younger sons were members of the military clerical order of the Knights of Saint-Jean-de-Jérusalem, the Knights of Malta. They have been counted as military men but added in parenthesis to the clerics to show how many were in clerical orders.

central administration; whereas only two older sons and three younger sons of the conseillers d'Etat of 1658 maintained comparable status in the robe.

Another striking difference between the two groups is that a very high proportion of the younger sons of the 1658 group became military officers or clerics, while none of the sons of the high officers on the sixteenth-century city council became soldiers and only six became clerics—two of whom held high robe offices at the same time. The fact that a third of the younger sons of the conseillers d'Etat became clerics (nearly two-thirds if we include the nine sons who were members of the military religious order of the Knights of Malta) and that more than another third became army officers suggests that the traditional stereotype of the noble family, sending its cadets off to early deaths on the battlefield or consigning them to the celibacy of the clerical estate to protect the family fortunes for the eldest, may have a validity for the seventeenth-century robe officers that it does not have for those of the sixteenth century.

Information available on the seventeenth-century descendants of the city councillors—grandsons, for the most part, of the group we are studying—reinforces the suggestion that clerical and military professions played a more prominent part in the family plans of seventeenth-century robe families. To take just one example, Martin de Bragelongne, *lieutenant civil* of the Châtelet of Paris and a city councillor from 1534 to 1569, fathered six sons. All six, born in the second quarter of the sixteenth century, became robe officers, married, and had children. Among them, these six sons had thirty-two sons, most of whom came of age in the early years of the seventeenth century.[61] The careers of twenty-nine of these sons are known: fourteen had office in the judiciary, the chancellory, and the king's household, ten took religious orders, five had military careers (including one knight of Malta), and one was a simple écuyer living nobly. In each branch of the family, the oldest son was a robe officer; the second son in all but one branch was likewise of the robe; none of the eldest sons was a cleric or a soldier. The latter positions uniformly went to the youngest sons. Only seventeen of the sons married, including four who probably married without the support of their families: two who left religious orders to marry and two army officers who married abroad and did not return to France. All of the eldest sons married. This one fecund family comes very close to the stereotype of the robe nobility

---

[61] François Alexandre Aubert de La Chesnaye-Desbois and Badier, *Dictionnaire de la noblesse*, s.v., "Bragelongne." Although La Chesnaye-Desbois is often an unreliable genealogical source, it does appear that the information on the Bragelongne family in the later sixteenth and early seventeenth centuries is reliable.

of Old Regime France. The descendants of other city councillors show similar patterns. While most of the sons of the
city councillors remained in robe office, married, and produced families, their grandsons—and particularly the cadets
of each line—appear to have been more likely to adopt military or clerical careers and more likely to die celibate.

These examples, while far from conclusive, suggest that
more systematic comparison of family structures of the sixteenth and seventeenth centuries would be profitable. There
are several factors that may have caused changes in the career
patterns of young men coming of age in the sixteenth century
and those who came of age in the seventeenth century. Among
these factors are the escalating price of robe office, the renewed enthusiasm for monastic life brought about by the
Catholic Reformation, and more generally, the state-building
practices of the Bourbon monarchs, which may have introduced a greater rigidity into the social structure. The patterns
discussed here suggest a greater dynamism in Renaissance
France. Only a thorough, comparative study of career patterns
and inheritance practices in the sixteenth and seventeenth
centuries can help us determine the extent of change and
understand both causal factors and effects. In the meantime,
however, we should obviously be wary of assuming that the
behavior patterns of French families were consistent over long
periods of time, any more than that they were consistent
throughout the diverse regions and the different social groups
of the state.

PART III

The Marriage Alliance

5. The Institution of Marriage

Tout cecy, combien à l'opposite
des conventions amoureuses!
—Montaigne

FOR THE sixteenth-century Frenchman, as for the believing
Catholic today, the sacrament of marriage joined man and
wife in a mystical, indissoluble union. For the early modern
state and society, however, the personal union of two unique
individuals had distinctly less importance than the social and
economic partnership engendered by the marriage vows. The
elite of sixteenth-century Paris would have agreed with Montaigne when he said, "we do not marry for ourselves, whatever we say; we marry just as much or more for our posterity,
for our family."[1] Like Montaigne, they believed in the arrangement of marriage by a third party and valued "connections and means" above the personal attributes and inclinations of the individuals to be wed.

These attitudes are well known, so well known, in fact, as
to seem commonplace. It is nevertheless worthwhile to examine more closely the role of "this sober contract"—to quote
Montaigne once again—in the context of the sixteenth-century Parisian family. Mutual benefit is at least as complex a
foundation for wedlock as mutual attraction, and we raise
more questions than we answer by simply labeling marriage
an alliance of families. In order to understand fully the institution of marriage, we must consider not only the nature of
the interests at stake but the role of the various members of
the family in determining priorities, identifying potential allies, and negotiating desired matches. Moreover, the role of

[1] Montaigne, *Essais*, bk. 3, chap. 5 (Frame, p. 646).

marriage must be considered from the perspective of the aims and structures of society as a whole as well as those of its constituent families.

In order to get a comprehensive picture of these Parisian marriages, it is necessary to piece together information from a variety of sources, each of which is incomplete in itself. In the first place, there is the important sixteenth-century legal issue, the question of laws designed to ensure parental consent to marriage. As humanists, magistrates, and delegates to the Estates General at Orléans and at Blois, Parisian notables played an important part in the sixteenth-century crusade to increase parental authority over marriage. The opinions they put forth disclose important aspects of their attitudes toward both family and state. Next are the personal qualities that were sought in a bride. What attributes besides "connections and means" were desired in the woman who would share a man's life and bear his children? What was the age for marriage, what were the rituals of courtship and marriage, and what were the roles of matchmakers and witnesses as well as those of the principal parties?

Marriage and Parental Authority

In 1556 Henry II proclaimed the right of parents to disinherit children who married without parental consent. The edict of 1556 accused those who wed secretly and against the wishes of their parents of irreverence and ingratitude, "disdain and condemnation of their fathers and mothers, transgression of the law and commandment of God, and offense against the laws of public honesty."[2] The edict thus intertwined three strands of moral authority: civil law, divine ordinance, and the natural law of respect for parents. It marked the first intervention of the French state in what had previously been considered a purely sacramental concern, subject to the regulation of church authorities. It also marked a major

[2] Isambert, *Lois*, 3:469: "Edit contre les mariages clandestins" (Paris, February 1556; registered March 1, 1556).

step toward a new conception of the role of the family as the foundation and support of the state and hence as a legitimate object of monarchical concern. It is this development, and in particular the contributions made by the Parisian elite, that interests us here. At issue is not only the role of the individual in the family but the role of the family in the state.

The idea that the consent of parents to the marriage of their children should be sought was not in itself new to the sixteenth century. Because of the importance attached to the marital tie and the transfers of property that usually occurred with marriage, it had long been customary for prospective brides and grooms whose parents were still living to seek parental approval of the marriages they contemplated, if indeed the union had not been arranged by the parents in the first place.[3] What was new in the sixteenth century was, rather, the demand for legislation that would force couples to obtain their parents' consent before marrying by threatening them with nullification of the marriage and/or disinheritance if they did not do so. This demand necessarily conflicted with Catholic doctrine, which held that the sacrament of marriage required only the solemn agreement of two individuals before God. The church, which claimed exclusive jurisdiction over marriage because of its sacramental nature, urged but refused to require the consent of parents, the presence of witnesses, or even the affirmation of a priest.[4] One of the major lines of development of the demand that parental consent be required thus lay in the humanist and later the Protestant criticism of Catholic church practices. Consequently the arguments over the issue are inevitably bound up with the larger religious conflicts of the century.

A second line of development lay in Roman law, which was increasingly studied by French jurists in the sixteenth century. In southern France, where the influence of Roman

---

[3] J. M. Turlan, "Recherches sur le mariage dans la pratique coutumière (xiie-xvie s.)," *Revue historique du droit français et étranger*, ser. 4, 35 (1957):478 501.

[4] *Dictionnaire de théologie catholique*, 9:2,235.

law had always been strongest, provisions requiring parental consent to marriage were written into the law of several regions in the early decades of the sixteenth century. In Bordeaux, for example, the customary laws were revised in 1520 to permit a father to deny his daughter all rights to his property if she married without his permission. The bodies of customary law published for Labourd in 1514, for Sôle in 1520, and for Limoges in 1551 all contained requirements for parental consent in which the influence of Roman law is apparent.[5]

In the writings of the humanists, the argument for parental consent to marriage was made first on the simple grounds of respect and reason. Marguerite of Angoulême, for example, warned that marriage "must not be undertaken lightly nor without the opinion of our closest relations."[6] Similarly, Erasmus counseled in his colloquies that a marriage was more likely to be happy if the parents had consented to it.[7] The humanist argument in favor of requiring parental consent attained its full vigor, however, only when it occurred in the broader context of the criticism of what were condemned as abuses in the Catholic church. Thus, for example, in the colloquy "The Virgin Averse to Matrimony," Erasmus took a much stronger position than he had on other occasions, arguing that the dogma that allowed children to take marital or religious vows without the permission of their parents was contrary to the dictates of nature, the law of Moses, and the teachings of Christ.[8] These arguments were repeated and amplified by both religious and juridical reformers. Calvin denounced the laws that recognized the marriage of children without the permission of their parents as unfair to man and God, and the jurist Jean de Coras argued that marriages con-

---

[5] Jules Basdevant, *Des Rapports de l'Eglise et de l'Etat dans la législation du mariage du Concile de Trente au Code Civil* (Paris, 1900), p. 3. Léon Duguit, "Etude historique sur le rapt de séduction," *Nouvelle Revue historique de droit français et étranger*, ser. 3, 10 (1886): 601-603.

[6] Marguerite d'Angoulême, queen of Navarre, *Heptaméron des Nouvelles* (Paris, 1853), 2:337.

[7] Erasmus, *Colloquies*, 1:223.

[8] Ibid., 1:235.

tracted without parental knowledge and consent were not only against the "law of God and of nature, but even of all human nature and law."[9]

Rabelais was still more outspoken. Pantagruel's attack on marriage without parental permission as contrary to "all law, sacred or profane and barbarous" at the end of the *Tiers Livre* repeats the earlier arguments with just a twist of humor. But Gargantua's tirade against the fraternity of "image-bearing molecatchers" carries the anticlerical argument to new extremes.[10] It also introduces an important element of the struggle by revealing just how closely the fear of misalliance was bound up with the demand that parental consent be mandatory. In a scarcely veiled attack on the ultramontane clergy, Gargantua accuses the "dreaded molecatchers" of having so perverted the laws of marriage in a certain unnamed country on the continent that "there is no scoundrel, criminal, rogue, or gallowsbird, no stinking, lousy, leprous ruffian, no brigand, robber or villain in their country, who may not snatch up any maiden he chooses—never mind how lovely, rich, modest or bashful she may be—out of her father's house, out of her mother's arms, and in spite of all her relations." Lamenting with the grieving parents the loss of daughters they had carefully nurtured and intended "in due course to marry to the sons of their neighbors and old friends," Gargantua goes so far as to justify the fathers who "have caught the ruffian together with his molecatcher and have cut them to pieces on the spot."[11]

The comic exaggerations of this tirade serve to point up

[9] Pierre Bels, *Le Mariage des Protestants français jusqu'en 1685* (Paris, 1968), p. 22. Michael A. Screech, *The Rabelaisian Marriage* (London, 1958), p. 49, citing Coras, *Paraphrase sur l'edict des mariages clandestinement contractez par les enfans de famille contre le gré et consentement de leurs pères et mères* (Paris, 1572), dedicatory letter of 1558. Charles Du Moulin, in his *Conseil sur le faict du Concile de Trente* (Lyons, 1564), used similar language, attacking marriage without parental consent as "contre les bonnes et anciennes loix civiles, et honnesteté publique" (fol. 19v°).

[10] Rabelais, *Tiers Livre*, chap. 48. All English language quotations from Rabelais are taken from *The Histories of Gargantua and Pantagruel*, trans. J. M. Cohen (London, 1955) and are cited as (Cohen, p. 418).

[11] Ibid., pp. 419-20.

the issue that lay at the heart of the matter, at least as far as the Parisian elite was concerned. Parental authority over marriage was necessary, it was argued, because otherwise daughters of good families might run off with "penurious and miserable curs" instead of marrying the well-bred and carefully raised children of neighbors and friends. It was not just the child but the entire lineage that was at stake. Gargantua's sympathies are not for the children but for the parents, the sad parents who "had looked forward to the birth of children from these happy marriages, who would inherit and preserve not only the morals of their fathers and mothers but also their goods and lands."[12] In a less exaggerated fashion, these same arguments occur repeatedly in the reasons Parisians gave for laws requiring parental consent to marriage.

According to Jacques-Auguste de Thou, for example, the momentous edict of 1556 against clandestine marriage was provoked by the frequency with which "marriages were contracted by persons of unequal condition, which dishonored and at the same time ruined the most considerable of houses."[13] De Thou used similar language in his account of a decision in which he participated as a special commissioner from the Parlement of Paris to that of Bordeaux in 1582. The case involved a young woman who had eloped with a man "of a condition quite inferior to her own." Caught before the marriage was consummated, the woman was sent back to her mother and the young man threatened with death if he tried to see her again. In de Thou's opinion, this decision was "necessary to reestablish the honor and validity of marriages, as in these times of disorder many clandestine ones are made, and because an example is needed to reprimand the insolence of ravishers who abuse the simplicity of ill-advised daughters of good families and dispose of them with impunity without the consent of their parents."[14]

As this case shows, the edict of 1556 did not end the

---

[12] Ibid.
[13] De Thou, *Histoire*, 3:183 (bk. 19).
[14] De Thou, *Mémoires*, p. 302.

problem of marriage without parental permission. Even had it been scrupulously observed, the law would not have satisfied the upper classes, since it applied only to the civil effects of clandestine marriages, it did not nullify them. The edict allowed parents to disinherit and revoke donations to sons under thirty and daughters under twenty-five who married without permission, and it denied the illicit couple the benefits they might claim by right of marriage. Even above these ages, the advice and counsel of parents had to be formally sought. The threat of disinheritance had been used informally as a sanction against undesirable marriage since medieval times. The edict of 1556, however, made the threat of disinheritance more effective by easing the parents' burden of proof. Previously parents had been required to demonstrate ingratitude and gross misbehavior on the part of the child as well as marriage without permission. Now proof of marriage without permission sufficed. Also the edict denied the child the right to challenge the disinheritance in court.[15]

The right to disinherit a child who married against the parental will apparently extended to the grandparents, too. This right was invoked on at least one occasion in a city councillor's family in the decades following the edict of 1556. In 1571 Hippolyte Viole disinherited her grandson Aignan Luillier, the eldest son of her daughter and the deceased city councillor Cosme Luillier, because he went against her orders and contracted marriage with a woman named Marie Gentian.[16] Unfortunately, the disinheritance document does not say what Marie's status was or why Hippolyte objected to her. There is, however, one particularly interesting aspect to the case. Aignan was clearly over the age of thirty at the time of his marriage. Although we do not know his precise date of birth, baptismal records for his younger siblings show that he

[15] Isambert, *Lois*, 13:469-71: "Edit contre les mariages clandestins" (Paris, February 1556). If a mother had married a second time, her permission was not required. On medieval practices: Turlan, "Pratique coutumière," p. 478.
[16] AN, Min. cen. VI:44 (11/4/71): *Exhérédation.*

was born in 1540 at the latest. This is confirmed by the fact that he was already a lawyer in Parlement in 1560, when his father's will named him co-executor of the estate and co-guardian of his siblings. In theory, then, he was only compelled to ask his grandmother's advice and counsel, which he apparently did since the fact that she forbade the match is explicitly stated. We do not know what the disinheritance cost Aignan. The only known sons of Hippolyte Viole and her husband, Aignan Cailly, vicomte de Carentan, died childless, and no other daughters are known, so it is possible that the loss was great. Whatever the sums involved, the act in itself is important because it demonstrates the force of the belief in the principle of familial authority. A grown man, a man whose father had eleven years earlier deemed him sufficiently responsible to be named a guardian of his brothers and sisters, could be disinherited for disobedience to his grandmother's wishes.[17]

The wealthy classes wanted to do more than disinherit disobedient children, however. They wanted marriages made without parental permission to be nullified. But Henry II refused to take any action that would have entailed intervention in the sacramental side of marriage. Moreover, he hoped that the matter would soon be resolved by the church at the Council of Trent. When the Estates General were called in 1560, both the Second and Third Estates included articles on clandestine marriage in their *cahiers des doléances*. The cahier

[17] Baptismal records for Luillier: BN, MSS fr. 32591 Saint-Paul and 32588 Saint-Jean-en-Grève. AN, Min. cen. III:100 (10/11/60): *Testament* of Cosme Luillier, Sgr. de Saulsay. There is no sign that Aignan challenged his grandmother's action. Hippolyte's testament appears in her same notary's records in 1573 (AN, Min. cen. VI:48 [30/1/73]), but there is no sign there of eventual forgiveness. Since Aignan had received more than ten years earlier his paternal inheritance and, presumably, the properties his mother had had as her dowry and from her father's estate, he should not have been financially dependent upon his grandmother. It is interesting, then, that Hippolyte claimed in disinheriting Aignan that she did not want "to treat him badly" and ordered her heirs to pay him an annual pension of £240 "in the form of foodstuffs." On the Cailly family: Henri de Frondeville, *Les Conseillers du Parlement de Normandie* (Rouen, 1960), p. 295.

of the Third Estate, presided over by the prévôt des marchands Guillaume de Marle as "the head of the capital and first city of the kingdom," asked that it be forbidden for anyone to marry outside his or her own parish and without having previously published banns. It further requested that curés be forbidden to marry individuals from outside the parish unless they were well known to them.[18] The demands went unmet.

The question of clandestine marriage was finally taken up by the Council of Trent in 1563. At the request of the French representatives, legislation that would have nullified marriages made without parental consent was very nearly adopted. When it was suggested that such legislation might be considered a concession to the doctrines of the Protestants, however, the cardinal of Lorraine and a number of his supporters abandoned the plan and it failed. The resolution eventually passed by the council, the *Decret Tametsi*, rebuked children who married without parental approval but pronounced anathema against anyone who declared a marriage null because such approval was lacking. As an attempt at compromise, the council did adopt certain measures similar to those proposed by the Third Estate at Orléans. Clandestine marriages, that is to say, marriages that took place without the proper parish priest, witnesses, or prior publication of the banns, were henceforth made illegal.[19] The decree thus went further than the edict of 1556 by making it more difficult for eloping couples to marry, but it failed to resolve the central issue by not insisting on parental consent.

In any event, since the decrees of the Council of Trent were not accepted in France for another thirty years, these provisions did not have the force of law in the kingdom. Indeed, because of the frequent antagonism between pro-Gallican par

---

[18] BN, MS fr. 4815: "Cayers generaulx des plaintes, doleances, et remonstrances . . ." (1560): "Cahier du 3ᵉ Etat," art. 40 (fol. 210). See also "2ᵉ cahier de la noblesse," art. 13 (fol. 183). On the role of the prévôt des marchands: *Reg. BV*, 5:80.

[19] *Dictionnaire de théologie catholique*, 9:2,235.

lementaires and the Tridentine clergy responsible for the *De-cret Tametsi*, juridical decisions in France relative to the question of marriage without parental consent are confused and often contradictory in the decades following the Council of Trent. In 1576, for example, the Parlement of Paris issued an *arrêt* upholding a marriage that had been nullified as clandestine on the grounds that banns had not been published and the marriage had not taken place before the priest in the couple's own parish church. Parlement judged the marriage valid and reproved the official of Soissons for recognizing the Tridentine decrees. The position of Parlement was, however, rendered ambiguous by the further order that the young couple return to Soissons and present themselves before the official to have their marriage again solemnized and to receive penance.[20] Though they strongly disapproved of clandestine marriage, the Gallican parlementaires were forced to acknowledge the legality of such unions, at least until 1579. At that time, the reforming edict of Blois eased the problem by incorporating measures against clandestine marriage into French law.

Many of the provisions of the edict of Blois that concerned clandestine marriage were drawn almost word for word from the cahier des doléances presented to the king by the Third Estate at the Estates General convened at Blois in November 1576. In accordance with tradition, the prévôt des marchands of Paris was elected to preside over the Third Estate. This important position thus fell to Nicolas Luillier de Saint-Mesmin, and with the Parisian lawyer Pierre Versoris, he is said to have dominated the proceedings.[21] The cahier drawn up at Blois repeated and amplified the articles on marriage from the cahier presented to the king at Orléans, not only asking for laws requiring that marriage take place in the proper parish, preceded by banns, and attended by witnesses, but specifying that priests who failed to make certain of the consent of the parents of minors they married should be liable to punish-

[20] Louet, *Arrests*, 2:117.
[21] L'Estoile, *Journal pour le règne de Henri III*, pp. 142 and 160.

ment as accomplices to the crime of *rapt* (abduction of a minor).[22] Additional articles went still further, asking that anyone who induced a minor to marry against the wishes of his or her parents be punished by death, even if consent was later obtained; that "extraordinary" punishment be prescribed for all accomplices to the crime; and that guardians be forbidden to consent to the marriage of minors without the advice and consent of the nearest relatives.[23] All of these measures were incorporated into the final edict, as were articles reaffirming earlier laws and forbidding notaries to receive any promises of marriage by *paroles de présent*. (Marriage by paroles de présent consisted simply of an exchange of marriage vows in the present tense and was considered a legally binding marriage by the Catholic church. A marriage contract in *paroles de futur* might be nullified by private agreement, though a party unilaterally renouncing such a contract risked legal action, but a marriage contract in paroles de présent could only be annulled by the church.[24])

Although one may suspect that whenever possible children who ran off to marry without their parents' consent were quietly dealt with by their families so as to avoid a public scandal, the harsh penalty of death for those who seduced and eloped with girls of good family was not an idle threat. L'Estoile recounts the case of Claude Tonart, a clerk in the household of a president of the Chambre des Comptes by the name of Bailly, who was sentenced to death by the *lieutenant civil* of the Châtelet in 1582 for having seduced Bailly's daughter and gotten her with child. The Parlement of Paris confirmed the sentence. The interest of the case for L'Estoile lay in the reaction of the Parisian populace, which obviously found the sentence too severe. As Tonart was led to the scaffold, his friends charged the Châtelet officers handling the execution and set Tonart free. Two officials were killed and others

[22] BN, MS fr. 10871: "Cahier des remonstrances présentées au Roi, aux Etats-Généraux de Blois, en 1577, par le Tiers Etat," art. 91.
[23] Ibid., arts. 166 and 167.
[24] Adhémar Esmein, *Le Mariage en droit canonique* (Paris, 1891), 1:139.

wounded in the scuffle. It is interesting to note that L'Estoile agreed with public opinion that the sentence was unwarranted, though he was careful to dissociate himself from the anger and seditious behavior of "an ignorant and flighty populace." L'Estoile, who came from a notable Parisian family, thought that all reasonable men would share his view for two reasons. In the first place, the couple had maintained throughout that they were legally married. Bailly's daughter insisted that she had not been seduced but had married Tonart (by paroles de présent) before bedding down with him. Secondly, "as for the supposed inequality, one could not and should not pay it any mind, for in addition to the fact that the offer his parents made [10,000-12,000 francs to buy him a higher position] made up for it (if it even existed), everyone knew that the mother of the girl was the daughter of a very mediocre merchant and her father the son of a petty functionary at the Châtelet, whom all of Paris had seen begging his livelihood and his bread."[25] In L'Estoile's opinion, had Tonart simply been allowed to marry the girl, he would have more than made up for his sins. What is most interesting about L'Estoile's account is the weight he gives to the question of the "presumed inequality" of the parties. As in the case de Thou described, it is the fact or the possibility of misalliance that is at the heart of the issue.

Though the Edict of Blois attempted to put an end to marriage without parental consent by pressuring priests to require parental approval, forbidding marriages in secret, and reinforcing the pecuniary penalties for marriages without permission, the issue of misalliance was not yet resolved. Secular courts still did not claim the power to nullify the sacrament of marriage, and ecclesiastical courts still firmly maintained that parental consent was not a requirement for valid marriage. However reprehensible, marriage without parental approval was legal. In the opinion of many parlementaires, this was an unfortunate state of affairs. Etienne Pasquier, for ex-

[25] L'Estoile, *Journal pour le règne de Henri III*, pp. 307-308. Further details on the incident are recounted in H. de Curzon, "Les Infortunés Amours d'Artuse Bailly, poésie inédite de 1583," *MSHP* 13 (1886):261-73.

ample, argued that the power to disinherit children for marrying without permission did more harm than good, for instead of separating the child from his undesirable spouse, it drove a wedge between parent and child. Instead of strengthening the family unit, it weakened it.[26]

Effective means to make parental consent a prerequisite for a legal marriage were not developed until well after the period that concerns us. By 1629 the Edict of Blois had been strengthened by the further declaration that marriages that violated it were "not validly contracted."[27] As the careful wording of this law indicates, the kings still purported to regulate only the contractual and not the sacramental aspect of marriage. When a similar law was enacted in 1639, a special stress was laid upon the punishment for abduction (*rapt*). The increasing willingness of the courts to assume that a child who had secretly eloped was the victim of abduction eventually resulted in an effective legal strategy by which the annulment of an undesirable marriage and the punishment of the presumed seducer (the undesirable spouse) could be procured.[28] By the eighteenth century, the charge of *rapt de séduction* was commonly and successfully invoked to break any marriage contracted by a minor of good family without parental consent. The theory was that only one who had been beguiled would commit the enormity of stealing away to marry without the approval of his parents. It was presumed also that the guilty party was the party of lower social standing, for the one of higher standing had nothing to gain by the marriage. A woman, even a minor, could thus be guilty of seducing and abducting a man, if he came from a better family than hers.[29]

[26] Pasquier, *Lettres*, bk. 3, letter 1. See also bk. 14, letter 15; bk. 22, letters 10 and 11.

[27] Isambert, *Lois*, 16:234-35: "Code Michaud," art. 39. See also *Lois*, 15:303: "Edit sur les plaintes . . . du Clergé" (December 1606).

[28] Ibid., 16:520: "Déclaration sur les formalités de mariage" (Saint-Germain-en-Laye, 16/11/1639).

[29] J. Ghestin, "L'Action des Parlements contre les 'mésalliances' aux xviie et xviiie siècles," *Revue historique de droit français et étranger*, ser. 4, 34 (1956):198.

While the theory of *rapt de séduction* evolved only slowly into an effective legal tool, we can see in it the logical product of the concern for the protection of the lineage already apparent in the sixteenth century. The fear of misalliance that generated this theory, clearly evident in the opinions of Pierre de L'Estoile and Jacques-Auguste de Thou, is already present in Gargantua's lament on the sad fate of parents whose carefully nurtured daughters are abducted by ruffians.[30] This fear was grounded in the belief that the tendency toward virtue and superior moral character was inherited. It was not mere snobbery or a wish for financial advantage that dictated the policy of marrying one's children to the offspring of friends but the belief that the children of good families were morally superior to those of obscure origin.

Indeed, as Arlette Jouanna has shown in her study of the idea of *race* in sixteenth- and early seventeenth-century France, this belief that virtue was inheritable was widely shared by the upper classes in the sixteenth century. It was, moreover, an important element in the theories that justified the hierarchical society of the early modern period and one of the key reasons why the monarchy took an interest in marriage law.[31] Jurists, social theorists, educators, and even doctors believed that superior bloodlines coupled with carefully planned education and marriages had brought certain family lines, or *races*, to a higher moral plane than that of common society. Social preeminence was the mark of innate superiority, and nobility was—or should have been—its public acknowledgment. The specific virtues that were thought to produce this superiority varied with the particular social background and aspirations of the theory's proponents. The list of virtues could be modified to serve the aims of the old nobility, the robe, or even the upper bourgeoisie. But whatever the context and content of the argument, it showed both an awareness of the hierarchical nature of the society and a desire to defend—if possible improve—the proponents' position in that society.

---

[30] Rabelais, *Tiers Livre*, chap. 48 (Cohen, p. 419).
[31] Arlette Jouanna, *L'Idée de race en France au xvie siècle et au début du xviie siècle* (Lille, 1976), 1:19, 138-39, 254, and passim.

It was not only in the emphasis on lineage that the six-teenth-century concern with parental control over marriage was a reflection of the larger concerns of political theorists and jurists. For some political theorists, parental authority was an analogy to and complement of monarchical authority. This analogy was a central element in their understanding of the French state. The thesis is perhaps best expressed in the *Commonwealth* by Jean Bodin, first published in 1576. Argu-ing that "the family, which is the source and origin of all republics, is the principal member of it," Bodin likened the authority of parents over their children to the authority of the king over his subjects. The family, like the republic, was governed by commandment and obedience, and strong fami-lies were necessary to a strong republic.[32] Bodin's parallel between paternal and monarchical authority was not new. Im-ages of the king as father of his country and the father as sovereign in his household can be traced back at least to the *Politics* of Aristotle.[33] The importance that Bodin attributes to the family as the foundation of the state is nevertheless significant, as is the emphasis he placed on the extent of both paternal and monarchical authority.

By rationalizing the importance of authoritarian family structure, political theorists such as Bodin were able to justify the monarch's interference in matters of private law that had previously been left to local custom and canon law. In the preamble to the 1639 law on marriage, the relationships be-tween the family and the state, between parental authority and monarchical authority, and between private law and pub-lic order expressed in 1576 by Jean Bodin are clearly evident:

As marriages are the seminary of states, the source and origin of civil society, and the foundation of families, which compose the republics that in principle regulate them, and in which the natural reverence of children toward their parents is the bond of the legit-imate obedience of subjects toward their sovereign, thus have the kings our predecessors judged it worthy of their care to make laws

---

[32] Jean Bodin, *Les Six Livres de la république* (Darmstadt, 1961; facsimile of Paris, 1583 ed.), p. 10.
[33] Aristotle, *Politics*, bk. 3, chap. 14.

regarding their public order, their apparent decency, their honesty, and their dignity.[34]

Seen in its broadest context, the issue of parental control over marriage concerned the state as well as the family. Like the emphasis on lineage and *race*, it was the expression of a society that was attempting to rationalize, justify, and even extend patterns of hierarchy and authority.

The Qualities of a Good Wife

The man who agreed with Montaigne that "we do not marry for ourselves" but "for our posterity" would necessarily choose his bride—or allow her to be chosen—according to rather different specifications from those important to the man who married for his own pleasure. Even if, with Montaigne, he attached more weight to "connections and means" than to "graces and beauty," he would want to be confident that the woman he wed had the necessary personal qualities to make a fitting wife and mother. What qualities would he seek? And what virtues would good parents try to instill into marriageable daughters?

If we look at the virtues attributed to the wives of the Parisian elite in letters, poetry, and epitaphs, it is not surprising that the characteristics that appear most often are passive and domestic virtues, qualities that strengthen the family, rather than beauty, intelligence, vivacity, or other personal characteristics, qualities that might charm the lover.[35] The first and absolute virtue demanded of these women was chastity. Above all else, it was demanded that the honor of a

[34] Isambert, *Lois*, 16:520: "Déclaration sur les formalités de mariage" (Saint-Germain-en-Laye, 16/11/1639).

[35] Ruth Kelso, *Doctrine for the Lady of the Renaissance* (Urbana, Ill., 1960), is the best general study of the Renaissance ideal of womanhood. The reader is referred, in particular, to her valuable bibliography of treatises, guidebooks, and tracts on women's education and women's roles. The sources cited below are only those that directly concern the families of the Paris city councillors.

bride be unstained.[36] The epitaph of Claude Bailly (the wife of the wine merchant and city councillor Louis Abelly), engraved in marble in the church of Saint-Leu, repeatedly describes her as "chaste" and "very virtuous" and calls upon the passer-by to hear of her "high principles" and "honorable name."[37] In Ronsard's epitaph for Marie Brachet (the wife of the city councillor and president of Parlement Jean Prevost), the personification of "Modesty and her sainted companions" weep at Marie's tomb, underscoring the virtue of chastity. Marie is praised, moreover, for having always followed the "honorable virtue that guided her life."[38]

Considering the fear of cuckoldry expressed in the popular literature of the time, it is not surprising that a woman's purity should be of primary concern. A man had, after all, his own reputation and his family's name to consider. The letter that Guillaume Budé wrote to a close friend, Louis Ruzé, *lieutenant civil* of the Châtelet and a city councillor until his death in 1531, whose wife had just run off with another man, is interesting in this regard. First commiserating with his friend over the unfortunate scandal, Budé ends by cele-

[36] One wife of a city councillor has left a reputation for something less than purity, but she may perhaps be considered the exception to prove the rule. Pierre Perdrier's wife Jeanne le Coq is said to have been the lawyer's wife whose dalliance with a "bien grand prince" is the subject of the twenty-fifth tale of Marguerite of Navarre's *Heptaméron*. Jeanne was not yet Perdrier's wife but rather the wife of Jacques Dixhomme ("plus extime que neuf hommes," as one manuscript variation has it); the "grand prince," of course, was Francis I. (Marguerite de Navarre, *L'Heptaméron*, ed. Michel François [Paris, n.d.], p. 472; *Journal d'un bourgeois de Paris sous le règne de François I*, ed. Ludovic Lalanne [Paris, 1854], p. 15.) Some of the verses and opinions L'Estoile cites concerning members of city councillor families mention cuckolded husbands, but there is no proof that these accusations had any basis other than a malicious desire for vilification of high officers of the king. (See, for example, *Journal de Henri III*, p. 109, a verse against Jean Le Charron; p. 533, an accusation against the daughter-in-law of Nicolas de Neufville; and p. 539, a verse against Nicolas Luillier's daughter Anne.)

[37] Maurice Vimont, *Histoire de l'église et de la paroisse Saint-Leu-Saint-Gilles à Paris* (Paris, 1932), pp. 163-64.

[38] Pierre de Ronsard, "Epitaphe de Marie Brachet," in his *Oeuvres complètes*, ed. Gustave Cohen (n.p., 1950), 2:530-31.

brating the happy day when Ruzé's wife departed from his house. Ruzé's friends, says Budé, rejoice for the sake of his honor. No longer will he have to live alongside a woman who was a constant source of worry and upon whom he had continually to keep a close eye. At a small price to his property (apparently she ran away with the family jewelry and silverware, too), he has avoided dishonor.[39]

Budé's letter was written before the scandal hit its peak; it would be interesting to know what he thought of subsequent events. The Bourgeois de Paris informs us that after two months of wandering through the countryside with her lover, his brother, and her maid, Ruzé's wife, Marie de Quatrelivres, returned to the capital, where she was taken into custody and sent to a convent to await trial. Ruzé wanted to see her deprived of her share in the community property of their marriage and accused her not only of debauchery and theft but of having committed incest with his nephew. The original sentence, however, was mild, condemning her only to three years in a convent, during which time the court was to have control of her properties. The two brothers, accused of theft and of violating the laws of marriage, were to be absolved if they agreed to indemnify Ruzé's losses and to pay the costs of the trial. Both sides appealed. The second verdict was more harsh. In December 1522 the Parlement condemned Marie to be beaten and deprived of her rights to community property and dower. She was then to have her head shaved and be placed in a convent for life, supported by the moderate pension her husband was ordered to pay. True to the classic double standard, her maid was also to be beaten, while the brothers were again absolved, though still required to reimburse Ruzé for the sums allegedly stolen.[40]

This fine tale of the wages of sin has an ambiguous ending. A short time later, Francis I gave Marie her freedom—perhaps because he found the sentence excessive, perhaps because of the pleas of her family, perhaps just because he had always

---

[39] Delaruelle, *Répertoire*, no. 107: Letter to Louis Ruzé (Nuits, 1/7/21).
[40] *Journal d'un bourgeois de Paris*, pp. 97-100.

liked women who showed more spirit than character. Whatever the reason, there is a revealing contrast between the severity of the magistrates and the cavalier attitude of the king. The contrast between the punishment meted out to Marie and her maid and the absolution of the two young men is also interesting. The fact that, as sons of a royal officer of Orléans, they came from good family doubtless helped influence the Parlement to treat a woman's crime as a young man's lark.[41]

Although the family honor was important in and of itself as a reason for demanding chastity of women, it was not the only reason for the demand. Beneath the concern for the family honor was the concern for the family property. A woman had to be chaste so that a man could be confident that the sons she bore were truly his. A married woman whose children were secretly fathered by another man not only deceived her husband, she robbed his rightful heirs of their lawful estate.[42] A widow who made a second marriage out of passion, lavishing her wealth on her new love, robbed her children of what was rightfully theirs.[43] A single woman who gave expensive gifts to a lover robbed her kin.

Besides chastity, the desirable attributes of married women most often mentioned in poetry and epitaphs were the benevolent virtues—loving, giving, and serving. The epitaph of Anne de Marle (the sister of the city councillor Guillaume de Marle), for example, attributes to her "a whole heart, gracious and benign" and praises her as a model of "nuptial friendship" and "cordial charity."[44] Claude Bailly's inscription lauds charity and piety alongside chastity and honor.

With a woman's life devoted so entirely to the responsi-

---

[41] Ibid., p. 100.

[42] Eustache Deschamps called this sort of deception "roberie commise par la puterie" (*Miroir de Mariage*, XC, verses 10,823-24). See Keith Thomas, "The Double Standard," *Journal of the History of Ideas* 20 (1959):211, on the relation between female chastity and property rights in English law.

[43] Isambert, *Lois*, 14:36-37.

[44] Emile Raunié and Max Prinet, *Épitaphier du vieux Paris* (Paris, 1890-1914), 1:178: Epitaph of Anne de Marle, wife of Gaillard Spifame (1529). The verse may be Clément Marot.

bilities of husband and children, it is not surprising that the other members of her family should occupy an important place even in her epitaph. The verse for Claude Bailly informs the reader that Claude died at the age of sixty-seven, a wife for fifty-two years and the mother of twenty-one handsome children, three of whom were still living. Similarly, the epitaph Ronsard composed for Marie Brachet tells that she bore eight sons. Indeed, more than half the poem recounts the virtues not of Marie but of her husband and two of her sons. Marie's own virtues are described only in very abstract terms. She is called the "ornament of her sex" and the "light in which all virtues shone first." Even her purity is only alluded to in the personification of modesty and the commendation of her "honorable virtue." Beyond this, we are told only her name and that she came from Orléans. On the other hand, her husband, a president of Parlement, is praised in very specific terms for his pursuit of justice and honor, his service to the king, and his just administration of the laws. Her sons too are lauded for their accomplishments and character.[45]

In view of the share of their lives that most women devoted to childbearing, it is only reasonable that acknowledgment of maternity should figure in their epitaphs. Though an extremely high infant mortality rate kept the average family from being very large, it was not unusual for a woman who lived through the childbearing years to give birth to more than a dozen children. Claude de Marle, the wife of the elder Augustin de Thou, bore her husband twenty-one children, fourteen of whom died young.[46] Marie Goyet, the wife of Jérôme de Bragelongne, gave birth to eighteen children and was lucky enough to raise nine of them.[47] Because women in

---

[45] The epitaph mentions only sons. I have not seen any indication that she also had daughters, but I cannot say for certain whether this was the case or whether her daughters were simply omitted from the epitaph. (*Oeuvres*, ed. Cohen, 2:530-31.)

[46] La Chesnaye-Desbois, *Dictionnaire*, s.v., "Thou."

[47] Bluche, *Magistrats du Parlement*, pp. 107-108; BN, MS fr. 32591 Saint-Paul: baptisms of children of Jérôme de Bragelongne and Marie Goyet.

this social group did not normally nurse their own infants and thus did not benefit from reduced fertility during lactation, the intervals between births for the more fecund members of this group were short.[48] In her first marriage, Renée Nicolay gave birth to ten babies in less than twelve years—a baby every 13.2 months.[49] Claude le Maçon, the second wife of Simon Teste, gave birth to nine children at intervals that averaged only 14.5 months, and Etiennette L'Escuyer gave birth to fifteen children at intervals of 15 months.[50] Somewhat more moderately, Jeanne Tronçon produced nine babies and Antoinette Lamy ten, at 17-month intervals, and Marie de Champagnes gave birth to fourteen children at 19-month intervals.[51] Even if the new babies were immediately put to nurse and there were servants to help with the older children, the burdens of pregnancy and motherhood were heavy for women who had the mixed blessing of fecundity.

From letters, educational treatises, and books of advice to young women, it is clear that the practical virtues expected of them were obedience and efficient household management. Compatibility between spouses was valued, for it was considered important that there be peace in the household. Usually, however, the ideal of compatibility is expressed in unilateral

[48] Léon Mirot, "Deux Livres de raison parisiens du xvi⁰ siècle," extract from *Mélanges en l'Honneur de M. Fr. Martroye* (Paris, 1940), p. 8; Montaigne, *Essais*, bk. 2, chap. 8 (Frame, pp. 290-91); David Hunt, *Parents and Children in History* (New York, 1970), pp. 100-109.

[49] Arthur Michel de Boislisle, *Histoire de la Maison de Nicolay* (Nogent-le-Rotrou, 1873-75), no. 195: Baptisms of children of Renée Nicolay and Dreux Hennequin.

[50] Le Maçon: Françoise Lehoux, "Le Livre de Simon Teste, correcteur à la Chambre des Comptes au xvi⁰ siècle," *Bulletin philologique et historique du Comité des travaux historiques et scientifiques* (1940-41), pp. 160-71. L'Escuyer: BN, D.b. 598 Sanguin, fols. 114-20: "Mémoire de la généalogie de nostre famille Sanguin."

[51] Tronçon and Lamy: BN, MS fr. 32591 Saint-Paul: baptisms for families of Jean Bochart and Thierry de Montmirail. Despite her fertility, Antoinette Lamy did not have any sons who lived to adulthood. Champagnes: BN, MS fr. 4752 Le Picart, pp. 207-209; and D.b. 429 de Marle, fols. 20-20v⁰.

rather than reciprocal terms, as a product of the wife's submissiveness rather than as a result of mutual understanding and compromise.[52]

Even among the elite, the sixteenth-century wife was expected to be an efficient manager of the domestic economy, not a lady of leisure. Running the town house for a wealthy family that employed a number of servants was itself not an inconsiderable administrative task, but many sixteenth-century wives, particularly the wives of robe officers, assumed responsibility for the management of the family's rural estates as well.[53] Pasquier's wife, for example, supervised the harvest and wine-making on their seigneury in Brie, while he devoted himself to his writing.[54]

Whenever possible, urban families owning rural estates preferred to import wine, vegetables, and other products of household consumption into the city from their country properties. If rural properties were extensive, managers were hired to collect rents and dues from the peasants or properties were leased in large blocks to *fermiers*, principal tenants who then subleased to the peasants who actually tilled the soil. Still, an eye had to be kept on the managers and tenants, and the portion of the estates that the family reserved for its own needs had to be closely supervised.

Anne Baillet gives some idea of the extensive responsibilities this supervision could entail in a note to her daughter-in-law Jeanne Luillier. Asking Jeanne to check up on her estates when she went out to the country, Anne specified that Jeanne was to oversee the wine-making at Goussonville, making certain the casks were filled and the presses in order,

[52] Typical is the advice of Michel de L'Hôpital to Renée of France on her marriage: "Votre patrie est désormais auprès de votre époux. Attachez vous à lui plaire." (Cited in E. Dupré La Sale, *Michel de L'Hospital avant son élévation au poste de chancelier de France* [Paris, 1875], pp. 131-32.) See also Jean Vauquelin's "Enseignements pour les filles à marier, traduits de Naumache, poète grec," in *Les Diverses Poésies*, ed. Julien Travers (Caen, 1869), 1:373-74.

[53] Bézard, *Vie rurale*, p. 108.

[54] Pasquier, *Lettres*, bk. 9, letter 11 (Thickett, *Lettres familières*, p. 164).

check on the house and mills at Bourneville and inspect some construction work in progress there. She was also to visit the fermiers of the estates at Silly-la-Poterie and Marolles, to be sure that they were taking good care of her properties and that they would pay what they owed, and to interview a new fermier for Bernonville. She had, moreover, to lease out the presses, make certain the woods were well guarded and the poaching had ceased, draw up an inventory of the movable properties at Bernonville, and compile a list of the poor who deserved charity at Bernonville and Silly. The only request Anne Baillet made of her son was that he be certain that the officers of seigneurial justice on her various estates were rendering justice properly, "according to God and reason."[55]

The ideal sixteenth-century wife used her natural gentleness to glove the firm hand with which she managed the family's affairs. Pasquier paid tribute to Jacqueline de Tulleu, the wife of Christophe de Thou, as a "woman who disposed herself wisely to her husband's wishes, which she knew how to manage so gently that she gained by long obedience this point on him, that he never believed so much in anyone else as in her." Since de Thou was interested only in the law and his books, Jacqueline de Tulleu managed all of the family properties. According to Pasquier, she handled the fermiers of the family's many seigneuries so kindly but so well that none ever quit on her and all became rich along with her.[56]

A woman's education was oriented toward these practical skills of household management; if her family was socially prominent, she might also be trained in singing, instrumental music, and other social graces. In at least a few households, influenced by the humanists, women were encouraged to develop their intellect beyond the level of literacy and computation required for domestic affairs. Madeleine de l'Aubespine, the daughter-in-law of the city councillor Nicolas de Neufville de Villeroy, even achieved a certain reknown for

[55] Boislisle, *Nicolay*, no. 165: note (n.d.) from Anne Baillet to Jeanne Luillier.
[56] Pasquier, *Lettres*, bk. 7, letter 10.

her literary endeavors. Her talent as a poet was commended by Ronsard.[57] The literary tastes of Charlotte de Livres and her daughter Anne Luillier are apparent in the inventory taken after the death of Charlotte's husband, Nicolas Luillier. The inventory lists more than forty books found in Anne's private sitting room and a dozen in that of Charlotte. While Anne favored history and popular romances such as *Amadis of Gaul*, Charlotte's library included Plato's *Symposium*, Aristotle's *Politics*, and St. Augustine's *Meditations*. Both women possessed French translations of the Bible. It is interesting, moreover, that though both Nicolas and the son who still remained at home had numerous law books in their studies, Anne had her own copy of the Paris customary law and Charlotte had two volumes of *Ordonnances* of the city of Paris. Unlike Nicolas's own library or that of his son, the books in the possession of his wife and daughter were almost exclusively in the vernacular.[58]

Michel de L'Hôpital did encourage his wife, who was interested only in music when they married, to take up the study of Greek and Latin, but she abandoned her studies for motherhood when her first child was born. L'Hôpital apparently regretted his wife's giving up her studies. In a letter to Renée of France upon her marriage he advised her to try to charm her husband with her learning.[59] The records do not show whether L'Hôpital likewise encouraged scholarly achievement in his only daughter, but it would seem that the other city councillor most known for his learning, Guillaume Budé, did not take much interest in his daughters' education.

---

[57] It is possible that there was more flattery than truth in Ronsard's praise, for he was often the recipient of the Neufvilles' largess. His epitaph for Madeleine's dead lap dog testifies to his adeptness at this sort of flattery ("Epitaphe de la Barbiche de Madame de Villeroy," in *Oeuvres complètes*, ed. Cohen, 2:541-43). Still, Madeleine was praised by several other poets for both her verse and her translations of Ovid.

[58] AN, Min. cen. LXVIII:56 (18/2/87): *Inventaire après décès* of Nicolas Luillier, Sgr. de Saint-Mesmin et de Boulancourt.

[59] Dupré La Sale, *Michel de L'Hospital*, pp. 131-32.

Citing the splendid example of the learned daughters of Thomas More, Erasmus expressed regret that Budé had not had the same audacity.[60]

Erasmus' letter to Budé is particularly interesting because it argues against the premises upon which most men in the sixteenth century based their opposition to the education of women. In the first place, Erasmus derided the common opinion that letters were useless or even a threat to chastity. In his view women were more likely to lose their virtue through ignorance than through knowledge "of to what dangers such a treasure was exposed." He also derided the common fear that women would be less docile if they had an education. No so, argued Erasmus: nothing is so inflexible as one who is ignorant.[61] Erasmus argued, moreover, that a woman who was educated would do a better job of raising her children, an argument that should have been persuasive in a society that placed so much emphasis on virtue inherited from parents and cultivated in the home. If his argument was not convincing, it was because the fear that educated women would despise the subjection of marriage was still more convincing.

The Age for Marriage

One way to ensure the docility of wives was to marry them while they were still girls and unsure of themselves. Fifteenth-century Italian physicians, for example, recommended brides of "girlish age" as more likely to conform with their husband's wishes.[62] It would appear, however, that the extreme youth of brides in Renaissance France has been exaggerated by historians who have looked only at the marriage

[60] Erasmus, *Correspondance*, p. 232 (no. 1233). On the other hand, McNeil, *Budé*, pp. 7-8, cites a Spanish humanist to the effect that Budé's wife was "learned" and adds that she knew enough Latin to "help her husband in the preparation of his books."

[61] Erasmus, *Correspondance*, p. 231 (no. 1233).

[62] Guido A. Guarino, ed. and trans. *The Albertis of Florence: Leon Battista Alberti's "Della Famiglia"* (Lewisburg, Pa., 1971), p. 123.

records of the high nobility.[63] The data on the councillors' families suggests that in this particular elite women most often married in their late teens or their early twenties. The mean age at marriage for the sixteen wives and daughters of city councillors for whom we know both the precise date of birth or baptism and the date of marriage was twenty years and three months; the median was nineteen years and three months. The youngest was sixteen; the oldest twenty-six. Among other families, however, we find at least one case of an "old maid" marrying for the first time in her thirties, and one case of a very early marriage. This was the daughter of Philippe Hurault de Cheverny and Anne de Thou, who was married in 1585 at the age of eleven. It would appear that the very ambitious Chancellor Cheverny was following patterns of alliance that were perhaps more common among the court nobility into which he married the child. The arrangements for the girl to marry the marquis de Nesle, of the old noble house of Laval, were concluded when she was but nine.[64] In any event, it is doubtful that the couple lived together as man and wife at so early an age. Cheverny does not go into details in the case of his daughter, but he mentions in regard to the marriage of his thirteen-year-old son to a girl of eleven that the marriage was "consummated between them according to their age," and then the bride went home with her family and the groom with his. They did not in fact begin life together until 1596, when Cheverny's son was twenty-one and his daughter-in-law nineteen.[65]

Despite the small number of cases, the figures on the average age at marriage of the daughters of the city councillors accord well enough with the results of comparable enquiries

---

[63] William Leon Wiley, *The Gentleman of Renaissance France* (Cambridge, Mass., 1954), p. 196; Huppert, *Bourgeois Gentilshommes*, p. 43; Georges Snyders, *La Pédagogie en France au xvii* et xviii* siècles* (Paris, 1965), p. 233.

[64] Cheverny, *Mémoires*, pp. 475 and 478. The idea that the high nobility married very young may, however, also be incorrect. See Jean Pierre Labatut, *Les Ducs et pairs de France au xvii* siècle* (Paris, 1972), pp. 36-38. Unfortunately, there are no comparable statistics on their brides.

[65] Cheverny, *Mémoires*, pp. 486 and 548.

for them to be accepted with some measure of confidence. For example, Burr Litchfield found the average age at marriage for thirty-six daughters of the Florentine patriciate wed between 1550 and 1599 to have been 19.0 years, and according to Jonathan Dewald, the average age at marriage for sixteen daughters of Rouennais parlementaires from the late sixteenth century was 19.9.[66] The comparable figure for the twelve known cases of city councillor daughters wed between 1550 and 1599 is 19.5.

These figures are also in line with the age recommended by both humanists and doctors as most fitting and healthful for marriage. Erasmus, for example, described virgins of seventeen to twenty as "in the flower of their age" and "ripe for wedlock" and urged them to marry while still "fresh and fair upon the tree." Etienne Pasquier warned that a girl should be married before her perfect ripeness had passed; he recommended twenty as the proper age. Medical opinion opposed both very early and very late marriage as detrimental to the production of healthy heirs. The physician Jean Liébault, for example, recommended seventeen to twenty-five as the prime age for a woman to conceive healthy, masculine heirs.[67]

The city councillors and their sons were considerably older when they married than were their daughters. The exact dates of birth or baptism and marriage are known for fifteen city councillors and their sons or sons-in-law. The mean age at marriage for this group is twenty-eight years; the median is twenty-seven years and eleven months. If we include another thirteen men for whom the year of birth and marriage but not the precise date is known, the mean rises to twenty-nine years and seven months and the median is likewise twenty-

---

[66] R. Burr Litchfield, "Demographic Characteristics of Florentine Patrician Families: Sixteenth to Nineteenth Centuries," *Journal of Economic History* 29 (1969):199; Dewald, *Provincial Nobility*, p. 278.

[67] Erasmus, *Colloquies*, 1:42, 219, 226. Pasquier, *Lettres*, bk. 22, letter 10 (Thickett, *Lettres familières*, p. 408). Jean Liébault: From *Trois Livres des maladies . . . des femmes*, cited in Gustave Fagniez, *La Femme et la société française dans la première moitié du xviie siècle* (Paris, 1929), p. 61.

nine.[68] The tendency for men to marry late is also shown in letters and other literary sources. Etienne Pasquier, for example, rejected the first offers that were made for the marriage of his eldest son on the ground that Théodore, who was but twenty-two and had just made his debut as a lawyer in Parlement, was simply too young. Writing to his friend Loisel of the proposal, Pasquier declared candidly that Théodore needed to learn to love women before he learned to hate them, and that to marry so young would ruin his chances for the future. Pasquier himself had married at thirty. Several years before his marriage, he composed the *Monophile*, in which he suggested that a man should marry at full maturity, or about thirty-five.[69] Michel de Montaigne married at thirty-three but approved "the suggestion of thirty-five, which they say is Aristotle's." He thought it was best not to marry young so that the age of the father and his needs at that age would not be "confounded" with the needs of his sons. He argued that "when a gentleman is thirty-five, it is not time for him to give place to his son who is twenty," while a man who postponed having children until he was himself mature could then retire when his sons were grown and turn over to them the bulk of his estate.[70]

With the possible exception of Pasquier's concern that a young man have some experience with life before he was saddled with a wife, the considerations concerning the age of marriage were oriented toward the good of the family rather

[68] Similar figures emerged from Labatut's study of the dukes and peers of France in the seventeenth century. For the period 1580-1660, the average age at marriage was 30 years 8 months. Most married between 25 and 35. Labatut concludes that most married after their careers were established but not necessarily after they had reached their peak (*Ducs et pairs*, pp. 36-38). The same was probably true of the city councillors.

[69] Pasquier, *Lettres*, bk. 7, letter B (Thickett, *Lettres familières*, p. 113). Still, Théodore married comparatively young, wedding at the age of 26 (*Lettres*, bk. 10, letter 8). The *Monophile* is excerpted in François Grudé, sieur de La Croix du Maine, *Les Bibliothèques françoises de La Croix du Maine et de Du Verdier, sieur de Vauprivas*, ed. Jean Antoine Rigolay de Juvigny (Paris, 1772-1773), 3:522. In the same work, Pasquier cites Plato's belief that a woman should not marry before she was eighteen or nineteen.

[70] Montaigne, *Essais*, bk. 2, chap. 8 (Frame, pp. 282-83).

than the inclinations of the individual. A woman should marry at an age that would allow her to produce healthy heirs, and a man at an age that would bring him to the union at full maturity and increase the interval between generations.

The result of these considerations was that the husbands in this social group were often ten or even fifteen years older than the women they wed. This age difference had important demographic consequences. Although women were more likely than men to die in the first few years of marriage because of the complications of childbirth,[71] a woman who survived these dangers might well outlive her husband by a good number of years. At least forty-six city councillors left widows, while in only twenty-one cases is it clear that the city councillor outlived his wife (or the last of his wives, if he married more than once). Some of these widows, moreover, outlived their husbands by several decades. The second wife of Jean Morin, for example, survived him by thirty-eight years; the widow of Augustin Le Prevost by thirty-six years. The role of widows in the management and partition of the family properties must therefore be given serious consideration. The important financial responsibilities which were, as we shall see, frequently assumed by widows in city councillor families stand out in sharp contrast to the traditional image of women as both juridically and physiologically unsuited to such tasks. Many widows also had to assume the important responsibility of choosing, or at least approving, the marriage partners of their children.

The age difference common between husband and wife must have had important psychological effects also. The fact that men of thirty were commonly wed to girls not yet twenty may help to explain some of the prevailing antifeminist tendencies. A young man of good family was encouraged to spend

[71] Lawrence Stone, *The Crisis of the Aristocracy* (Oxford, 1965), pp. 589-90, found the chance of women dying in the first fifteen years of marriage almost double that of men. He also found that over one-third of all first marriages lasted less than fifteen years because of the premature death of one of the spouses.

his twenties completing his education and beginning his career. Many men from wealthy families also found a chance to travel, attending several universities in the south of France and Italy, following the court or taking up service in the household of a family patron, or simply wandering from relative to relative and task to task. There was a large peer group of unmarried males, and many of the most popular pastimes for young men, from hunting to scholarship, took place in an atmosphere of hearty masculine companionship. No doubt illicit love and sexual adventure also had their place in these self-centered and even self-indulgent years. When a man of such background took a bride not yet out of her teens—a bride who had, moreover, been brought up under the strict eye of a mother or governess whose main concern had been to protect her from unseemly knowledge or worldly experience—it was perhaps inevitable that he should assign to himself a role of authority in the family that denied even the possibility of partnership.

If the husband and wife were considerate and perceptive, it was possible for a marriage to overcome the initial handicaps of age difference and role stereotypes. We know from a few touching letters and epitaphs that marriage could include devoted love and trust.[72] The relationship which eventually developed in a marriage depended more upon the character of the two individuals who were bound together than upon the expectations with which the union was begun. An able and devoted wife might in time earn her husband's love, if indeed she cared to seek it. A husband and wife might also be drawn together by their shared love for the offspring of the marriage—though conflict over the children could also, of course, have the opposite effect. In the long run, however, the nature of the union was determined less by personal compatibility than by a deeper concern for the continuation and advancement of the lineage.

[72] See, for example, Pasquier's grief on the death of his wife (*Lettres*, bk. 14, letter 6), or the epitaphs of Mathieu Chartier and Jeanne Brinon (Raunié, *Epitaphier*, 1:63).

The Rituals of Betrothal and Marriage

Marriages arranged by third parties naturally involved a very different sort of courtship from those that resulted from the mutual attraction of the individuals to be wed. Unfortunately, however, journals and diaries give us few insights into the courtship and betrothal customs of the sixteenth-century Parisian elite. A few scattered comments indicate that at least occasionally a degree of affection developed between suitors and their prospective brides before a marriage was arranged.[73] Jacques-Auguste de Thou, for example, relates how a marriage was nearly made between his father and Marguerite de Beaune and how, even though the alliance did not take place, "the friendship of two such virtuous persons, founded on so legitimate a subject, always persisted." After Marguerite found favor at court, she did her best to help advance de Thou's career. She also made her "good friend" (as she called him) executor of her estate and left him a prayerbook she had received from Claude of France. This he always kept "among his most precious jewels."[74]

Most accounts, however, leave an impression that a great deal of distance and formality was maintained, not only between the prospective bride and groom but between those who arranged the match. Jacques-Auguste de Thou's description of the arrangements for his own first marriage contrasts sharply with his more sentimental account of his father's old attachment. The original suggestion for Jacques's alliance came from mutual friends whom he describes as *entremetteurs* ("go-betweens"). Principal among them was the personal doctor of both Jacques's widowed mother and his future mother-in-law, the widow of François Barbançon de Cany. He also mentions that the bride's brother-in-law was a close friend and encouraged the match. The doctor's role seems largely to have consisted of speaking so often and so highly of Madame de Cany

[73] André Le Fèvre d'Ormesson, *Journal d'Olivier Lefèvre d'Ormesson*, ed. Pierre Adolphe Chéruel (Paris, 1860), 1:ix.
[74] De Thou, *Mémoires*, p. 318.

and her daughter to Jacques's mother that he created a "great eagerness" for the marriage. The role of the *entremetteurs* stopped short of an actual proposal of marriage and the negotiation of financial accords. "To observe the proprieties," the marriage proposal was made by Jacques's senior brother-in-law, Philippe Hurault, who, accompanied by Jacques and "several persons of distinction," called upon Madame de Cany in her hôtel in the faubourg Saint-Germain and obtained her consent to the match. The formalities of the arrangements take precedence here over the personal relationships; de Thou tells us nothing about the woman who was the object of these negotiations.[75]

It is only logical that the arrangement of a marriage should appear as primarily a business negotiation. The marriage of a son or daughter was not only of major financial concern to a family, it was an important step both socially and politically. For officers of the crown, the political aspect could be crucial. Alliances with those who had the ear of the king or powerful persons at court were particularly valued, of course, but it was also important in these times of factional strife to avoid alliances that might compromise favor already gained. Thus, for example, Jean Morin nearly broke off arrangements for the marriage of his daughter to Michel de L'Hôpital when he discovered that L'Hôpital's father had been implicated in the treason of the connétable de Bourbon, whose personal physician he had been. When the archbishop of Aix had originally proposed L'Hôpital as a potential son-in-law, Morin had been attracted to the idea. He had not met the young man but was impressed by what he had heard of him. Still, when he learned of the connection with the connétable, he backed quickly away. In a letter to Chancellor du Bourg, Morin wrote that he had halted "as soon as I knew that he was the son of the doctor to Bourbon, . . . I would prefer the death of myself and of my daughter rather than encourage here the least suspicion and cause myself to lose all the good will that it pleases the King and you to bear me." Only when du Bourg was

---

[75] Ibid., pp. 323-24.

able to reassure Morin that Michel de L'Hôpital was in no way personally implicated in the treason did he agree to the marriage.[76]

Although we may be certain that some sort of discussion of the young woman's dowry and the suitor's "prospects" began as soon as a courtship looked serious, the formal signing of the marriage accords often occurred only a month or less before the wedding itself.[77] The signing of the marriage contract was an important occasion, and it was common among the Parisian elite for a dozen or more close friends and relations of the bride and groom to be present for the event. The contracting parties usually included only the parents or guardians of the bride and groom, if they were underage, and the couple themselves, although other friends or relatives who made financial contributions to the marriage might also be included. If one or both parents of an underage bride or groom were dead, then, in addition to the guardian or guardians, the contract normally listed the nearest relatives as "advising and consenting" to the match. As we have seen, after 1579, guardians were forbidden to marry off their wards without the advice and consent of the nearest relatives, and even before that time, it was customary to seek such consent. Sometimes individuals are listed as "consenting" even though their consent does not appear to have been legally required. The consent of parents of sons who had reached majority, for example, is often specified. Most often, however, the attending relatives whose consent was not legally required are described as having given "advice and counsel," "advice," or merely having "attended." These distinctions could be important if the contract was later challenged.

The circle of kin representing the interests of the bride in

---

[76] Dupré La Sale, *Michel de L'Hospital*, pp. 68-70, citing BN, Coll. Dupuy 193, 194, fol. 27.

[77] See, for example, Mirot, "Livres de raison," p. 7. Jacques Taranne signed his marriage contract May 9, was affianced May 15, and was married on May 23, 1529. Marie Palluau and Pierre Luillier signed their marriage contract on January 19 and were wed on February 21, 1569 (BN, Carrés 479 Palluau, fol. 180 [19/1/69]: extract of marriage contract; MS fr. 32587 Saint-Eustache [21/2/69]: marriage).

a marriage contract usually outnumbered those gathered on the groom's behalf, probably because the bride was more often in a position of legal and financial dependency. The average bride had five or six relatives, including her parents, who signed the marriage contract on her behalf; the average groom only four.[78] It is no doubt indicative of the age difference between spouses that the fathers of half of the eighty-three brides for whom we have wedding contracts were still living and present for the signing of the contract, while this was true of only one-third of the grooms. The mothers of the brides were also present somewhat more often than were the mothers of grooms.[79]

A particularly important aspect of kinship shown by the marriage contracts of the city councillors' families is the bilateral nature of relationships. Kin related through the paternal and maternal lines signed the marriage contract in approximately equal numbers. This is true of both brides and grooms. Analysis of baptismal records reinforces the conclusion that the families of the city councillors retained a close association with the matrilineal as well as the patrilineal kin, at least where the formal ceremonies of life were concerned.[80]

[78] Based on eighty-three marriage contracts or reliable extracts: brides were supported by an average of 5.5 persons, grooms by 4.0. First-time brides had slightly higher averages than those making second or third marriages. There was no significant change in these figures over the second half of the sixteenth century. There appear to be fewer persons outside the principal parties signing in the first half of the sixteenth century, but contracts for this period are not sufficiently numerous for a reliable average to be calculated.

[79] Fathers of forty-two brides (50.5%) were present; fathers of twenty-seven grooms (32%) were present. Mothers of forty-six brides (53%) were present; mothers of thirty-six grooms (43%) were present.

[80] Evaluation of baptismal records for 156 children born into city councillor families shows that approximately 57% of the children had at least one godparent who can be identified as a paternal grandparent, aunt, uncle, or cousin by blood or marriage, while about 51% had at least one godparent of comparable relation on the maternal side. The family situation among the Parisian elite consequently looks very different from the patriarchal and patrilineal family described by Robert Muchembled on the basis of marriage contracts for Artesian nobles in the late sixteenth century ("Famille, amour et mariage: mentalités et comportements des nobles artésiens à l'époque de Philippe II," *Revue d'histoire moderne et contemporaine* 22 [1975]:252).

After the contract was signed, the engagement was formally celebrated. This usually took place in the presence of the close family and friends of the couple at the parish church where the marriage was to take place, although sometimes with permission from the bishop the ceremony was allowed to take place at home.[81] The formal betrothal frequently preceded the wedding itself by only about a week. Most sources describe the marriage ceremony during this period as having taken place "before the church door," followed by a mass in the church itself.[82] Persons who were well known or of high standing sometimes married after midnight, as did Jacques-Auguste de Thou, "to avoid the crowds."[83] Others may have taken more pleasure in the public aspects of the ceremony. Jacques Taranne, a général des monnaies and distant relative of several city councillors, gives the processions to and from the church pride of place in the account of his wedding in his *livre de raison*. Taranne was conducted from his lodgings on the Ile-de-la-Cité by two of his relations, first to the home of his bride and then to the church of Saint-Merry, where the wedding was to take place. Two other city notables conducted him back to his home. (Presumably his new bride was with him, but she is not mentioned.)[84]

Taranne's account makes no mention of a wedding supper, but Etienne Pasquier provides a glimpse into the festive side of marriage in a letter to his friend René Hennequin de Sermoises on the preparations for the alliance between his eldest son, Théodore, and Geneviève Mangot. Although he grumbled about the expense and the confusion in his household, Pasquier nevertheless betrayed a certain pride and pleasure in the uproar. Particularly interesting is his insistence that it was the young couple who demanded all of the fuss. Though the match was arranged by the parents, the bride and groom were far from passive participants in the events that followed.

---

[81] See, for example, Mirot, "Livres de raison," p. 7.

[82] Philippe Ariès, *Centuries of Childhood* (New York, 1962), p. 398; Esmein, *Mariage en droit canonique*, 1:179.

[83] De Thou, *Mémoires*, p. 324.

[84] Mirot, "Livres de raison," p. 7.

Comparing marriage to childbirth and the father's role in preparing the wedding to the mother's labor pains, Pasquier complained that "I have never seen so much disturbance in the house: silk merchants, jewelers, tailors, bootmakers, shoemakers, caterers, bakers, tapestry makers, cooks, violin players, musicians, and a thousand other idlers." Pasquier added that the difference is that women in childbirth are aided by midwives (*sages-femmes*), while in these events the wise have no say "and it is only the young (I do not dare say the greatest fools) who hold sway. . . . If the fathers and mothers wish to bring some sobriety and temperance into the affair, suddenly the children cry that the festivities are for them, that they have only a day or two to themselves, and that we don't remember what it is like to be young."[85]

Though it appears that in the highest levels of society the wedding feast most often occurred in the home of the bride's family, there was no firm rule on this point. Marriage contracts sometimes specify that the costs of the wedding are to be divided between the two families, or that the bride's family will give the groom a certain sum to help him pay for the nuptial celebration, or even that the groom alone is to pay the costs.[86] Erasmus and other reformers frequently complained of the extravagance of wedding festivities. One clear case of extravagance among the councillors' families has already been mentioned in an earlier chapter. That was the wedding supper for one of the daughters of Claude Marcel held at the Hôtel de Guises in 1577. According to Pierre de L'Estoile, the masked ball that followed the wedding supper, graced by Henry III and thirty princesses and ladies of the court dressed in cloth of silver and gem-encrusted white silk, dissolved into such licentious confusion that the well-bred women and girls were constrained to leave.[87]

[85] Pasquier, *Lettres*, bk. 10, letter 8 (Thickett, *Lettres familières*, pp. 182-83).

[86] AN, Y89, fol. 230v° (10/1/43), for example, specified that the groom, a lawyer in Parlement and counselor in the Eaux and Forêts be given 4000 écus as his wife's dowry. From this sum, he was to outfit his wife according to his tastes and to pay the costs of the wedding dinner and supper.

[87] L'Estoile, *Journal pour le règne de Henri III*, p. 157.

In any case, the marriage of Marguerite Marcel was clearly an anomaly in the social circles frequented by the city councillors. More typical might be the wedding of Nicolas Luillier with Charlotte de Livres in 1552. According to the marriage contract of the couple, Nicolas de Livres, the bride's father, was to pay for the cost of the wedding, an expense estimated at £800. To get some idea of the magnitude of the sum, it might be compared to Charlotte's dowry, which totaled £16,000, a handsome but by no means extraordinary sum for that date.[88] On the other hand, it might also be compared to the wage paid a manual laborer. In 1552, a manual laborer in the building trades earned approximately 4 sous a day. It would have taken him nearly fifteen years to earn £800.[89] Somewhat more moderately, the £500 given Catherine Barthelemy, the niece of four merchants on the city council, for the expenses of her wedding in 1572 to a counselor in the Parlement of Rennes would have taken more than three-and-a-half years for a manual laborer earning the then current wage of 10 sous a day.[90]

The cost of the festivities underscores the ceremonial importance of the contracting of a new alliance. Beneath the joyous trappings of the marriage celebration, the solemnity of the event is never far from view. It is clear, for example, in Pasquier's analogy with childbirth. Whatever the joy of the occasion, sending your children out from your house "to enter into a new life" was, like giving birth, serious business.[91]

[88] AN, Y98, fols. 293-95 (18/6/52).
[89] Micheline Baulant, "Le Salaire des ouvriers du bâtiment à Paris de 1400 à 1726," *Annales* 26 (1971):482.
[90] Ibid. AN, Y112, fol. 312 (19/2/72).
[91] Pasquier, *Lettres*, bk. 10, letter 8.

6. Marriage in the City Councillors' Families

Encore maintenant pour faire un mariage,
On songe seulement aux biens et au lignage.
—Nicole Estienne

AS WE HAVE SEEN, it was the practical value of marriage as an institution designed to protect and promote the family and its patrimony that mattered most. The personal bond between husband and wife and the ability of the union to satisfy the emotional and physiological needs of the marriage partners were clearly secondary. Within this context, marriage appears quite naturally as an alliance between families rather than individuals. It is important therefore to examine in more detail just how these alliances worked among the families of the city councillors. Because, as Roland Mousnier has pointed out, "a man married less a woman than the social status of her father,"[1] we shall first examine the alliances in terms of the comparative professional standing of husbands and their fathers-in-law.

The Marriages of the City Councillors

Analysis of the 105 marriages known to have been made by the ninety city councillors confirms the theory that a man most often married the daughter of a man whose professional and social standings were very close to his own. It is difficult to quantify this information in order to display it in tabular form, although Table 11 attempts to do just this, because a

[1] Roland Mousnier, "Recherches sur les structures sociales parisiennes en 1634, 1635, 1636," *Revue historique*, no. 507 (1973), p. 38.

marriage alliance was arranged with a number of factors in mind—not all of which are perceivable from a distance of four centuries. The occupation of the husband-to-be at the time of the marriage may have been less important than his prospects for future advancement, prospects that were largely but not entirely determined by the professional standing of his father. A lawyer in Parlement who was the son of a president of the court might make a very different marriage from that of a lawyer in Parlement who was the son of a merchant. The alliance might also be affected, of course, by the size of the dowry, the beauty of the bride, and the age and previous marital status of both parties. For the time being, however, it is only the professional nexus that concerns us.

To serve as a basis for analysis, I have set down the marriages of the city councillors in cross-tabular form. Table 11 compares the professions of the city councillors' fathers-in-law at the time of the marriages between their daughters and the city councillors with those of the councillors themselves at the time of the marriage or shortly thereafter (offices purchased with funds provided at the time of the marriage have been included, because they would in all probability have figured into the premarital agreements and were thus inherent in the understanding the contracting parties had of one another).

As can be seen from Table 11, the professional standing of the fathers of 78 of the 105 women married by the city councillors (74%) is known.[2] Of these, thirty-five (44%) belonged to the same professional category as their sons-in-law, the city councillors. And if we bear in mind that there was not much difference between the respect accorded a secrétaire du roi and that accorded a counselor in Parlement, and that nobles who

[2] Of the city councillors whose father-in-law's profession is not known, half are merchants. I would be surprised if more than one or two of these merchants' wives were not the daughters of merchants, but it has not been possible to document this suspicion. In three other cases, the bride's father is not known because the woman was a widow, and in Parisian contracts, a widow is more commonly described by her deceased husband's quality than by that of her father.

TABLE 11

Marriages of the City Councillors

Occupation of city councillor at time of his marriage	Occupation of father-in-law at the time of marriage of his daughter with city councillor							Total
	High office	Middle office: courts	Middle office: administration	Low office & liberal professions	Nobles without office	Bourgeois & merchants	Not known	
High office	1	—	—	—	—	—	1	2
Middle office: courts	4	12	2	3	3	2	2	28
Middle office: administration	1	6	—	4	—	1	4	16
Low office & liberal professions	1	6	1	9	2	1	6	26
Nobles without office	—	1	1	—	1	—	1	4
Bourgeois & merchants	—	—	1	3	—	12	13	29
Total	7	25	5	19	6	16	27	105

exercised no office had a standing that depended on the age of the family's titles, the previous positions held by family members, and the family's connections, it is apparent that few marriages involved any measurable inequality between the parties.

Moreover, if we take into consideration the career expectations of those men who appear to have married into higher social and professional groups, we can often explain away the apparent inequality. René Baillet, for example, was but a counselor in Parlement when he married the daughter of Jean Brinon, a president of the Parlement of Rouen. Baillet's father, however, was a president of the Parlement of Paris, and it was only a matter of time before René was to step into the same position. When Baillet's first wife died shortly after their marriage, he was able to make a second prestigious marriage on the basis of the same expectations, marrying the daughter of the maître des requêtes (and city councillor) André Guillart.

There is, however, another factor which must be considered in evaluating these apparently unequal matches, and that is the element of family standing and reputation that was not directly connected with professional activities. Though it is easiest, particularly for quantitative analysis, to treat a man's social standing as a direct product of his professional achievements, we know that the esteem in which a man or a family was held depended also upon less easily measured factors. Among such factors were the length of time the family was known in the city, the other alliances it had contracted, and the reputation of its members for honesty and probity. Participation in civic affairs, for example, improved a family's standing in the city. While the aspects of social standing unrelated to a man's occupation were not of sufficient weight to preclude a charge of *mésalliance* if a marriage took place between persons of vastly disparate occupational groups, they could, I think, serve to erase any taint of inequality when the professional difference was not great.

For example, the marriage of Claude Aubery, a merchant, with the daughter of a secrétaire du roi (and city councillor), Jean Palluau, cannot be considered an unequal match, despite the disparity in professional standing. Aubery's father had served in the municipal administration alongside Palluau, who had moreover been a merchant himself before purchasing the office of secrétaire du roi in 1549. There are, moreover, indications of previous connections between members of the Aubery and Palluau clans. The Palluaus, in short, came from very much the same social milieu as the Auberys.[3]

A similar case is the 1550 marriage of Philippe Le Lievre, a lawyer in Parlement and the first member of a well-known merchant family to enter the liberal professions, with the

[3] BN, D.b. 36 Aubery, fol. 96v°; AN, P.o. 2187 Palluau, no. 22; BN, MS fr. 32838 Saint-Gervais: baptism of Philippe Aubery (22/5/54).

daughter of Louis Gayant, seigneur de Varastre and a counselor in Parlement.[4] Marie Gayant's dowry of £7,000 was rather small for a parlementaire's daughter in 1550, but it was not so small that it can be assumed that she was married to a man of lesser standing in order to save on expenses. Nor is it likely that Philippe had expectations of soon becoming a parlementaire himself. He does not appear to have possessed either a large fortune or (at least according to his colleague at the Paris bar, Etienne Pasquier) impressive professional talents.[5] It is more probable that the match was founded on an old friendship between the two families. Like the Le Lievres, the Gayants had been cloth merchants in Paris.[6] Philippe's father-in-law, Louis Gayant, was the first member of the family to acquire royal office. Furthermore, the Gayants, like the Le Lievres, were active in city politics. Louis Gayant was prévôt des marchands in 1546, while Philippe's father, Claude Le Lievre, was a city councillor. An alliance between the children of these local notables would thus have seemed both suitable and logical.

The same crucial quality of family background figures in certain marriages in which the city councillor took a bride whose father's standing was somewhat less than his own. Nicolas Le Clerc, for instance, a counselor in Parlement destined to be a president of the court of Requêtes (and the son of a procureur général in the Grand Conseil) married a merchant's daughter. The bride, however, Marguerite Croquet, was the daughter of the city councillor Pierre Croquet and thus a

---

[4] There were Le Lievres in Parlement in the sixteenth century, but they do not appear to have had close family ties with the Le Lievres on the city council.

[5] Antoine Loisel, "Pasquier, ou Dialogue des Avocats du Parlement de Paris," in *Profession d'Avocat*, ed. André Marie Jean Jacques Dupin (Paris, 1832), 1:233. For Le Lievre's fortune, see BN, P.o. 1718 Lièvre, nos. 283, 286-87: marriage contract of Philippe Le Lievre and *partage* of some of his parents' properties; AN, Min. cen. XCI:158 (23/11/1600): *partage* of estate of Philippe Le Lievre and Marie Gayant.

[6] *Reg. BV*, 1:218.

member of an old and important merchant family whose connections went beyond the commercial sphere. The fact that
Le Clerc's mother, Madeleine Barthelemy, was a member of
a family of merchants and officers closely related to the Croquets must also have lessened the distance between the two
parties and made the match seem suitable.[7] The alliances of
Guillaume Budé (while a secrétaire du roi) with the daughter
of a retired merchant and of Jean Luillier de Boulancourt
(while a maître des comptes) with the daughter of a merchant
from Troyes are comparable. Both the Le Lieur family into
which Budé married and the Hennequin family with which
Luillier allied himself could boast of branches in robe office
as well as in commerce, and both had prestigious connections
among the Parisian elite. Both families were wealthy, and
while it is probable that Budé and Luillier profited financially
from their marriages, neither marriage can be considered a
mésalliance contracted solely for economic reasons.[8]

As was pointed out in chapter two, there was a high rate
of endogamy among the municipal notability. Fifty-two percent of the wives taken by the city councillors (55 of 105)
were members of families whose names appear on lists of sixteenth-century prévôts des marchands, échevins, and city
councillors. The rate is significantly higher if we look at just
those marriages that involved some sort of professional inequality.[9] Sixty-nine percent (eleven of sixteen) of the marriages in which the city councillor had a professional standing
clearly lower than his father-in-law and 64% (seven of eleven)

---

[7] BN, P.o. 944 Croquet and 780 Le Clerc à Paris. AN, Y114, fol. 169v°
(*donation* of 13/12/70) helps straighten out the Croquet/Barthelemy family
trees.

[8] Luillier/Hennequin: *Actes de François I*, 6:731 (no. 22716) and 5:537
(no. 17437); BN, D.b. 354 Hennequin, fol. 187v° (3/10/20): extract of
partage of estate of Michel Hennequin—the quality of Michel and his son
Oudart are effaced in this document. Budé/Le Lieur: Foisil, "Budé," p.
285n, citing BN, Cabinet d'Hozier 312.

[9] Middle court and middle chancellory offices are not distinguished for
purposes of this comparison, and nobles who held no office are not included.

of the alliances in which the councillor's standing was higher than that of his father-in-law were made with the daughters of Parisian families that could count at least one member among the prévôts des marchants, échevins, and city councillors of the sixteenth century. These figures on endogamy are extremely important. The fact that the families of the city councillors intermarried frequently *despite* professional disparities indicates a tacit recognition and perpetuation of a civic elite distinct from the social hierarchies created by monarchical office.

Indeed, the common tie of participation in municipal office links more city councillors to their fathers-in-law than does a common occupation. The rate of endogamy among the municipal elite as a whole equals or exceeds that of any of the occupational groups to which the city councillors belonged except for the merchants, three-quarters of whom (twelve of sixteen) married the daughters of other merchants. Although fifteen out of twenty-seven (55%) of the men who were officers of the sovereign courts at the time of their marriage married the daughters of magistrates, only six (22%) married the daughters of officers of the court to which they themselves belonged. Only two out of nine lawyers in Parlement married daughters of their colleagues, and not one of the thirteen men who held office as secrétaire du roi at the time of their marriages wed the daughter of a secrétaire du roi.

The rate of endogamy among the city councillors' children, though not as high as that among the councillors themselves, was nevertheless significant. Forty percent (45 of 113) of the known marriages of city councillors' sons and 35% (55 of 155) of the known marriages of city councillors' daughters allied them with Parisian families active in the affairs of the Hôtel de Ville. Indeed, these figures would be higher if it were not necessary for purposes of consistency to adhere to the limited definition of civic elite that requires that a member of the same paternal family (defined by patronym) have held office as prévôt des marchands, échevin, or city councillor during the sixteenth century. Such old Parisian families as the Lallement and the Longuejoue, both of which were active in fifteenth-century politics, are excluded by this rather rigid definition.[10] One aspect of endogamy that deserves special mention is the tendency of certain families repeatedly to form alliances among themselves. Many of these marriages must have been within the degrees of consanguinity forbidden as incestuous by the church, though the records rarely show whether or not papal dispensations were obtained. According to canon law, the prohibited degrees of consanguinity included all relatives down to the great-great-grandchildren of a common great-great-grandparent.[11] Kin by marriage were supposed to be counted like blood relations, but it appears that the requirement for dispensation may have been less strictly enforced where there was no blood tie. Whether or not dispensations were obtained, certain families did show a strong tendency to intermarry. The Croquets and the Barthelemys, for example, repeatedly intermarried over at least three generations. Two sons and a daughter of Denis Barthelemy married two daughters and a son of Jean Croquet. Denis himself took a Croquet for his second wife, and two of Jean Croquet's grandchildren, daughters of a son who had not already married into the Barthelemy family, married Barthelemys. The Croquets also intermarried repeatedly with the Gobelins, the Perrots, and other families prominent in the Parisian mercantile elite. In fact, three of Jean Croquet's children, the three who did not marry Barthelemys, married into the Gobelin family.[12]

[10] At least twenty-six additional sons and daughters-in-law can be identified as members of old Parisian families according to a manuscript list of the "Origines de toutes les anciennes familles de Paris" in the Institut Catholique de Paris, MS fr. 215.

[11] Flandrin, *Familles*, pp. 29-32, discusses the "tree of consanguinity." The family papers of the Chomedy family, for example, mention that dispensation was received for the marriage of Jérôme Chomedy to his fourth cousin Madeleine Tanneguy. The genealogy shows they had common great-great-grandparents (BN, P.o. 759 Chomedy, nos. 26-27).

[12] BN, P.o. 944 Croquet, 206 Barthelemy, and 2242 Perrot à Paris, passim (all contain inconsistencies and errors); AN, Min. cen. XX:76 (10/3/68): *Inventaire après décès* of Jean Croquet; AN, Y88, fol. 173 (12/8/42);

Alliances between the Croquet and Barthelemy Families
over Three Generations

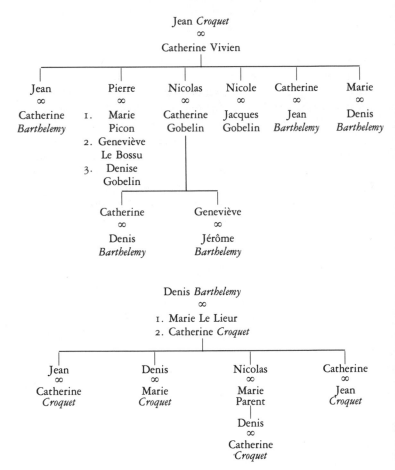

Jean *Croquet*
∞
Catherine Vivien

Jean	Pierre	Nicolas	Nicole	Catherine	Marie
∞	∞	∞	∞	∞	∞
Catherine	1. Marie	Catherine	Jacques	Jean	Denis
Barthelemy	Picon	Gobelin	Gobelin	*Barthelemy*	*Barthelemy*
	2. Geneviève				
	Le Bossu				
	3. Denise				
	Gobelin				

Catherine   Geneviève
∞   ∞
Denis   Jérôme
Barthelemy   *Barthelemy*

Denis *Barthelemy*
∞
1. Marie Le Lieur
2. Catherine *Croquet*

Jean	Denis	Nicolas	Catherine
∞	∞	∞	∞
Catherine	Marie	Marie	Jean
Croquet	*Croquet*	Parent	*Croquet*

Denis
∞
Catherine
·*Croquet*

One of the most interesting cases of recurrent intermarriage is the Luillier/Nicolay/Hennequin connection. In 1552 Jean Luillier de Boulancourt married Renée Nicolay, to whom he was already linked by many kinship ties. Luillier's first wife, Anne Hennequin, had been the sister of Renée's first husband, Dreux Hennequin. Renée had, moreover, served as godmother to one of the daughters of Jean and Anne back in 1538, and Jean had been godfather to one of her sons in 1549. Just four months before she married Jean, one of Renée's brothers had married another of Jean's daughters, and eight years later, in 1560, Renée's youngest brother, married the youngest of Jean Luillier's daughters by his first wife. [13]

Patterns of repeated alliance can also be traced among the Longueil and Montmirail clans and several other sets of city families of both mercantile and officerial standing. Few families, however, appear to have carried the practice of intermarriage to the extent shown by the Croquet/Barthelemys or the Nicolay/Luilliers. It is not clear whether there was a financial advantage to this sort of alliance. Anthropologists have found that in primitive societies certain sorts of cross-cousin marriage were useful for the purpose of retaining properties that would otherwise have passed out of the family with marriage. [14] That would not appear to have been the case in these Parisian families. Dowries, even in endogamous marriages, were often in cash, and, as we shall see, the customary laws

AN, Y114, fol. 169vº (13/12/70); AN, Y122, fols. 34-35vº (15/7/80); *Reg. BV*, 2:149.

[13] BN, MS fr. 32588 Saint-Jean: marriages of Luillier/Nicolay; Hennequin/Nicolay; baptism of children of Luillier/Hennequin. AN, Y105, fol. 93 (2/1/52); AN, Y105, fol. 95vº (6/5/64); Boislisle, *Nicolay*, no. 195: Hennequin/Nicolay baptisms. It is interesting, moreover, that Jean Luillier was, literally, old enough to be Renée Nicolay's father, even though she was already a widow with nine children when he married her. His first marriage took place in 1520, the same year as Renée's parents were wed. Moreover, his son Nicolas was married in 1552, the same year as Renée and Jean. This overlapping of generations gives a special character to these early modern families; it also creates serious difficulties for the historian who is trying to set the genealogical record straight!

[14] John Rankine Goody and S. J. Tambiah, *Bridewealth and Dowry*, (Cambridge, 1973), pp. 27-31.

of the Paris area gave other sorts of protection to family properties. It is certainly possible, even probable, that some intermarriages were contracted because a family wished to see a kinsman rather than an outsider benefit from the marriage portion of a rich heiress. Still, it would seem from a study of contracts in the city councillors' families that social and not merely economic reasons underlay the tendency toward repeated endogamy. It was best, everyone agreed, to marry someone whose character and lineage were known, and who was better known than one's own kin?

Obviously, there was a danger in carrying this logic too far. A family needed outside alliances to extend its contacts and strengthen its position in society. Families that intermarried too exclusively would find themselves isolated and insecure. In the long run, the soundest policy would be to broaden one's alliances yet remain within a known and thus, presumably, a safe group. This, it would seem, is what the families of the civic elite, intermarrying frequently but not exclusively, tried to do.

The Marriages of the City Councillors' Children

In most respects, the patterns of alliance found among the sons and daughters of the city councillors resemble those found among the city councillors themselves. We have already seen that the rate of intermarriage among families holding civic office was somewhat lower for the children of the city councillors than for the councillors themselves but that it still equaled 35 to 40%. The patterns of professional endogamy among children also resemble those of the city councillors in their general outlines. The largest proportion of marriages joined a father and son-in-law of approximately equal standing, and few marriages joined families of markedly different status. These generalizations are true of both sons and daughters. There are, however, some subtle differences between the marriage patterns of the male and female children of the city councillors. These patterns deserve attention, for they suggest that some modifications may be necessary in the commonly held theory that the daughters of wealthy merchants and robe officers in early modern France frequently married into higher social circles because of their attractive dowries, while the sons of nobles and officers often had to marry beneath themselves in order to be on the receiving end of the larger dowry offered in an unequal match.[15]

Evidence on merchant families tends to confirm this theory of hypergamy of daughters. The occupations of nineteen sons-in-law of merchants and bourgeois de Paris on the city council are known. Only eight of these sons-in-law were merchants. Six were low-level officers or lawyers in Parlement at the time of the marriage, and five were counselors in the sovereign courts. Two of the sons-in-law eventually went on to become presidents of the sovereign courts. Nearly half of the daughters of the members of liberal professions and low-level officers on the city council also married into higher social circles. Seven out of seventeen known sons-in-law in this group were middle-level officers of the robe at the time of marriage, and one was a high robe officer. Two of the middle-level officers eventually attained high office.

There is, however, a generational aspect to this hypergamy of daughters that is frequently overlooked. The fourteen daughters of merchants and low-level officers whose husbands became officers of ennobling rank in the sovereign courts were not isolated heiresses who married "above themselves" but members of upwardly mobile families. All but one of the fourteen had at least one brother who was upwardly mobile, and ten had at least one sister who likewise married into the middle or high robe. Indeed, four of the merchants' daughters who married robe officers were the daughters of just one man, Pierre Croquet.

The family of Pierre Croquet illustrates well the case of parallel upward mobility taking place simultaneously among siblings. The royal officers who married four of Croquet's

[15] Mousnier, "Structures sociales," p. 39. Dewald, *Provincial Nobility*, pp. 268-75, has also challenged this theory.

daughters apparently held low or middle-level positions at the time of their marriages. All, however, went on to ennobling office, and two eventually became presidents of Parlement. Croquet's only son became a secrétaire du roi, a position that, although less prestigious than those of two of his brothers-in-law, nevertheless represented a considerable achievement for the son of a merchant.[16] Most of the family's advancement came after Croquet's death, and it is probable that the eventual success of Croquet's offspring was due at least in part to the influence of the senior brother-in-law, Nicolas Le Clerc. It was, for example, Le Clerc who became guardian of Croquet's minor daughter, Geneviève, upon her father's death, and therefore it was most likely Le Clerc who later arranged for Geneviève's marriage to Nicolas Longueil du Rancher.[17]

Analysis of the marriages of other city councillors' families also suggests that it was not just the social status of the bride's father that a man sought in marriage but the social and political connections provided by whichever members of the bride's near family were in positions of power and esteem. In the family of Jean Morin, for example, there is a strong suggestion that a woman's in-laws might be of more crucial concern to her suitors than her father's status. Morin died in 1548, ten years after the marriage of his eldest daughter to Michel de L'Hôpital, but while the children he had by his second wife were still young. It seems evident that Jean Tambonneau, who married Guillemette Morin, Jean Morin's younger daughter, in 1563 was more interested in the opportunity to

[16] It is doubtless significant that three of the four husbands of Croquet's daughters—Nicolas Le Clerc, Claude Perrot, and Nicolas Longueil du Rancher—were members of families long active in Parisian politics. Apparently Croquet's son never married. Croquet also had a fifth daughter, much older than the others, who was married in 1559 to François Perrot, the son of the merchant Nicolas and a bourgeois de Paris. I have omitted discussion of them here because François and Nicole were both Protestants, and the normal course of François's career—whatever that might have been—was cut off by his active participation in the Protestant dissent.

[17] Reg. BV, 6:453 and 453n; BN, P.o. 944 Croquet and 780 Le Clerc à Paris.

TABLE 12
Marriages of the City Councillors' Sons who Held Robe Office[a]

Occupation of father-in-law	No. of marriages	% of total
High or middle robe officer	32	70%
Low office, liberal profession	3	7
Noble: no office, military, courtier	8	17
"Seigneur de . . ."	1	2
Merchants, bourgeois	2	4
Total	46	100%

[a] City councillors' sons holding high or middle robe office at the time of their marriage. Percentages calculated from son's peak achievement do not differ significantly.

acquire kinship ties with the chancellor of the realm than he was in the position of Guillemette's long-deceased father.[18]

In the case of the sons of merchants and low-level officers, the determining factor in marriage was clearly the son's own occupation and expectations and not his father's status. The son of a merchant who was himself a merchant took a merchant's daughter for his bride. Thus, for example, the eldest son of the merchant Claude Le Lievre remained in commerce and married the rich widow of another merchant; the youngest son became a lawyer in Parlement and married the daughter of a counselor in that court.[19] The same pattern holds true for the sons of the middle and high robe officers, except that, insofar as the father's status was often a mark of his son's expectations, it also entered into the calculations. It is no surprise to learn that the best marriages were made by the sons of high officers who themselves held important positions. Table 12 summarizes information on the marriages of councillors' sons who held positions in the high and middle levels of the sovereign courts and the royal bureaucracy and indi-

[18] AN, Y126, fol. 272v° (14/1/85): *donation* by Marie Morin, widow of Michel de L'Hôpital, to Guillemette Morin, wife of Jean Tambonneau, and Pierre Morin, her brother and sister. See also BN, MS fr. 32585 Saint-Landry: baptism of 1543; BN, P.o. 2054 Morin, Sgrs. de Paroy, no. 136; AN, Y124, fol. 199 (9/1/67).

[19] BN, P.o. 1718 Lièvre, no. 281 (28/1/43); no. 283 (1/1/50).

cates the importance of intermarriage within these circles. As Table 12 shows, 70% of the sons who held robe office are known to have married daughters of officers of ennobling rank in the courts and bureaucracy.

The daughters of robe officers also married most often at this high level, but there may have been a somewhat greater tendency to marry at lower levels. A comparison of tables 12 and 13 shows that a higher proportion of daughters (15%) than of sons (7%) married into low-level officerial families. If we had more information on the alliances with men qualified as noblemen and "seigneurs de . . . ," we would undoubtedly find some prestigious matches in this group. Most such alliances could not, however, be considered truly hypergamous. As we have seen from the careers of the city councillors and their sons, noble titles, military commissions, and even offices at the court were within reach of men only recently ennobled and do not in themselves guarantee an aristocratic pedigree. As for the comparison between sons and daughters, we can see that sons too married into the families of noblemen and men qualified as "seigneurs de. . . ." Indeed, we can be confident of the nobility of a larger proportion of the sons' spouses than of the daughters'. Finally, even within the ranks of the robe, the sons appear to have made somewhat better matches than the daughters. All six of the sons who were

TABLE 13
Marriages of the Daughters of Robe Officers[a]

Occupation of son-in-law	No. of marriages	% of total
High or middle robe officer	63	60%
Low office, liberal profession	16	15
Noble: no office, military, courtier	10	10
"Seigneur de . . ."	15	14
Merchant, bourgeois	1	1
Total	105	100%

[a] City councillors who were high or middle robe officers at the time of their daughter's marriage. Calculated from son-in-law's occupation at the time of marriage. Percentages calculated from son-in-law's highest level of achievement do not differ significantly.

high robe officers at the time of their weddings and who married within the courts and central bureaucracy wed daughters of high robe officers, while twenty-seven daughters of high robe officers were wed to men of middling status in the robe and only six married high officers. However, this disparity was largely ironed out by the time both sons and sons-in-law attained their peak careers.

Thus, while we do not find much evidence of hypergamous marriage on the part of the daughters of robe officers, we do find that, for the most part at least, they married well. The sons too married well, perhaps even better than the daughters. This is true of younger sons as well as older, a finding that reinforces the conclusions of an earlier chapter on the comparative success of older and younger sons in their careers. In the twenty-one families for which enough is known of the marriages of two or more sons to permit comparison, there is only one case in which the eldest son apparently made the best alliance. In four cases a younger son clearly made the better marriage, and in sixteen cases the eldest and younger brothers made approximately equal marriages.

Apparently, it was not common among city councillors' families for only the eldest sons to marry while younger sons remained unwed. As pointed out earlier, it is difficult to establish the number of celibates with any certainty. Some children undoubtedly disappeared from the record because they left no progeny, others may appear to have been celibate simply because records of their marriages have not been found. Nevertheless, the family histories that are known argue against the belief that younger sons were left unwed. We have seen that there were not a large number of city councillors' sons who followed clerical professions. Sons with secular careers who remained celibates are even more rare. Only six are known. Although it may merely reflect a bias in the sources, it is interesting that four of the six were eldest sons.

The fact that younger sons and daughters were not denied the possibility of a good alliance on the grounds of their order of birth or sex may well have helped reduce friction among siblings. If only the eldest son could advance socially through his career and his marriage, there would inevitably have been tensions between the firstborn and his younger brothers and sisters, who could not hope to share in his success. The possibility of parallel upward mobility for sons and daughters would have reinforced a sense of familial unity and encouraged a desire to assist rather than to compete with one's siblings.

Demographic patterns among the Parisian elite show the marriage of daughters to have contributed to the success of sons. Since the councillors' daughters were usually married at about the age of twenty, sons-in-law were often acquired at a point when the sons of the family were still youths or just at the start of their careers. Therefore, if they were men of standing, the sons-in-law could aid the sons of the house in their professional pursuits. It was precisely this consideration that Etienne Pasquier had in mind when he advised his son Nicolas to choose a son-in-law who was well placed in the same career his sons were entering so he could aid them in their advance.[20]

It would be pointless to paint a deceptively harmonious picture of sibling relationships in the city councillors' families. As will appear, there was ample occasion for family conflict, and the special legal privileges enjoyed by the eldest son in noble families had a major role in these conflicts. It is important, however, to appreciate the fact that, whatever the privileges of primogeniture when it came to the division of noble estates, the firstborn sons of this particular elite did not by virtue of their careers and marriages automatically move into social circles to which their younger siblings could not find admittance.

Although quarrels could and did occur over relationships generated by marriage, the marriage practices in these families were in essence unifying and not divisive forces. The very process by which a mate for one's children was chosen, and

[20] Pasquier, *Lettres*, bk. 22, letter 11 (Thickett, *Lettres familières*, pp. 413-14).

the actual ceremonies involved, helped reinforce the bonds of family. This was true not only on the level of the individual family but across the Parisian elite as a whole. Believing that virtue was first inherited from parents and then enhanced by a careful upbringing and education, they deliberately married their children with the equally well nurtured offspring of their oldest friends and neighbors. Like the parents of whom Gargantua speaks, they hoped thereby to produce children "who would inherit and preserve not only the morals of their fathers and mothers, but also their goods and properties."[21] Confident of their private virtues and public services, they consciously intermarried with families that shared the same heritage and the same values. In doing so, the Parisian elite reinforced its prestige and its power in the city and the state. In doing so, city families built the dynasties that were to dominate the sovereign courts and the royal bureaucracy down to the end of the Old Regime.

[21] Rabelais, *Tiers Livre*, chap. 48 (Cohen, ed., p. 419).

PART IV

The Family Estate

7. The Marriage Contract

Le vray truchement de la loy, c'estoit l'usage.
—Pasquier

IF A FAMILY was to prosper over a long period, it had not
only to acquire prestigious positions and alliances but also to
manage its wealth in such a way that both stability and growth
were assured. The most vulnerable points in the family's economic cycle occurred with the marriages and deaths of its
members. These occurrences necessitated the reassessment of
the rights and needs of individuals within the family and the
reapportionment of family assets to meet these rights and
needs. Because these matters were considered too important
to be left to individual discretion, a body of customary law
had gradually evolved to regulate the division of resources
when new family relationships were created by marriage and
old ones dissolved by death. Based on the common understanding of local usage, the customary law allowed the individual a degree of freedom to deviate from conventional practice as long as the deviation was explicit and did not violate
any of the essential principles on which the customary laws
were based. Within limits, the laws could be adapted to suit
individual needs and strategies for success. To understand how
the city councillors and their families sought to protect and
promote their standing and wealth, one must look at the use
they made of the complex provisions of the customary law.

There is another facet of the relationship between the city
councillors and the customary law of the Paris region that is
of interest here. This is their public role as men responsible
for the codification, interpretation, and application of these
laws. As lawyers and magistrates, humanists and legal scholars, many city councillors and members of their immediate

families took part in events that made the sixteenth century one of the most exciting periods in the evolution of private law in France. Forty of the ninety city councillors included in this study were at some point in their careers lawyers or counselors in the lower jurisdiction of the Châtelet or the higher court of Parlement. The larger circle formed by their sons and sons-in-law includes such noted jurists as Pierre Pithou and Claude Dupuy.[1] Other members of these families had a less central but nevertheless significant role as local notables whose understanding of the customary usages had both a direct and an indirect effect on the development of the law.[2]

The Parisian Elite and the Evolution of Civil Law

The first codification of civil law for the Paris region was not made until 1510, when the king appointed a special commission to compile and record the laws regarding persons and properties customarily followed in the area under the jurisdiction of the Châtelet. Rather than arresting the slow evolution of the law, codification of the local customs stimulated their further development and widened their influence. French legal scholars, inspired simultaneously by their studies of Roman law—studies that owe much to the pioneering work of Guillaume Budé on the Pandects—and by a nascent national sentiment that sought to purge "foreign" influences in favor of presumably Gallic customs, went to work on the newly codified customs.[3] Their commentaries pointed out a number of inconsistencies and inadequacies. As the customs of other regions were codified, they were compared with Parisian laws, and a debate broke out in legal circles over the desirability of unifying civil law in a common code for all of France. The

---

[1] Pierre Pithou married Catherine Palluau, the daughter of Jean Palluau. Claude Dupuy married Claude Sanguin, the daughter of Jacques Sanguin.

[2] On the influence of Parisian notables on the customary laws in the Middle Ages, see Guy Fourquin, "Le Droit parisien de la fin du Moyen Age: Droit des 'notables,' " *Etudes d'histoire du droit parisien*, ed. François Dumont (Paris, 1970), pp. 375-95.

[3] Kelley, *Language, Law, and History*, pp. 53-80.

royal commissioners responsible for the codification of regional customs had been explicitly enjoined to respect the particularities of local practice. With a few exceptions, this had been done. Still, jurists eager to see the power of the monarchy enhanced by a common body of law pressed for reforms that would have created a greater unity. For most of these jurists, Parisian law was the model against which others were measured and around which a common law might eventually take shape. There was consequently a special interest in the laws of the Paris area and an increased pressure to reform aspects of the 1510 codification that were considered ambiguous or outmoded. These pressures resulted in a full-scale revision of the Parisian customary law in 1580. Legal particularism eventually triumphed, and France was not to have a unified code of civil law until after the Revolution, but the *Nouvelle Coutume* produced by the 1580 revisions of Parisian law remained a standard for French jurists throughout the Old Regime. Interpreted and reinterpreted by countless jurists in the centuries that followed, the customary laws of Paris exerted an influence even on the Code Civil that today is still the law in France.[4]

The importance of these events as far as the local elite is concerned lies in the fact that the codification and revision of the law were by their very nature processes in which local usage was elevated to the status of law rather than processes in which the law was handed down from higher authorities. The mandate of the royal commissioners was to discover and record the law, not to make it. To do this, they had to call together representatives of the local estates and stage an inquest. Not surprisingly, the records of the inquests held in 1510 and 1580 indicate that the city councillors and their relatives played a prominent role in these proceedings. They were present not only as bourgeois representatives of the Hôtel de Ville and as officers of the Châtelet but as noblemen

[4] Olivier-Martin, *Histoire de la coutume*, 1:58-67; René Filhol, *Le Premier Président Christofle de Thou et la réformation des coutumes* (Paris, 1937), pp. 127-37.

possessing seigneuries within the jurisdiction of the Prévôté and Vicomté of Paris. In 1580, for example, five city councillors attended the meetings as delegates from the Hôtel de Ville, and more than a dozen members of this group or their sons attended personally in their capacity as noblemen who held the rights of high justice on their estates. Many others, as well as councillors' widows and daughters, who were of course not permitted to attend in person, were represented by *procureurs*, or solicitors. Even many of the solicitors bore names that mark them as members of notable Parisian families.[5]

Members of the local elite also had special roles in these proceedings by virtue of their prominence as royal officers and magistrates. Christophe de Thou, the first president of the Parlement of Paris and a city councillor for more than forty years, presided over the reformation of the Paris customary law in 1580. By that time, de Thou had devoted more than twenty years to the codification and reformation of local customs, and his role in this process was unequaled.[6] Thibault Baillet, also a president of Parlement and father of the city councillor René Baillet, had presided over the codification of Parisian law in 1510, and the city councillors Christophe de Harlay and Jean Prevost I were commissioned with the reformation of various regional customs.[7] Michel de L'Hôpital also helped further the codification and reform of regional customs while he was chancellor.[8]

Members of the Parisian elite not only helped to codify and execute the law, they participated in the legal system as litigants in civil and occasionally criminal suits, as court-appointed agents for the administration of protected persons and

[5] The procès-verbaux for the codification of 1510 and the reformation of the laws in 1580 are reprinted in Charles Antoine Bourdot de Richebourg, *Nouveau Coutumier général* (Paris, 1724), 3:18-19, and 56-66.

[6] Filhol's *Christofle de Thou* presents an excellent account of his activities in this regard.

[7] Baillet: Bourdot de Richebourg, *Coutumier*, 3:18; Harlay: Filhol, *Christofle de Thou*, p. 41; Prevost: *Actes de François I*, 1:328 (no. 1765).

[8] Salmon, *Society in Crisis*, p. 158, argues that L'Hôpital probably would have preferred to see the regional customs replaced by a national code.

properties, and as members of an institution known as the family council. The family council was a formal gathering of kin that was called before the *lieutenant civil* of the Châtelet or one of his officers when it was necessary to make important decisions regarding the affairs of minors who had no legally appointed guardian or whose guardian was unable to act in the situation at hand. The most frequent reason for the calling of a family counsel was to choose a guardian and to settle the financial affairs of a minor whose mother or father had died, but family councils were also required for the legal emancipation of minors from parental authority and for certain decisions involving children under guardianship.[9]

The members of the Parisian elite were thus involved with the legal system in many different ways and on many different levels. As the example of the family council shows, an individual could be called before the law in an advisory capacity in private as well as in public matters. It seems reasonable to assume that this involvement with the legal system encouraged a belief that the law was an organic entity, shaped by the needs of those that it served, and therefore particularly well suited to those needs. One who looked upon the law in this way would necessarily consider it deserving of his respect, although he might be willing to deviate from it when he thought it would serve his own purposes.

In many respects this is the position that was reached, albeit in a far more intellectual manner, by Etienne Pasquier in his studies of the law. As Donald Kelley has shown, Pasquier represents the culmination of the movement of legal humanism in France, a movement that may be considered as having begun with Budé's *Annotations on the Pandects* and that is characterized by an increasing awareness of historical change and cultural relativity.[10] In a letter to the jurist Choppin,

---

[9] Olivier-Martin, *Histoire de la coutume*, 1:195-99; Guillaume de Lamoignon, *Recueil des Arrêtés* (Paris, 1777), pp. 4-17. Title IV of Lamoignon's *Arrêtés* deals with guardianships. It must be remembered, however, that the *Arrêtés* represented a program for reform and not a statement of the laws as they existed.

[10] Kelley, *Language, Law, and History*, especially pp. 271-309.

Pasquier compared the law to a mother bear who gradually shapes her cubs by licking them; so it was that the laws were polished with time and use, "and that is why they say that the true interpreter of the law is custom."[11] In another letter, he praised the practice in customary law areas of holding inquests to clarify dubious points in the law: "Since customs were formed gradually in each province according to the diversity of our characters, it seems appropriate in cases of obscurity or doubt to have recourse to people close to us, who by their proximity would seem to conform to [symbolisent] our manners and character and so to our customs."[12]

We can also see in Pasquier that a belief in legal particularism was not necessarily founded upon opposition to the monarchy—which Pasquier strongly supported—but could have its origins rather in the conviction that the king's duty to administer justice included the obligation to respect the diversity of local customs.[13] Not all Pasquier's friends, the jurists who frequented the circles of de Thou and Dupuy, agreed with him on this last point. Antoine Loisel and Pierre Pithou both believed that a unified law would provide an important bastion for monarchical power.[14] Christophe de Thou must be judged more by his actions than his words, but scholars have generally concluded that, while he may in principle have favored a unified law, for the most part he did respect local particularities in his capacity as commissioner for the reform of regional customs.[15] Whether or not these jurists agreed on the desirability of a common code of private law for all of France, the debate in legal circles over the role of the custom-

[11] Pasquier, *Lettres*, bk. 6, letter 2 (Thickett, *Lettres familières*, p. 73).
[12] Ibid., bk. 9, letter 1, as translated by Kelley, *Language, Law, and History*, p. 289.
[13] Ibid., bk. 6, letter 2.
[14] Kelley, *Language, Law, and History*, pp. 247, 260-61.
[15] Filhol, *Christofle de Thou*, passim. See especially pp. 62-67 and 84-94. In Filhol's opinion, the commissioners used their power indirectly to influence the law in the direction of greater commonality, but the deviations from traditional practice were relatively minor and could not be enacted over the opposition of the local population.

ary law stimulated thought about the origins, nature, and purpose of the law in general and thus contributed to an increased sensitivity to its role in both public and private life.

The relationship between the Parisian elite and the local legal system is significant for what it reveals about their concept of family, as well as their concept of the law. The family council in particular demonstrates how the family functioned in its broadest sense as a formal institution. The council was supposed to consist of the nearest relatives over twenty-five years of age. They were to be evenly distributed between the maternal and paternal lines, with at least three members representing each line. In the large families of the Parisian elite there were often ten or more persons assembled for a family council.

A good example of the family council in action is a case from 1585 involving a child whose mother had remarried without naming another guardian to share her responsibility for the child's financial affairs, as she was required to do. The boy's paternal uncle, Claude de Hacqueville, had the family council called. Ten paternal uncles and cousins and five from the maternal line assembled before the counselor of the Châtelet designated to handle the affair, Nicolas de Longueil. Four other relatives, at least three of them from the paternal side, failed to appear. The boy's mother, Jeanne Le Prevost, did not attend, although women were allowed in family councils, but sent a solicitor in her stead. The solicitor protested that Jeanne had not been asked to name her nearest relatives before the gathering was called and that consequently the maternal line was underrepresented. A new meeting was called, with four additional members of the maternal line invited. The second gathering chose Claude de Hacqueville, the boy's paternal uncle, as his guardian to the age of twenty, despite Jeanne's protests, conveyed again through her solicitor. The family council also took care of certain financial matters that remained to be settled from the marriage between Jeanne and the deceased Pierre de Hacqueville so that the estate could be freed from any claims she might make on it.[16]

The rights and obligations implicit in kinship extended beyond the immediate family to more distant relatives in both the paternal and maternal lines, even to those who were only connected by marriage. For instance, Jean Du Drac, listed among the relatives attending the Hacqueville family council as one of the "paternal cousins," was in fact but the husband of a cousin of the child's deceased father. It is significant, too, that a formal family council was called when a child had lost even one parent—as in this case—not only when a child was doubly orphaned. In many cases the calling of the family council and the consent of the judge were simple formalities, and the person appointed guardian was the child's nearest relative. If the mother died and the father was still living, he was automatically made the legal guardian of his children; if the father died a surviving mother could not be denied guardianship except for serious reasons or if the father had designated another guardian in his testament.[17] Still, the existence of the family council was important. It provided legal recognition and reinforcement for a system of kinship that distributed the obligation to look out for the interests of one's kin relatively widely among the family members, while at the same time, and without apparent contradiction, it made parental authority a central premise of family relations.

The consent of the nearest relatives to the marriage of a child under guardianship was a direct extension of the responsibilities of the family council. The presence and counsel of a wide circle of family members at the signing of a marriage contract that did not require their consent was a symbolic expression of the same concept of kinship. It is significant that the assembled family bore witness to the financial arrangements for marriage as well as to the vows themselves.

---

[16] AN, Y3879 (9/7/85): election of tuteurs for Nicolas de Hacqueville, son of the deceased Pierre de Hacqueville, sieur de Pomponne, and Jeanne Le Prevost.

[17] Olivier-Martin, *Histoire de la coutume*, 1:195.

The bride's father and mother, if they were still living, were solely responsible for determining the dowry she was to receive. It seems likely, however, that the presence of other members of the family—among them the children who were already wed and their spouses—exerted a tacit pressure on the parents to treat all of the children in the family fairly and according to standards that were accepted in at least their own social circles.[18] Just what were those standards, and how did they relate to the public standards that were expressed in the customary laws of the region?

To answer these questions we shall have to look at the laws that governed the disposition of family properties and at the actual practice in city councillor families as shown in their marriage contracts, lifetime donations, and post-mortem divisions of property. All of these aspects of the division of the patrimony are closely related in both law and practice. They overlap in complex fashion. Marriage contracts, for example, were concerned not only with the lifetime aspect of marriage—the promise to marry and the possessions brought to the marriage—but with the separation of the estates upon the death of either or both of the spouses. If the affianced couple had parents who were still living or whose estates had not yet been divided, the rights of the young couple to the future successions of these parents were also set out in the marriage contract.

Except among the very poor it was the norm to have the promise of marriage and the financial arrangements for the union formally drawn up and notarized. Derived mainly from the customary practices of the region and usually drawn up according to standardized models, a marriage contract was nevertheless written to meet the individual needs and situation of the couple to be wed. Regional customs could be modified or specifically renounced in the contract, as long as there was no violation of the fundamental principles from

[18] Olivier-Martin (*Histoire de la coutume*, 2:371) also concludes that the dowry is influenced by family pressures and does not reflect the will of the head of the household alone.

which the custom was derived.[19] It is along this line between convention and individuality that the interest of the marriage contracts of the city councillors and their families lies. Before undertaking an analysis of marriage contracts of city councillors and their families, however, it is necessary to understand the customary laws that regulated the properties of married couples in the Prévôté and Vicomté of Paris.

Customary Laws Regarding Marriage

Since the sacrament of marriage was regulated by canon law, customary law regulated only the temporal effects of marriage. The most important function of the customary laws was to define which possessions of a husband and wife were community properties and which were lineage properties. In theory, community properties were those in which the spouses shared equally and from which the daily needs of their common household were met, while lineage properties, called *propres*, were properties a person received from his parents and were intended to pass on intact to his nearest blood relations. In practice, however, it was often difficult to keep the two kinds of property separate. Therefore a whole body of laws evolved defining the nature of properties and the property rights of husbands and wives and their respective heirs. Complex as these provisions are, it is vital to understand the way in which a concern for the protection of patrimony was translated into law.

Unless otherwise specified in the marriage contract, a couple who married in the region of the Paris customs possessed in common both real and personal property acquired during the course of the marriage. The only exceptions were: inherited properties or properties that were the gift or legacy of a direct relative (*propres*), real properties acquired through one's own labor or through the gift of a collateral relative before the time of marriage (*acquêts*), and property later given to one

[19] Gabriel Lepointe, *Droit romain et ancien droit français* (Paris, 1958), p. 380.

of the spouses with the express provision that it not become community property. *Propres* were kept separate from community property because they were subject to different rules of devolution. A surviving spouse was entitled to half the community property, but the rights of husbands and wives to the lineage properties of their mates were strictly limited. The laws regulating the disposition of lineage properties were more restrictive than the laws regulating the disposition of acquired properties because of the assumption that the *propres* belonged to the family line. The individual was considered more their custodian than their owner. For this reason, the laws of the Paris region permitted an individual to bequeath freely only one-fifth of his or her *propres*. The remainder had to be divided among the nearest kin according to the customary rules of succession. Because they were considered to belong to the lineage, *propres* could only be inherited by the nearest blood relations, and it was thus necessary to ensure that they would return to the family of origin in the event that a marriage produced no new line of descent.[20]

During marriage, the husband had full responsibility and authority for the management of the community property. He could dispose of it as he chose without the consent or even the knowledge of his wife (although he could later be prosecuted for fraud if he enriched himself or his own heirs at the expense of the community property).[21] The husband could not, however, dispose of his wife's lineage properties, her *propres*, without her consent, nor could she dispose of her own *propres* without her husband's authorization. A contract signed by a married woman without her husband's express authorization was void. (A woman whose husband was insane

[20] Paris *Coutumier* of 1580 (hereafter "N.C."), arts. 220 and 246. Inheritances from lineal relatives and gifts in advance of succession from these relatives were considered *propres* whether they occurred during marriage or not. Collateral inheritances made during marriage were *conquêts* of the community and not *propres* unless the decedent specifically provided that they became *propres* of the party receiving them. See also Lepointe, *Droit romain*, pp. 375-76, on *propres*.

[21] N.C., art. 225.

or absent for a long period of time could, however, get permission from the court to dispose of property and enter into legal agreements.)[22]

In principle, the community property was divided into two equal portions upon the death of one of the spouses. One portion went to the survivor and the other to the heirs of the deceased. It was, however, permitted for a widow to renounce her right to the community property, recuperating only her *propres*, any *acquêts* which preceded the marriage, and her dower rights on her deceased husband's estate.[23] The right to renounce the common property, originally permitted to noblewomen in order to free them from ransoms and other obligations contracted by husbands who went off to fight in the Crusades, was extended to commoners in many sixteenth-century customs. In Paris, the codification of customary law made in 1510 specified noblewomen; the revised law of 1580 allowed all widows to renounce their rights to the marital community.[24] According to most commentaries on the customary law, the right to renounce the community property was a privilege accorded the wife as a counterbalance to her legal incapacity during marriage. Having had no say in the success or failure of the joint economic enterprise, she was free to disclaim the fruits or failures of her husband's labors. Even if the widow accepted her share of the common property, her *propres* were protected by laws that limited her responsibility for debts contracted by her husband.[25] In the eyes of some commentators, these privileges benefited the wife unduly; she

[22] N.C., arts. 223, 225, 226.

[23] N.C., arts. 229 and 237.

[24] Bourdot de Richebourg, *Coutumier*, 3:23; Paris *Coutumier* of 1510 (hereafter "A.C."), art. 115. Claude Le Prebstre (*Questions notables de droict* [Paris, 1645], p. 11) and Jean Tronçon (*Le Droict françois et coustume de la prevosté et vicomté de Paris* [Paris, 1643], p. 483) discuss the reasons for the law. (Both Le Prebstre and Tronçon are descendants of city councillors included in this study.) Lepointe, *Droit romain*, pp. 388-89, cites Loisel's opinion that it was Jean-Jacques de Mesmes, *lieutenant civil* in Paris, who was most responsible for the extension of the law to commoners.

[25] N.C., arts. 221, 228; Olivier-Martin, *Histoire de la coutume*, 2:245.

did not share the risks her husband took but stood only to gain.[26] Besides a right to half the community property, a widow had a subsistence right that allowed her to claim the lifetime usage of certain lineage properties of her husband. In Parisian law the customary widow's right, called her dower (*douaire*), equaled one-half of the husband's *propres* and included *propres* bequeathed to him after marriage as well as those he possessed at the time of the wedding.[27] So important was the right to a dower that it existed even if there was no marriage contract. A marriage contract could, however, specify instead of the customary dower a fixed amount payable in one sum or as an annual income, called a *douaire préfix*. The fixed dower could be larger or smaller than the customary dower, but whatever the sum agreed upon in the marriage contract, the widow assigned a fixed dower had no right to choose instead the customary dower unless she had been explicitly given this option. While a customary dower always returned to the husband's heirs upon the widow's death, a *douaire préfix* was occasionally specified as nonreturnable.[28] A woman did not lose her dower if she remarried, although she could lose it for adultery or debauchery.[29]

The importance of a woman's dower rights went beyond the question of subsistence in widowhood. These rights constituted an important check on a husband's freedom to dispose of his *propres*. According to the customary law, the wife's dower had priority over any debts the husband contracted. In

[26] François Bourjon (*Le Droit commun de la France et la coutume de Paris*, new ed. [Paris, 1770], cited in Lepointe, *Droit*, p. 389) and Olivier-Martin (*Coutume*, 2:243) referred to marriage as a "société léonine où la femme garderait toutes les chances de gain sans toujours courir les risques de perte." The same idea, including the reference to marriage as a "société léonine" in which the wife has all the advantages is expressed in the *cahier des remonstrances* of the Third Estate at Blois (BN, MS fr. 10871, fols. 111-12).

[27] N.C., art. 248.

[28] N.C., arts. 247 and 248; discussed in Etienne Pasquier, *L'Interprétation des Institus de Justinien* (Paris, 1847), p. 355; and Claude de Ferrière, *La Science parfaite des notaires* (Paris, 1682), p. 88.

[29] Lepointe, *Droit romain*, p. 406.

practice, then, creditors usually insisted that a husband secure his wife's agreement to any alienation of his *propres*.[30] Moreover, if there were children, the dower did not cease with the wife's death. The customary law provided that the dower became the *propres* of the children born of the union, and neither father nor mother could sell or mortgage such properties to the prejudice of their children. As we shall see, the right of children to their mother's dower could serve as a valuable tool in the protection of lineage properties.

One of the principles upon which the institution of community property was based required that a woman at the time of marriage contribute some of her own properties to the marital community. According to a seventeenth-century guide for notaries, a man could declare all of his possessions *propres* and exempt them from the community of goods if he chose, because he contributed to the community through his labor. A woman, on the other hand, was ordinarily expected to enter at least a quarter if not a third of her goods as community property. If she had no cash or *meubles* (personal property, or movables), a portion of her real property was to be declared movables by convention and left to the disposition of her husband.[31] It is important, then, in studying marriage contracts to look not just at the total sum a woman brought to marriage—the dowry, if she was not yet in possession of her own property—but at the amount that entered into the marital community and the terms under which this community property was to be terminated. As we shall see in studying the marriage contracts of the city councillors' families, the

[30] In the seventeenth century, theory caught up with practice, and the wife was said to have a "legal mortgage" on her husband's *propres*. In practice, however, the wife's legal claim on her husband's estate was already established in the sixteenth century. See Olivier-Martin, *Histoire de la coutume*, 2:236; and Le Pointe, *Droit romain*, p. 396, for the seventeenth century. For the sixteenth century, see contracts of the city councillors' families, such as AN, Y105, fols. 93-95 (2/1/52): Luillier/Nicolay, which specifies that all of Antoine Nicolay's properties are mortgaged ("hypothèquées") to cover his wife's dower rights. Most of the contracts assign the dower rights on some or all of the husband's properties.

[31] Ferrière, *Parfait Notaire*, p. 77.

importance of the contractural arrangements for the protection of the patrimony lay less in the size of the dowry than in the maze of carefully worded clauses enumerating *propres* and ensuring their return to the line from which they came in the event the union produced no issue. The total size of the dowry, however, was important because of its relationship to the parental estate. The portion often given a man in marriage if his parents were still living was important for the same reason. In the medieval law of the Paris region, a child who was married by his parents and did not remain in residence with them was normally given a marriage portion in lieu of inheritance. Only children who were still a part of their parents' household, those who, unmarried or married, were still living under the same roof and contributing their labor to the common wealth, qualified to share in the parental succession.[32] Over time, however, it became common to allow children who had been dowered off to return to the parental succession if they returned (*rapportant*) any sums they had received or deducted these sums from their share of the parental estate. Until the codification of the customs in 1510, this privilege had to be specifically granted in a marriage contract.[33] After 1510, the right to return to the parental succession was the rule in Parisian law, and a parent who did not wish a child to have this privilege had to require that the child explicitly renounce his rights to later successions in his marriage contract.[34]

It was not permissible to renounce rights to future successions except by the terms of a marriage contract. Indeed, the laws of the Paris area, unlike the laws of Anjou, Maine, and

---

[32] Olivier-Martin, *Histoire de la coutume*, 2:146, more generally, 2:141-62.

[33] Bourdot de Richebourg, *Coutumier*, 3:23. François Olivier-Martin, "Les Manuscrits de Simon Marion et la coutume de Paris au xvie siècle," *Travaux juridiques et économiques de l'Université de Rennes* 7 (1920):179.

[34] A.C., art. 123; N.C., art. 304. A major study providing a comparative perspective on this practice is Jean Yver, *Egalité entre héritiers et exclusion des enfants dotés* (Paris, 1966). See especially pp. 15-23 regarding the development of this privilege in the Parisian law.

other regions, never did expressly permit this renunciation in any form.[35] But it was not forbidden either. The practice was at least tolerated in Paris, and some Old Regime jurists looked on it most favorably, particularly if it was a daughter who renounced her rights in favor of a son.[36] Louet, for example, argued that the renunciation of successions by daughters in favor of sons was justified not only by the "natural presumption" that parental affection would prevent a mother or father from treating any of their children unfairly but by a "political reason." This was the "public interest served by the conservation of families, the possessions of which should be conserved and distributed to the males, who uphold the splendor and dignity of the house whose name and arms they bear, rather than the daughters, who cause these possessions to pass into a strange hand and family."[37] Since the renunciation of parental successions in marriage contracts has thus been linked directly to the protection of the lineage, it will be important to see if this was a strategy commonly employed in city councillors' families.

Besides requiring the renunciation of a future succession, there was another way that parents could use marriage contracts and marriage portions to nullify the normal rules of succession. This was by allowing a child the option of keeping his or her marriage portion in lieu of inheritance. Article 307 of the revised laws of 1580 expressly permitted any child who wished to keep gifts received from parents at marriage or any other occasion to keep these gifts by abstaining from the parental succession. There is no comparable article in the codification of 1510, but most historians and jurists have assumed that this right was implicitly granted in the customary provision, "Il ne se porte heretier qui ne veut."[38] Charles Du

---

[35] Lepointe, *Droit romain*, p. 453.

[36] Ferrière, *Parfait Notaire*, p. 97; Bourjon, *Droit commun*, 1:909-11.

[37] Louet, *Arrests*, 2:816. He is paraphrasing here the *Coutume* of the Marche. Le Prestre, *Questions notables*, pp. 60 and 62, also justifies this law on the basis of the "conservation of families."

[38] A.C., art. 130; N.C., art. 315. Before 1510, the option of returning

Moulin, one of the most authoritative commentators on the 1510 laws was, however, of the contrary opinion, believing any gifts given children in advance of inheritance had to be returned to the succession or renounced.[39] For added safety it was thus common for parents explicitly to offer their children the option of keeping gifts or returning them to share in the succession. Careful drafting of marriage contracts and deeds of gift was essential for parents who wished to avoid customary restrictions on the disposal of their property and at the same time avoid family quarrels.

One other set of clauses in marriage contracts affected the distribution of the patrimony. These were the provisions that allowed parents marrying their children to write into the children's marriage contracts clauses that prevented the division of the parental community until after the death of both parents.[40] The law, supposedly written to encourage parents to marry off their children by allowing them a financial advantage if they did so, permitted the surviving parent to enjoy the movables and the immovables acquired during marriage (*conquêts*, as *acquêts* made during marriage were usually called) by the deceased spouse as long as he or she did not remarry.[41] This provision was important because it was an exception to the rule that a married couple could not make one another gifts of their property. A fiancé could give a gift to his intended bride and vice versa, but such gifts were not allowed after marriage. It was feared that the emotional bond between the spouses would cause them to favor one another at the expense of their lineal relations.[42] The only gifts that were permitted were reciprocal donations (*dons mutuels*) of movables and *conquêts* of the community property and the usufruct of

---

to the succession did not exist unless specifically extended in the marriage contract.

[39] Du Moulin, cited in Tronçon, *Droict françois*, p. 673.
[40] N.C., art. 281.
[41] Lepointe, *Droit romain*, p. 415.
[42] Olivier-Martin, *Histoire de la coutume*, 2:287-94.

the *propres*. But after 1510 even *dons mutuels* were forbidden in the Paris law if a couple had any living children.[43] Only in the marriage contracts of their children could parents make one another gifts of their property.

It should be apparent from this survey of customary laws regarding marriage that the negotiation of a marriage involved some complex bargaining. A man was interested not just in the total size of the dowry his bride would bring but in the amount that would be subject to his immediate and direct control as part of the community property. Depending upon his own financial situation and current needs, he would weigh his bride's prospects for future inheritance against the sum to be paid the night of the marriage, the traditional moment for the payment of dowries. He would also have to decide how to provide for the support of his wife if he died. Should he allow her the customary dower, the usufruct of half his *propres*? Or should he specify a fixed sum, in which case he could probably expect that the wealthier the woman he sought to marry, the more splendid the style of life she would expect to maintain as a widow. The bride's father, on the other hand, would want to contribute enough to the community property to provide the comforts and style of living he wished for his daughter without jeopardizing any more of the patrimony than was necessary. Wishing to maintain the family's dignity and advance the grandchildren he expected from the union, he would want to abet and not hinder the ambitions of his son-in-law. At the same time, he would want to be sure that any profits derived from his daughter's wealth would enrich his own lineage and not strangers. Moreover, the parents of both bride and groom, if they were still living and intended to contribute to the support of the young couple, would have to balance out the needs and desires of

[43] Bourdot de Richebourg, *Coutumier*, 3:24. The reasons for this change are given in art. 161 of the procès-verbal made in 1507 prior to the codification of the law and published by François Olivier-Martin ("Un Document inédit sur les travaux préparatoires de l'Ancienne Coutume de Paris," *Nouvelle Revue historique de droit français et étranger* 42 [1918]:218-19).

the couple to be wed against the needs of their own community and their promises and hopes for other offspring.

The Financial Arrangements for Marriage in the City Councillors' Families

Clearly, these complex considerations cannot be reduced to simple charts and maxims. Quantitative evaluation of the dowries and dowers given in the councillors' families can yield a certain insight into the comparative financial statuses of these families, but most of the provisions in marriage contracts cannot be analyzed in quantitative terms. My primary aim, rather, is to evaluate the contracts that I have found in broader terms, seeking to understand in what ways the basic elements of the customary law were respected and in what ways they were evaded. What special clauses and guarantees occur most often, and what considerations seem to have dominated in the negotiation of marriage for this particular social group?

The evaluation that follows is based primarily on the examination of seventy complete marriage contracts (fifty-six of which concern the city councillors, their parents, and their children, and fourteen of which concern their brothers and sisters, stepchildren, and grandchildren). Contracts from the period 1550 to 1580 are the most numerous. Only ten complete contracts date from the first half of the sixteenth century, and only fifteen of the seventy contracts date from after the reform of the customary law in 1580.[44] Information on the financial arrangements for marriage was also drawn from an additional forty summaries or extracts of contracts concerning the marriages of the city councillors, their sons, and daughters.

Before embarking upon an analysis of the more complex clauses in these contracts, let us look at the total sums in-

[44] 1550-1559: 12 contracts; 1560-1569: 17 contracts; 1570-1579: 16 contracts; 1580-1589: 9 contracts; 1590-1599: 6 contracts.

volved in the dowries brought to the marriages of the city councillors and their children. Although the total cash value of a woman's marriage portion was frequently not specified in the contract, particularly if the dowry included real properties or extensive personal possessions, an approximate value or a guaranteed minimum value was sometimes stated for houses, country estates, jewelry, and other tangibles given at the time of marriage. It is thus possible to calculate dowries for a total of fifty-eight marriages: sixteen in which the bride was the daughter of a merchant, twenty-eight in which she was the daughter of a royal officer who claimed at least personal nobility or of a nobleman who did not hold royal office, and fourteen in which she was the daughter of a high officer of the crown.

Only marriage portions that were properly speaking "dowries," that is to say, portions given in lieu of or in advance of inheritance and not marriage portions that represent the settlement of the estates of deceased parents, have been counted here. I have, however, counted those cases in which only one parent was alive at the time of the marriage because the final reckoning of the estate of the deceased parent was so often not made until after the final break-up of the marital community with the death of the second parent. Children who had come into their parental inheritances were frequently able to bring much larger sums to marriage than were those who still had one or both parents living. Thus, for example, Jean Luillier gave his daughter Catherine a dowry of £30,000 on her marriage to Thibault Nicolay in 1561. When Catherine remarried five years later, she was able to offer her new husband, Pierre de Saint-André, a much larger amount. Her father had died in the meantime, and her brother guaranteed that her rights in the recently divided parental estate would equal at least £70,000.[45]

---

[45] Boislisle, *Nicolay*, no. 200: marriage contract of Thibault Nicolay and Catherine Luillier (11/1/60-61). Approximately £19,000 of the £30,000 given in marriage was to represent Catherine's share in the estate of her deceased mother. Luillier also promised her an additional £10,000 on his

Even after eliminating the distortion produced by comparing dowries with what were in fact inheritances, we find an enormous variation in the size of the dowries given in the city councillors' families. Denis Tanneguy, a lawyer in Parlement, gave his daughter Ursine only £2,000 for her marriage in 1563 to Denis Lambin, a lecturer in Greek at the University of Paris. In addition Tanneguy offered to lodge the young couple and a servant in a room in his house and to feed them at his table for a year after their marriage.[46] By contrast, the daughter of Pierre Hennequin, a president in Parlement, brought a dowry of £50,000 to her husband, Olivier Le Fèvre d'Eaubonne, in 1591.[47] In order to appreciate the magnitude of the sums involved, it might be useful to express these dowries in terms of their purchasing power or as wage equivalents. Conversion into wheat prices is perhaps the most accurate measure, given the current state of our knowledge of sixteenth-century prices. In 1563, £2,000 would have purchased 271 *sétiers* (more than thirty-two tons) of first quality wheat on the Paris grain market. In spite of the raging inflation, which brought wheat prices in 1591 to more than four times what they had been in 1563, £50,000 would have purchased 1,498 sétiers (nearly 180 tons) of wheat in that year. Or, to use wage equivalents, the £2,000 paid Tanneguy's daughter in 1563 would have hired twenty-four unskilled laborers in the building trades for a year. The £50,000 paid Hennequin's daughter in 1591 would have hired 309.[48]

---

death if she chose not to come to the succession. AN, Min. cen. LXXXVI:66 (10/9/66). In addition to her parental inheritance, Catherine would receive a dower of £400 per year on the estate of her first husband.

[46] AN, Min. cen. VIII:259 (2/11/63). Although no value was given for the year of room and board, a comparison with other contracts suggests that this service might have been valued at about £100, £200 at the most. See for example, AN, Y98, fols. 222v°-24v° (23/1/53-54): Pommereul/ Guybert. This is not a city councillor's family. I know of no comparable arrangement for members of this group except for the marriage of the first daughter of Claude Le Prestre, which involved a mercantile partnership as well as a residential arrangement (AN, Min. cen. VIII:205 [9/8/49]).

[47] AN, Min. cen. VI:47 (21/1/91).

[48] Micheline Baulant, "Le Prix des grains à Paris," *Annales* 23 (1968):538. In a more recent article on "Prix et salaires à Paris au xvie siècle" (*Annales*

TABLE 14
Dowry Values in the Families of the City Councillors
(Expressed in livres tournois)

Period Included	Merchant or Bourgeois			Middle-Level Officer or Noble, No Office			High Officer		
	No.	Mean	Median	No.	Mean	Median	No.	Mean	Media
1525-1549	4	4,225	3,850	7	8,800	8,000	1	12,000	–
1550-1574	10	7,150	6,500	15	13,553	13,500	6	24,667	25,00
1575-1599	2	18,500ª	18,500ª	6	16,267	15,500	7	31,143	30,00
Total	16	7,838	6,000	28	12,946	12,000	14	27,000	30,00

Status of Father of the Bride

ª The mean and median for merchant daughters after 1575 are skewed by the small number of ca
and the unusually high dowry given in one of the cases.

A composite picture of dowries in city councillors' families
for the fifty-eight marriages for which dowries can be calculated is presented in Table 14. Because a comparison of the
dowries received by city councillors and those received by
their sons to those given their daughters revealed no consistent differences in size or nature, I have included all three
groups—the city councillors, their sons, and their daughters—in Table 14. For the sake of consistency, the status
categories here are based on the standing of the bride's father.

It is clear from Table 14 that, at least until the last quarter
of the century, the average dowry given a merchant's daughter was distinctly lower than that given the daughter of a
middle-level officer of the crown or a nobleman who held no
office, while the dowries given this latter group fell even further short of the dowries given the daughters of high officers
of the crown. It is also clear (or it appears so at first glance)
that dowries rose markedly over the course of the century.
The average dowry in middle-level officerial families in the
second quarter of the century was less than £9,000. In the
third quarter of the century this figure rose to over £13,500,

31 [1976]:992), Baulant gives the equivalent of the sétier of sixteenth-
century Paris as approximately 240 pounds of *froment*. On wage equivalents,
see Baulant, "Salaire des ouvriers," p. 483.

TABLE 15
Dowries Expressed as Sétiers of Grain on the Paris Market
(Five-year moving averages)

				Status of Father of the Bride				
	Merchant or Bourgeois			Middle-Level Officer or Noble, No Office			High Officer	
Period Included	No.	Mean	Median	No.	Mean	Median	No.	Mean	Median
1525-1549	4	1,352	1,434	7	2,646	2,577	1	4,196	—
1550-1574	10	1,456	1,216	15	2,102	1,816	6	4,321	4,245
1575-1599	2	2,356[a]	2,356[a]	6	1,934	2,118	7	2,908	2,616

[a] The mean and median for merchant daughters after 1575 are skewed by the small number of cases and the unusually high dowry given in one of the cases.

and by the last quarter of the century, it was over £16,000. Dowries for merchant families and for the highest level of officers would appear to have risen comparably, but we have fewer cases and a poorer distribution by which to judge them.

Since this was a period of severe and widespread inflation, however, the inflationary rate, as far as can be determined, must be taken into account if the upward trend in dowries is to be properly understood. This is done in Table 15, which reduces dowries to their equivalent value in grain prices on the Paris market. Grain prices are not a perfect measure of inflation. Ideally, a standard index would include a variety of products, manufactured as well as foodstuffs. Such an index is not available for this period, however, while Micheline Baulant's tables of annual average wheat prices in the Paris Halles do provide consistent and reliable statistics on this one item.[49] Using the tables compiled by Baulant, the fifty-eight dowries used for Table 14 have been reduced to their equivalent in first quality wheat. To reduce the annual fluctuation produced by the hazards of drought, cold, and other circumstances only indirectly related to the general inflation, wheat prices used for these computations have been based on five-year moving averages, rather than on the annual figures in

[49] Baulant, "Prix des grains," p. 538.

Baulant's tables. Means and medians have then been calculated for these "wheat equivalents" to produce a table resembling Table 14 except that the dowries are expressed as sétiers of wheat rather than as livres tournois.

As Table 15 shows, the increase in the size of dowries is illusory, at least as compared to the inflation of grain prices. Indeed, there appears to have been a drop in the purchasing power of the average dowry given in middle-level officerial families between the first and second halves of the century and among the high officers between the third and fourth quarters of the century, although the relatively small number of cases makes these conclusions more tentative than one might like. Moreover, Baulant's research on prices of other commodities in sixteenth-century Paris suggests that wheat prices climbed more rapidly than any other items and, consequently, that deflation according to a "wheat standard" may be somewhat misleading.[50] While a certain amount of caution must go into the interpretation of these figures, it does appear from Table 15 that the increase in dowries was most probably a response to the general inflation of the period. Other factors—an increasing desire for social display, for example—may have entered into the picture, but economic factors alone appear to provide a sufficient explanation for the trend.

The effects of the inflation can, moreover, be seen on the level of individual families. Table 16 shows the rise in marriage portions in the family of the merchant Claude Le Prestre between the marriage of his first child in 1549 and his seventh in 1572. Expressing the dowries as grain parities does not prove them precisely equal, but it does diminish the difference between early dowries and later ones. In any event, perfect equality is not to be expected; Le Prestre's perception of the general rate of inflation would necessarily differ from the inflation charted in Baulant's tables of grain prices. Nevertheless, the relationship that emerges from these calculations suggests an attempt to take inflation into account in dowering the children.

[50] Baulant, "Prix et salaires," pp. 945-51.

TABLE 16
Dowries in the Family of the Merchant Claude Le Prestre, Adjusted for
Inflation

Marriage	Date	Marriage portion (£)	Average wheat price (£ per sétier) (5-yr. moving avge.)	Ratio
Daughter	1549	3,500	3.31	1,057
Son[a]	1556	4,000	3.86	1,036
Daughter	1558	6,000	4.12	1,456
Daughter	1563	6,000	5.68	1,056
Daughter	1565	6,000	7.31	821
Daughter	1569	7,500	6.60	1,136
Daughter	1572	8,000	10.11	791

SOURCE: AN, Min. cen. LIX:21 (9/8/99): *Inventaire après décès* of Marguerite Bastonneau.

[a] This is the sum Le Prestre gave his son toward his marriage, not the bride's dowry.

The question of how siblings were dowered is an important one. Unfortunately, relatively complete series of marriage contracts exist for only a few large families. In several families for which such series do exist, however, the pattern of marriage portions increasing gradually over time, without distinction between sons and daughters, is repeated. The merchant Nicolas Perrot, for example, gave £5,000 apiece to sons who married in 1552 and 1556, while a son and a daughter who married in 1559 each received £6,000.[51] In some families, the larger portions given younger children were offset by later donations to siblings already married. Louis Huault de Montmagny, for example, gave his eldest daughter £12,000 when she married in 1566; his second daughter received £13,000 in 1571, and his third £14,000 in 1573. In 1574, however, additional gifts were made to the older daughters to equalize their dowries with that of the younger one.[52]

[51] BN, P.o. 2242 Perrot à Paris, no. 8 (21/4/52): Perrot/Parent; no. 13 (22/11/56): Perrot/Boullenger; no. 19 (?/5/59): Perrot/Chouart; no. 20 (13/6/59): Croquet/Perrot.

[52] AN, Min. cen. VI:79 (17/12/77): *Inventaire après décès* of Louis Huault de Montmagny. Other examples of equalizing donations: BN, P.o. 1859

A majority of sons had already received at least one parental succession by the time they married, and it was consequently less common for sons to receive a major parental gift on the occasion of marriage than it was for daughters. Still, it would seem that there are some perceptible differences between the marriage portions that were given sons and those given daughters. It appears that a son, unless he was from a mercantile family, was more likely to receive property or annuities than a daughter, who was more likely to be given a flat cash sum. Sons of merchants, however, appear frequently to have received cash. This may be because cash was what a young merchant needed most, or it may be because mercantile wealth was more often liquid and less often invested in real properties than was the wealth of a royal officer or nobleman. Some sons of noblemen received control of noble estates at the time of their marriage; others did not receive the property but were guaranteed their rights to share eventually in the parental estate as eldest son and principal heir.[53] On the whole, however, it does not appear that marriage was the primary occasion for transferring their inheritance rights to sons.

Furthermore, it does not appear that marriage was often an occasion for inducing daughters to renounce their rights to succession, despite the customary laws permitting such a step. Only one of the marriage contracts I have found for the councillors' families entails the renunciation of a future succession, and that renunciation was voided less than six months after the wedding because of the great love and affection borne the bride by her grandmother and guardian.[54] The daughters of

---

de Marle, no. 170 (7/1/85): Marle/Rinces; AN, Y124, fol. 432v° (17/3/83): Hennequin/Bragelongne/Parent; AN, Y118, fol. 39v° (22/12/76): Marle/Le Maistre.

[53] Occasionally daughters also had clauses in their marriage contracts that guaranteed that none of the other children in the family would be given any unfair advantage in the succession, but these clauses were most often included for eldest sons of living parents. See, for example, AN, Y111, fols. 435v°-37v° (4/3/71): Dubois/Prudhomme; and Y111, fols. 155-56 (5/4/68): Neufville/Clausse; BN, Nouveau d'Hozier, 15 Aubery, fols. 4-4v° (7/9/70): Aubery/Vivien.

[54] AN, Y100, fols. 87-89v° (26/1/73); and Y115, fol. 11 (30/9/74).

another city councillor were apparently also compelled to renounce their rights to their mother's succession in their marriage contracts, but they too were later readmitted to the
inheritance.[55]

If renunciation of rights to succession does not often appear
in marriage contracts, explicit clauses allowing daughters to
return to their successions if they returned the dowry do.
Although it was not necessary after the codification of the
customary law in 1510 to state explicitly that a child might
return to the parental successions as long as any gifts were
returned or their value declared and deducted, many of the
marriage contracts involving couples who had living parents
do make this statement. Mentioning the right to return to
the succession may simply be a carry-over from the precodi-
fication period, when children who were dowered off could
not inherit without this explicit provision. It seems, however,
that a clause covering this point served several rather more
important functions. In the first place, it usually gave the
couple the option of returning to the succession or not. Although most jurists were of the opinion that this option was
already implicit in the Paris customs, the law was not clear
on this point, and the clause gave an added guarantee of
freedom of choice. Second, the clause could be used to extend
the right of return to properties lying outside the boundaries
of the Paris customs in areas where this right was not customarily extended. Third, the clause permitted parents to specify
what portion of the dowry was assigned on the estate of which
parent. The dowry of Radegonde Burdelot, for example, was
entirely derived from the estate of her deceased father. She
did not need to return any of it in order to partake of her
mother's inheritance.[56]

Parents could draw the dowry from whatever source they

[55] It is possible, though not proven, that the daughters were recalled by
their mother, Louise de Selve, the widow of Etienne de Montmirail, because of the death of their only brother, Lazare de Montmirail, whom the
renunciation would have been intended to benefit, in about 1570. Léon
Mirot, *Inventaire analytique des hommages rendus à la Chambre de France* (Melun, 1932-1945), nos. 957 and 958.
[56] BN, P.o. 1859 de Marle, no. 68 (3/2/26-27).

chose; it could even come out of the community property, if there were sufficient funds. The source from which the dowry was drawn was less significant than the fact that it could be returned in exchange for a share of the succession. Among the city councillors' families, the marriage portion was consistently seen as an advance on future successions and not a substitute for them. The stereotype of the daughter who was "dowered off" to preserve the patrimony for the sons merits reappraisal. Though this practice may have been common in other regions, other social groups, or at other times in history, it does not appear to have been a popular strategy for the protection of the patrimony among this mid-sixteenth-century Parisian elite.[57]

There is, however, one important way in which the marriage contracts of the city councillors' families commonly affected the distribution of the parental estates. This was in the insertion of a clause allowing a surviving parent to keep possession of the property of the deceased parent for his or her lifetime. As we have seen, customary law permitted a surviving parent, unless he or she remarried, to retain the community property of the deceased spouse. Aymar Nicolay and Anne Baillet put such a clause into the marriage contract of their son Antoine. Antoine received an annuity of £1,000 in advance of his inheritance and promised in return that as long as one or the other of his parents was living neither he nor his heirs would demand any of the movables or acquired immovables which his parents possessed. He would leave these properties to the surviving parent to enjoy.[58]

Some parents, however, went beyond the limits of the customary law by requiring that the dowered child promise to

---

[57] It does not appear to have been a popular strategy among Parisian families in the second half of the eighteenth century, either. Studying the marriage contracts of Parisian notaries in the second half of the eighteenth century, Jacques Le Lièvre failed to find *any* cases of daughters renouncing future successions upon receipt of their dowry (*La Pratique des contrats de mariage chez les notaires au Châtelet de Paris de 1789 à 1804* [Paris, 1959], pp. 74-75).

[58] AN, Y105, fols. 93-95 (2/1/52).

demand no accounting whatsoever of the estate of a deceased parent as long as one parent survived.[59] This was contrary to the customary law because a parent did not have any right to the deceased spouse's *propres*. An example of this sort of illegal clause can be seen in the contract for the marriage of Denise Perrot, in which she promised her mother and father that the survivor could retain all of her share of the properties, both movables and immovables, of the first to die.[60] Jacques Le Lièvre, studying notarial practice in the marriage contracts of eighteenth-century Parisians, found similar clauses in which parents claimed the right to retain each other's succession in its entirety. According to Le Lièvre, the right to retain only community property, as the law provided, was generally not respected. He points out the nullity of such clauses but adds that "the notaries seem to count on the *good faith* {his italics} and the loyalty of the dowered children."[61] The same appears true of the sixteenth-century Parisians studied here.

Almost unanimously, members of the city councillors' families allowed their properties to be regulated according to the community property laws of the Prévôté and Vicomté of Paris. Although some specified that properties outside the jurisdiction of the Prévôté of Paris should be divided according to the laws of the region in which they were located, most of these properties lay within the large central area of France in which community property laws closely resembled those of the capital.[62]

In the marriage contracts of the city councillors' families, the proportion of the dowry entering into the community

[59] AN, Y134, fol. 212 (20/12/94): Longueil/Selve; Y109, fols. 76v°-79 (14/8/68): Longueil/Montmirail; and Y131, fols. 73v°-75 (20/12/87): Luillier/d'O; Min. cen. LXXVII:30 (6/11/69): Hennequin/Le Grand. BN, P.o. 2242 Perrot à Paris, no. 7 (2/4/52) Perrot/Parent.

[60] BN, P.o. 2242 Perrot à Paris, no. 19 (?/5/59) Perrot/Choart.

[61] Le Lièvre, *Contrats de mariage*, pp. 72-74.

[62] See G. Fortin, *Conference de la coustume de Paris avec les autres coustumes de France* (Paris, 1651), pp. 171-74, for a comparison of Parisian laws on community property with laws of other regions. Even in written law areas, a couple could choose community property if they wished. Only the Norman law forbade it. See also Ferrière, *Parfait Notaire*, pp. 75-76.

property was determined more by agreement between the parties involved than by the nature of the funds or properties. If the dowry consisted mainly of real properties, it was necessary in the marriage contract to designate a share of these properties movables, so that sufficient funds would enter into the marital community to provide for the day-to-day household expenses. Often, however, particularly if at least one of the bride's parents was still living, the dowry consisted primarily of cash or other liquid assets rather than real properties. In this case, in order to prevent the liquid assets from entering the community, as would have happened under the customary law, the contract usually specified that a certain sum be employed in *rentes*, lands, or other investments and treated as *propres* of the bride.

The device of artificially creating *propres* was especially important for the protection of venal offices and *rentes constituées*, two forms of wealth common in elite families. Considered movables in Paris law prior to 1580, offices and *rentes* were nevertheless frequently designated *propres* in the marriage contracts of city councillor families, thus ensuring their return to the family of origin if the marriage produced no children. This device became unnecessary after the reformation of the laws in 1580. Legally designated immovables, offices and *rentes* were henceforth subject to the stricter rules that applied to the disposal and inheritance of real properties. [63]

In the contracts for the city councillors' families, the proportion of the dowry specified as *propres* of the bride varies

---

[63] N.C., arts. 93-95. The legal situation of *rentes* is complex in the sixteenth century. Annuities secured by alienation of land or houses (*rentes foncières*) were considered real property (*immeubles*) rather than movables (*meubles*) because the property transaction on which they were founded involved alienation of a real property. By extension, annuities produced by alienation of a sum of money in return for a perpetual income (*rentes constituées*) were also deemed immovables by the late sixteenth century. Art. 94 of the 1580 *Coutume* specified that *rentes constituées* were *immeubles* until repurchased, when they reverted to the status of *meubles*, unless belonging to a minor when repurchased or reemployed in other *rentes* or heritages, in which case they remained *immeubles*. The best work on the subject is Bernard Schnapper's *Les Rentes au xvi*ᵉ *siècle* (Paris, 1957).

from less than a third to more than three-fifths.[64] In many cases, it would appear that more than half the dowry became community property, a proportion well in excess of the quarter or third recommended in Ferrière's guide for notaries.[65] This was probably because the anticipated parental successions could be counted upon later to increase the wife's *propres*.

One can well imagine how a marriage contract generous in community properties but meager in *propres* might represent a compromise acceptable to both the potential husband and the parents of the bride (or the surviving parent, if one had died). The husband would receive a goodly sum on the eve of the marriage, a sum which, as community property, could be spent or invested as he pleased. The bride's father and mother, on the other hand, would retain control over the bulk of the *propres* throughout their lifetime. The husband's interest in the *propres* of his wife was not negligible, however. Far from it. The man whose wife brought seigneuries, houses, and other real properties to the marriage could enjoy the display that the bounty provided and even certain of the profits from these properties.[66] Though he could not dispose of the *propres* without his wife's consent, a husband who had his wife's confidence probably had little trouble securing this permission. As long as he could replace the *propres* if necessary, the husband would in practice have had considerable freedom to manipulate them as he chose. Indeed, a family could do little to protect a complaisant wife from a spendthrift husband, especially if he squandered his own properties along with hers.[67]

---

[64] Only cases in which the bride had at least one parent still living are considered here. If the parental successions had previously been divided, the total value of the properties brought to marriage is seldom indicated in these contracts.

[65] Ferrière, *Parfait Notaire*, p. 77.

[66] Lepointe, *Droit romain*, p. 375; "fruits" of the *propres* during marriage were considered *meubles*.

[67] AN, Y94, fol. 261 (16/3/49) recounts the complaints of the mother-in-law of Germain Teste, brother of the city councillor Simon Teste, against the way he squandered his estate and that of his wife and thereby caused his wife to die "desnuée de tous biens." Lehoux, "Simon Teste," pp. 150-

In an attempt to protect a wife's *propres*, a clause was often written into the marriage contract requiring the husband to reinvest any funds obtained from the sale of his wife's *propres* in *propres* of equivalent value. This clause was important because otherwise the money received for the *propres* would have been treated as movables, and even though the wife or her heirs were entitled to the value of the sale, the special protection given *propres* would have been lost. It was further specified that if this reinvestment had not occurred by the death of one of the spouses the surviving wife or the heirs of a deceased spouse could recuperate the value of her *propres* from the community property. If the community property did not suffice, the remainder could be taken from the husband's *propres*—providing, of course, that enough of his *propres* remained to make up the losses.

A wife who wished to put a stop to a husband's squandering of her *propres* could resort to the law. If she could prove her charges, she might be granted a legal separation of property (*séparation des biens*), which would allow her to administer her own business affairs (though she still could not alienate her *propres* without permission from her husband).[68] Still, if a husband could not or would not make good his wife's losses, she had little recourse. If the husband had blatantly violated any laws protecting her property, a legal suit was possible, but few families would have welcomed the public scandal that would have inevitably ensued.

In order to protect a daughter's *propres* from possible misuse (as well, of course, as to continue to enjoy these properties themselves), cautious parents might have sought to convince the potential son-in-law not to demand too much in the way of *propres* at the time of marriage, offering as recompense a generous sum toward the community property.[69] In order,

---

53, gives further details on Germain Teste, including the fact that he served a prison term for debt and fraud.

[68] Lepointe, *Droit romain*, pp. 385-87.

[69] Pierre Croquet used a different solution to the same problem. He specified in his daughter's marriage contract that he retained the manage-

then, to reassure the potential husband that the daughter's expectations of future inheritances were justified, marriage contracts not infrequently included clauses specifying a certain sum that the daughter and her husband could later take from the parental estate if they chose to abstain from the succession. These clauses guaranteed that the inheritance would provide an acceptable supplement to the dowry. Thus, for example, Jeanne Le Viste promised her daughter, Marie Robertet, and son-in-law, André Guillart, £18,000 cash (one-third of which was to be designated *propres*) on the eve of their wedding plus an additional annuity of £800 (equal to £9,600 at the current interest rate) on her death. If Marie and André chose, however, they could return the dowry on her death and share in Jeanne Le Viste's succession according to customary law.[70] The promise of the £800 annuity was thus merely a guarantee of a minimum sum to be received later.

Over the course of time, Parisians worked out an ingenious way to protect the large sums that went into the community property as well as the *propres* of daughters given in marriage. As we have seen, the customary law allowed a widow to renounce her rights to the community property, taking only her *propres* and the dower her husband accorded her. Though this right was not automatically extended to commoners in the Prévôté of Paris until 1580, it was usually written into marriage contracts of commoners and nobles alike throughout the century. By the second half of the century, however, the right to the retrieval of marriage portions was very often extended to allow a widow or her heirs to reclaim not only her *propres* but a major share or even all of her dowry and any later gifts and inheritances that had come to her. The contract for the marriage of Jacques de Longueil and Catherine de Montmirail in 1568, for example, specified that Catherine, if

---

ment of the *propres* he gave her for her marriage as long as he lived (BN, P.o. 2242 Perrot à Paris, no. 20 [13/6/59]).

[70] AN, Y97, fol. 440v° (8/7/51): Robertet/Guillart; similarly, BN, P.o. 1859 de Marle, nos. 106-12 (4/6/65): Marle/Vielpont; AN, Y105, fols. 93-95 (2/1/52): Nicolay/Luillier; and Y134, fols. 212-13v° (20/12/94): Selve/ Longueil.

she outlived Jacques, could renounce her right to the community property and take back the entire £15,000 her father gave her as a dowry, along with any immovables she later acquired by inheritance, without being held responsible for any of the debts charged against the marital community.[71] Without this provision, Catherine would have been entitled, according to the customary law to only £6,000, the value of the *propres* designated in her dowry, plus any *propres* later received from parental successions, had she chosen to renounce her right to the community property. Any collateral successions would have fallen into the community property unless they had been specifically designated as *propres*. Because it guaranteed that a woman could take out of a marriage virtually everything she brought to it, a clause such as this was of tremendous significance.

A distinction was usually made between the rights accorded a woman who outlived her husband, with or without progeny, and the rights accorded the heirs of a woman who predeceased her husband and left no progeny. Whereas the widow was frequently allowed to take back all of her dowry and inheritances, the heirs of a married woman who died childless were in general allowed by the marriage contract to reclaim only a part of the dowry, though still more than that portion allotted them by customary law. A part of the dowry— anywhere from about 10% to about 40%—was retained by the husband. Apparently it was considered only fair that if the marriage failed in its reproductive purpose the wife's family foot the bill for her room and board and for the expenses of the marriage.[72] These clauses, however, did recognize a family's right to get back more than the often minimal *propres* stipulated in the dowry in the event that no direct heirs were

---

[71] AN, Y109, fols. 76v°-79 (14/8/68). Comparable clauses can be found in the majority of contracts for the second half of the sixteenth century.

[72] For example, if Anne Luillier outlived her husband, Jacques d'O, seigneur du Baillet, she could take back the entire 10,000 écus she brought to the marriage; on the other hand, if she died first, her heirs were entitled to only 6,000 écus (AN, Y131, fols. 73v°-75 [26/12/87]).

produced by the match and thus prevented the passage of her properties to her husband's line.

Whereas a wife who survived her husband virtually always was accorded her customary right to accept the community property if she chose, her heirs if she died childless were frequently denied this right. Thus, in the contract of Jacques de Longueil and Catherine de Montmirail, it was specified that if Catherine died childless, Jacques would return £12,000 of the £15,000 given Catherine in marriage and be quit of any debts to her family. In this case, it does not appear that either Catherine's heirs or Jacques had any option in the disposition of the community property if she died childless. Much of the time, however, the option to return the properties of a childless wife rather than to share the community property with her heirs rested with the surviving husband; occasionally it was the heirs who had the option. In any event, the principle of separation of properties underlies all of these possibilities. The party who retained the option had, of course, a certain advantage. Nevertheless, a wife's family was likely to be more interested in ensuring the recovery of the funds invested in the fruitless marriage than in the possibility of making a profit off the match. The husband's position would probably depend on where he saw his own advantage. The right to return a wife's dowry, or most of her dowry, rather than allowing her heirs to share in the community goods can be seen as the counterpart of the wife's right to renounce the common property. Just as a widow might wish to avoid responsibility for any losses incurred by her husband's mismanagement of the marital community, so a widower might wish to deny his wife's family the profits made from its effective management.

The provisions regarding the separation of properties when a childless marriage ended, then, varied according to the individual contract. Each family sought to protect its own interests, but the specific way in which this was done depended on the value and nature of the properties involved. Special arrangements for the break-up of the community property of marriages that failed to produce heirs became increasingly common as the century progressed. Marriage became less an affair of common custom and more one of private contract.[73]

It should be pointed out, however, that although regulating the financial relationship in marriage more explicitly through their contractual agreements than did the customary law, the city councillors and their families were not trying to subvert the law. The special provisions they added were not in conflict with its underlying principles. Community property, for example, had always been negotiable in the Parisian law. Besides, the community property laws were intended to benefit primarily the married couple and their descendants, not collaterals or ascendants who happened to inherit because the marriage was childless. The principle of separation of properties was already an important one in the local customs. The actions of the city councillors' families carried these principles further; they did not violate them. In theory, separation of properties was effected through the laws defining *propres* and the requirement that they always be passed to the nearest heir of the bloodline from which the property originated. In practice, however, and primarily because of the nature of the wealth given in dowries, the laws regarding *propres* had no longer seemed sufficient to protect a family's investment in marriage. It had thus proved useful to tamper with the meaning of *propres*, separating the concept from its original identification with immovable family properties by artificially creating *propres* from *meubles* and, conversely, allowing specified real properties to be treated as *meubles*. With the addition of the complex clauses we have been considering, a family could prevent properties given a daughter in marriage from falling into other hands without sacrificing the basic system of community property.

Designation of artificial *propres* could, of course, also be used to protect the properties a man brought to marriage. A second way to protect the husband's properties was to employ

---

[73] Lepointe, *Droit romain*, p. 380, draws a similar conclusion.

the fixed dower. It will be recalled that a wife had a right to the usufruct of one-half of her husband's *propres* to support her during widowhood, unless her marriage contract assigned her instead a fixed sum or annuity. Among the councillors' families, it would appear that throughout the century the fixed dower was the rule and the customary dower the exception. Virtually every contract gave at least the option of a fixed dower, usually an annuity, and only about a quarter of the contracts allowed a widow the option of a customary dower. Although there was a wide range in the value of the fixed dowers assigned in the marriage contracts of the city councillors' families, a dower equal to approximately one-third of the dowry was the most common practice.[74] The fixed dower in the city councillors' families nearly always consisted of an annuity rather than a lump sum, but the possibility to repurchase the annuity was usually stipulated.[75] Occasionally a widow was allowed to pass a fixed dower on to her own heirs if there were no children born of her marriage, but in the great majority of cases the dower, whether fixed or customary, returned to the husband's nearest relatives on the widow's death, as the law provided.

The advantage of the fixed dower was that it did not weigh solely on a man's *propres*, as the customary dower did. A man's heirs could pay the widow's dower out of the deceased's share of the community property, their own movables, or any other source they chose rather than leaving the widow in possession of half the *propres* of the deceased. Even though these properties would be returned on the widow's death, the family of

---

[74] In fifty-seven marriage contracts for which the proportion of dower to dowry can be calculated, the mean was 38%, the median 33%. Forty-two percent of the contracts had a dower that was between 30% and 35% of the total dowry. Natalie Davis has found that, similarly, the "normal" dower in Lyons in the sixteenth century was one-third of the dowry. An individual could alter this in either direction in a marriage contract, but changes were made with an awareness of the norm.

[75] Seventy-seven dowers were given as *rentes constitutées* or *foncières*, five as lump sums. Repurchase was usually at the *denier douze* (twelve times the annual rate), as was common with *rentes* at the time, but there were exceptions in both directions.

a man who died childless might wish to ensure their more immediate return. Consider, for example, how galling it would have been for a man to watch the widow of an older brother who had died childless and young live out her long life in the manor house that was his own proper inheritance. She might remarry and bear another man's children there, and he could do nothing but wait.[76]

The fact that the customary dower might someday be claimed encumbered half of a man's lineage properties, hindering his freedom to dispose of his properties and otherwise manipulate his wealth in search of better investments. To the parent who feared a careless son might dissipate his patrimony, the restriction imposed by the customary dower was of course an advantage. The very intention of the dower, as evidenced by the fact that it was given to the wife only as usufruct but to the children as *propres*, was the conservation of family properties. To the man who wanted not only to conserve his estate but to use his resources and extend his fortune, however— and we must number the larger part of the civic elite in this group—this was precisely its disadvantage.

When it was permitted at all by the marriage contract, the customary dower was often subject to restrictions. For example, although a widow's dower right was not normally lost by remarriage, Madeleine de Montmirail was allowed the customary dower only so long as she remained a widow. She was, moreover, allowed only the fixed dower if there were children living when her husband died.[77] Denise de Neufville and Marie Hennequin were likewise allowed the customary

[76] Olivier-Martin, in *Histoire de la coutume*, 2:286, sees less sympathy for dowers in the sixteenth century than in earlier centuries. As reasons for this disfavor he cites the influence of Roman law, which did not know the dower, as well as the inequity of the dower right's being continued despite remarriage. There was also criticism that husbands, eager to please their wives and knowing that they would personally never have to pay the dower, were overly generous in these settlements in marriage contracts, leaving unreasonable burdens on the patrimony.

[77] AN, Y112, fols. 302v°-303v° (16/9/71): Champront/Montmirail.

dower only if childless.[78] The reasoning presumably was that the customary dower might interfere with the full enjoyment of inheritance rights by any children of the union. Other families reasoned differently, denying the right of customary dower to a childless widow but permitting it to a widow with children, reasoning perhaps that the widow with children could be expected to administer her dower with the best interests of her children—the eventual heirs to the property—in mind.[79]

The controls placed on dowers, like the controls placed on dowries, thus varied from contract to contract. What is clear, however, in all of these various aspects of marriage contracts is the careful consideration and, one must imagine, the serious negotiation that went into them. Extending and adapting the local customary law to their own needs, the city councillors' families found ways to preserve the principle of community property that was traditional in the Paris customs while at the same time ensuring that the lineage properties of the two families brought together in marriage would not be confounded, dissipated, or appropriated by those who had no legitimate claim to them. In the complex maze of clauses that make up the marriage contracts of the Parisian elite, we find the best evidence of their understanding of the nature of this alliance and its ultimate aim, the protection and extension of the family's name and patrimony.

[78] AN, Y111, fols. 133-36 (3/4/68). Neufville/Clausse, AN, Min. cen. VII:47 (28/1/91): Hennequin/Le Fevre.

[79] For example, AN, Y110, fols. 63-65v° (7/8/69): Hennequin/Hennequin; Y131, fols. 73v°-75 (20/12/87): Luillier/d'O.

8. Inheritance: Dividing the Family Estate

Car amour descent aux enfans
Des peres, beau filz, or m'entens:
L'amour aux peres ne remonte
Des enfans.
—Eustache Deschamps

WHEN A MEMBER of the Parisian elite died, the funeral was traditionally celebrated with great pomp. Members of the household were outfitted with new mourning clothes, masses were said, candles were lit, and alms were distributed to the poor. A cortege, which usually included representatives of the mendicant orders, children from local orphanages, and poor people who mourned professionally for a few sous, as well as friends and family, followed the casket to the cemetery or church where the deceased was laid to rest among the tombs of his ancestors.[1] If the deceased was a city councillor, the members of the Bureau de la Ville were expected to take part as a company in the cortege, and a dozen torches emblazoned with the city arms were borne aloft to show the respect due the city's officers. If he was as important a man as Christophe de Thou, one might have found the king himself among the spectators to the procession.[2]

When death took the head of the household, a private rit-

[1] Typical testaments setting out funeral observances: AN, Min. cen. III:100 (10/11/60): *Testament* of Cosme Luillier, Seigneur de Saulsay; BN, P.o. 547 Budé, nos. 80-96 (28/3/1600): *Testament* of Marye Nepveu, widow of Dreux Budé.

[2] On the city corps: *Reg. BV*, 5:78 (19/11/60). The city officers were rebuked for having failed to turn out for the funeral of Cosme Luillier. On the funeral of de Thou: Pasquier, *Lettres*, bk. 7, letter 10; L'Estoile, *Journal pour le règne de Henri III*, pp. 309-311.

ual of great importance followed the public ceremonies, as the heirs gathered around the locked chest in which the family papers were kept to discover the estate that was to be theirs.[3] This scene of the heirs gathered around the family papers may be said to symbolize the inheritance process in the Paris region. The process that began with the opening of the locked chest ended with the heirs assembled once again for the final signing of the papers that formalized the divisions of property. These papers then joined the other important documents under lock and key, and all passed into the safekeeping of the senior heir.

There were other ways that the division of the patrimony could take place. An individual could dispose of his or her estate personally through lifetime gifts or, within limits, through testamentary bequests. The choice between lifetime partition of one's property and post-mortem succession was an important one in Parisian law, for it was to a large degree a choice between naming one's own heirs and allowing them to be named by custom. At the heart of this choice lay the now familiar tension between favoritism and equality, between the belief that the family resources should be concentrated in but a few hands and the belief that siblings should be treated similarly. In order to understand the dilemma this choice posed and why post-mortem succession was ultimately preferred among the city councillors, we must look more closely at the letter of the law, its spirit, and its application in the families of the city councillors.

The Laws of Inheritance

As we have seen, the freedom of the individual to dispose of family properties was closely regulated by customary law because of the firm conviction that properties inherited from one's parents belonged less to the individual than to the fam-

---

[3] Boislisle, *Nicolay*, no. 173: note on succession of Anne Baillet (11/10/83); BN, MSS DuPuy, no. 615: *Mémoires de Mr Philippes Hurault, Evesque de Chartres*, fol. 14v°.

ily line—past, present, and future. The rules controlling the succession of children to their parents' estates were especially clearly defined. The basic premise of these laws was equality, although the eldest son was allowed a certain advantage, called a *droit d'aînesse*, where noble properties were concerned. According to the Paris customary law, nonnoble properties transmitted by direct succession were to be divided equally among the heirs. Parents were forbidden to employ donations, testaments, or contracts to favor one of the heirs over his siblings.[4] Noble properties were so divided that the eldest son received two-thirds if there was but one other heir or one-half if there were two or more other heirs. A single younger sibling received the remaining third of the noble properties; if there were more younger siblings than one, they shared equally in the remaining half of the noble property.[5] The eldest son also received a special share of the noble properties in the succession of each parent called a *préciput*, which consisted of the principal manor house, its garden, and a piece of adjoining land of roughly an acre.[6] Except for these special privileges given the eldest son in the inheritance of noble properties, daughters and sons had equal rights in their parents' successions.

As in most legal systems, however, there were ways to avoid even those restrictions that were apparently the most rigid. Many of the restrictions applied only to post-mortem divisions of property; donations (*donations à vie*) could be made with more freedom to individuals who did not stand to inherit, and some properties could be disposed of by testamentary bequest. With a special knack for arguing all sides of an issue, Parisian lawyers and commentators on the customary law attempted to justify both the apparent inflexibility of the

---

[4] N.C., arts. 302 and 303.

[5] N.C., arts. 15 and 16. It is important to note that it was the noble status of the properties and not the person that counted for successions.

[6] N.C., art. 14. Article 17, however, guaranteed that the eldest son owed his younger siblings recompense if the *préciput* absorbed the family's heritage to the point that the younger children were deprived of the minimum share the law guaranteed them. This article was new in the 1580 *Coutume*.

rules of succession and the acknowledged loopholes in these laws. The basic rule that children should share equally was said to promote harmony among siblings, while the privileges of the eldest in noble families were held to serve as a necessary bulwark to preserve the greatness of families on which the crown most depended.[7] The right to evade the rule of equality among siblings was justified as the natural prerogative of parents to demonstrate a special preference for the most deserving of their children.[8]

The testament, the principal instrument of inheritance in areas like southern France where the influence of Roman law was strong, was not favored in the Paris area. The Paris law allowed only limited testamentary bequests. A person could dispose as he pleased of all personal property and all real property that he had himself acquired in his testament, but he could dispose freely of only one-fifth of the real properties he had inherited or received from lineal relations as gifts or legacies (*propres*). The remaining four-fifths of the *propres*, called the *réserve héréditaire*, had to be divided among the nearest relations according to the rules of intestate succession.[9] While a man whose wealth was largely self-acquired could allocate most of it as he chose by means of testamentary bequests, a man whose wealth was largely inherited found his liberty to dispose of it severely restricted by these rules. He could gain more liberty by a process known as "declassifying" *propres*. This was the exchange of family properties for properties of comparable value, which by virtue of the exchange would no

[7] Tronçon, *Droict françois*, pp. 654-55, is typical of the attitude toward equality of heirs. Filhol, *Christofle de Thou*, p. 171, credits Tiraqueau with removing the droit d'aînesse from the sphere of strictly feudal law by justifying it according to the principle of conservation of families. Cujas, cited in Louet, *Arrests*, 1:406, also defended the advantages of the eldest son on the ground that he is the perpetuator of the family name.

[8] Typical again is Tronçon, *Droict françois*, p. 657, though he does warn elsewhere (p. 655) that the right to favor one child should be used prudently.

[9] N.C., art. 292. See also Olivier-Martin, *Histoire de la coutume*, 2:316-17.

longer have been considered *propres*.[10] Such a procedure might have been useful for certain types of *propres*—*rentes* and minor properties, for example—but to trade away the lands and manors that constituted the family's principal heritage just in order to dispose of the wealth as one wished would have been so contrary to the best interests of the family that it was seldom if ever employed. Moreover, this maneuver was sometimes prevented by conditions laid down when the *propres* were acquired. Marriage contracts and donations often included a clause specifying that the *propres*, if alienated, had to be replaced by properties of equal value that were subsequently to be treated as *propres*. The use of testaments to avoid the customary rules of succession was also restricted by a law that forbade a legatee from being simultaneously an heir of the estate.[11] A favored child bequeathed the disposable share of the estate could not share with the other heirs in the *réserve*.

With respect to donations, the revised laws of 1580 gave children explicitly the option of retaining donations made in advance of parental succession and then abstaining from the succession.[12] As was previously pointed out, this option was not mentioned in the codification of 1510, but most jurists accepted it as implicit in the statements against forced heirship.[13] In any event, parents could—and frequently did— offer this option in marriage contracts and other donations of property. If the child chose instead to share in the parental succession, the return of all lifetime donations was required.

The freedom to dispose of family properties through lifetime donations was limited, however, by the *légitime*, which guaranteed the children in a family a minimum share in the parental properties. According to the revised laws of 1580, each child was legally entitled to one-half the share that he or she would have had in the estate of a parent or other

---

[10] Ralph E. Giesey, "Rules of Inheritance and Strategies of Mobility in Prerevolutionary France," *American Historical Review* 82 (1977):276 and 276n.

[11] N.C., art. 300; A.C., art. 121.

[12] N.C., art. 307.

[13] See chapter 7, nn. 38 and 39.

ascendant if there had been no donations, testamentary bequests, or other special dispositions of property beyond the payment of the debts and funeral expenses of the deceased.[14] For example, if a man had three children, the légitime of each was one-sixth of his total estate minus his debts and funeral expenses.

The légitime, derived from Roman law, was a new development in sixteenth-century customary law. Introduced into the customary law of Chartres, Sens, and other areas near Paris in the first decades of the sixteenth-century, it was officially incorporated in the Paris laws in 1548 as a result of a special *enquête par turbe* (an inquest that was the traditional method of determining customary practice) conducted by the Parlement of Paris.[15] According to the sixteenth-century jurist Charles Du Moulin, the légitime was introduced in recognition of the need to make sure that all of the children of a family were treated fairly. In the opinion of the legal historian François Olivier-Martin, it was primarily designed to limit the prerogatives of the eldest son in noble inheritances where the *préciput* due the firstborn would have absorbed the whole of the estate (where, for example, the entire inheritance consisted of one manor house).[16]

Whatever the original intention of the légitime, it is not clear whether this device was beneficial or inimical to the portion of the younger children in the long run. It did guarantee that younger children would not be deprived of a share in the parental estate. In practice, however, it may have tended to reduce the share normally allotted to the younger children by creating a new idea of the "rights" of each child that

[14] N.C., arts. 298 and 307.
[15] Olivier-Martin, "Manuscrits de Simon Marion," p. 169.
[16] Olivier-Martin, *Histoire de la coutume*, 2:362; Filhol, *Christofle de Thou*, p. 178. The laws of many regions ran contrary to the reformed law of Paris on this latter point, however, preferring the rights of the firstborn to those of his younger siblings. According to Louet, *Arrests*, 1:406, although it seems rigorous and contrary to the laws of equity thus to favor the eldest, this is justified according to "une raison politique, que le nom, l'éclat, la splendeur, la dignité de la famille se conserve et se perpetuë en la personne des aisnez."

differed from the older customary ideas of equality and primogeniture. To the extent that people came to believe that they had fulfilled their obligation to the younger children by allowing them their légitime instead of their customary inheritance, the tradition of equality and consequently the position of the younger children deteriorated.

Even before the introduction of the légitime, the dower rights of the children ensured that each had some claim on the paternal estate. A child could, if he chose, renounce his succession and claim instead a share of the douaire promised his mother in her marriage contract. Whether or not this was a wise move depended upon the size of the dower if the dower was fixed, the value of the inherited real properties in the paternal estate if the dower was customary, and the extent of the debts on the estate. It also depended upon the child's position in the family, for there was no droit d'aînesse on the dower. If there were three children in the family and their mother had been given the customary dower, the dower right of each child was equal to one-sixth of the father's *propres*. This could be less than the same child's légitime, which was equal to one-sixth of the acquired real properties and movables as well as one-sixth of the *propres*. On the other hand, if there were large debts outstanding on the estate, it could be more. Unlike the légitime, which was calculated after the payment of debts, the dower rights of the wife and children took precedence over all other claims on the estate. The children of a spendthrift might have been well advised to choose the dower over the légitime.[17]

The rules of succession for grandchildren were modeled on those of parental succession. Articles 138 of the codification of 1510 and 319 of the revised codification of 1580 permitted children who outlived a parent to succeed in the place of the parent to the grandparental estate. The grandchildren, said to "represent" their deceased parent, divided among themselves the portion that would have devolved upon the parent

[17] Pasquier, *Justinien*, pp. 357-58, discusses a lawsuit involving dower rights claimed by the son of the city councillor Olivier Du Drac de Beaulieu.

they represented according to the normal rules of direct succession.[18] The right to *représentation* was new in the 1510 codification of the law. Previously it had been necessary to insert into a child's marriage contract the right of grandchildren to represent their parents in the grandparental successions.[19] Du Moulin and other sixteenth-century jurists argued in favor of the inclusion of representation clauses in the reform of customary laws that did not already contain them on the grounds of common justice, but Du Moulin also slyly pointed out that the absence of a representation clause furthered parental authority by discouraging children from marrying without parental approbation.[20] Although there is some merit in Du Moulin's argument, the representation clause did have one rather serious flaw as a weapon against a rebellious child: if a representation clause was written into the marriage contract of one child, all of the siblings of that child were legally entitled to the same right.[21] It might thus be argued that the representation clause better served the function of ensuring the equality than the exclusion of heirs.

On the other hand, the 1510 article on representation altered customary practice in favor of the descendants of the eldest son by allowing them the right to their father's droit d'aînesse.[22] Prior to 1510 children permitted to represent their parents in the grandparental succession were denied this right.[23]

[18] Bourdot de Richebourg, *Coutumier*, 3:23.

[19] Olivier Martin, "Travaux préparatoires," p. 116. Articles 131 and 133 of the procès-verbal of the commission that met in 1507 to begin codification of the customary law show the old state of the law. The manuscript, however, suggests that these laws were not commonly observed.

[20] Filhol, *Christofle de Thou*, pp. 225-35. According to Filhol, this note appears in the customary laws of Auxerre, Amiens, the Boulenois, Hainault, and others. Representation clauses figured in the marriage contracts of several city councillors, probably because these families had properties in regions that did not yet automatically allow representation. See, for example, AN, Y105, fols. 93-95 (2/1/52): Nicolay/Luillier.

[21] Bourdot de Richebourg, *Coutumier*, 3:23.

[22] The eldest son of the eldest son in turn claimed a droit d'aînesse on the father's share. If the eldest son left only daughters, they could still claim the droit d'aînesse due their father, but they divided it among themselves without reference to age. A.C., arts. 134 and 139; N.C., arts. 314 and 324. See also Lepointe, *Droit romain*, p. 445.

[23] Olivier-Martin, "Manuscrits de Simon Marion," pp. 180-81.

Instead they shared equally in the estate with surviving aunts and uncles or the children who represented them. The inclusion of a droit d'aînesse in the 1510 article on representation suggests an increased interest in protecting noble estates from the abrupt fragmentation that might otherwise have been caused by the premature death of the eldest son.

Collateral succession differed from direct succession in several respects. In the first place, a distinction was made between the heirs to the *propres* and the heirs to the personal property and acquired real property. The nearest collaterals of the same degree shared equally the personal and acquired properties, while the *propres* could go only to collaterals of the same line as the person who had originally acquired the property. The provenance of each inherited property thus dictated its heirs, according to the principle of *paterna paternis, materna maternis* (that which comes from the paternal line returns to the paternal line; that which comes from the maternal line returns to the maternal line).[24] The second difference was the way in which noble properties were divided. While nonnoble properties were divided equally among the heirs of like degree regardless of sex, in the partition of noble properties, males inherited to the exclusion of females of like degree. Brothers inherited to the exclusion of sisters, nephews to the exclusion of nieces, and so forth. There was no right of representation in collateral inheritance—sisters succeeded before the sons of deceased brothers, nieces before the sons of deceased nephews[25]—nor was there a droit d'aînesse in collateral successions. Male heirs shared the noble properties equally. According to jurists, this was because a decedent who left no direct heirs had been free during his lifetime to make gifts of his properties to collateral relatives if he so desired.[26] The laws that prevented parents from favoring one of their children did not apply to collateral relatives. There was, for example, no requirement of *rapport* attached to collateral inher-

---

[24] N.C., arts. 325, 327-28; A.C., arts. 145-57.
[25] N.C., arts. 320 and 331; A.C., art. 149.
[26] Lepointe, *Droit romain*, p. 448.

itances, so the recipient of gifts from a brother, uncle, or other collateral could still be an heir to the estate.[27] Because collateral inheritances could be manipulated more freely than direct inheritances, they could play an important part in a family's management of its wealth.

Although collateral inheritance thus differed in many respects from the distribution of properties to direct heirs in the Paris customary law, the fundamental principles underlying collateral and direct inheritance were the same. In both cases, the heirs had equal rights to nonnoble properties, while males were favored in the inheritance of noble properties, and in both cases, the provenance of inherited properties determined their distribution. Moreover, these fundamental principles remained unchanged despite modifications made in inheritance laws by the codification of 1510 and the reformation of 1580. The right of dowered children to return to the parental succession and the right of grandchildren to represent their parents in the grandparental succession, for example, were incorporated into the law in 1510 as extensions of the principle of equality. The right of a child to a share in the family properties was considered to extend past marriage and even death, when it passed intact to any living descendants. Furthermore, inclusion of the rights of *rapport* and *représentation* changed the law without necessarily altering the common practice. Indeed, because the very basis of the customary law was common practice, the law could not have been changed without a prior change of practice.

The Estates of the City Councillors

Documents concerning the successions of the city councillors reveal some of the complexity of the problems inherent in the partition of the patrimony. Although notarial records enable us to go beyond legal theory and to reach at least a partial understanding of the use to which the laws of inher-

[27] N.C., art. 301.

itance were put, we are prevented from making a quantitative evaluation of the inheritance practices of the city councillors' families by the paucity and the frequent ambiguity of available sources.

The basic documents concerning the division of estates, the *partages*, are frequently incomplete and misleading.[28] They often include only real properties, although inventories after death show that wealthy Parisian families normally possessed cash, jewelry, tapestries, and other personal property of considerable value. Furthermore, the *partages* do not always specify the value of properties returned to the succession, listing only the difference between the value of the properties advanced to each child. Children who did not return to the succession are not mentioned, nor is mention usually made of *partages* involving other properties from the same estate. Different types of property and properties in different regions were frequently divided in separate *partages*, and the researcher can seldom be confident that all of the relevant documents have been found. Thus, the full value of the estate cannot usually be computed, and without a knowledge of the full value of the estate, it is of course impossible to judge the equity of its distribution.

The alternative to post-mortem succession, the partition of the estate during the lifetime of the parent, is even more difficult to evaluate with respect to the size of the estate and the equity of distribution. When properties were divided by gift, the value of the properties was not normally included in the conveyance. Indeed, in some lifetime *partages*, such as that made by André Guillart among his three children, only the properties given the younger children were identified. A blanket statement assigned the remainder to the eldest as his droit d'aînesse.[29] It can never be assumed, moreover, that such di-

[28] Giesey, "Rules of Inheritance," p. 288n, citing Jean Meyer (*La Noblesse bretonne* [Paris, 1966], 1:128), suggests that the records of successions may have been deliberately kept evasive and incomplete in order to protect family privacy.

[29] AN, Y107, fols. 245-48 (21/9/66): *partage* of André Guillart, Seigneur du Mortier.

visions of property were the final word. Though it was in theory impossible to revoke these donations, there were grounds on which a revocation could be—and was—justified.

Marie de Dormans, for example, revoked the donation of property that she had made to her son Jacques de Longueil at the time of his marriage when she discovered that he had conspired with his sister and brother-in-law to benefit himself and them at the expense of the heirs of her eldest son. According to Marie's statement of revocation, Jacques had convinced her that the children of her deceased firstborn had benefited unduly in the succession of their grandfather, Marie's husband. In order to make up for this, Marie was coaxed by Jacques, his sister and brother-in-law, and his future father-in-law to increase Jacques's marriage portion through a donation of all of her acquired real property. Marie made the donation, but a year later she discovered that Jacques and his sister had agreed to split between them any donations she made. The pleas Jacques's sister and her husband had made on his behalf had thus in fact been for their own financial benefit as well as his. Denouncing this deceit, Marie stated that she had always loved her children equally and intended for them all to come equally to her succession according to the customs of the region. She then revoked the donation and guaranteed the children of her eldest son their legal share of her estate.[30]

Receipt of further gifts or the decision to return to the succession could also alter the effect of a donation, as could the decision of other heirs to challenge the donation in court. As André Guillart recognized (he had himself engaged in years of lawsuits with his brother and sister over the parental estate), it was quite possible that the division of property ordered in the *partage* would not hold up if one of the children applied instead for his customary share of the estate.[31]

[30] Marie was justified in her accusation of conspiracy. A week before the wedding contract was signed, Jacques, his sister, and his brother-in-law Nicolas Berruyer signed a notarized agreement to divide between them any future donations made to either by their mother. AN, Y109, fols. 59/60 (6/8/68); Y109, fols. 76-79 (14/8/68); Y109, fols. 261-62v° (12/2/69).

[31] AN, Y107, fols. 245-48 (21/9/66). André Guillart's partage made pro-

Whatever the difficulties in assessing the records of inheritance practice in the city councillors' families, it is clear that the rules of intestate succession prescribed by the customary law were favorably viewed and commonly followed.[32] Letters and memoirs as well as legal documents express a preference for intestate succession and, except for the special rights of the eldest, equality of heirs. Demographic realities also favored customary, post-mortem *partages*. Large lifetime donations appear to have seldom been made to children who were not yet grown, and the high mortality rate deprived many children of their parents at an early age. In most cases, the estate of a parent who died young was held in trust by the surviving parent and/or other guardians and then divided according to custom at a later date.

The *partages* for the city councillors' estates confirm, moreover, that if a person did not act during his lifetime to avoid the rigid rules of the customary law his estate was fairly and impartially divided after his death. The *partages* were the work of professionals, who assessed the value of the real and personal property of the deceased and divided it into lots. Marriage portions and gifts were scrupulously accounted for, and except for the share of noble properties given the eldest son, all of the lots were equal. The traditional practice was to bring a small child in off the street to draw the lots that

---

vision for the younger children to get the légitime if the *partage* was broken, but he added that he did not wish that to happen. See also BN, 4° Fm 14302, Simon Marion, *Factums et mémoires*. Collection de factums, fols. 111-31.

[32] Though only a handful of complete *partages* have been recovered for the city councillors' families, it has been possible to determine through extracts included in marriage contracts and other family papers that the properties of many if not most city councillors on all social levels were in fact divided according to post-mortem *partages* to which all the living descendants reported. For example, AN, M622, Dossier d'O (2/10/64): extract of *partage* of Nicolas de Livres and Marie Du Drac (original no longer extant); BN, D.b. 354 Hennequin, fol. 187v° (18/5/59): extract of *partage* of properties left by Oudart Hennequin and Jeanne Michon, with reference to *partage* of 31/7/58; BN, P.o. 1718 Lièvre, nos. 286-87 (18/2/58 to 27/4/60): procès-verbaux regarding estate division of Charlotte Menisson, widow of Claude Le Lievre.

assigned the shares to their respective heirs, but sometimes the heirs simply agreed among themselves who got which lot. In either event, the law was respected.[33]

The division of the estate of Guillaume de Courlay illustrates the process involved. Two appraisers spent three days evaluating the properties left by Courlay and his wife and dividing the office, *rentes*, and lands the couple had owned into three lots for Courlay's three children. According to the *partage*, the lots were to be "the most just and equal possible." In the course of their task, the appraisers visited all of the houses and outbuildings the family owned in the vicinity of Vitry, south of Paris. The boundaries and area of each piece of arable soil were recorded and, in order to determine the proper value of these fields, local peasants were consulted. The Courlay children also had a say in the appraisal process. They decided among themselves, for example, that a farm valued at 1,400 écus by the appraisers was overestimated and should instead be valued at 1,200 écus. After the properties were surveyed, the eldest son was given as his droit d'aînesse one-half of the family's fief of Malassis. The remainder of the properties and *rentes* were then divided into thirds. Courlay's daughter, who had been given a dowry of 8,000 écus upon her marriage, returned one-third of this sum to each of her two brothers.[34] Except for the droit d'aînesse of the eldest, the three portions were as nearly equal as it was possible to make them.

Interestingly, in the Courlay *partage*, the special advantage

[33] Typical *partages* are AN, Min. cen. XCI:158 (23/11/1600): *partage* of properties of Philippe Le Lievre; BN, P.o. 886 de Courlay, fols. 55-109 (4/12/93): *partage* of properties of Guillaume de Courlay and Marie Le Cointe. Traditional practice described in AN, Min. cen. XIX:243 (4/6/69): *partage* of estate of Martin de Bragelongne and Marie de Chesnart.

[34] It is perhaps worth pointing out that Marie de Courlay's dowry of 8,000 écus was equal to 19% of the total estate of Guillaume de Courlay and his wife at their death. Though we cannot know how Courlay's financial situation changed in the ten or so years between Marie's wedding and his death, it does help place the question of dowries into perspective to think of the burden the marriage of a daughter placed on a man like Courlay, a husband and the father of two young sons.

given the eldest son amounted to less than 1% of the total estate. Although the Courlays claimed noble status, noble lands made up only a miniscule portion of the family properties.[35] The droit d'aînesse of Jean-Baptiste de Courlay, representing half of the fief of Malassis and consisting of properties scattered around the villages of Vitry, Ivry, and Villejuifve, amounted to only 350 écus out of an estate valued at 42,100 écus.[36] The family also owned a fief called "la Robinette," but its value must have been even smaller, for Jean-Baptiste allowed it to be divided between his sister and brother as a nonnoble property in exchange for their permitting him to take the other half of Malassis as part of his share of the estate. There was apparently no manor attached to the fief, and the house Jean-Baptiste inherited in the village of Vitry is appropriately described as a farm house. The property consisted primarily of stables and outbuildings for livestock, and the living quarters for the human inhabitants of the farm were neither large nor elaborate. The farm (valued at 1,600 écus) together with the neighboring fields given to Jean-Baptiste (123 *arpents* of nonnoble tenures valued at 1,353 écus) plus the fief of Malassis amounted to about a third of his share in the estate. The largest part of Jean-Baptiste's inheritance— about half the total—consisted of *rentes* on the Hôtel de Ville, the clergy, and individuals. A one-third interest in the office of *tabellion royal* at Etampes, valued at 1,453 écus, made up most of the remainder. The composition of the portions given Courlay's younger son, François, and his daughter, Marie, is known in less detail, but it is clear that each received a house and lands as well as *rentes*.

Although the droit d'aînesse of Jean-Baptiste de Courlay

[35] Guillaume de Courlay was a notaire and secrétaire du roi. His two sons did not hold noble office, but the eldest, Jean-Baptiste, styled himself "écuyer, Sieur de Malassis, Vitry, Ivry, et Villeneuve en partie," and the younger, François, called himself "écuyer, Sieur de Thiaiz."

[36] The size of the fief is not specified, but, assuming the fields of Malassis were equal in value to the other fields the family owned in the vicinity (11 écus per *arpent*), the droit d'aînesse would have consisted of about 64 *arpents* and the total fief of 128 *arpents*, or roughly 128 acres.

may have been unusually small, the process involved in the Courlay *partage* is typical. The employment of professional appraisers, the return of previous gifts, and the agreement of all of the heirs at each step in the partition were common to intestate property divisions.

From a study of the estates of the city councillors, it appears that equality among the heirs was more likely to be undermined by gifts of property than by testamentary bequests. Parisians used the testament primarily to prescribe the desired funeral rites—the place of burial, the masses to be said after death, the gifts to the poor, and the clerics who were to take part in the cortege.[37] Minor bequests to servants and to relatives who did not otherwise stand to inherit were common, and occasionally the right to bequeath personal and acquired real properties to a friend or relative was exercised. Ordinarily, however, the bulk of the estate was left to be divided according to the normal rules of intestate succession.

In a letter to the legist René Choppin, Etienne Pasquier used this preference for intestate successions in the Paris customary law to underscore the regional variations in French law and to make the point that "the true interpreter of the law is usage."[38] The case Pasquier used to illustrate this point involved the succession of Catherine de Montmirail, the widow of the city councillor Jacques de Longueil. Pasquier represented one of the daughters of Catherine and Jacques in a suit brought in the Parlement of Paris over a testamentary bequest

---

[37] Chaunu, *La Mort*, pp. 225-26 and 288-92, gives a good background on testamentary practice in sixteenth-century Paris. A typical testament is that of Marie Neveu, the third wife and widow of Dreux Budé (BN, P.o. 547 Budé, nos. 80-96 [28/3/1600]). By contrast to the elaborate ritual prescribed by Marie Neveu, Guillaume Budé's testament requested a very simple funeral to take place at night. About the division of his estate, Budé writes that "de cette forme testamentaire n'est besoing de disposer de mes biens, veu le nombre des enfans que je laisse" (Ravenel, "Testament," pp. 225-27). Michel de L'Hôpital wrote that, "Premièrement, je veulx et ordonne que tous mes biens et héritages viennent à ceulx auxquelz ilz appartiennent par les loyz et coustumes du pays. . . ." (*Oeuvres complètes*, ed. Pierre Joseph Spiridion Duféy [Paris, 1824-1826], 2:525).

[38] Pasquier, *Lettres*, bk. 6, letter 2 (Thickett, *Lettres familières*, p. 73).

made to her by her mother that her siblings refused to honor. According to Pasquier, the legacy was perfectly legal and involved only personal and acquired properties that the mother was free to give. "I had the customary law, along with the explicit will of the mother," explained Pasquier, "but I did not have the general sentiment of the judges for me." Pasquier lost the suit because his client's siblings convinced the court that "it was beneficial for children to divide equally the properties of their mother," and the judges, equating "natural piety" with an "arithmetic equality among the children," decided that this principle was more important than the wish of a mother to gratify one of her daughters.[39] As Pasquier discovered, customary practice and the principles from which usage was derived outweighed the letter of the law. In this case at least, the principle of equality was judged more important than the freedom to dispose by testament. Pasquier had no doubt that had the same case been brought before the Parlement of Toulouse, in a region more favorable to testamentary bequests, the judges would have reached the opposite conclusion.

The desire that siblings should benefit equally is often mentioned in the marriage contracts, donations, and *partages* of the city councillors and their families. Louise de Selve, the widow of the city councillor Etienne de Montmirail, recalled to her succession the married daughters who had previously renounced their inheritance rights so that all of her daughters would share as equally as possible.[40] Catherine Hennequin made a special donation to her eldest daughter, Claude Parent, the wife of Jean de Bragelongne, in order to make her wedding portion equal to that given her stepsister.[41] The reason most often specified in these contracts is the desire to promote peace and love among the children. Jacqueline de Marle put a finer point on the matter. By equalizing the sums

[39] Ibid., p. 74.
[40] AN, Y116, fol. 11 (30/9/74); Y115, fol. 420v° (24/4/74).
[41] AN, Y124, fols. 432v°-34 (17/3/83).

given her sons and daughters, she hoped to avoid "any future occasion for lawsuits among them."[42]

The sentiment in favor of equality is also conveyed in the donations that Jacqueline de Tulleu, the widow of Christophe de Thou, made to her son Jacques-Auguste after he renounced his religious orders to marry. In 1585 Jacqueline gave Jacques a house and properties at la Villette and at Aubervilliers, near (now within) Paris. The donation was explicitly justified on the ground that Jacques had not had "as much of an advance on the estate of the deceased President as had her other children."[43] Several years later, Jacqueline, who had apparently retained the management of the paternal properties after the death of her husband, decided that, as successor to the office held by his father, Jacques-Auguste should inherit the family house in Paris rather than the country properties that had been ceded him by his siblings and in-laws when he renounced religious orders. This change was effected by means of a testamentary bequest that gave Jacques the paternal house and some other properties on the condition that he take over the care of the monuments to the family in the parish church and execute some charitable bequests included in the testament. Jacques was obviously worried about the reaction of his siblings to this bequest, however, for he pointed out in his memoirs that all of this passed in the view and with the knowledge ("au vu et au su") of the other heirs. He also claimed to have persuaded his mother to insert a clause specifying that, if the other children thought Jacques's share of the estate was too large after the charitable bequests were taken care of, his share was to be adjusted to meet their approval. In his own, inimitably self-righteous style, Jacques added, "It was unnecessary that de Thou had that clause inserted against the will of his mother: after the *partages* none of the heirs complained of the donation or of the legacy that

[42] AN, Y102, fol. 230 (15/4/61): Paillart; Y109, fols. 261-62v° (12/2/69): Dormans/Longueil; Y90, fol. 77v° (8/8/44): Luillier/Quatre-Livres; Y118, fol. 39v° (22/12/36): Marle/Le Maistre.

[43] AN, Y126, fol. 370 (3/4/85).

his mother had made him; they all found that nothing had happened without justice and agreed that he had exactly observed the law to *do unto others as you would have them do unto you* [emphasis in original]."[44]

Although we should not mistake the rhetoric of equality for its reality, the frequency with which such phrases as "a fair and just division of property," "an equal love," and "a desire to promote harmony" occur in contracts, memoirs, and legal treatises of sixteenth-century Parisians indicates that the traditional equality of siblings in the Paris customary law was an important foundation of patrimonial politics among this sixteenth-century urban elite.

Evidence of a countervailing tendency to favor the eldest son or another child above and beyond his share of the family properties should not, however, be ignored. Gifts that favored one child were expressly permitted in the Paris customary law as long as they were gifts effective during the parent's lifetime and not bequests to be claimed only after the parent's death. Such gifts were employed by some of the city councillors to keep intact properties that would otherwise have been divided by intestate succession. Christophe de Harlay, for example, confirmed in his testament of July 1573 that he had previously given to his eldest son, Achilles, his seigneury of Beaumont, his house in Paris, and his office of president in Parlement. Leaving his younger son, Charles, the seigneury of Dollot, Christophe left only *rentes* to the children of his two deceased daughters. In order to ensure obedience to his wishes, Christophe added that if his daughters' children quarreled with Charles over their share of the estate, the bequest of *rentes* to them was to be revoked and the *rentes* given to Charles in addition to his other share.[45] It is not clear just

---

[44] De Thou, *Mémoires*, pp. 324-25.

[45] AN, Y114, fol. 242v° (1/7/73). It is interesting that the only conflict predicted was between the younger son and the heirs to the daughters. BN, Carrés 331 Harlay, fols. 114-18, further illustrates the disparity between the way Harlay treated his sons and the way he treated his daughters. One of the daughters received only 1,000 écus for her marriage. The other received 4,000 écus. Achilles received all of the above-mentioned properties

what weight these conditions would have had in a courtroom, but certainly the members of a family would have felt a strong moral obligation to honor such an exact and firm expression of the paternal will. In any event, the intention here seems clear. By giving his eldest son both his office and his most important seigneury, Christophe would ensure the continuance of the status that his own ascension to the presidency of Parlement had given the family. The bequest to the younger son allowed Charles to retain intact a property that would otherwise have had to be shared with the children of his sisters.[46]

One can sympathize with the efforts many parents made to preserve intact their feudal heritages or at least their most valuable seigneuries. Historians who have studied noble landholding in the Paris region have generally concluded that the droit d'aînesse was relatively weak there, too weak to prevent the "morseling" of fiefs in the Paris basin.[47] If no special action was taken to prevent a fief or seigneury from being divided according to the regular rules of noble succession, it would in just a few generations be reduced to an absurd patchwork of tiny holdings. A case in point is the seigneury of Onsenbray. In 1538, less than fifty years after Onsenbray was acquired by Marie Guillart's great-grandfather Jacques de Hacqueville, her husband did homage on her behalf for a share of the property that had diminished to one-sixth of one-seventh of one-third of the seigneury.[48] The seigneury having passed through three successive generations of women, this portion was particularly small, but even the share of the property that made up the droit d'aînesse would have diminished

in advance of inheritance plus a *rente* of £700 (equal to a capital of 2,800 écus). Achilles' bride, Catherine de Thou, brought £20,000 (6,666-⅔ écus) to the marriage.

[46] Other donations that apparently favored eldest sons: AN, Y131, fols. 193v°-96 (22/3/89): *donation* by Jean Palluau to his son Denis; AN, Y102, fol. 230 (15/4/61): *donation* by Jacques Paillart to his children. In both cases the advantage to the eldest is open to question, however.

[47] See, for example, Fourquin, *Campagnes*, pp. 118-20; and Bézard, *Vie rurale*, p. 71.

[48] Mirot, *Hommages*, no. 4,119.

after three generations to only one-eighth of the original seigneury.

In the Budé family one can see both the struggle against
partition of a seigneury and its seeming inevitability. The
seigneury of Yerres, acquired in 1452 by the grandfather of
Guillaume Budé, was passed on intact to Guillaume's father
and then to his eldest brother, Dreux, despite the fact that
there were many children in the family. When Dreux died,
Yerres was divided among his eight children. By law, the
eldest son, Jean, received half, and after his death in 1558
his widow succeeded in reassembling the fragments that had
gone to other heirs. The unification survived only until her
death, when the property was split between her two sons,
Dreux (the city councillor) and Pierre. Pierre, as the younger
son, received only a third. His third was again divided for
his two sons, and the two pieces, no longer worth holding
onto, passed out of the family. The two-thirds that went to
Dreux were passed intact to his eldest son, Eustache, but
Eustache left no male heirs, so the property was divided between his daughters.[49]

The case of Yerres is more typical than exceptional. Records of the noble lands in the Paris region show that seigneuries were continually being divided and, somewhat less frequently, reassembled.[50] Too numerous offspring, failure of
the male line, financial hardship, or the acquisition of other,
more desirable properties could all cause a property to be
divided, and seigneuries that were repeatedly partitioned over
several generations often ended in other than family hands. A
principal reason, then, for tampering with the customary partition of the patrimony was to preserve the integrity of a
family's noble estates.

---

[49] Lebeuf, *Paris*, 5:214-15. Foisil, "Guillaume Budé," p. 287n, cites
records found in the Archives of Seine and Oise, Series A, 1010, to the
effect that the seigneury of Yerres included a walled and crenelated château,
a garden of four *arpents*, 28 *arpents* of tillable soil, and 456 *arpents* of woods
and brush in 1504, shortly after Guillaume Budé's brother Dreux inherited
it.

[50] Mirot, *Hommages*, passim.

Aside from the special provisions sometimes used to prevent excessive partition of noble properties, departures from
the customary rules of succession in the families of the city
councillors seem to have occurred more frequently in the
transmission of properties by childless collaterals, heiresses,
or the parents of hieresses than in the transmission of property
from father to son.

In the Guillart family, the donation of property from an
unmarried son to a married son was used over two successive
generations to increase the fortune of the male line at the
expense of the female line. The marriage contract of André
Guillart contained a clause by which his older brother, Louis,
the bishop of Chartres, renounced in André's favor all that
was to come to him of the paternal estate.[51] The renunciation
was repeated the day after the *partage* of André's father's estate
in 1538. To guard against their sister Marie's objection that
one could not dispose of his droit d'aînesse, a fictitious sale
was arranged in 1544 by which Louis sold his inheritance to
a third party for £13,000 and André recovered the properties
several months later for £13,004 according to the laws of
retrait lignager (which permitted the repurchase of alienated
family properties according to strict rules of precedence).[52] A
lawsuit brought by Marie was apparently unsuccessful, and
her ultimate share of the parental estate was composed almost
entirely of properties that had belonged to her mother. The
same ploy was used in the next generation. André specified
in the *partage* of noble properties he made in 1566 among his
three children that the share given his younger son, Charles,
who had taken religious orders and become bishop of Chartres
in succession to his uncle Louis, should return to his other
son on the bishop's death.[53] André's daughter, Isabeau, the
wife of the city councillor René Baillet, does not appear to

[51] BN, 4°Fm 14302, Marion, *Factums et mémoires*, fols. 113-15. Discussed in Jouanna, "Guillart," p. 244.

[52] Ibid. On the laws of *retrait lignager*, see Olivier-Martin, *Histoire de la
coutume*, 2:320-43.

[53] AN, Y107, fols. 245-48 (21/9/66).

have challenged this clause, perhaps because her legal grounds were weaker since there was no droit d'aînesse involved, perhaps simply because she had seen the failure of her aunt's efforts.

Donations by clerics and elderly persons who apparently did not hope for progeny of their own are by far the most frequent of the fraternal and avuncular donations, but occasionally there are donations by nonclerics of still marriageable age.[54] Germain and Guillaume de Marle (sons of the city councillor Germain de Marle) contracted in 1549 that if the first to die left no heirs then all of the properties inherited from their father should go to the other.[55] François Aymeret gave his brother Jean the family's principal seigneury of Gazeau, near Niort, on the condition that Jean "legitimately marry an honest woman suitable to his estate and house."[56] François claimed the donation was valid even if he himself later married and had children, but it is not certain that the courts would have upheld him in this matter. In any event, it seems likely that François had no intention of marrying. A week after the donation of Gazeau, he made over to Jean all of his rights to his mother's estate, and it is unlikely that a man who was planning to have a family of his own would thus dispose of virtually his entire patrimony.[57]

[54] Clerics: AN, Y100, fol. 112 (17/1/59): Luillier; Y101, fol. 72 (24/1/59): Luillier; Y91, fol. 293 (11/1/46): Vivien; Y91, fol. 318v° (22/2/46): Vivien; Y86, fols. 79-80 (8/1/38): Du Drac; Y86, fol. 146 (26/10/32): Du Drac; Y94, fol. 328 (30/4/49): Arbaleste; Y111, fol. 50v° (1/1/57): de Thou; Y111, fol. 219v° (13/2/71): de Thou. Nonclerics: Y86, fol. 313v° (14/7/35): Livres/Longueil; Y89, fol. 239 (7/4/44): Burdelot; Y113, fol. 183 (8/6/71): Du Drac.

[55] AN, Y95, fol. 66 (18/10/49); also Y102, fol. 215v° (20/12/50); BN, Carrés 414 Marle (20/1/46): *partage* of Germain de Marle (father). Germain (son) did die without heirs, and this donation allowed Guillaume to receive the seigneury of Thillay, which had been given Germain as his droit d'aînesse. Guillaume appears as "Seigneur de Thillay" just a year after the donation, and it appears likely that the donation was thus made on Germain's deathbed as a means of holding together the family's principal estates.

[56] AN, Y107, fol. 86 (9/6/66).

[57] AN, Y107, fol. 207v° (18/6/66).

It should be pointed out, however, that fraternal donations and bequests were not always motivated by fraternal feeling. In the donation Regnault Clutin made to his brother Charles of all of the properties coming to him from the estates of his parents and deceased siblings, it is explicitly agreed that Charles was in return to pay off the many debts that Regnault had contracted. The brothers were acting to keep the properties in the family and to avoid their dispersal among Regnault's creditors.[58]

It should also be pointed out that rather than always favoring eldest sons collateral donations sometimes even excluded them. Robert de Harlay gave his nephew Charles de Harlay, the younger son of city councillor Christophe de Harlay, the fief and lands of la Mothe-Saulnier with the understanding that the donation was to be nullified if Charles, through the death of his older brother Achilles, became the eldest son and principal heir of Christophe.[59] Jacques Luillier, a cleric, gave his brother Jean Luillier de Boulancourt his rights to the succession of Marie Coeur, their mother, with the explicit provision that the properties were to be divided among Jean's legitimate children "by equal portions and as nonnoble family properties." There would be no droit d'aînesse, and daughters were to share equally with sons.[60] A similar refusal to favor the males, let alone the eldest male, in collateral inheritance also appears in the declarations of Louis de Marle by which he allowed the children of his deceased sister Claude de Marle to represent her in his succession, even though the Paris law did not normally allow representation among collateral relatives. Louis offered the right of representation to Claude's daughter, Barbe de Thou, as well as to her sons.[61] Clearly personal preference and personal ideas of justice thus played a definite part in collateral inheritance. The properties of family members who died without

[58] AN, Y90, fol. 281 (9/3/45).
[59] AN, Y92, fol. 215v° (1/1/45).
[60] AN, Y100, fol. 112 (17/1/59).
[61] AN, Y102, fol. 306v° (15/7/61); Y102, fol. 38 (11/7/61).

direct heirs could be used to bolster the estate of the firstborn son, but this was by no means the only—or even the most popular—way of disposing of these properties among the families of the city councillors.

In the disposition of the estates of heiresses, we also find some exceptions to the standard rules of inheritance. When a noble family failed to produce a son, a substitute heir was sometimes chosen from among the children of a daughter, if there was one, or the nephews, if there were no daughters. This child was then given the family's most important properties on the condition that he adopt the name and arms of the line that would otherwise have become extinct. The marriage contract of Jean Perdrier and Charlotte de Sains, for example, provided that Charlotte was to receive the seigneuries of Laas and Escrennes, near Orléans, on the condition that the couple's first son adopt the name of Charlotte's maternal family, the Salazars, and become the "seigneur de Laas."[62] Similarly, Jeanne Le Viste, sole heir to the properties of her father, Antoine Le Viste, a maître des requêtes and seigneur de Fresnes, gave her son Florimond Robertet lands she had inherited near Lyons on the condition that he bear the name and arms of the Le Viste family or at least combine them with the Robertet arms. Florimond was also required to marry, and Jeanne reserved the right to choose which of his sons should bear the name Le Viste.[63] In most sixteenth-century documents, the city councillor Nicolas de Neufville de Villeroy appears as "Nicolas Le Gendre," the name he adopted in order to fulfill the terms of the will of his great uncle, Pierre Le Gendre. Le Gendre, a *trésorier de France*, seigneur d'Alaincourt and Magny, and a very wealthy man, named de Neufville his universal heir but required that he adopt the Le Gendre family name. While de Neufville did submit to the condition himself, his children later got permission from the king to retain the Neufville family name instead.[64] Even Michel

---

[62] AN, Y98, fol. 359 (21/3/53).
[63] AN, Y96, fol. 327v° (5/5/51); Y106, fol. 273v° (15/10/61).
[64] *Reg. BV*, 6:21n.

de L'Hôpital had either the personal vanity or the family pride to wish to have his name borne by his posterity even though he had no sons. In his testament, L'Hôpital requested that his grandsons add his family name to their surname "Hurault." He wished the memory of his name to remain with his family, in the hope that his achievements would inspire his grandsons to achieve a like degree of honor. Besides, he added, there were so many "Huraults."[65]

L'Hôpital's concern for the transmission of his family name should serve as a reminder that the patrimony of the city councillors included more than money, lands, and other tangibles. The family name and reputation were a part of the patrimony, too. Ties of patronage and clientele, prestigious alliances, and social and political honors formed a heritage that could be drawn upon by all of the heirs alike, a heritage that could, despite division, become more fruitful with each new generation.

By way of summary then, because all of the children were bearers of the family name and heirs to its reputation, it was deemed neither just nor wise to deprive them of a fair share of the family properties. Moreover, family solidarity was valued in both theory and practice, and to preserve a sense of solidarity, it was necessary to avoid any cause for quarrel among siblings and their spouses. This end could best be met, it was believed, by leaving the partition of the family property to the laws of the land rather than to the parental will. As Montaigne concluded, "In general the soundest distribution of our estate when we die seems to me the one prescribed by the custom of the country. The laws have thought about this better than we; and it is better to let them err in their choice than rashly to run the risk of erring in ours."[66] While the specific customs of the Bordelais, to which Montaigne was in all probability referring here, were not those of Paris, many of the city councillors would nevertheless have been of the same mind.

[65] L'Hospital, *Oeuvres*, 2:526.
[66] Montaigne, *Essais*, bk. 2, chap. 8 (Frame, p. 289).

Despite the soundness of this reason, some men, Montaigne included, eventually succumbed to the temptation to choose a favored heir. And as the example of the Guillart family shows, when the will was there, the law could be bent. It is impossible to tell just how often this happened. The evidence suggests, however, that intestate succession and adherence to customary law was the more general rule among the city councillors. The emphasis in memoirs, contracts, and correspondence is on equality and a just balance among the heirs, and the marriages and careers of the younger children do not indicate that they were disadvantaged. The eldest son did have certain prerogatives, but these privileges, guaranteed by law and honored by tradition, do not appear to have been themselves sources of tension in the family. Among the city councillors' families, at least, the evidence suggests that tension was felt only when the rights given one child—eldest or younger—were in excess of the customary share.[67]

[67] See, for example, Louet, *Arrests*, 1:413-15, regarding Bocharts and Bragelongnes.

9. Widowhood, Remarriage, and the Protection of the Patrimony

> Le second mariage estant au dire de
> Platon, une calamité domestique. . . .
> —Georges Louet

BECAUSE so many people died at an early age, it was very common for a marriage to be terminated by death before all of the children were grown.[1] The tendency to prolong the period of childbearing until it was ended naturally by death or menopause, coupled with the fact that most women were married to men eight years or more their senior, meant that widows were often left with young children. At least one-third of the city councillors died leaving a widow with minor children to raise. It is important therefore to consider the problems posed by widowhood and by the need to protect the properties of minors until they were able to manage their own affairs. These problems were especially acute when a widowed parent remarried, for the protection and management of the patrimony was further complicated by the introduction of stepparents and stepsiblings.

The Administration of the Estates of Minors

The first order of business after the death of a parent was the calling of a family council to nominate an official guardian to be responsible for the financial and legal affairs of any

[1] Studying the English aristocracy for the sixteenth and seventeenth centuries, Lawrence Stone found that one child out of every three had lost at least one parent by the age of fourteen. The figures for the city councillors' families appear comparable (Stone, *Family*, p. 58, based on data for fig. 16 of *The Crisis of the Aristocracy*).

minors. There were several distinct but overlapping forms of guardianship. The most fundamental form was the *tutelle et curatelle*. The *tuteur et curateur* assumed official responsibility for the legal and financial affairs of the minor, and in addition to administering the property, was responsible for the child's education and preparation for a career or marriage. The tutelle normally continued until the minor was twenty-five, the age of full majority, or in the case of a female, until her marriage. At this time, a full accounting of the tuteur's administration was required to be presented to the court.[2] Another form of guardianship gave a surviving parent or, if the family was noble, a grandparent the option of assuming a form of administration of the child's property more profitable to the guardian. This was called the *garde noble* or the *garde bourgeoise*. It allowed the *gardien* to enjoy the usufruct of the minor's property as compensation for the expenses incurred in the minor's upbringing and education. The gardien could be simultaneously the tuteur, or the two positions could be split, in which case it was the tuteur who represented the child in legal actions.[3] Because the garde noble and the garde bourgeoise left more room for misuse of the estate of the minor than did the tutelle, the rules governing the selection of gardiens were more restrictive than those governing the selection of tuteurs.

The tuteur was appointed by a court of law on the recommendation of the family council. As was pointed out previously, the family council could be expected to name the nearest living relative, and the judge's approval of the tuteur was primarily a formality in the sixteenth century. A surviv-

---

[2] Olivier-Martin, *Histoire de la coutume*, 1:195-99. Under certain circumstances, a person could assume responsibility for his or her affairs before the age of twenty-five. Magdaleine de Marle, granddaughter of the city councillor Guillaume de Marle, was allowed to administer her own properties at the age of nineteen. Both of her parents had died, and in order to avoid the time and expense of a full inventory of the parental estate, she received permission from the king and courts to have her nearest relatives proceed immediately to give her a share of the parental properties (BN, P.o. 1859 de Marle, no. 195).

[3] On the garde bourgeoise and the garde noble: Lepointe, *Droit romain*, pp. 424-26; Leprestre, *Questions notables*, p. 557.

ing father was always named tuteur of his children, and a mother could only be excluded for serious reasons or if the father had named another tuteur in his testament. If the mother was not yet of age herself or if she remarried, a co-tuteur had to be named. Apparently, it was not uncommon for the new husband to be chosen as co-tuteur.[4] In cases where there was a possible conflict between the legal or financial rights of the tuteur and those of the child, a special substitute (*tuteur subrogé*) was appointed to represent the child.[5]

Although the naming of the nearest relative as tuteur was almost automatic, family politics and expectations of inheritance must sometimes have played a part in the decision of whom to appoint as tuteur. When Thibault Nicolay, the younger son of the first president of the Chambre des Comptes, died three years after his marriage in 1560, his mother, Anne Baillet, rather than his widow, Catherine Luillier, was named *tutrice* of his fifteen-month-old daughter. Catherine retained the physical custody of the child and, although only twenty when Thibault died, could nevertheless have been named co-tutrice. Since the infant was an heiress, however, it is not surprising that Anne Baillet, who had shown a strong hand in the management of her family's affairs since the death of her husband in 1553, should have wished to maintain sole control over her grandchild's paternal estate. She continued in later years to play a dominant role in her granddaughter's upbringing. In 1572 Catherine, who had remarried but was again widowed, had to promise that if she married yet again she would relinquish custody of her daughter at Anne's re-

---

[4] Claude Tudert was tuteur to his stepsons François and Jean Aymeret (Ernest Coyecque, *Recueil d'actes notariés relatifs à l'histoire de Paris et ses environs* [Paris, 1905-1923], 2:102). David Blandin was tuteur to his stepdaughter Marie de Neufville (AN, Y123, fols. 513-14v° [25/6/72] Aymeret/Neufville). Jean Luillier was tuteur for his stepchildren, the children of Renée Nicolay and Dreux Hennequin (AN, Min. cen. LXXXVI:53 [10/5/60]: *Constitution de rente*).

[5] Olivier-Martin, *Histoire de la coutume*, 1:196. The *tuteur subrogé* might also represent the child when the regular tuteur presented the accounts of his guardianship. See, for example, BN, D.b. 92 Besançon, fol. 138 (11/10/44): extract of *registres du greffe du Châtelet*.

quest, and when the child was married in 1578 it was her grandmother and not her mother who supplied the dowry and was a principal in the contract. Catherine was merely present among the other relatives who gave their "advice and consent" to the match.[6] This nevertheless appears to have been a relatively rare situation. Among the city councillors' families, a surviving mother was almost always named tutrice of her children if her husband died.[7]

While any close relative could in theory be named tuteur, only parents and grandparents could be named to the garde noble. In the fifteenth century, close collateral relatives could also be named, but this practice was no longer permitted when the law was codified in 1510, because it was believed that collaterals often despoiled the properties of minors entrusted to their care.[8] The garde bourgeoise was still more restrictive than the garde noble, being permitted only to parents. The garde bourgeoise also differed from the garde noble in that it ended sooner, terminating when the male ward was fourteen and the female twelve, instead of when the males were twenty and the females fifteen, as did the garde noble. Moreover, parents who accepted the garde bourgeoise of their children were required to make an inventory of the estate and to post a bond, while no similar guarantee was required of parents or grandparents accepting the garde noble. On the point of remarriage, however, the law was the same for both. The 1510 codification of the Paris law forbade parents who

[6] AN, Y105, fol. 95vº (4/2/63). AN, 3AP 10 and 12 contain numerous documents relating to Anne Baillet's administration of Nicolay family affairs. Boislisle, *Nicolay*, pp. 262-64: note of 5/4/72 and marriage contract of 16/9/78: Vaudetar/Nicolay.

[7] For example: AN, Min. cen. VI:79 (17/12/77): *Inventaire après décès* of Louis Huault de Montmagny; BN, P.o. 886 de Courlay, no. 30; P.o. 780 Le Clerc à Paris, no. 305; P.o. 1859 de Marle, no. 69; P.o. 3026 Viole, no. 87; AN, Y129, fol. 247 (11/9/87): Hennequin. An exception: BN, P.o. 2187 Palluau, no. 20: Jean Palluau is listed as tuteur of his brother Claude's children in a *quittance* of 4/1/60, even though the children's mother was still alive.

[8] Bourdot de Richebourg, *Coutumier*, 3:22: procès verbal of 1510. See also Olivier-Martin, "Travaux préparatoires," p. 214.

remarried to keep the garde of their children. This provision was added to the law on the ground that parents who remarried frequently used revenues belonging to the children of a former marriage to support a second husband or wife or the children of a subsequent marriage and that this resulted in "great loss and misfortune."[9]

All of these restrictions on the garde noble and the garde bourgeoise stemmed from fear that the child's properties might be misappropriated. Only parents, or grandparents if they were noble, could be trusted to have the child's best interests at heart, and even they could not be trusted when a new spouse came into the picture. There was also some distrust of tuteurs. The *Pourmenade du Pré aux Clercs*, a popular satire of Parisian morals dating from the early seventeenth century, pictured tuteurs purchasing offices and lands for themselves, while their poor defenseless wards cried for a morsel of bread.[10]

In theory, the requirement for a formal accounting of the tutelle should have prevented any misappropriation of funds. The tuteur not only had to present written accounts to an examining officer of the Châtelet, but that official might visit the properties to judge for himself of their worth.[11] The tuteur could be held responsible for any misuse of funds or properties. In practice, however, it appears that the legal requirement for a formal accounting of the tutelle was not always fulfilled, particularly if the tuteur was the child's parent. In a number of marriage contracts from city councillor families, the dowry of the bride or the marriage portion of the groom was given with the express condition that the child not demand an accounting of the tutelle. Denise de Longueil had to promise her mother, Catherine de Montmirail, that she and her husband would not ask for an accounting of the estate of Denise's father, Jacques de Longueil, as long as

---

[9] Bourdot de Richebourg, *Coutumier*, 3:23; A.C., arts. 99 and 101; Olivier-Martin, "Manuscrits de Simon Marion," pp. 177-78.

[10] *La Pourmenade du Pré aux Clercs* (n.p., 1622), p. 17.

[11] For example: BN, D.b. 92 Besançon, fol. 138 (11/10/44): Extract of the *registres du greffe civil du Châtelet*.

Catherine lived. There were similar clauses in the marriage contracts of Nicolas Luillier's daughter Anne and Pierre Hennequin's daughter Marie. And a clause of like intent appeared in the testament of Michel de L'Hôpital, who made his wife the administrator of all his possessions, even though his only child was a married woman in her thirties. L'Hôpital stated that he was confident that his wife's management would be to the profit of his heirs, and he forbade them to ask her to account for her stewardship.[12]

Like the clause appearing in marriage contracts by which parents had their children promise not to demand division of the parental estate until after the death of both parents, the clause forbidding heirs to demand an accounting of the estate of a deceased parent appears to have depended for its observance less on law than on traditions of obedience and respect for parents. Whether or not there were explicit agreements to this effect, it appears to have been possible for a surviving parent to continue to administer the properties of a deceased parent long after all of the children had come of age. André Guillart, for instance, retained control over his wife's properties for thirty-six years after her death in 1530.[13] He did not fail to provide well for his children. He gave his daughter Isabeau a handsome dowry on her marriage in 1542, his son André was given his own office of maître des requêtes when he married in 1551, and his son Charles succeeded to Louis Guillart's position as bishop of Chartres in 1552, but it was not until 1566 that André at last allowed his wife's properties to be divided among his then middle-aged children.[14] During this thirty-six-year period, Guillart not only retained the profit

---

[12] AN, Y134, fol. 212 (20/12/94): Longueil/Selve; Y131, fols. 73vº-75 (26/12/87): d'O/Luillier; AN, Min. cen. VII:47 (28/1/91): Le Fèvre/Hennequin. L'Hospital, *Oeuvres*, 2:425-26. The term that L'Hôpital used when referring to his wife's administration was "tutelle and curatelle," the term that normally referred to the guardianship of minors and other incompetents.

[13] Jouanna, "Guillart," p. 239, citing *acte de création de tutelle* of 23/6/30.

[14] AN, Y107, fols. 245-48 (21/9/66); Y97, fols. 44vº-48 (8/7/51) Guillart/Robertet.

from his wife's properties, he enjoyed the increased authority
that control of the maternal properties gave him. Moreover,
when the properties eventually were divided, it was not according to the will of the children's long-deceased mother or
the dictates of the customary law, but according to the design
of André Guillart himself. The product of Guillart's design
has already been seen. By using cash and the properties of his
deceased wife to make up the share of the estate descending
to his daughter, Guillart was able to concentrate the patrilineal properties in the hands of his sons. Then, by means of a
donation between the sons, he was able to increase further
the share of the eldest.[15]

It is in the Guillart family that the potential effect of the
manipulation of the properties of a deceased spouse can be
seen most clearly. But many other examples of the practice
of withholding partition of all or many of the properties of a
deceased spouse can be cited. Pierre Croquet gave his eldest
daughter £10,000 for her wedding, "in advance of an accounting" of the estate of her deceased mother. The mother,
Marie Picon, had been dead twenty years; Pierre had been
twice remarried; and yet there had been no accounting of her
estate.[16] Jeanne Du Pré, the widow of Jean Tronçon, gave her
eldest son, François, the family's seigneury of Couldray for
his marriage in 1560. The donation, which had to be returned to the succession when a formal *partage* was made, was
given "in advance of inheritance both of the successions already fallen to the aforesaid Messire François Tronçon from
his deceased father and brothers as well as those yet to fall."
Jean Tronçon had died eleven years earlier. Apparently it was
not intended that a formal *partage* should be made until after
the death of his widow.[17]

The fact that widows as well as widowers could retain control over the estate of a deceased spouse is very important. It
demonstrates that the basis for the laws that subjected wives

[15] See Chapter 8, n. 31.
[16] BN, P.o. 2242 Perrot à Paris, no. 20; P.o. 944 Croquet, no. 49.
[17] AN, Y107, fols. 213v°-17 (17/3/60).

to the legal authority of their husbands lay less in the supposed incompetence of women than in the belief that each family should have one and only one head. This, at any rate, was the argument of the sixteenth-century jurists André Tiraqueau and Charles Du Moulin, who attributed the legal incapacity of married women to the need to uphold marital authority.[18] Olivier-Martin was of the same opinion. In his view, the subjection of married women to the authority of their husbands in sixteenth-century Parisian law "expresses above all the sentiment of a whole era and a whole society that loved hierarchy and authority too much not to introduce them, without great nuances, into marriage as into the family. Marital absolutism, like paternal absolutism, flourished in an atmosphere in which monarchical absolutism sounded the key."[19] This same belief in order and hierarchy allowed a woman, on the death of her husband, to take up the authority that he had dropped. It was inconceivable that a family not have a head, and it is striking evidence of the importance of the nuclear family in this society that, whatever the allegiance to the idea of lineage, it was the widow rather than a representative of the male line who was most often designated to fill the role of head of the family.

As a widow, a woman entered for the first time in her life into the full possession of her own property and control over her own person. If she was named tutrice of her minor children, she also assumed a responsibility for their property and persons. Indeed, even if she had no children, she might, as executor of her spouse's testament and/or as the beneficiary of the reciprocal donation of personal and acquired real properties permitted in the Paris law, assume important responsibilities for the administration of her deceased husband's affairs. The experience that allowed women to take on these

---

[18] Jacques Bréjon, *André Tiraqueau, 1488-1558* (Paris, 1937), pp. 110-11; Paul Ourliac and Jehan de Malafosse, *Histoire du droit privé* (Paris, 1973), 3:147-48.

[19] Olivier-Martin, *Histoire de la coutume*, 2:258. Olivier-Martin also mentions the influence of Roman law, which treated women more like children than did French law.

important duties can only have been acquired in years of informal participation in or even supervision of the family's financial affairs. The difference between the role of estate manager under the husband's authority and the assumption of that role under her own authority should not, however, be underestimated. The situation of the widow is ironic. As Nancy Roelker has pointed out, "the literature depicts widowhood as the worst calamity that can befall a woman, but, in fact, it provided the optimum condition for feminine autonomy."[20]

Although certain elements in the customs of the Paris region, such as the community property laws and the traditions of intestate succession, may have made it likely that a surviving widow would be allowed to administer her husband's property, the practice does not appear to have been unique to the Paris area.[21] Citing the example of a royal officer who died "needy and overwhelmed with debts at fifty," while his mother "in her extreme decrepitude was still enjoying all his property by the will of his father," Montaigne sharply criticized the "error of judgment" of fathers who, "not content with depriving their children during their long lifetimes of the share they naturally ought to have had in their fortunes, . . . afterwards also leave to their wives this same authority over all their possessions and the right to dispose of them

---

[20] Roelker, "Appeal of Calvinism," p. 397. Stone, *Family*, pp. 24-25, presents a very different view of the position of women in sixteenth- and seventeenth-century England, as do Herlihy and Klapisch-Zuber for fifteenth-century Florence (*Les Toscans et leurs familles* [Paris, 1978]).

[21] The community property laws, by which all properties acquired by purchase or collateral inheritance during marriage were the joint property of the spouses, would appear to have favored the role of widows as managers of the family properties. Rather than partitioning the community property after the death of one spouse, it was often more convenient to leave it intact, particularly if there were minors for whom the property had to be administered and who would eventually succeed to the entire estate. Moreover, although inherited properties and acquired properties were juridically distinct, the actual pieces of property involved were often interconnected. Records of the estates of the city councillors show that married couples often acquired further parcels of land in the fields or seigneuries belonging to one spouse as *propres*.

according to their fancy." Montaigne went on to specify that
it was right to leave the administration of the paternal estate
to the mother while the children were minors, but he thought
that, once they were of legal age, the children (presumably
he refers only to the males) "will have more wisdom and
ability than his wife." The wife should be given ample means
of support, since it was unseemly to leave a mother dependent
on the discretion of her children, but the property itself should
go to the heirs.[22]

Remarriage and Protection of the Patrimony

The freedom enjoyed by widows in sixteenth-century France
was such that there was considerable fear that family properties rightfully belonging to the children of one marriage might
be misappropriated to the benefit of a second spouse or the
children of a second marriage. This concern found expression
among the educated in moral treatises, private memoirs, and
literature, and more popularly, in the charivaris that sometimes mocked those who took a new husband or wife.[23] It
found expression also in the laws on marriage, which were
changed early in the sixteenth century to restrict the rights
of widowed parents to the use of the property of their deceased spouses and, later, to restrict their right to dispose of
even their own properties.

Prior to the codification of the customary laws in 1510,

---

[22] Montaigne, *Essais*, bk. 2, chap. 8 (Frame, pp. 288-89).

[23] Erasmus, in his colloquy on "The Funeral," has a dying husband counsel his wife on remarriage: "If the weakness of the flesh shall call otherwise,
know that my death releases you from the marriage bond, but not from
the obligation you have in my name, and in your own, of caring for our
children" (in *Ten Colloquies*, ed. and trans. Craig R. Thompson [Indian-
apolis, 1957], pp. 110-11). Jacques-Auguste de Thou applauded the Edict
on Second Marriages (1560) as a "very judicious law" in his *Histoire* (3:580-
81), and in his memoirs tells of the foolish remarriage of the daughter of
the Chancellor Birague with a much younger man (*Mémoires*, p. 315). On
charivaris, see Natalie Z. Davis, "The Reasons of Misrule," in her *Society
and Culture in Early Modern France* (Stanford, 1975), pp. 97-123, especially
pp. 106-107 and 116-17.

noble persons could keep any personal property belonging to
a deceased spouse if they paid the funeral expenses and any
personal debts of the deceased. In 1510 this prerogative was
limited to persons without children because of complaints
that the survivors too often remarried and deprived the children of the first marriage of their properties to benefit the
offspring of the second marriage.[24] This is the same argument
that was used to oppose the right of a surviving parent to
continue the garde noble or garde bourgeoise after remarriage.[25] According to Olivier-Martin, unwillingness to contribute to the upkeep of another spouse and another's children
also caused some opposition to dower rights in the sixteenth
century, but the laws on dowers remained unchanged. A widow's dower did not cease with remarriage.[26] It is possible that
the tendency to give fixed dowers was reinforced by the sentiment against dowers, however. A cash dower was more im-
personal than one that consisted of family properties; and the
potential humiliation to the family of seeing it benefit a second husband was less acute.

By mid-century, public opinion was building in favor of
further restriction of the property rights of persons who remarried, and in 1560 a royal edict on second marriages was
published at the instigation of the new chancellor, Michel de
L'Hôpital. According to Jacques-Auguste de Thou, the final
impetus for the law was provided by a public scandal involving "one of the richest widows in Paris." The widow, identified as Anne Dalegre or d'Alligre, had recently turned over
all of her possessions to a new young husband, "whom she
loved to distraction; her foolish passion prevented her from
seeing that he sought only her possessions and not her person." Her seven children received only the portion she could
not by law deny them.[27] The Edict on Second Marriages,
registered in Parlement on August 5, 1560, aimed at pre-

[24] Bourdot de Richebourg, *Coutumier*, 3:23.
[25] Olivier-Martin, "Manuscrits de Simon Marion," p. 177.
[26] Olivier-Martin, *Histoire de la coutume*, 2:286.
[27] De Thou, *Histoire*, 3:581. Louet, *Arrests*, 2:637.

venting such situations by forbidding a widow to make any donation to a second husband that was larger than the smallest portion given one of her children or grandchildren. She was also forbidden to give her new husband any goods that had been given her by her first husband; these gifts had to be reserved for her children by her first marriage.[28]

Although the royal edict was originally aimed strictly at women, in consideration of the "weakness of that sex," it was extended to apply also to men by an *arrêt* of Parlement in 1578.[29] According to the sixteenth-century jurist Georges Louet, this was because "the principle motive and reason behind the edict was less the flightiness, weakness, and infirmity of the feminine sex than the interest of the children and the conservation of houses and families, . . . a reason that applies to men as well as to women."[30] As Louet pointed out, this reason was written into the edict itself. Like other instances of royal intervention into the sphere of family law, the Edict on Second Marriages was justified on the ground that public order was necessarily founded on strong families. Excessively large donations to a second spouse were said to cause family strife and to end in "the desolation of good families, and consequently the diminution of the strength of the state." Citing the example of the ancient emperors, who had passed comparable laws for the "police, repose, and tranquility of their subjects," the edict justified royal action in hitherto private affairs.[31]

The fear of misalliance already implicit in the arguments for the Edict on Second Marriages became explicit when the case against widows remarrying was again taken up in 1576 at the Estates General of Blois. Considering the Edict on Second Marriages to have proven ineffective, the representatives of the Third Estate at Blois complained that scandals

[28] Isambert, *Lois*, 14:36-37: *Edit sur les secondes noces* (Fontainebleau, July 1560; registered in Parlement August 5, 1560).

[29] René Filhol, "L'Application de l'Edit des Secondes Noces en pays coutumier," *Mélanges Roger Aubenas* 9 (1974):295-99.

[30] Louet, *Arrests*, 2:636.

[31] Isambert, *Lois*, 14:36-37.

continued to occur and demanded stronger remedies. Widows continued to be sought after by "voracious ne'er-do-wells," who, even though they had been denied large donations of property as a result of the Edict on Second Marriages, influenced the widows they wed to sell off properties acquired during their previous marriages to the detriment of their children. The Third Estate asked the king to forbid widows to sell any real properties acquired during a previous marriage to the prejudice of their children. They further complained of widows with children who "frivolously and foolishly remarried with persons unworthy of their condition, and, which is worse, some with the valets and servants of their dead husbands," and asked that such women be forbidden to alienate any of their properties.[32]

The Edict of Blois did not take up these recommendations, although it did forbid widows to marry persons "unworthy of their condition."[33] To reinforce the royal legislation, an article was added in the reformation of the Paris customary law in 1580 restating the Edict on Second Marriages and adding several further restrictions.[34] Even this action did not solve the problem, however. In 1593, for example, Michel Sevyn, a counselor in the Parlement of Paris, entered a suit in Parlement to gain control of the finances of his mother, who at the age of fifty-eight had just run off with a soldier twenty-three years old, and a penniless foreigner to boot. Sevyn and his two younger brothers seem not to have been alone in finding themselves in this humiliating position.[35]

The seduction of rich widows by young fortune hunters has doubtless occurred in nearly every society, but the intensity

[32] BN, MS fr. 10871: "Cahier des remonstrances," fols. 111-12, arts. 417 and 418.

[33] Ordonnance de Blois, art. 182.

[34] N.C., art. 279; see also Filhol, *Christofle de Thou*, pp. 161-62; and Olivier-Martin, *Histoire de la coutume*, 2:299. Olivier-Martin concludes that the further restrictions of the 1580 *Coutume* did not add up to much.

[35] Maugis, *Parlement*, 3:274, citing the requête of Michel Sevyn of May 11, 1593. Sevyn, the son of a *correcteur* in the Chambre des Comptes, had extensive family ties among the Parisian elite.

of the public outrage over this issue in the mid-sixteenth century is striking. The publication of the Edict on Second Marriages was one of the first acts Michel de L'Hôpital took as chancellor; and even before this time, Christophe de Thou and the other parlementaires working on the redaction of regional customs were concerning themselves on a local level with the issue of second marriages.[36] Like the move to prevent clandestine marriage that was taking place at the same time, the move to restrict the freedom of widows to dispose of their property reveals a strong fear of misalliance and a desire to protect the patrimony, strengthen the ties of lineage, and promote the role of the family as the basis for an orderly and powerful state.

Remarriage in City Councillor Families

The marriage contracts of members of city councillor families who married for the second time show two different and potentially conflicting views of property rights in remarriage. On the one hand, the inclusion of carefully worded clauses outlining the property rights of minor children and the agreements relating to their support indicates a conscious effort to avoid family conflict and to provide fairly for all. On the other hand, these marriage contracts permitted parents who remarried to retain a control over the disposal of their own properties and those belonging to their children that sometimes exceeded the limits placed on remarried parents by customary law and royal legislation.

Widows and widowers who had children and remarried commonly drew up inventories of their possessions at that time, so it would be clear from the outset which properties had been acquired prior to the second marriage.[37] While or-

[36] De Thou, *Histoire*, 3:580. Filhol, *Christofle de Thou*, p. 159, citing the customary laws of Laon, Reims, and Châlons.

[37] AN, Y126, fol. 338v° (27/2/85): Du Drac/Le Charron (only the wife's possessions are inventoried here, though the husband was also previously married and had a son). AN, Y124, fol. 186 (20/8/82): Paillart/Bochart; Y126, fol. 405v° (16/1/85): Bourgeois/Paillart.

dinary expenses such as food and clothing for the children of
previous marriages were normally paid from the community
property of the subsequent marriage, major costs such as education and entry into careers or marriage were paid from
funds held in trust by the children's guardian or from the
propres of the surviving natural parent.[38] A further solution to
the problem of keeping separate properties of two alliances
was to limit the rights of children from one marriage to the
community property of a subsequent marriage. For example,
the contract between Guillaume Larcher and Marguerite Par-
faict specified by her children by Claude Le Sueur should have
no rights in the new marital community. Larcher was required to reimburse her children for her share of the community property if she died before he did, however, either by
making a lump sum payment of £1,000 or by giving them
one-quarter of her acquired properties from the marriage. In
addition, her children from her earlier marriage might claim
all of the properties that Marguerite brought into the marriage.[39]

Pierre Viole du Chemin, a widower with several children
made similar commitments when he married Marguerite Bataille in 1578. Pierre and Marguerite each placed only 3,000
écus into the community established for their marriage, and
Pierre swore that the 3,000 écus did not include any properties belonging to his deceased wife or the children of his
first marriage. He added that those children would therefore
have no rights to the community property of the new marriage. He further specified that he had the garde noble of his
children and would continue to administer their affairs separately from those of his second family.[40] By law he should
have been required to relinquish the garde noble of his children upon remarriage. Apparently, however, the law was not

[38] AN, Min. cen. LXXXVI:66 (10/9/66): Luillier/Saint-André;
LXXXVI:30 (2/5/52): Luillier/Nicolay; Y107, fols. 213v°-17 (17/3/60):
Tronçon/Monthelon.
[39] AN, Min. cen. III:105 (27/11/62).
[40] AN, Y102, fols. 48-49v° (12/8/78).

strictly enforced. Marguerite de Monthelon likewise retained her claim to the garde noble of her children by Louis de L'Estoile despite her marriage in 1560 to François Tronçon. At the time she married Tronçon, she promised to relinquish her right to keep the profits of her children's property so long as they did not demand a legal accounting of her guardianship, but she threatened that if they did demand an accounting she would take back all of her rights under the laws of the garde noble.[41]

Another case in which a contract for remarriage violated the provisions of the customary law is the marriage contract of Jean Luillier and Renée Nicolay. They promised one another that the survivor should enjoy the lifetime use of all of the real properties acquired during the marriage as long as the regular upkeep and repair of these properties was paid. This clause was clearly illegal. Donations between husband and wife, even if reciprocal, were forbidden in the Paris customary law if a couple had children. Jean and Renée had a total of fourteen children by previous alliances, and they subsequently had three in common. When Jean died in 1563, his heirs naturally protested against Renée's intention of keeping the acquired real properties for her use. They also protested that some of her dower claims were excessive. The heirs argued that in his marriage contract Jean had disposed of properties that he was not free to give. They cited the royal edict limiting donations made in second marriage and pointed out that the donations were in any event null because the marriage contract had not been registered at the Châtelet as the law required. To avoid a lawsuit and settle the dispute among "parens et amys," Renée agreed to renounce some of her more excessive dower claims and to give up her claim to Jean's share of the properties acquired during the marriage. Ironically, two of the children on whose behalf the protests were made were married to Renée's brothers. Multiple ties of kinship were no guarantee that mutual interest rather than per-

[41] AN, Y107, fols. 213v°-17 (17/3/60).

sonal interests would be served where family properties were
at stake.[42]

The *partage* that discloses this dispute between Renée Nicolay and her stepchildren further shows that Jean Luillier
had not lived up to the promises he made in the marriage
contracts of his daughters by his first wife to provide them
with the properties due from their maternal inheritance.[43] As
this case shows, even a parent who remarried could retain
control of properties to which he or she had no legal right.
The accepted principles of authority and hierarchy in the family made it difficult for children to claim their properties from
parents who did not voluntarily yield them.

There is little specific evidence to illuminate the nature of
the relationship between stepparents and their stepchildren in
the city councillor's families. Few records of donations and
testamentary bequests to stepchildren are to be found in the
archives. Marguerite Bataille, the wife of Pierre Viole, gave
his three sons by his first marriage all of her movables up to
the sum of £25,000 plus her rights to two collateral inheritances because of the "bonne amytie" she had for them.[44]
Marie Neveu, the third wife of Dreux Budé, gave £150 to
each of the six children Budé had by a previous wife.[45] Though
the evidence is slight, such donations appear to be the exception rather than the rule, especially in the case of stepparents
who had children of their own by other marriages. There is
little to suggest that stepparents, whatever the degree of affection they bore their stepchildren, felt any particular financial obligation to these children beyond the fulfillment of the
contractual agreements of the marriage and compliance with
the customary law.

The inheritance rights of children of successive marriages

[42] AN, Min. cen. LXXXVI:30 (2/5/52); LXXXVII:139 (23/7/63): *Inventaire après décès* and *partage* of Jean Luillier.
[43] Boislisle, *Nicolay*, no. 200: Marriage contract of Thibault Nicolay and
Catherine Luillier (11/1/60); AN, Y105, fols. 93-95 (2/1/52): Antoine Ni-
colay/Jeanne Luillier.
[44] AN, Y128, fol. 91 (14/9/86); Y129, fol. 11 (2/5/87).
[45] BN, P.o. 547 Budé, nos. 80-96.

followed the now familiar principle of separation of properties. The question of direct succession, in theory at least, was simple. Except for the droit d'aînesse, which belonged to the eldest son of the first marriage, half brothers and sisters shared equally in the estate of their common parent but could make no claim on the estate of stepparents. In practice, it was sometimes difficult to keep the community properties of successive alliances separate. Still, the only claim that stepchildren could make on the estate of stepparents was for property rights owing to their deceased mother or father. They had no direct claim on their own behalf.

The relationship between full and half siblings in collateral inheritance is somewhat more complex. *Propres* could, of course, only be inherited by brothers and sisters who were themselves of the lineage of the ascendant by whom the property had originally been acquired. All other real and personal properties were divided equally among full and half siblings. Let us suppose that a woman had six children, three by her first marriage and three by her second. If a child of the first marriage died without descendants, the patrilineal properties were split between the two siblings who had the same father, while the matrilineal properties and all other properties were divided equally among the five survivors without regard to the full or half relationship. The law thus prevented the transmission of *propres* outside of the lineage through remarriage. At the same time, it avoided polarizing the family and setting the children of successive marriages against one another by refusing where properties other than *propres* were concerned to place the rights of children of the same marriage above those of children who shared only the same mother or father. In this fashion, the laws regulating the division of property in collateral inheritance among siblings and half siblings struck a balance between the dual objectives of protecting lineage properties and maintaining harmony within the family.[46]

In collateral as well as in direct inheritance, in remarriage

[46] Olivier-Martin, *Histoire de la coutume*, 2:389-91.

as well as in first marriage, we find these same considerations of separation of lineages and family harmony. Though there was undoubtly some abuse of the customary laws, and there certainly were family quarrels, the traditional rights of inheritance would seem in general to have provided, in practice as in theory, a sound basis for family politics.

It is significant that the principal deviation from the customary law observed in city councillor families concerned parents who retained control over properties that legally belonged to their children. Children found it difficult to press claims for dowries that remained unpaid or parental successions that remained undivided. This was perhaps an inevitable consequence of the presumption the law made that parents would necessarily have the best interests of their children at heart. Moreover, because of the hierarchical structure of the family and the overriding respect for parental authority, it was difficult for children to oppose their parents and for jurists to conceive of a need for mechanisms that might strengthen the position of children relative to that of parents. A perceptive observer like Montaigne might recognize an abuse of legitimate authority in a parent who retained properties due his child, but for the most part, the prevailing theories of the hierarchical family operated in favor of the parents rather than the children.[47] Only where remarriage was involved was the possibility of a conflict of interest between parent and child recognized.

[47] Montaigne, *Essais*, bk. 2, chap. 8 (Frame, p. 288).

Conclusion. The Politics
of Patrimony

CONSCIOUS of their status and confident of their role in both city and monarchy, the families of the city councillors of sixteenth-century Paris constituted one of the most important elites in the French kingdom. Their high standing and the stability of their position were maintained through the dextrous use of a variety of formal and informal mechanisms. For analytical purposes, it has been necessary to isolate these mechanisms and examine separately the ways in which civic office, professional advancement, marriage, and the partition of the family estate contributed to the acquisition and maintenance of the councillors' position. In practice, however, these mechanisms were mutually reinforcing. They functioned together and overlapped.

Underlying the city councillors' conception of their place in society was their belief in a social system that was orderly, hierarchical, and stable, but not entirely static.[1] Personal experience strengthened this belief. Wealthy merchants and bourgeois regularly entered into the king's service, and through office in the royal bureaucracy, they or their descendants attained the marks and privileges of noble status. The line between noble and roturier was not clearly drawn, and the possibility of social ascent through service to the king was a real one.

Whether bourgeois or noble, the city councillors and their families accepted the importance of monarchical institutions in shaping the social hierarchies of the state. Guillaume Budé,

[1] Claude de Seyssel has provided a good description of this social system in his treatise for Francis I, *Le Monarchie de France* (ed. Jacques Poujol [Paris, 1961], pp. 124-26).

for example, because he thought it important for the advancement of his family, was willing to serve at court himself and to bring up his sons to aspire to royal office even though he strongly disliked the courtier's life. The conception the city councillors had of social success was not, however, limited to the receipt of royal favor or the attainment of noble status. The social and political institutions of the monarchy existed side by side with the social and political institutions of her capital city, and the aspirations of the Parisian elite were conditioned by the local experience as well as the monarchical superstructure. In sixteenth-century Paris, at least until the period of the League, civic and monarchical institutions worked well in tandem, and the mutual benefits of their cooperation helped further the ambitions of the Parisian elite. The officers of the Hôtel de Ville assisted the king in various capacities. They helped to keep order in the capital; they collected taxes and helped fill the royal coffers through the sale of *rentes*; and in elaborate ceremonies welcoming heads of state into the city, they helped promote the majesty of the French monarchs. Local prestige and royal recognition were the dual rewards of this service.

Although it might thus be argued that the city officers served themselves better than they served their fellow Parisians, it would be unfair to assume that the city officers were motivated only by selfish aims. Civic service, like participation in religious and charitable activities, had an important place in the ethical code of the Parisian elite. Despite the prestige, many men found municipal office in Paris a time-consuming, wearying, and essentially thankless task. Yet they served in those positions. Again the example of Guillaume Budé is apt. Budé accepted office as prévôt des marchands even more reluctantly than he had accepted office at court. Four months after he took over as prévôt des marchands in August 1522, Budé was moved to complain to Erasmus that the function "has about as much to do with me as war or commerce with literature!" The job, he wrote, "has stolen from me more than four months of study, of tranquility, of gaiety," and he was simultaneously bored to death, furious, and worried by his lack of experience.[2] Budé accepted the position because he felt obliged to do so, just as he had accepted the post at court because he felt that he owed it to his family and to his fellow men of letters. Deeply imbued with the principles of civic humanism, Guillaume Budé thought it essential to disprove the accusation that men of a scholarly bent were unsuited to the active life through the example of his own willingness to serve.[3]

While Budé's willingness to accept office in his city and his state may have derived at least in part from a learned appreciation of the principles of civic humanism, the ethic of public responsibility was deeply rooted in the Parisian elite. Inherent in the conception of an orderly, hierarchical, and stable society was the belief that certain men were born and bred to assume certain roles in the affairs of polity and society. The families of these men were the essential building blocks of which both municipality and monarchy were structured. Family background as well as personal qualifications determined the suitability of a person to perform certain functions in society, and the concept of lineage as a determinant of social standing played a crucial role in the social system of the city councillors.

A family took pride in the age of its name, the prestige of its alliances, the probity of its men, and the virtue of its women. An honorable reputation brought increased access to civic honors, professional advancement, and prestigious social circles. At the same time, mockery and castigation of those who rose too high too fast or married outside suitable social circles served to curb excessive ambition and to support traditional mores. Consider, for example, the sardonic tone with which L'Estoile disposed of the pretensions of the Bailly fam-

---

[2] Erasmus, *Correspondance*, pp. 235-36 (letter of December 14, 1522). An epidemic of plague struck the city shortly after Budé took office, which must have rendered the job of the city officers even more difficult than usual.

[3] Delaruelle, *Répertoire*, no. 87: letter to Leonicus (Romorantin, 18/3/21).

ily in their opposing the marriage of Bailly's daughter to Claude Tonart. In response to their accusations of Tonart's low social standing, L'Estoile cited the humble origins of Bailly himself and those of his wife, "the daughter of a very mediocre merchant."[4]

When informal regulating mechanisms such as regard for family honor or the pain of public humiliation appeared to fail, the powers of the law and the authority of the king were summoned to the defense of the social order. The legislation affecting marriage that began in 1556 was aimed at preventing a crime that was seen as an affront to the whole social order—the crime of misalliance. In the edict of 1556, the monarch justified intervention in private law on the ground that marriage without parental permission was not only a transgression of God's laws but an offense against public decorum.[5] Similarly, the edict of 1560 concerning second marriages was justified on the ground that imprudent and ill-considered remarriage by widows was causing the "desolation of good families and consequently the diminution of the power of the state."[6] Registered in Parlement with unusual haste, these and later laws regulating marriage were greeted with approval by the king's officers and others of high standing. Indeed, if the king's officers had any objection to the new laws regulating marriage, it was that they did not go far enough. Pressing for further legislation, they encouraged the monarchy in its concern for public order to entertain a more authoritarian and patriarchal view of both state and family.

While the city councillors and others of their social standing encouraged certain extensions of monarchical authority, they condemned others as abusive. In 1575, for example, a delegation of city officers and other notable Parisians condemned the "iniquity" caused by venal office. Deploring the

---

[4] L'Estoile, *Journal pour le règne de Henri III*, pp. 307-308.

[5] Isambert, *Lois*, 13:470: *Edit contre les mariages clandestins* (Paris, February 1556; registered March 1, 1556).

[6] Ibid., 14:36: *Edit sur les secondes noces* (Fontainebleau, July 1560; registered August 8, 1560).

exercise of judicial office by those who were ignorant and unqualified and by those who sought financial profit, the city's delegation also remonstrated with the king against the evils inherent in the unrestrained multiplication of royal office. The situation was such, they claimed, that one could say of the kingdom as it was said of the Emperor Hadrian that he died of too many doctors.[7] There was, of course, a serious discrepancy between the public stance and the private actions of the officeholders. At the same time that they were lobbying to defend the security and the integrity of their own positions, they were trafficking in the very commerce they deplored. Purchasing higher offices for themselves, procuring additional offices for their sons, and endeavoring to guarantee the rights of their heirs to continue in these offices, the king's officers ignored the contradictions in their own behavior and seized upon any opportunity to consolidate the position of their own families in the royal bureaucracy.

The external conditions favorable to social and professional advancement for the city councillors in the mid-sixteenth century were strengthened by family structures. Ties of blood and alliance reinforced the sense of community from which the confidence and pride of the royal officers were in large measure derived. In addition, the tendency toward endogamy among old city families helped create a sense of identifiable community and thus fostered the existence of a local elite that overlapped but was nevertheless distinct from the officerial elite of the monarchy. These family ties served a direct and practical purpose, providing a useful network for the communication of information and favors. As has been shown, many royal offices were not passed directly from father to son but were instead circulated within a fairly closed circle. Even if they did not inherit office, the sons of royal officers were favorably placed to acquire prestigious offices by virtue of their families' standing and influence.

The ties created by endogamous marriage were strength-

---

[7] *Reg. BV*, 7:314.

ened by the bilateral family structure of the Parisian elite. A
married woman retained important ties with her family of
birth, and the relationship between in-laws was an important
one. The evidence has shown that maternal kin played important roles in the life of a family. They were witnesses to
marriages in approximately equal numbers with paternal kin
and were chosen as godparents only slightly less frequently
than paternal kin. Their presence at family meetings for the
choice of guardians and for other serious family business and
the frequency with which significant donations of property
and money and resignations of office involved persons related
through the female line indicate that the role of the maternal
family was not merely ceremonial.

The desirability of a good working alliance between in-laws
is further reflected in the change in inheritance laws in 1510
that allowed married children to return to the parental succession. The daughters of the Parisian elite were not "dowered
off" but retained an important economic interest in their family of birth. The laws, moreover, accorded daughters a right
to the parental estate equal to that of the sons, except where
the special prerogatives of the eldest son in noble inheritances
were concerned. Although there are indications that parents
may sometimes have tried to increase the portion of the estate
due one son or more, the very fact that daughters had a strong
and legitimate claim on the parental properties is significant.

The attempt to balance the privileged position of the eldest
son in noble inheritances with the fundamental rule of equality among heirs is also significant. City councillors, however
desirous of the elevation of their families, were not willing to
sacrifice the younger children to the success of the eldest.
Legal records as well as literary sources emphasize the need
to promote amity among siblings through equal treatment
and a just balance among heirs. The careers and marriage
patterns observed among the city councillors' children further
indicate that any advantage that might have been given the
eldest did not cost the younger sons their chance for professional success nor the daughters their chance for a good

marriage. Cooperation among siblings was a more important strategic device for the advancement of the family than concentration of resources, and adherence to local custom was advocated as the surest way to guarantee this cooperation.

In time, the particular combination of political, social, and intellectual forces that enabled the families of the city councillors of mid-sixteenth-century Paris to consolidate and improve their position in the city and in the monarchy broke down. The sixteenth-century expansion of the royal bureaucracy and the movement to transform both civic and monarchical office into hereditary holdings took place at a time when social hierarchies were sufficiently fluid to allow upward mobility for persons who had respected parentage, ample funds, and friends in high places. The city councillors studied here were able to take advantage of this favorable conjuncture to promote their own careers and those of their children. This state of affairs was self-limiting in certain respects, however.

A sense of common interest and a desire to perpetuate the prestige that came from participation in civic affairs encouraged the formation of a hereditary elite in city office. Election of city councillors became increasingly rare in the second half of the sixteenth century, as the large majority of offices changed hands by resignation rather than by election. There is reason to believe that city offices were sometimes even sold. In any event, the development of a hereditary caste of municipal officers through intrafamilial resignations is evident. The example of proprietary office in the royal bureaucracy was undoubtedly influential in this process.

The spread of venal office in the French monarchy between the reigns of Francis I and Henry III had a dual effect on the civic elite in Paris. It not only encouraged the tendency toward hereditary office in the municipality, it simultaneously increased the opportunities for upward mobility for persons whose wealth and status allowed them to acquire the new monarchical offices. In doing so, it led inevitably to the domination of the Paris city council by a narrower and more prestigious elite. Merchants had composed a small but significant fraction of the city council during the reign of Francis I; by the reign of Henry III, they had been virtually eliminated from this high position in the city. The merchants who had made it into the ranks of the city councillors were generally successful in promoting themselves and their families into the officerial elite within a brief period of time. Already at the pinnacle of the mercantile community when they entered civic office, these merchants used their administrative experience, social contacts, and the prestige of high municipal office to facilitate the transition of their families to officerial status in the monarchy. With the closing of membership in the city council to merchants in the last third of the sixteenth century, this integrative mechanism no longer functioned.

There were other factors that may have prevented later generations of ambitious Parisians from acceding to higher status through the means used by the families studied here. The long-term effects of the general price inflation of the sixteenth century may by the end of the century have had important consequences for the management of patrimonial resources. As the price of royal office escalated, so too increased the magnitude of the fortune necessary to support the lifestyle expected of an officer of the crown.[8] Even wealthy families may have found it increasingly difficult to maintain their status without consolidating a major share of the family resources in the hands of the eldest son.

Less easily defined but nonetheless important were the changes wrought in the structure of society and the system of values by the prolonged turmoil of the religious and civil wars. J.H.M. Salmon has aptly described the period of religious wars as "the crucible in which some of the competing forces from an earlier age were consumed in the fire and others blended and transmuted into new compounds: it is the matrix for all that came after."[9] Under this stress, the principles of

[8] Giesey, "Rules of Inheritance," pp. 284-85, estimates that "a fortune five to six times greater than the value of the office itself was necessary to support the style of life it required."

[9] Salmon, *Society in Crisis*, p. 13.

order, authority, and hierarchy became more rigid. Stronger but less elastic, these principles were relied on increasingly to support monarchical authority, while the complex old networks of extended kinship and corporate affiliation and the old ethic of public service were weakened. Even that most essential building block of state power, the family, took on a new character as the forces of monarchical absolutism found their echo in patriarchal authority. The new piety of the Catholic Reformation accorded well with this conservative and authoritarian trend.

For the elite of mid-sixteenth-century Paris, however, these changes were of no moment. The families of the city councillors had made good use of a favorable conjuncture of social, economic, and political factors to secure their position and that of their descendants in the hierarchies of both city and state. The increasing rigidity of social and political hierarchies tended to strengthen the position of those already at the top, while the increasing prestige of the royal bureaucracy lengthened the distance that separated officers of the crown from the milieu from which they had sprung. The dominant families of sixteenth-century Paris were well situated to play an important role in the subsequent history of the city and the monarchy.

List of City Councillors,
1535-1575

City councillor	Dates	Other city office[a]	Professional activities		Principal estates
			Early career	Peak career	
Abelly, Louis	71-06[b]	E	Marchand, bourgeois	Bourgeois	Trilleport, Trousay
Aubery, Claude	69-87		Marchand, bourgeois	Secrétaire du roi	Trilleport, Trousay
Aubery, Jean	64-69	E	Marchand, bourgeois	Marchand, bourgeois	Gazeau, Velluyre
Aymeret, Raoul	32-36		Conseiller au Parlement	Conseiller au Parlement	Sceaux, Tresmes
Baillet, René	42-52		Conseiller au Parlement	Président au Parlement	
Barthelemy, Denis	48-57	Q, E	Marchand, bourgeois	Marchand, bourgeois	
Barthelemy, Jean	33-53	Q, E	Marchand, bourgeois	Bourgeois	Plessis-Belleville
Besançon, Louis	33-37		Conseiller au Parlement	Conseiller au Parlement	
Bochart, Jean	41-54		Greffier des Requêtes	Conseiller au Parlement	Champigny, Noroy
Boucher, Jacques	33-38		Elu	Maître des comptes	
Bragelongne, Jérôme de	69-94		Trésorier de l'Extraordinaire des Guerres	Secrétaire du roi	
Bragelongne, Martin de	34-69	E, PM	Conseiller au Châtelet	Lieutenant particulier au Châtelet	Charonne
Bragelongne, Thomas de	38-65	E	Conseiller au Châtelet	Lieutenant criminel au Châtelet	La Celle, Charmoy
Braillon, Louis	36-41		Docteur en médecine	Médecin ordinaire du roi	
Budé, Dreux	74-87		Secrétaire du roi	Notaire et secrétaire au Parlement	Yerres
Budé, Guillaume	?-40	PM	Secrétaire du roi	Maître des requêtes	Marly-la-Ville
Chomedy, Jérôme	65-84		Avocat au Parlement	Avocat au Parlement	Germenoy
Courlay, Guillaume de	53-83[c]	E	Secrétaire du roi	Contrôleur de l'audience du roi	Malassis, Vitry
Courtin, Jean	36-53	E	Auditeur en la Chambre des Comptes	Auditeur en la Chambre des Comptes	Bois-le-Vicomte

Name	Dates		Office (earlier)	Office (later)	Location
Cressé, Simon	65-77	E	Bourgeois	Général des monnaies	Chaillot
Croquet, Jean	49-68	Q, E	Marchand, bourgeois	Bourgeois	
Croquet, Pierre	53-72		Marchand, bourgeois	Marchand, bourgeois	
Du Drac, Adrien	32-71		Secrétaire du roi	Conseiller au Parlement	
Du Drac, Olivier	71-75		Conseiller au Parlement	Maître des requêtes	Ay, Beaulieu
Du Gué, Nicolas	59-71c		Avocat du roi en la Cour des Aides	Avocat du roi en la Cour des Aides	Ay, Beaulieu
Guillart, André	34-49	PM	Conseiller au Parlement	Maître des requêtes	Le Mortier
Guyot, Claude	48-76	PM	Secrétaire du roi	Président en la Chambre des Comptes	Charmeaux
Hacqueville, Nicolas	31-42	E	Avocat au Parlement	Lieutenant général de la Prévôté de la Marchandise	Attichy
Harlay, Christophe	32-36		Conseiller au Parlement	Président au Parlement	Beaumont
Hennequin, Oudart	49-57		Marchand, bourgeois	Maître des comptes	Boinville
Hennequin, Pierre	57-77		Conseiller au Parlement	Président au Parlement	Boinville
Huault, Louis	69-76		Noble, no office	Noble, no office	Montmagny
La Place, Nicolas de	73-01		Conseiller au Parlement	Conseiller aux Requêtes	Saint-Suplix
Larcher, Gervais	33-43	E	Marchand, bourgeois	Marchand, bourgeois	
Larcher, Guillaume	43-71	E	Marchand, bourgeois	Bourgeois	
Le Breton, Jean	72-89b		Avocat au Parlement	Avocat au Parlement	Evry-en-Brie
Le Charron, Jean	72-77	PM	Conseiller au Parlement	Président en la Cour des Aides	
Le Clerc, Nicolas	72-08b		Conseiller au Parlement	Président des Requêtes	Saint-Martin
Le Coirte, Antoine	40-53	E	Conseiller au Châtelet	Conseiller au Châtelet	
Le Lieur, Germain	34-46	E	Marchand, bourgeois	Marchand, bourgeois	
Le Lieur, Jean	47-49	E	Marchand, bourgeois	Marchand, bourgeois	
Le Lieur, Robert	?-47	Q	Marchand, bourgeois	Marchand, bourgeois	
Le Lievre, Antoine	48-53		Marchand, bourgeois	Marchand, bourgeois	
Le Lievre, Claude	?-48	Q, E	Marchand, bourgeois	Marchand, bourgeois	
Le Lievre, Philippe	53-98b		Avocat au Parlement	Avocat au Parlement	
Le Prestre, Claude	69-94b	E	Marchand, bourgeois	Marchand, bourgeois	

City councillor	Dates	Other city office[a]	Professional activities		Principal estates
			Early career	Peak career	
Le Prevost, Augustin	75-85	E	Avocat au Parlement	Notaire et secrétaire au Parlement	Brevant, Malval
Le Sueur, Claude	54-61	E	Marchand, bourgeois	Bourgeois	La Croix
Le Sueur, Jean	61-68	E	Marchand, bourgeois	Marchand, bourgeois	
Le Sueur, Nicolas	68-71		Greffier en la Cour des Aides	Secrétaire du roi	Osny
L'Hôpital, Michel de	46-61		Conseiller au Parlement	Chancelier	Vignay
Livres, Nicolas de	37-64	PM	Secrétaire du roi	Secrétaire du roi	Vienne, Ravenel
Longueil, Jacques de	68-69		Noble, no office	Maître de l'Hôtel du Roi	Sèvres
Lormier, Guy	53-59	E	Secrétaire du roi	Maître des comptes	L'Espine
Luillier, Cosme	52-60	E	Général des monnaies	Général des monnaies	Saulsay
Luillier, Jean	?-63	PM	Maître des comptes	Président en la Chambre des Comptes	Boulancourt, Saint-Mesmin
Luillier, Nicolas	63-83[b]	PM	Conseiller au Châtelet	Président en la Chambre des Comptes	Boulancourt
Marcel, Claude	64-90[b]	E, PM	Marchand, bourgeois	Intendant, contrôleur général des finances	Saint-Mesmin
Marle, Germain de	?-37	PM	Général des monnaies	Général des monnaies	Thillay
Marle, Guillaume de	60-64	PM	Maître des Eaux et Forêts	Maître de l'Hôtel du Roi	Versigny
Montmirail, Charles	?-40	E	Avocat au Parlement	Avocat au Parlement	Vaudoire
Montmirail, Etienne	33-49	PM	Conseiller au Parlement	Maître des requêtes	Montmirail, Fourqueux
Montmirail, Thierry	40-68		Noble, no office	Noble, no office	Chambourcy, Vaudoire
Morin, Jean	?-48	PM	Conseiller au Châtelet	Lieutenant civil au Châtelet	Paroy
Neufville, Nicolas de	68-72	PM	Secrétaire du roi	Conseiller au conseil privé	Villeroy
Paillart, Jacques I	38-66	E	Noble, no office	Noble, no office	Jumeauville
Paillart, Jacques II	66-01[b]		Avocat au Parlement	Avocat au Parlement	Jumeauville

Palluau, Claude	52-54		Marchand, bourgeois	Marchand, bourgeois	Palluau, L'Erang
Palluau, Jean	54-89[b]	E	Marchand, bourgeois	Secrétaire du roi	Bobigny
Perdrier, Pierre	36-52		Greffier de l'Hôtel de Ville	Secrétaire du roi	Carneaulx, Courtil
Perrot, Nicolas I	57-63	PM	Conseiller au Parlement	Marchand, bourgeois	
Perrot, Nicolas II	63-91[b]		Marchand, bourgeois	Conseiller au Parlement	
Poulain, Pierre	71-72	E	Conseiller au Parlement	Secrétaire du roi	Morsans, Villabry
Prevost, Bernard	71-85[b]		Conseiller au Parlement	Président au Parlement	Saint-Cyr
Prevost, Jean I	31-37		Conseiller au Parlement	Président au Parlement	Saint-Cyr, Villabry
Prevost, Jean II	37-71		Secrétaire du roi	Président en la Cour des Aides	
Saint-Germain, Robert	74-75		Secrétaire du roi	Notaire et secrétaire au Parlement	Livry
Sanguin, Jacques	69-87[b]	E	Général des Eaux et Forêts	Lieutenant général des Eaux et Forêts	Roquencourt
Sanguin, Jean	55-73	E	Secrétaire du roi	Contrôleur des Guerres	Santenay
Sanguin, Pierre	73-74		Auditeur en la Chambre des Comptes	Maître des requêtes	
Tanneguy, Denis	61-65	E	Avocat au Parlement	Avocat au Parlement	
Teste, Simon	31-38	E	Auditeur en la Chambre des Comptes	Correcteur en la Chambre des Comptes	
Thou, Augustin I de	?-36	PM	Avocat au Parlement	Président au Parlement	Bonneuil
Thou, Augustin II de	75-76	E, PM	Avocat du roi au Châtelet	Président au Parlement	Abbeville
Thou, Christophe de	37-82[d]	PM	Avocat au Parlement	Président au Parlement	Bonnoeil, Cély
Tronçon, Jean	34-49	PM	Conseiller au Châtelet	Conseiller au Parlement	Couldray
Voile, Pierre I	32-55		Conseiller au Parlement	Conseiller au Parlement	Athis
Voile, Pierre II	55-73		Conseiller au Parlement	Conseiller au Parlement	Athis
Vivien, René I	49-55		Secrétaire du roi	Secrétaire du roi	St. Maur, la Mothe
Vivien, René II	71-74		Secrétaire du roi	Correcteur en la Chambre des Comptes	La Mothe

[a] PM: Prévôt des marchands; E: Echevin; Q: Quartenier.
[b] Resigned *en survivance* at earlier date.
[c] Removed from office 1569-1571 as Protestant.
[d] Held office 1537-1576, again 1578-1582.

Bibliography

Principal Manuscript Sources

Archives nationales (Paris)
 M series   Genealogical dossiers and *preuves de Malte.*
 Y series   Châtelet records, in particular Y98-134: *insinuations* of
  notarial contracts, 1539-1600.
 Minutier central   Notarial records.
Bibliothèque nationale (Paris)
 Genealogical collections

	Pièces originales.
	Dossiers bleus.
	Carrés d'Hozier.
	Cabinet d'Hozier.
	Nouveau d'Hozier.
	Chérin.

Fonds français
 4815   *Cahiers* of Estates General of 1560.
 10871   *Cahiers* of Estates General of 1576.
 11692   Tax roll of £300,000 raised in 1572.
 18661   Genealogies of Parisian families.
 32138-39 Genealogies of royal officers.
 32356   Genealogies of Parisian families—Hozier.
 32359   Officers of the Hôtel de Ville—Chevillard.
 32585-94 Extracts of parish records—Guiblet.
 32838-39 Extracts of parish records—Saint-Gervais.
 32840   City councillors.
 32991   Cour des Aides.
Nouvelles acquisitions
 11854-82 Genealogical materials—Fleury Vindry.
 11904   Confraternity of "la Monnoye."
Collection Dupuy
 615   Memoirs of Philippe Hurault, bishop of
  Chartres.

632   Testament of Jacques-Auguste de Thou.
Collection de Factums
4°Fm14302   Simon Marion, *Factums et mémoires.*

Published Genealogical Sources and Bibliographical Tools

Barroux, Marius. *Les Sources de l'ancien état civil parisien. Répertoire critique.* Paris, 1898.

Bigot de Monville, Alexandre. *Recueil des présidents, conseillers, et autres officiers de l'Echiquier et du Parlement de Normandie, 1499-1550.* Edited by G. A. Prévost. Rouen, 1905.

Bluche, J. François. *L'Origine des magistrats du Parlement de Paris au xviiie siècle.* Mémoires publiés par la Fédération des sociétés historiques et archéologiques de Paris et de l'Ile-de-France, nos. 5-6 (1953-1954). Paris, 1956.

Brièle, Léon. *Inventaire sommaire des archives hospitalières antérieures à 1790.* Paris, 1882-1889.

C. d'E. A. [Chaix d'Est-Ange]. *Dictionnaire des familles françaises anciennes ou notables à la fin du xixe siècle.* 20 vols. Evreux, 1903-1929. [Useful despite inaccuracies.]

Clouzot, Etienne, ed. *Répertoire des sources manuscrites de l'histoire de Paris. Dépouillement d'inventaires et de catalogues.* 3 vols. Paris, 1915.

Compardon, Emile, and Alexandre Tuetey. *Inventaire des registres des insinuations du Châtelet de Paris. Règnes de François I et Henri II.* Histoire générale de Paris. Paris, 1906.

Coyecque, Ernest. *Recueil d'actes notariés relatifs à l'histoire de Paris et ses environs.* 2 vols. Paris, 1905-1923.

Delaruelle, Louis. *Répertoire analytique et chronologique de la correspondance de Guillaume Budé.* Paris, 1907.

Dollinger, Philippe; Philippe Wolff; and Simonne Guenée. *Bibliographie d'histoire des villes de France.* Paris, 1967.

Etat des inventaires des archives nationales, départmentales, communales, et hospitalières au 1er janvier 1937. Paris, 1938.

Frondeville, Henri de. *Les Conseillers du Parlement de Normandie. Recueil généalogique établi sur la base du manuscrit Bigot de la Bibliothèque de Rouen.* Rouen, 1960. [Useful despite inaccuracies.]

————. *Les Présidents du Parlement de Normandie (1499-1790). Recueil généalogique établi sur la base du manuscrit Bigot de la Bibliothèque de Rouen.* Rouen and Paris, 1953. [Useful despite inaccuracies.]

Hozier, Charles René d'. *Armorial de la généralité de Paris.* Published by Jacques Meurgey de Tupigny according to the manuscript in the Bibliothèque nationale. Mâcon, 1965-1967.

Jurgens[-Connat], Madeleine. *Documents du Minutier central concernant l'histoire de la musique (1600-1650).* Paris, [1967].

————. "Inventaires des bibliothèques contenus dans les inventaires après décès du Minutier central des notaires parisiens. Xvi^e siècle." Typescript available at AN, Minutier central.

La Chesnaye-Desbois, François Alexandre Aubert de, and Badier. *Dictionnaire de la noblesse.* 3rd ed. 19 vols. Paris, 1863-1877. [Highly inaccurate.]

Lacombe, Paul. *Bibliographie parisienne. Tableaux de Moeurs (1600-1880).* Paris, 1887.

Meurgey, Jacques Pierre, baron de Tupigny. *Guide des recherches généalogiques aux Archives nationales.* Paris, 1956.

Mirot, Léon. *Inventaire analytique des hommages rendus à la Chambre de France.* 2 vols. in 3. Melun, 1932-1945.

Saffroy, Gaston. *Bibliographie généalogique, héraldique, et nobiliaire de la France des origines à nos jours. Imprimés et manuscrits.* 2 vols. Paris, 1968-1970.

Soliday, Gerald L., ed. *History of the Family and Kinship: A Select International Bibliography.* Millwood, N.Y., 1980.

Trudon des Ormes, A. "Notes sur les prévôts des marchands et échevins de la ville de Paris au xviiie siècle (1701-1789)." *Mémoires de la Société de l'histoire de Paris et de l'Ile-de-France* 38 (1911): 107-223.

Tuetey, Alexandre. *Inventaire analytique des Livres de couleur et des Bannières du Châtelet de Paris.* Histoire générale de Paris. 2 vols. Paris, 1899-1907.

————. *Testaments enregistrés au Parlement de Paris sous le règne de Charles VI.* Published by the Comité des travaux historiques. Mélanges historiques; choix de documents; vol. 3. Paris, 1886.

Vilar-Berrogain, Gabrielle. *Guide des recherches dans les fonds d'enregistrement sous l'ancien régime.* Paris, 1958.

Published Primary Sources

[Ableiges, Jacques d']. *Le Grand Coutumier de France.* Edited by Edouard René Lefebvre de Laboulaye and Rodolphe Dareste de La Chavanne. Paris, 1514; reprint ed., Paris, 1868.

Académie des sciences morales et politiques, Paris. *Collection des ordonnances des rois de France: Catalogue des actes de François Ier.* 10 vols. Paris, 1887-1908.

Alberti, Leone Battista. *The Family in Renaissance Florence, a Translation of "I Libri della Famiglia."* Edited and translated by Renée Neu Watkins. Columbia, S.C., 1969.

Aubigné, Théodore Agrippa d'. *Histoire universelle.* Edited by Alphonse de Ruble. 10 vols. Paris, 1886-1907.

——. *Oeuvres complètes.* Edited by Eugène Reaume and F. de Caussade. 6 vols. Paris, 1873-1892.

Barillon, Jean. *Journal.* Edited by Pierre de Vaissière. 2 vols. Paris, 1897.

Blanchard, François, and Jean-Baptiste l'Hermite-Souliers. *Les Eloges de tous les premiers presidens du Parlement de Paris depuis qu'il a esté rendu sedentaire jusqu'à present.* Paris, 1645.

Bodin, Jean. *Les Six Livres de la république.* Darmstadt, 1961; facsimile of Paris, 1583 edition.

Boislisle, Arthur Michel de. *Chambre des Comptes de Paris. Pièces justificatives pour servir à l'histoire de ses premiers présidents (1506-1791).* Nogent-le-Rotrou, 1873.

——. *Histoire de la Maison de Nicolay.* 2 vols. Nogent-le-Rotrou, 1873-1875.

Bonnardot, François; Alexandre Tuetey; Paul Guérin; et al. *Registres des délibérations du Bureau de la Ville de Paris.* Histoire générale de Paris. Vols. 1-7. Paris, 1883-1893.

Bourdot de Richebourg, Charles Antoine. *Nouveau Coutumier général.* 4 vols. Paris, 1724.

Bourjon, François. *Le Droit commun de la France et la coutume de Paris.* 2 vols. New ed. Paris, 1770.

Bournon, Fernand, ed. "Chronique parisienne de Pierre Driart, chambrier de Saint-Victor (1522-1535)." *Mémoires de la Société de l'histoire de Paris et de l'Ile-de-France* 22 (1895):67-178.

Brièle, Léon. *Collection de documents pour servir à l'histoire des hôpitaux de Paris.* 4 vols. Paris, 1881-1887.

Brillon, Pierre Jacques. *Dictionnaire des arrêts ou Jurisprudence universelle des Parlemens de France et autres tribunaux.* 6 vols. New ed. Paris, 1727.

Brodeau, Julien. *Commentaire sur la coustume de la prevosté et vicomté de Paris.* 2 vols. Paris, 1658.

Brulart, Nicolas. "Journal des choses plus remarquables . . . (1559-

1569)." In *Mémoires de Condé*, edited by Denis François Sécousse, 1:2-211. Paris, 1743-1745.

Budé, Guillaume. *Epistolae*. [Paris, 1520].

————. *Epistolae . . . posteriores*. [Paris, 1522].

————. *Epistolarum Latinarum, Lib. V*. [Paris, 1531].

Les Caquets de l'accouchée. Recueil général suivi de l'Anti-Caquet. Paris, [1890].

Catherine de Médicis. *Lettres*. Edited by Hector de la Ferrière and Baguenault de Puchesse. 11 vols. Paris, 1880-1909.

Cheverny, Philippe Hurault, comte de. *Mémoires*. Nouvelle Collection des mémoires pour servir à l'histoire de France. Edited by Joseph François Michaud and Jean Joseph François Poujoulat. Ser. 1, 10:461-576. Paris, 1838.

Choppin, René. *Commentaire sur les coustumes de la prevosté et vicomté de Paris . . . divisé en trois livres et traduict en nostre vulgaire sur la dernière impression de l'an 1603*. Paris, 1614.

Coras, Jean de. *Paraphrase sur l'edict des mariages clandestinement contractez par les enfans de famille, contre le gré et consentement de leurs peres et meres*. Paris, 1572.

Coutumes de la prevosté et vicomté de Paris avec les notes de M. C. du Moulin . . . ensemble les observations de Messieurs J. Tournet, Jacques Joly, et Charles Labbé. Vol. 2. Paris, 1691.

Curzon, H. de. "Les Infortunés Amours d'Artuse Bailly, poésie inédite de 1583." *Mémoires de la Société de l'histoire de Paris et de l'Ile-de-France* 13 (1886):261-73.

Davis, James C., ed. and tr. *Pursuit of Power: Venetian Ambassadors' Reports on Turkey, France, and Spain in the Age of Philip II*. New York, 1970.

Deschamps, Eustache. *Oeuvres complètes*. Edited by Gaston Raynaud. 11 vols. Paris, n.d.; reprint ed., New York, 1966.

Des Maisons, M. F. *Nouveau Recueil d'arrests et réglemens du Parlement de Paris*. Paris, 1667.

Dictionnaire des ennoblissemens, ou Recueil des lettres de noblesse depuis leur origine, tiré des Registres de la Chambre des Comptes & de la Cour des Aides de Paris. 2 vols. in 1. Paris, 1788. [Unreliable.]

Du Moulin, Charles. *Conseil sur le faict du Concile de Trente*. Lyons, 1564.

————. *Les Notes de maistre Charles Du Moulin sur les coutumes de France. Mise par matières*. Paris, 1715.

Erasmus, Desiderius. *The Colloquies of Erasmus.* Translated by N. Bailey. 2 vols. London, 1878.

———. *La Correspondance d'Erasme et de Guillaume Budé.* Translated by Marie Madeleine de La Garanderie. Paris, 1967.

Fagniez, Gustave. "Fragment d'un répertoire de jurisprudence parisienne au xvᵉ siècle." *Mémoires de la Société de l'histoire de Paris et de l'Ile-de-France* 17 (1890):1-94.

———. "Mémorial juridique et historique de Mᵉ Guillaume Aubert, avocat au Parlement de Paris, avocat général à la Cour des Aides (deuxième moitié du xviᵉ siècle)." *Mémoires de la Société de l'histoire de Paris et de l'Ile-de-France* 36 (1909):47-82.

Favier, Jean. *Les Contribuables parisiens à la fin de la guerre de Cent Ans. Les Rôles d'impôt de 1421, 1423, et 1438.* Hautes Etudes médiévales et modernes, no. 11. Geneva and Paris, 1971.

Félibien, Michel, and Guy Alexis Lobineau. *Histoire de la Ville de Paris.* 5 vols. Paris, 1725.

Ferrière, Claude de. *La Science parfaite des notaires, ou le moyen de faire un parfait notaire.* Paris, 1682.

Filmer, Robert. *Patriarcha and Other Political Works.* Edited by Peter Laslett. Oxford, 1949.

Fortin, Gilles. *Conference de la Coustume de Paris avec les autres coustumes de France, et les ordonnances et arrests expositifs de quelques articles d'icelles, avec les notes de M. C. du Moulin.* Paris, 1651.

Fournier, Edouard, ed. *Variétés historiques et littéraires. Recueil de pièces volantes, rares, et curieuses en prose et en vers.* 10 vols. Paris, 1855-1863.

Gallia Christiana in provincias ecclesiasticas distributa. 16 vols. Paris, 1715-1865.

Guérin, Paul. "Délibérations politiques du Parlement et arrêts criminels du milieu de la première guerre de religion (1562)." *Mémoires de la Société de l'histoire de Paris et de l'Ile-de-France* 40 (1913):1-116.

Hurault, Philippe, Abbé de Pontlevoy and Bishop of Chartres. *Mémoires.* Nouvelle Collection des mémoires pour servir à l'histoire de France. Edited by Joseph François Michaud and Jean Joseph François Poujoulat. Ser. 1, 10:579-614. Paris, 1838.

Isambert, François André, et al. *Recueil général des anciennes lois françaises depuis l'an 420 jusqu'à la Révolution de 1789.* 29 vols. Paris, 1822-1833.

Joly, Claude, ed. *Divers opuscules tirez des memoires de Antoine Loisel, ausquels sont joints quelques ouvrages de Baptiste du Mesnil, de Pierre Pithou*. Paris, 1652.

"Journal de ce qui s'est passé en France durant l'année 1562, principalement dans Paris et à la Cour." *Revue Rétrospective*. Ser. 1, 5 (1834):81-116, 168-212.

Journal d'un bourgeois de Paris sous le règne de François I (1515-1536). Edited by Ludovic Lalanne. Paris, 1854.

La Croix du Maine, François Grudé, sieur de. *Les Bibliothèques françoises de La Croix du Maine et de Du Verdier, sieur de Vauprivas*. New ed. Edited by Jean Antoine Rigolay de Juvigny. 6 vols. Paris, 1772-1773.

La Fosse, Jean de. *Journal d'un curé ligueur*. Paris, [1865].

Lamare, Nicolas de. *Traité de la police*. 4 vols. Paris, 1705-1738.

Lamoignon, Guillaume de. *Recueil des Arrêtés*. New ed. Paris, 1777.

La Place, Pierre de. *Commentaires de l'estat de la religion et république soubs les Rois Henry et François seconds, et Charles neufieme* (1565). Choix de chroniques et mémoires sur l'histoire de France. Edited by J.A.C. Buchon. Paris, 1836. 2:1-200.

La Planche, Louis Régnier, sieur de. *Histoire de l'estat de France, tant de la république que de la religion sous le règne de François II*. Edited by Edouard Mennechet. 2 vols. Paris, 1836. [Vol. 2 contains the treatise "Du grand et loyal devoir, fidelité, et obeissance de Messieurs de Paris envers le roy et couronne de France," otherwise known as the "Livre des Marchands," often attributed to Régnier de La Planche.]

Le Bret, Cardin, *Recueil d'aucuns plaidoyez faits en la Cour des Aydes . . . ensemble un Plaidoyé dudit seigneur et arrest intervenu sur iceluy en la Cour de Parlement contre les enfans qui se marient sans le consentement de leurs peres et meres*. Paris, 1625.

Lehoux, Françoise. "Le Livre de Simon Teste, correcteur à la Chambre des Comptes au xvie siècle." *Bulletin philologique et historique du Comité des travaux historiques et scientifiques* (1940-1941), pp. 137-99.

Le Maistre, Gilles. *Oeuvres*. 2nd ed. Paris, 1673.

Le Prestre, Claude. *Questions notables de droict, decidees par plusieurs arrests de la Cour de Parlement, et distribuees par centuries. . . . Ensemble un traicté des mariages clandestins*. Paris, 1645.

Le Roux de Lincy, Antoine Jean Victor. *Recueil de chants historiques français depuis le xiie jusqu'au xviiie siècle*. Ser. 2: xvie siècle. Paris, 1842.

Le Roux de Lincy, Antoine Jean Victor, and Lazare Maurice Tisserand. *Paris et ses historiens aux xive et xve siècles. Documents et écrits originaux.* Histoire générale de Paris. Paris, 1867.

L'Estoile, Pierre de. *Journal de L'Estoile pour le règne de Henri III (1574-1589).* Edited by Louis Raymond Lefèvre. Paris, 1943.

————. *Journal de L'Estoile pour le règne de Henri IV.* Edited by Louis Raymond Lefèvre and André Martin. 2 vols. Paris, 1958.

"Lettre de Guillaume Poyet relative au mariage de Michel de l'Hospital." *Bulletin historique et scientifique de l'Auvergne*, no. 12 (1882): pp. 128-33.

L'Hospital, Michel de. *Oeuvres complètes.* Edited by Pierre Joseph Spiridion Duféy. 5 vols. Paris, 1824-1826; reprint ed., Geneva, 1968.

Loisel, Antoine. *Institutes coutumières.* Paris, 1637.

————. "Pasquier, ou Dialogue des Avocats du Parlement de Paris." In *Profession d'Avocat: Recueil de pièces concernant l'exercise de cette profession*, edited by André Marie Jean Jacques Dupin, 1:147-259. Paris, 1832.

La Louenge des femmes. Invention extraite du Commentaire de Pantagruel sus l'Androgyne de Platon. Lyons, 1551. Reprint ed., edited by Michael A. Screech. New York, 1967. [Probable author: Thomas Sébillet.]

Louet, Georges. *Recueil de plusieurs arrests notables du Parlement de Paris.* 2 vols. Paris, 1712.

Loyseau, Charles. *Cinq livres du droit des offices.* Paris, 1610.

————. *Traité des ordres et simples dignitez.* Cologne, 1613.

Malingré, Claude. *Les Antiquitez de la ville de Paris.* Paris, 1640.

Marguerite d'Angoulême, queen of Navarre. *L'Heptaméron des nouvelles.* 3 vols. New ed. Paris, 1853-1854.

Le Ménagier de Paris. Traité de morale et d'économie domestique composé vers 1393, par un parisien pour l'éducation de sa femme. 2 vols. Paris, 1847.

Mirot, Léon. "Deux Livres de raison parisiens du xvie siècle." Extract from *Mélanges en l'honneur de M. Fr. Martroye.* Published by the Société nationale des antiquaires de France. Paris, 1940.

Montaigne, Michel Eyquem de. *The Complete Essays of Montaigne.* Translated by Donald M. Frame. Stanford, 1958.

————. *Essais.* Edited by Albert Thibaudet. Paris, 1950. [Based on the Bordeaux edition.]

Olier, Nicolas Edouard. *Journal de Nicolas-Edouard Olier, conseiller au Parlement, 1593-1602*. Edited by L. Sandret. Paris, 1876.

Olivier-Martin, François. "Un Document inédit sur les travaux préparatoires de l'Ancienne Coutume de Paris." *Nouvelle Revue historique de droit français et étranger* 42 (1918):192-227.

————. "Les Manuscrits de Simon Marion et la coutume de Paris au xvie siècle." *Travaux juridiques et économiques de l'Université de Rennes* 7 (1920):135-240.

Ordonnances des rois de France de la troisième race, recueillies par ordre chronologique. 21 vols. Paris, 1723-1849.

Ormesson, André Le Fèvre d'. *Journal d'Olivier Lefèvre d'Ormesson.* Collection de documents inédits sur l'histoire de France. Edited by Pierre Adolphe Chéruel. Ser. 3: histoire politique. Vols. 1 and 2. Paris, 1860.

Paschal, Pierre de. *Journal de ce qui s'est passé en France durant l'année 1562 principalement dans Paris et à la cour.* Société d'histoire de France. Publications. Série antérieure à 1789. Paris, 1950.

Pasquier, Etienne. *L'Interprétation des Instituts de Justinien.* Paris, 1847.

————. *Lettres familières.* Edited by Dorothy Thickett. Paris, 1974.

————. *Les Oeuvres.* 2 vols. Amsterdam, 1723.

La Pourmenade du Pré aux Clercs. N.p., 1622.

Les Quinze Joies de mariage. Edited by Jean Rychner. Geneva and Paris, 1963.

Rabelais, François. *Oeuvres complètes.* Edited by Jacques Boulenger and Lucien Scheler. [Paris], 1955.

Raunié, Emile, and Max Prinet. *Epitaphier du vieux Paris. Recueil général des inscriptions funéraires des églises, couvents, collèges, hospices, cimetières et charniers depuis le Moyen Age jusqu'à la fin du xviiie siècle.* Histoire générale de Paris. 4 vols. Paris, 1890-1914.

[Ravenel, J.] "Testament de Guillaume Budé (1536)." *Bulletin de la Société de l'histoire de France.* 2e partie, 2 (1835):225-27.

Ribbe, Charles de. *Une Famille au xvie siècle d'après des documents originaux.* 3rd ed. Paris, 1879.

Ronsard, Pierre de. *Les Oeuvres: Texte de 1587.* Edited by Isidore Silver. 8 vols. Chicago, 1966-1970.

Roye, Jean de. *Journal, connu sous le nom de Chronique scandaleuse 1460-1483.* Edited by Bernard de Mandrot. 2 vols. Paris, 1894.

Ruble, A. de. "Journal de François Grin, religieux de Saint-Victor (1554-1570)." *Mémoires de la Société de l'histoire de Paris et de l'Ile-de-France* 21 (1894):1-52.

Sales, François de. *Introduction à la vie dévote*. In his *Oeuvres*, edited by André Ravier and Roger Devos. [Paris], 1969.

Sauval, Henri. *Histoire et recherches des antiquités de la ville de Paris*. 3 vols. Paris, 1724.

Seyssel, Claude de. *La Monarchie de France*. Edited by Jacques Poujol. Paris, 1961. [First published in 1515.]

Sieber, L. "Description de Paris par Thomas Platter le jeune, de Bâle (1599)." *Mémoires de la Société de l'histoire de Paris et de l'Ile-de-France* 23 (1896):167-225.

Tessereau, Abraham. *Histoire de la Chancellerie*. Paris, 1710.

Thou, Jacques-Auguste de. *Histoire universelle depuis 1543 jusqu'en 1607*. 16 vols. London, 1734.

————. *Mémoires*. Nouvelle Collection des mémoires pour servir à l'histoire de France. Edited by Joseph François Michaud and Jean Joseph François Poujoulat. Ser. 1, vol. 11. Paris, 1838.

Tronçon, Jean. *Le Droict françois et coustume de la prevosté et vicomté de Paris ou il est fait rapport du droict romain . . . avec les arrests donnez en interpretation d'icelles*. 4th ed. Paris, 1643.

Vauquelin, Jean, sieur de la Fresnaie. *Les Diverses Poésies*. 2 vols. Edited by Julien Travers. Caen, 1869.

Vidier, Alexandre; Léon Le Grand; Paul Dupieux; and Jacques Monicat. *Comptes du domaine de la ville de Paris*. Histoire générale de Paris. 2 vols. Paris, 1948-1958.

Villeroy, Nicolas de Neufville de. *Mémoires d'Estat par Monsieur de Villeroy*. Nouvelle Collection des mémoires pour servir à l'histoire de France. Edited by Joseph François Michaud and Jean Joseph François Poujoulat. Ser. 1, vol. 11. Paris, 1838.

Vives, Juan-Luis. *Vives' Introduction to Wisdom: A Renaissance Textbook*. Edited by Marian Leona Tobriner. New York, 1968.

Secondary Works

Ariès, Philippe. *L'Enfant et la vie familiale sous l'ancien régime*. Paris, 1960. [Translated by Robert Baldick as *Centuries of Childhood: A Social History of Family Life*. New York, 1962.]

Ascoli, Peter M. "The Sixteen and the Paris League, 1585-91." Ph.D. dissertation, University of California at Berkeley, 1972.

Audiat, Louis. "Un fils d'Estienne Pasquier, Nicolas Pasquier, . . . lieutenant général à Cognac." *Bulletin de la Société archéologique et historique de la Charente*, ser. 4, 9 (1873-1874):3-296.

Babeau, Albert. *La Ville sous l'ancien régime.* Paris, 1880.

Babelon, Jean Pierre. *Demeures parisiennes sous Henri IV et Louis XIII.* Paris, 1965.

Barnavi, Elie. *Le Parti de Dieu. Etude sociale et politique des chefs de la Ligue parisienne, 1585-1594.* Louvain, 1980.

Bart, Jean. "L'Egalité entre héritiers dans la region dijonnaise à la fin de l'ancien régime et sous la Révolution." *Mémoires de la Société pour l'histoire du droit et des institutions des anciens pays bourguignons, comtois et romands* 29 (1968-1969):65-78.

—————. *Recherches sur l'histoire des successions ab intestat dans le droit du Duché de Bourgogne du xiii⁰ à la fin du xvi⁰ siècle.* Paris, 1966.

Bascou-Bance, Paulette. "La Condition des femmes en France et les progrès des idées féministes du xvi⁰ au xviii⁰ siècles." *L'Information historique* 28 (1966):139-44.

Basdevant, Jules. *Des Rapports de l'Eglise et de l'Etat dans la législation du mariage du Concile de Trente au Code Civil.* Paris, 1900.

Baulant, Micheline. "Le Prix des grains à Paris." *Annales. Economies, sociétés, civilisations* 23 (1968):520-40.

—————. "Prix et salaires à Paris au xvi⁰ siècle. Sources et résultats." *Annales. Economies, sociétés, civilisations* 31 (1976): 954-95.

—————. "Le Salaire des ouvriers du bâtiment à Paris de 1400 à 1726." *Annales. Economies, sociétés, civilisations* 26 (1971):463-83.

Bels, Pierre. *Le Mariage des Protestants français jusqu'en 1685. Fondements doctrinaux et pratique juridique.* Paris, 1968.

Benedict, Philip. *Rouen during the Wars of Religion.* Cambridge Studies in Early Modern History. Cambridge, England, 1981.

Berkner, Lutz K. "The Stem Family and the Developmental Cycle of the Household: An Eighteenth-Century Austrian Example." *American Historical Review* 72 (1972):398-418.

Berty, Adolphe, and Henri Legrand. *Topographie historique du Vieux Paris. Région du Louvre et des Tuileries.* Histoire générale de Paris. 2 vols. Paris, 1866-1868.

Bézard, Yvonne. *La Vie rurale dans le sud de la région parisienne de 1450 à 1560.* Paris, 1929.

Bieler, André. *L'Homme et la femme dans la morale calviniste.* Geneva, 1963.

Bitton, Davis. *The French Nobility in Crisis: 1560-1640.* Stanford, 1969.

Bloch, Jean Richard. *L'Anoblissement en France au temps de François I.* Paris, 1934.

Bluche, J. François. *Les Magistrats du Parlement de Paris au xviiie siècle (1715-1771)*. Paris, 1960.

—————, and Pierre Durye. *L'Anoblissement par charges avant 1789*. 2 vols. Les cahiers nobles, nos. 23-24. [La Roche-sur-Yon, 1962].

Boinet, Amédée. *Les Eglises parisiennes*. Vol. 1: *Moyen Age et Renaissance*. Paris, 1958.

Boislisle, Arthur de. "Le Quartier Saint-Honoré et les origines du Palais-Cardinal." *Mémoires de la Société de l'histoire de Paris et de l'Ile-de-France* 36 (1909):1-46.

—————. "Topographie historique de la seigneurie de Bercy, par Charles-Henri de Malon, seigneur de Bercy." *Mémoires de la Société de l'histoire de Paris et de l'Ile-de-France* 8 (1881):1-94.

Boulay, César Egasse du. *Historia Universitatis parisiensis*. 6 vols. Paris, 1665-1673.

Bourdieu, Pierre. "Les Stratégies matrimoniales dans le système de réproduction." *Annales. Economies, sociétés, civilisations* 27 (1972): 1,105-25.

Bourgeon, Jean Louis. "L'Ile de la Cité pendant la Fronde. Structure sociale." *Mémoires de la Fédération des sociétés historiques et archéologiques de Paris et de l'Ile-de-France* 13 (1962):23-144.

Bréjon, Jacques. *André Tiraqueau, 1488-1558*. Paris, 1937.

Brémond, Henri. *Histoire littéraire du sentiment religieux en France depuis la fin des guerres de religion jusqu'à nos jours*. 11 vols. Paris, 1916-1933.

Britton, Edward. "The Peasant Family in Fourteenth-Century England." *Peasant Studies* 5 (1976):2-7.

Brucker, Gene. *The Civic World of Early Renaissance Florence*. Princeton, 1977.

Calliat, Victor, and Antoine Jean Victor Le Roux de Lincy. *Eglise Saint-Eustache à Paris*. Paris, 1850.

Carsalade du Pont, Henri de. *La Municipalité parisienne à l'époque d'Henri IV*. Collection histoire des institutions, vol. 4. Paris, [1971].

Castan, Yves. *Honnêteté et relations sociales en Languedoc, 1715-1780*. Paris, 1974.

Cazelles, Raymond. *Nouvelle Histoire de Paris de la fin du règne de Philippe Auguste à la mort de Charles V, 1223-1380*. Paris, 1972.

Champion, Pierre Honoré Jean Baptiste. *Paris au temps de la Renaissance. L'Envers de la tapisserie: le règne de François Ier*. Paris, 1935.

————. *Paris au temps de la Renaissance. Paganisme et réforme: Fin du règne de François Ier. Henri II.* Paris, 1936.

————. *Paris au temps des guerres de religion. Fin du règne de Henri II. Régence de Catherine de Médicis. Charles IX.* Paris, 1938.

Chaunu, Pierre. *La Mort à Paris: Xvi^e, xviie, et xviiie siècles.* Paris, 1978.

Chénon, Emile. *Histoire générale du droit français et privé des origines à 1815.* 2 vols. Paris, 1929.

Chojnacki, Stanley. "Dowries and Kinsmen in Early Renaissance Venice." *Journal of Interdisciplinary History* 5 (1975):571-600.

————. "Patrician Women in Early Renaissance Venice." *Studies in the Renaissance* 21 (1974):176-203.

Church, William F. *Constitutional Thought in Sixteenth-Century France.* Cambridge, Mass., 1941.

Coornaert, Emile. *Les Français et le commerce international à Anvers: Fin du xve-xvie siècle.* Paris, 1961.

Coquerel, Athanase Josué. *Précis de l'histoire de l'Eglise Réformée de Paris. Première époque, 1512-1594. De l'Origine de l'église à l'Edit de Nantes.* Paris and Strasbourg, 1862.

Cougny, M. E. *Etudes historiques et littéraires sur le Parlement de Paris. De la philosophie chez les jurisconsultes du xvie siècle et en particulier chez Simon Marion.* Paris, 1865.

Couperie, Pierre, and Madeleine Jurgens. "Le Logement à Paris au xvie et xviie siècles: Une Source, les inventaires après décès." *Annales. Economies, sociétés, civilisations* 17 (1962):488-500.

Daumard, Adeline, and François Furet. *Structures et relations sociales à Paris au milieu du xviiie siècle.* Paris, 1961.

Davis, Natalie Zemon. "Ghosts, Kin, and Progeny: Some Features of Family Life in Early Modern France." *Daedalus* (Spring, 1977: "The Family"), pp. 87-114.

————. *Society and Culture in Early Modern France: Eight Essays.* Stanford, 1975.

Delachenal, Roland. *Histoire des avocats au Parlement de Paris: 1300-1600.* Paris, 1885.

Delaruelle, Louis. *Guillaume Budé: Les Origines, les débuts, les idées maîtresses.* Geneva, 1970.

Denière, Georges. *La Juridiction consulaire de Paris; 1563-1792. Sa Création, ses luttes, son administration intérieure, ses usages, et ses mœurs.* Paris, 1872.

Dent, Julian. *Crisis in Finance: Crown, Financiers, and Society in Seventeenth-Century France.* New York, 1973.

Deronne, Elianne. "Les Origines des chanoines de Notre Dame de Paris de 1450 à 1550." *Revue d'histoire moderne et contemporaine* 18 (1971):1-16.

Desjardins, Albert. *Les Sentiments moraux au xvie siècle.* Paris, 1887.

Desmaze, Charles. *Le Châtelet de Paris. Son organisation, ses privilèges (1060-1862).* Paris, 1863.

Dessert, Daniel. "Finances et société au xviie siècle: A propos de la Chambre de Justice de 1661." *Annales. Economies, sociétés, civilisations* 29 (1974):847-82.

Devyver, André. *Le Sang épuré. Les Préjugés de race chez les gentilshommes français de l'ancien régime (1560-1720).* Brussels, 1973.

Dewald, Jonathan. *The Formation of a Provincial Nobility: The Magistrates of the Parlement of Rouen, 1499-1610.* Princeton, 1980.

————. "Magistracy and Political Opposition at Rouen: A Social Context." *Sixteenth Century Journal* 5 (1974):66-78.

Deyon, Pierre. *Etude sur la société urbaine au xviie siècle: Amiens, capitale provinciale.* Paris, 1967.

Dickerman, Edmund H. *Bellièvre and Villeroy: Power in France under Henry III and Henry IV.* Providence, 1971.

Diefendorf, Barbara B. "Widowhood and Remarriage in Sixteenth-Century Paris." *Journal of Family History* (forthcoming).

Dollinger, Philippe. *The German Hansa.* Translated by D. S. Ault and S. H. Steinberg. Stanford, 1970.

Doucet, Roger. *Les Bibliothèques parisiennes au xvie siècle.* Paris, 1956.

————. *Les Institutions de la France au xvie siècle.* 2 vols. Paris, 1948.

Douglas, Richard M. "Talent and Vocation in Humanist and Protestant Thought." In *Action and Conviction in Early Modern Europe. Essays in Memory of E. H. Harbison,* edited by Theodore K. Rabb and Jerrold E. Seigel, pp. 261-98. Princeton, 1969.

Doumergue, E. "Paris protestant au xvie siècle, 1509-1572." *Bulletin de la Société de l'histoire du protestantisme français* 45 (1896):113-32.

Dubief, Henri. "Les Opérations commerciales de Louis Guillart, évêque de Tournai, puis de Chartres en 1524." *Revue du Nord* 43 (1961):149-54.

Duguit, Léon. "Etude historique sur le rapt de séduction." *Nouvelle Revue historique de droit français et étranger,* ser. 3, vol. 10 (1886).

Dumolin, Maurice. *Etudes de topographie parisienne*. 3 vols. Paris, 1929-1931.

Dupont-Ferrier, Gustave. *Etudes sur les institutions financières de la France à la fin du Moyen Age*. Vol. 1: *Les Elections et leur personnel*. Vol. 2: *Les Finances extraordinaires*. [Paris], 1930-1932.

————. *Les Officiers royaux des bailliages et sénéchaussées et les institutions monarchiques locales en France à la fin du Moyen Age*. Bibliothèque de l'Ecole des hautes études. Sciences historiques et philologiques, vol. 145. Paris, 1902.

————. *Les Origines et le premier siècle de la Cour du Trésor*. Nouvelle Série d'études sur les institutions financières de la France à la fin du Moyen Age. Paris, 1936.

————. *Le Personnel de la Cour du Trésor (1310-1520)*. Special edition of the Annuaire/Bulletin de la Société de l'histoire de France, 1935-1937. Paris, 1938.

Dupré La Sale, Emile. *Michel de L'Hospital avant son élévation au poste de chancelier de France (1505-1558)*. Paris, 1875.

Duret-Robert, François. "La Dame à la Licorne." *Connaissance des Arts*, no. 269 (1974), pp. 27-34.

Edelstein, Marilyn M. "The Social Origins of the Episcopacy in the Reign of Francis I." *French Historical Studies* 8 (1974):377-92.

Erlanger, Philippe. *St. Bartholomew's Night. The Massacre of Saint Bartholomew*. Translated by Patrick O'Brian. New York, 1962.

Esmein, Adhémar. *Le Mariage en droit canonique*. 2 vols. Paris, 1891.

Estèbe, Janine. *Tocsin pour un massacre. La Saison des Saint-Barthélemy*. Paris, 1968.

Fagniez, Gustave. *La Femme et la société française dans la première moitié du xviie siècle*. Paris, 1929.

Favier, Jean. *Nouvelle Histoire de Paris. Paris au xve siècle (1380-1500)*. Paris, 1974.

————. "Une Ville entre deux vocations, la place d'affaires de Paris au xve siècle." *Annales. Economies, sociétés, civilisations* 28 (1973):1,245-79.

Favreau, Robert. "Les Changeurs du royaume sous le règne de Louis XI." *Bibliothèque de l'Ecole des chartes* 122 (1964):216-51.

Febvre, Lucien. *Amour sacré, amour profane: Autour de l'Heptaméron*. Paris, 1971.

————. *Au Coeur religieux du xvie siècle*. Paris, 1957.

Ferté, Jeanne. *La Vie religieuse dans les campagnes parisiennes (1622-1695)*. Paris, 1962.

Filhol, René. "L'Application de l'Edit des Secondes Noces en pays coutumier." In *Mélanges Roger Aubenas (Recueil de mémoires et travaux publié par la Société d'histoire du droit et des institutions des anciens pays de droit écrit)* 9 (1974):295-99.

――――. *Les Avocats au Parlement de Paris dans la seconde moitié du seizième siècle.* Barreau de Poitiers. Discours prononcé à la séance solonnelle de réouverture de la conférence des avocats stagiaires le 3 février 1934. Poitiers, 1934.

――――. *Le Premier Président Christofle de Thou et la réformation des coutumes.* Paris, 1937.

Flandrin, Jean Louis. *Familles: Parenté, maison, sexualité dans l'ancienne société.* Paris, 1976.

Fosseyeux, Marcel. "L'Assistance parisienne au milieu du xvie siècle." *Mémoires de la Société de l'histoire de Paris et de l'Ile-de-France* 43 (1916):83-128.

Foster, Frank F. "Politics and Community in Elizabethan England." In *The Rich, the Well Born and the Powerful. Elites and Upper Classes in History*, edited by Frederic Cople Jaher, pp. 110-38. Urbana, Ill., 1973.

Fournel, Jean François. *Histoire des avocats du Parlement et du barreau de Paris depuis S. Louis jusqu'au 15 octobre 1790.* 2 vols. Paris, 1813.

Fourquin, Guy. *Les Campagnes de la région parisienne à la fin du Moyen Age: Du Milieu du xiiie siècle au début du xvie siècle.* Paris, 1964.

――――. "Le Droit parisien de la fin du Moyen Age: Droit des 'notables.' " In *Etudes d'histoire du droit parisien*, edited by François Dumont, pp. 375-95. Paris, 1970.

Fraguier, Louis, marquis de. *Une famille parisienne.* Paris, 1963.

Franklin, Alfred Louis Auguste. *Les Corporations ouvrières de Paris du xiie au xviiie siècles.* Paris, 1884.

Franklin, Julian H. *Jean Bodin and the Sixteenth-Century Revolution in the Methodology of Law and History.* New York, 1963.

Frégier, Honoré Antoine. *Histoire de l'administration de la police de Paris depuis Philippe Auguste jusqu'aux Etats-généraux de 1789.* 2 vols. Paris, 1850.

Friedl, Ernestine. "The Position of Women: Appearance and Reality." *Anthropological Quarterly* 40 (1967):97-108.

Galpern, A. N. *The Religions of the People in Sixteenth-Century Champagne.* Harvard Historical Studies, vol. 92. Cambridge, Mass., 1976.

Gascon, Richard. *Grand Commerce et vie urbaine au xvie siècle: Lyon et ses marchands (environs de 1520-environs de 1580)*. Paris, 1971.

——. "Immigration et croissance urbaine au xvie siècle: L'Exemple de Lyon." *Annales. Economies, sociétés, civilisations* 25 (1970):988-1,002.

Gaudemet, J. "Législation canonique et attitudes séculières à l'égard du lien matrimonial au xviie siècle." *Xvii^e Siècle*, nos. 102-103 (1974), pp. 15-30.

Ghestin, Jacques. "L'Action des Parlements contre les 'mésalliances' aux xviie et xviiie siècles." *Revue historique de droit français et étranger*, ser. 4, vol. 34 (1956), 74-110, 196-224.

Giesey, Ralph E. "Rules of Inheritance and Strategies of Mobility in Prerevolutionary France," *American Historical Review* 82 (1977): 271-89.

Glasson, E. *Le Parlement de Paris. Son Rôle politique depuis le règne de Charles VII jusqu'à la Révolution*. 2 vols. Paris, 1901.

Goody, John Rankine, ed. *The Developmental Cycle in Domestic Groups*. Cambridge Papers in Social Anthropology, no. 1. Cambridge, England, 1969.

——, and S. J. Tambiah. *Bridewealth and Dowry*. Cambridge Papers in Social Anthropology, no. 7. Cambridge, England, 1973.

——; Joan Thirsk; and E. P. Thompson, eds. *Family and Inheritance. Rural Society in Western Europe, 1200-1800*. Cambridge, England, 1976.

Goubert, Pierre. *L'Ancien Régime*. Vol. 1: *La Société*. Vol. 2: *Les Pouvoirs*. Paris, 1969, 1973.

Gouesse, Jean-Marie. "La Formation du couple en Basse-Normandie." *Xvii^e Siécle*, nos. 102-103 (1974), pp. 45-58.

——. "Parenté, famille, et mariage en Normandie aux xviie et xviiie siècles." *Annales. Economies, sociétés, civilisations* 27 (1972): 1,139-54.

Gourmelon, Roger. "Etude sur le rayonnement commercial des marchands drapiers parisiens au xvie siècle." *Bulletin philologique et historique (jusqu'à 1610) du Comité des travaux historiques et scientifiques*, 1961 (1963), pp. 265-75.

Graham, Victor E., and W. McAllister Johnson. *The Paris Entries of Charles IX and Elisabeth of Austria, 1571*. Toronto, 1974.

Greven, Philip J., Jr. *Four Generations: Population, Land, and Family in Colonial Andover, Massachusetts*. Ithaca, 1970.

Guenée, Bernard. *Tribunaux et gens de justice dans le bailliage de Senlis à la fin du Moyen Age (vers 1380-vers 1550)*. Paris, 1963.

Guiffrey, Jules. "Les Gobelins, teinturiers en écarlate au faubourg Saint-Marcel." *Mémoires de la Société de l'histoire de Paris et de l'Ile-de-France* 31 (1904):1-92.

Haag, Eugène, and Emile Haag. *La France protestante*. 10 vols. Paris, 1846-1859.

Harding, Robert R. *Anatomy of a Power Elite: The Provincial Governors of Early Modern France*. New Haven, 1978.

Hayden, J. Michael. *France and the Estates General of 1614*. Cambridge, 1974.

—————. "The Social Origins of the French Episcopacy at the Beginning of the Seventeenth Century." *French Historical Studies* 10 (1977):27-40.

Haye, E., Abbé. "Notes historiques sur Chartres et le diocèse pendant l'épiscopat de Louis et de Charles Guillart (1525-1553, 1553-1573)." *Mémoires de la Société archéologique d'Eure-et-Loir* 10 (1896):241-72, and 423-60.

Herlihy, David. "Some Psychological Roots of Violence in the Tuscan Cities." In *Violence and Civil Disorder in Italian Cities, 1200-1500*, edited by Lauro Martines, pp. 129-54. Berkeley and Los Angeles, 1972.

—————, and Christiane Klapisch-Zuber. *Les Toscans et leurs familles: Une Etude du catasto florentin de 1427*. Paris, 1978.

Héron de Villefosse, René. *Bourgeois de Paris*. Paris, 1941.

Hervier, Dominique. "Un Serviteur de Louis XII et François Ier. Pierre Le Gendre et son inventaire après décès, 1524." *Bibliothèque d'humanisme et renaissance* 33 (1971):647-57.

Hexter, John H. *The Vision of Politics on the Eve of the Reformation. More, Machiavelli, and Seyssel*. New York, 1973.

Hogrefe, Pearl. "Legal Rights of Tudor Women and their Circumvention by Men and Women." *Sixteenth Century Journal* 3 (1972):97-105.

Holmès, Catherine E. *L'Eloquence judiciare de 1620 à 1660: Reflet des problèmes sociaux, religieux, et politiques de l'époque*. Paris, 1967.

Hufton, Olwen. "Women and the Family Economy in Eighteenth-Century France." *French Historical Studies* 9 (1975):1-23.

Huisman, Georges. *La Juridiction de la municipalité parisienne de Saint Louis à Charles VII*. Bibliothèque d'histoire de Paris, vol. 3. Paris, 1912.

Hunt, David. *Parents and Children in History: The Psychology of Family Life in Early Modern France*. New York, 1970.

Huppert, George. *Les Bourgeois Gentilshommes: An Essay on the Definition of Elites in Renaissance France*. Chicago, 1977.

————. *The Idea of Perfect History. Historical Erudition and Historical Philosophy in Renaissance France*. Urbana, Ill., 1970.

Imbart de la Tour, Pierre. *Les Origines de la Réforme*. 4 vols. Paris, 1905-1935.

Jacquart, Jean. *La Crise rurale en Ile-de-France, 1550-1670*. Paris, 1974.

Jassemin, Henri. *La Chambre des Comptes de Paris*. Paris, 1933.

Jeannin, Pierre. *Les Marchands au xviᵉ siècle*. Paris, 1957. [Translated by Paul Fittingoff as *Merchants of the Sixteenth Century*. New York, 1972.]

Jouanna, Arlette. *L'Idée de race en France au XVIème siècle et au début du XVIIème siècle: 1498-1614*. 3 vols. Lille, 1976.

Kelley, Donald R. *Foundations of Modern Historical Scholarship: Language, Law, and History in the French Renaissance*. New York, 1970.

————. *François Hotman; A Revolutionary's Ordeal*. Princeton, 1973.

————. "Martyrs, Myths, and the Massacre: The Background of St. Bartholomew." *American Historical Review* 77 (1972):1,323-42.

Kelso, Ruth. *Doctrine for the Lady of the Renaissance*. Urbana, Ill., 1960.

Kent, Francis William. *Household and Lineage in Renaissance Florence. The Family Life of the Capponi, Ginori, and Rucellai*. Princeton, 1977.

Kraus, Michael J. "Patronage and Reform in the France of the Préréforme: The Case of Clichtove." *Canadian Journal of History* 6 (1971):45-68.

Labatut, Jean Pierre. *Les Ducs et pairs de France au xviiᵉ siècle: Etude sociale*. Paris, 1972.

Lafon, Jacques. *Les Epoux bordelais: Régimes matrimoniaux et mutations sociales, 1450-1550*. Paris, 1972.

Lambert, Edouard. *De L'Exhérédation et les legs faits au profit des héritiers présomptifs*. Paris, 1895.

Laplanche, Jean de. *La Réserve héréditaire dans l'ancien droit français*. Paris, 1925.

Larmour, Ronda. "The Grocers of Paris in the Sixteenth Century: Corporations and Capitalism." Ph.D. dissertation, Columbia University, 1963.

Laslett, Peter. "La Famille et le ménage: Approches historiques."
    Annales. Economies, sociétés, civilisations 27 (1972):847-72.
————, and Richard Wall, eds. *Household and Family in Past Time.*
    Cambridge, England, 1972.
Lavedan, Pierre. *Histoire de Paris.* 2nd ed. Paris, 1967.
Lebeuf, Abbé. *Histoire de la ville et de tout le diocèse de Paris.* Edited
    by M. Augier. 7 vols. Paris, 1883-1893.
Lebrun, François. *La Vie conjugale sous l'ancien régime.* Paris, 1975.
Lecaron, Frédéric. "Les Origines de la municipalité parisienne." *Mé-
    moires de la Société de l'histoire de Paris et de l'Ile-de-France* 7 (1880):
    79-174; 8 (1881):161-272.
Lefebvre-Teillard, Anne. *Les Officialités à la veille du Concile de Trente.*
    Paris, 1973.
Lehoux, Françoise. *Gaston Olivier, aumônier du roi Henri II, 1552:
    Bibliothèque parisienne et mobilier du xvi*ᵉ *siècle.* Paris, 1957.
————. *Médecins à Paris: Le Cadre de vie des médecins parisiens aux
    xvi*ᵉ *et xvii*ᵉ *siècles.* Paris, 1976.
Le Lièvre, Jacques. *La Pratique des contrats de mariage chez les notaires
    au Châtelet de Paris de 1789 à 1804.* Paris, 1959.
Lemercier, Pierre. *Les Justices seigneuriales de la région parisienne de
    1580 à 1789.* Paris, 1933.
Lepointe, Gabriel. *Droit romain et ancien droit français: Régimes ma-
    trimoniaux, liberalités, successions.* Paris, 1958.
Le Roux de Lincy, Antoine Jean Victor. *Histoire de l'Hôtel de Ville
    de Paris. Suivie d'un essai sur l'ancien gouvernement municipal de cette
    ville.* Paris, 1846.
————. *Recherches sur la grande confrérie Notre-Dame aux prêtres et
    bourgeois de la ville de Paris.* Paris, 1844.
Le Roy Ladurie, Emmanuel. "Structures familiales et coutumes
    d'héritage en France au xvie siècle: Système de la coutume." *An-
    nales. Economies, sociétés, civilisations* 27 (1972):825-46.
————, and Pierre Couperie. "Le Mouvement des loyers parisiens
    de la fin du Moyen Age au xviiie siècle." *Annales. Economies, so-
    ciétés, civilisations* 25 (1970):1,002-23.
Lespinasse, René de. *Les Métiers et corporations de la ville de Paris.* 3
    vols. Paris, 1886-1897.
Litchfield, R. Burr. "Demographic Characteristics of Florentine
    Families: Sixteenth to Nineteenth Centuries." *Journal of Economic
    History* 29 (1969):191-205.

Lougee, Carolyn C. *Le Paradis des Femmes: Women, Salons, and Social Stratification in Seventeenth-Century France.* Princeton, 1976.

McNeil, David O. *Guillaume Budé and Humanism in the Reign of Francis I.* Travaux d'humanisme et renaissance, no. 142. Geneva, 1975.

Magne, Emile. *Paris sous l'Echevinage au xvii* siècle.* Paris, 1960.

Major, J. Russell. "The Crown and the Aristocracy in Renaissance France." *American Historical Review* 69 (1964):631-45.

————. *The Deputies to the Estates General in Renaissance France.* Studies presented to the International Commission for the History of Representative and Parliamentary Institutions, no. 21. Madison, Wis., 1960.

————. *The Estates General of 1560.* Princeton, 1951.

————. *Representative Institutions in Renaissance France, 1421-1559.* Madison, Wis., 1960.

Mandrou, Robert. *Introduction à la France moderne (1500-1640). Essai de psychologie historique.* Paris, 1961.

Maquet, Adrien. "Histoire de l'Etang-la-Ville." *Mémoires de la Société de l'histoire de Paris et de l'Ile-de-France* 11 (1884):208-48.

Marion, Marcel, *Dictionnaire des institutions de la France aux xvii* et xviii* siècles.* Paris, 1923; reprint ed., Paris, 1972.

Martin, Xavier. *Le Principe d'égalité dans les successions roturières en Anjou et dans le Maine.* Travaux et recherches de l'Université de droit, d'économie, et de sciences sociales de Paris. Série sciences historiques, no. 23. Paris, 1972.

Martines, Lauro, *Lawyers and Statecraft in Renaissance Florence.* Princeton, 1968.

Maugis, Edouard. *Histoire du Parlement de Paris de l'avènement des rois Valois à la mort d'Henri IV.* 3 vols. Paris, 1913-1916; reprint ed., New York, 1967.

Michaud, Hélène. *La Grande Chancellerie et les écritures royales au 16*^e *siècle, 1515-1589.* Paris, 1967.

Mieck, Ilja. "Die Bartholomäusnacht als Forschungsproblem. Kritische Bestandsaufnahme und Neue Aspekte." *Historische Zeitschrift* 216 (1973):73-110.

Miron de l'Espinay, Albert. *François Miron et l'administration municipale de Paris sous Henri IV, de 1604 à 1606.* Paris, 1885.

Molho, Anthony. "Politics and the Ruling Class in Early Renaissance Florence." *Nuova Rivista Storica* 52 (1968):401-20.

Monter, E. William. "Historical Demography and Religious History in Sixteenth-Century Geneva." *Journal of Interdisciplinary History* 9 (1979):399-427.

Mousnier, Roland. *Etat et société sous François I et pendant le gouvernement personnel de Louis XIV*. 2 vols. Cours de Sorbonne. Paris, 1966.

————. "L'Evolution des institutions monarchiques en France et ses relations avec l'état social." *Xvii^e Siècle*, nos. 58-59 (1963), pp. 57-72.

————. *Les Hiérarchies sociales de 1450 à nos jours*. Paris, 1969.

————. *Les Institutions de France sous la monarchie absolue, 1598-1789*. Vol. 1: *Etat et Société*. Vol. 2: *Les Organes de l'Etat et la Société*. Paris, 1974, 1980.

————. *Paris au xviie siècle*. 3 vols. in 1. Paris, 1961.

————. *La Plume, la faucille, et le marteau*. Paris, 1970.

————. "Recherches sur les structures sociales parisiennes en 1634, 1635, 1636." *Revue historique*, no. 507 (1973), pp. 35-58.

————. *La Vénalité des offices sous Henri IV et Louis XIII*. Rouen, 1945. [2nd ed.: Paris, 1971.]

————, et al. *Le Conseil du Roi de Louis XII à la Révolution*. Paris, 1970.

Mouton, Léo. *La Vie municipale au xvie siècle. Claude Marcel, prévôt des marchands, 1520-1590*. Paris, 1930.

Muchembled, Robert. "Famille, amour, et mariage: Mentalités et comportements des nobles artésiens à l'époque de Philippe II." *Revue d'histoire moderne et contemporaine* 22 (1975):233-61.

Normand, Charles. *La Bourgeoisie française au xviie siècle. La Vie publique, les idées et les actions politiques. Etude sociale*. N.p., 1908.

Nouaillac, Joseph. *Villeroy: Secrétaire d'Etat et ministre de Charles IX, Henri III, et Henri IV (1543-1610)*. Paris, 1909.

Olivier-Martin, François. *Histoire de la coutume de la prévôté et vicomté de Paris*. 2 vols. Paris, 1922-1926.

————. *Histoire du droit français des origines à la Révolution*. Paris, 1946.

Ormont, H. "Notes sur la famille de Guillaume Budé." *Bulletin de la Société de l'histoire de France* (1885), pp. 45-50.

Ourliac, Paul, and Jehan de Malafosse. *Histoire du droit privé*. 3 vols. Paris, 1968-1973.

Pasquier, Emile, Abbé. *Un Curé de Paris pendant les guerres de religion; René Benoist, le pape des Halles, 1521-1608*. Paris, 1913.

Picot, Georges. "Recherches sur les quarteniers, cinquanteniers et dizainiers de la ville de Paris." *Mémoires de la Société de l'histoire de Paris et de l'Ile-de-France* 1 (1874):132-66.

Pillorget, René, and Jean de Viguerie. "Les Quartiers de Paris aux xviie et xviiie siècles." *Revue d'histoire moderne et contemporaine* 17 (1970):253-77.

Pirenne, Henri. *Medieval Cities: Their Origins and the Revival of Trade.* Translated by Frank D. Halsey. Princeton, 1952.

Plattard, Jean. *Guillaume Budé (1468-1540) et les origines de l'humanisme français.* Paris, 1966.

————. "L'Invective de Gargantua contre les mariages contractés 'sans le sceu et adveu des parents' (Tiers Livre, chap. 48)." *Revue du seizième siècle* 14 (1927):381-88.

Plessis de Grenédan, Joachim du. *Histoire de l'authorité paternelle et de la société familiale en France avant 1789.* Paris, 1900.

Pommeray, Léon. *L'Officialité archidiaconale de Paris aux xve-xvie siècles.* Paris, 1933.

Power, Eileen. "The Position of Women." In *The Legacy of the Middle Ages,* edited by Charles George Crump and Ernest Fraser Jacob, pp. 401-33. New York, 1936.

Pradel, Charles. "Un Marchand de Paris au xvie siècle (1560-1588)." *Mémoires de l'Académie des sciences, inscriptions et belles-lettres de Toulouse,* ser. 9, 1 (1888):327-51; 2 (1890):390-427.

Ranum, Orest. *Paris in the Age of Absolutism, An Essay.* New York, 1968.

Richet, Denis. "Aspects socio-culturels des conflits religieux à Paris dans la seconde moitié du xvie siècle." *Annales. Economies, sociétés, civilisations* 32 (1977):764-89.

————. *La France moderne: L'Esprit des institutions.* Paris, 1973.

Robiquet, Paul. *Histoire municipale de Paris.* Vol. 1: *Depuis Les Origines jusqu'à l'avènement de Henri III.* Vol. 2: *Règne de Henri III.* Vol. 3: *Règne de Henri IV.* Paris, 1880-1904.

Roelker, Nancy L. "The Appeal of Calvinism to French Noblewomen in the Sixteenth Century." *Journal of Interdisciplinary History* 2 (1972):391-418.

————. *Queen of Navarre: Jeanne d'Albret, 1528-1572.* Cambridge, Mass., 1968.

Romier, Lucien. *Jacques d'Albon de Saint-André, maréchal de France, 1512-1562.* Paris, 1909.

————. *Le Royaume de Catherine de Médicis.* 2 vols. Paris, 1922.

Rosset, Philippe. "Les Conseillers au Châtelet de Paris de la fin du xviiᵉ siècle, étude d'histoire sociale." *Mémoires publiés par la Fédération des sociétés historiques et archéologiques de Paris et de l'Ile-de-France* 21 (1970):173-292; 22 (1971):233-302.

Rothrock, George A. "Officials and King's Men: A Note on the Possibility of Royal Control of the Estates General." *French Historical Studies* 2 (1962):504-10.

Roupnel, Gaston. *La Ville et la campagne au xviiᵉ siècle: Etude sur les populations du pays dijonnais.* Paris, 1955. [1st ed.: 1922.]

Salmon, J[ohn] H. M. "The Paris Sixteen, 1584-1594: The Social Analysis of a Revolutionary Movement." *Journal of Modern History* 44 (1972): 540-76.

———. *Society in Crisis: France in the Sixteenth Century.* New York, 1975.

———. "Venal Office and Popular Sedition in Seventeenth-Century France." *Past & Present*, no. 37 (1967), pp. 21-43.

Schalk, Ellery. "The Appearance and Reality of Nobility in France during the Wars of Religion: An Example of How Collective Attitudes Can Change." *Journal of Modern History* 48 (1976):19-31.

Schnapper, Bernard. *Les Rentes au xviᵉ siècle. Histoire d'un instrument de crédit.* Affaires et gens d'affaires. Centre des recherches historiques. Paris, 1957.

Schochet, Gordon J. *Patriarchalism in Political Thought. The Authoritarian Family and Political Speculation and Attitudes; Especially in Seventeenth-Century England.* New York, 1975.

Screech, Michael A. *The Rabelaisian Marriage: Aspects of Rabelais's Religion, Ethics, and Comic Philosophy.* London, 1958.

Shennan, J. H. *The Parlement of Paris.* Ithaca, 1968.

Siegel, Paul N. "Milton and the Humanist Attitude towards Women." *Journal of the History of Ideas* 11 (1950):42-53.

Slater, Miriam. "The Weightiest Business: Marriage in an Upper-Gentry Family in Seventeenth-Century England," *Past & Present*, no. 72 (1976), pp. 25-54.

Soman, Alfred, ed. *The Massacre of St. Bartholomew: Reappraisals and Documents.* International Archives of the History of Ideas, no. 75. The Hague, 1974.

Snyders, Georges. *La Pédagogie en France au xviiᵉ et xviiiᵉ siècles.* Paris, 1965.

Spont, Alfred. *Semblançay (?-1527). La Bourgeoisie financière au début du xviᵉ siècle.* Paris, 1895.

Stocker, Christopher. "Office as Maintenance in Renaissance France." *Canadian Journal of History* 6 (1971):21-44.

Stone, Lawrence. *The Crisis of the Aristocracy: 1558-1641.* Oxford, 1965.

————. *The Family, Sex, and Marriage in England, 1500-1800.* New York, 1977.

Strauss, Gerald. *Nuremberg in the Sixteenth Century.* New York, 1966.

Sutherland, Nicola Mary. *The French Secretaries of State in the Age of Catherine de Medici.* [London], 1962.

Thomas, Keith. "The Double Standard." *Journal of the History of Ideas* 20 (1959):195-216.

Timbal, P. C. "L'Esprit du droit privé au xviie siècle." *Xvii^e Siècle,* nos. 58-59 (1963), pp. 30-39.

Trudon des Ormes, A. "Notes sur les prévôts des marchands et échevins de la ville de Paris au xviiie siècle (1701-1789)." *Mémoires de la Société de l'histoire de Paris et de l'Ile-de-France* 38 (1911):107-223.

Turlan, J. M. "Recherches sur le mariage dans la pratique coutumière (xiie-xvie s.)." *Revue historique du droit français et étranger,* ser. 4, 35 (1957):477-528.

Venard, Marc. *Bourgeois et paysans au xviie siècle: Recherche sur le rôle des bourgeois parisiens dans la vie agricole au sud de Paris au xviie siècle.* Les Hommes et la terre, vol. 3. Paris, 1957.

Veyrasset-Herren, Béatrice, and Emmanuel Le Roy Ladurie. "La Vente foncière autour de Paris au xviie siècle." *Annales. Economies, sociétés, civilisations* 23 (1968):541-55.

Vidal, Pierre, and Léon Duru. *Histoire de la corporation des marchands merciers grossiers, joailliers, le troisième des Six Corps de la ville de Paris.* Paris, 1911.

Vidier, A. "Les Marguilliers laïcs de Notre-Dame de Paris (1204-1790)." *Mémoires de la Société de l'histoire de Paris et de l'Ile-de-France* 40 (1913):117-402; 41 (1914):131-346.

Vimont, Maurice. *Histoire de la rue Saint-Denis de ses origines à nos jours.* Vol. 1. Paris, 1936.

————. *Histoire de l'église et de la paroisse Saint-Leu-Saint-Gilles à Paris.* Paris, 1932.

Vovelle, Michel. *Piété baroque et déchristianisation en Provence au xviiie siècle. Les Attitudes devant la mort d'après les clauses des testaments.* Paris, 1973.

Wheaton, Robert Bradford. "Bordeaux before the Fronde: A Study of Family, Class, and Social Structure." Ph.D. dissertation, Harvard University, 1973.

———, and Tamara K. Hareven, eds. *Family and Sexuality in French History*. Philadelphia, 1980.

Wiley, William Leon. *The Gentleman of Renaissance France*. Cambridge, Mass., 1954.

Wolfe, Martin. *The Fiscal System of Renaissance France*. New Haven, 1972.

Woodward, William Harrison. *Studies in Education during the Age of the Renaissance*. Cambridge, Mass., 1965.

———. *Vittorino da Feltre and other Humanist Educators*. Cambridge, Mass., 1964.

Yver, Jean. *Egalité entre héritiers et exclusion des enfants dotés; Essai de géographie coutumière*. Paris, 1966.

Zeller, Gaston. *Les Institutions de la France au xvie siècle*. Paris, 1948.

Index

Coutume, Paris: (*cont.*)
216, 242, 242n, 245, 256, 291
Cressé, Simon (*city councillor*),39n, 85
Croix de Gastines, 79n, 105-106,
106n
Croquet: family, 197, 199; Jean
(*city councillor*), 41, 42, 71n;
Jean (father of city councillors
Jean and Pierre), 199; Marguerite, 196; Nicolas, 77-79, 79n,
80; Nicole, 77, 79, 80n, 204n
Pierre (*city councillor*), 40, 60,
78; election as échevin, 99, 99n;
daughters of, 77, 109n, 196,
203-204, 244-45n, 285; tax assessment, 48, 48n, 50
Cujas, Jacques, 255n

Dalegre, Anne, 289
Davis, Natalie Zemon, 249n
Decret Tametsi, 163
Denière, Georges, 103
Dewald, Jonathan, xxvn, 181
disinheritance, 161, 167
Dixhomme, Jacques, 171n
dizainiers (Hôtel de Ville), 6
Dollot (seigneury), 270
Dollu, René, 109n
donations (*donations à vie*), 254,
256, 262-63; to collaterals,
274-76; between husband and
wife, 229-30, 294
Dormans, Marie de, 263, 263n
dower (*douaire*): customary, 225-
26, 230, 249, 250-51; in city
councillor families, 249-51,
294; fixed (*préfix*), 225, 230,
249; relation to dowry, 249,
249n; and remarriage, 289;
rights of children to, 226, 258
dowry (*dot*), 226-27, 230, 239-40,
242; in city councillor families,
232-237, 265n; protection of,
245-47

drapers, 48, 48n, 92, 93n, 98
droit d'aînesse, 254-55, 254n, 258,
259-60, 265-66, 296
Du Drac: family, 36n, 37, 57, 73,
89; Adrien, vicomte d'Ay (*city
councillor*), 39n, 58, 63-64, 71,
72n, 73, 142n; Jean, 220; Marguerite, 74n; Olivier (*city councillor*), 58, 74, 258n
Du Gué, Nicolas (*city councillor*),
39n, 74, 80
Du Moulin, Charles, 159n, 228-
29, 257, 259, 286
Du Pré, Jeanne, 285
Dupuy, Claude, 214, 214n, 218

Eaux et Fôrets (court of), 45
échevins (Hôtel de Ville), xvii, 8n,
19, 34, 42n; role of, 6, 12, 27;
selection of, 14-15, 19, 21, 99
education: humanist ideas on, 114-
20; of women, 177-79
elite, Parisian, xvi, xxii, xxiv-xxvi,
4
Elizabeth of Austria, 102
Enfants Rouges (Enfants de Dieu),
71
enquête par turbe, 257
Erasmus, 158, 179, 181, 190,
288
Erlanger, Philippe, 108
Escrennes (seigneury), 276

family: bilateral structure of, 39,
188, 188n, 303; defined, xxi;
residential patterns of, 61-62,
63; in relation to state, xxi,
157, 169, 228, 255, 286, 290,
292, 300, 301, 306
family council, 217, 219-20, 279-
80
fathers, 120-24, 143
Faulcon, Claude de, 17
Ferrière, Claude de, 243

350

sons: careers of eldest and younger,
144-51; favoring of eldest, 238,
270-71, 278, 303; legal rights
of eldest, 254, 255n, 257,
257n, 259-60, 259n, 265-66
Soulas, Jean, 73
Stains (seigneury), 67
Stone, Lawrence, 120n, 183, 279n
successions, *see* inheritance

taille, 24, 53
Tambonneau, Jean, 204
Tanneguy: Denis (*city councillor*),
39n, 233; Madeleine, 199; Ursine, 233
Taranne, Jacques, 189
taxes, 8, 8n, 12, 22-29; assessment of 1572, 48, 49-51, 51n,
61, 63; collection of, 92; farming of, 91-92
testaments, 253, 255-56, 267,
267n
Teste: Germain, 243-44n; Simon
(*city councillor*), 175, 243
Thillay (seigneury), 274n
Thou, de: family, 36, 37, 86,
129, 147, 180; Anne, 180; Augustin I (*city councillor*), 60; Augustin II (*city councillor*, son of
Augustin I), 99n, 132, 141,
144; Barbe, 275; Catherine,
271n; Marguerite, 146; Nicolas,
bishop of Chartres, 128-29,
130, 133
    Christophe (*city councillor*),
xvii, 60, 67, 72n, 185, 252;
career of, 85, 86, 144; and family, 124, 130-31, 132-33, 148,
177, 269; and the law, xx, 216,
218, 292
    Jacques-Auguste, 56, 121,
185-86, 189, 269; opinions on
marriage, 160, 288n, 289; vocation of, 124-25, 130-34, 141

Tiers Livre (Rabelais), 159
Tiraqueau, André, 255, 286
Tonart, Claude, 165-66, 301
trésoriers généraux de France, 57
Tronçon: family, 73; François,
30n, 285, 294; Jean (*city councillor*), 30n, 39n, 73, 146, 285;
Jean (father of city councillor
Jean), 73; Jean (son of city
councillor Jean), 30n; Jeanne,
175
Troussay, le (seigneury), 55
Tudert, Claude, 281n
Tulleu, Jacqueline de, 64n, 177,
269
tutelle et curatelle, *see* guardianship
tuteurs, 280-81, 281n, 283

University of Paris, 7

venality: in city office, 16-17,
16n, 17n, 301-302, 304; in
royal office, xix, 17, 28, 92,
122, 242, 304
Vergerio, Pietro Paolo, 114-15
Versoris, Pierre, 164
Vigny, François de, 16
Villeroy, *see* Neufville, Nicolas de
Villers-Cotterets, ordinance of,
xviii
Viole: family, 36, 37, 67; Hippolyte, 161-62, 162n; Pierre I,
sieur d'Athis (*city councillor*),
142n; Pierre, sieur du Chemin,
293, 295
Vitry (seigneury), 70, 265, 266
Vivien, René I (*city councillor*),
142n
vocation: humanist ideas on, 114-
19; religious, 118, 125, 126,
131

widows, 246-47, 249-51, 282,
285-86; in city councillor fami-

Library of Congress Cataloging in Publication Data

Diefendorf, Barbara B., 1946-
Paris city councillors in the sixteenth century.
Bibliography: p. 313.
Includes index.
1. Paris (France). Hôtel de ville—Officials and employees—History.
2. Paris (France)—Officials and employees—History.
3. Elite (Social sciences)—France—Paris—History. I. Title.
JS5123.D53   1982   305.5'2'0944361   82-47591
ISBN 0-691-05362-6   AACR2